بسم الله الرحمن الرحيم

Engaging Muslim Students in Public Schools

What Educators Need to Understand

Michael Abraham

Abraham Education ◆ abrahameducation.com

TABLE OF CONTENTS

HOW TO READ THIS BOOK..1

Footnotes and Sourcing...1

About Generalizations...2

Arabic Words and Diacritical Markings.......................................4

PROLOGUE..6

Chapter 1: NEED AND JUSTIFICATION IN EDUCATIONAL RESEARCH 9

Religious Diversity is Neglected in Preservice Training.........................9

Teacher Evaluation 13

Child Development 14

Experience of Muslims Students in Public Schools 14

Chapter 2: HISTORY OF MUSLIMS IN AMERICA AND ITS LOCALITIES 17

Islam and African Americans 17

Converts and Community in the 20th Century 18

Transition to Sunni Islam 21

Conclusion..24

Earliest Immigrant Waves...24

Racial Classification of Arabs and South Asians...26

Professional Class of Muslim Immigrants 28

Important to Understand about Professional Class Immigrants...................31

Refugees..36

Iraqis...37

Somalis 42

Conclusion..53

Chapter 3: ISLAMIC BELIEF AND CONNECTIONS TO STUDENTS & FAMILIES...57

Sources of Islam..57

The Qur'an 57

Hadith & Sunnah 58

Importance of The Prophet's Companions and Early Followers..............59

Music, Capitulation, and Insight from Understanding Islamic Sources........61

Conclusion...74

The Core of Islam 74

The First Pillar - Monotheism 76

The First Pillar cont'd - Uniqueness, Omnipotence, and Metaphysical Cause. 78

The First Pillar - Prophets and Messengers....................................86

The Second Pillar - Salāh (obligatory prayer) 99

The Third Pillar - Zakāt (obligatory charity)..................................105

The Fourth Pillar - Fasting the Month of Ramadan 111

The Fifth Pillar - The Pilgrimage to Mecca (Hajj)...........................125

Islam and Race 129

The Tenets of Belief...146

Motherhood and attitudes towards females.................................154

Shyness..161

The Divine Decree and Critical Thinking..163

Islam and Personal Subjectivity..168

Two Hadith for the Classroom..170

Chapter 4: TECHNICALITIES OF FOLLOWING ISLAM -
ACCOMMODATIONS AND COLLISION IN THE SCHOOLS...........175

Salāh - Accommodations..175

Time - When the prayer happens..177

Time - Wudū': Preparatory Ritual Washing (ablution) 181

Time - The Process and Duration of Praying...................................185

Space - Where the Prayer Happens 190

Jummah - The Friday Congregation 198

Ramadan Fasting Times 203

Scheduling Considerations for the School......................................205

Family Involvement at School..209

Bathroom Habits...213

Culinary Habits...215

Clothing & Hijab...216

Family Gender roles...229

    The Male as a Provider and Boy's Motivation...235

Chapter 5: LEARNING IN MOSQUES & IMPLICATIONS IN MODERN EDUCATION...239
Behavioral Aspects...242

    Consequences...242

    Considerations Regarding Problematic Behavior...247

    Conclusion...261

Learning Incongruences & Areas of Utilization...261

    Qur'an Memorization learning...263

    Lecture based learning...272

Scaffolding Reading Comprehension...279

    Scaffolding Math...302

    Phonics...304

    Direct Instruction vs. Student Centered Teaching...309

    Conclusion...316

Chapter 6: TEXTS THAT FEATURE MUSLIMS...317
Books that are offensive to religious sensibilities...321

Books where Muslims are cast as victims...322

Books where Muslims are Tokenized...323

Refugee and Immigrant narratives...324

Books that authentically honor and relate religious identity...325

Chapter 7: FINAL CONSIDERATIONS...334
EPILOGUE...345
REFERENCES...347

HOW TO READ THIS BOOK

This book is meant to be read cover to cover. Books in the field of education are often styled to be used as reference sources, while others are pure narratives, and many struggle with being somewhere in between. Books that skew to the reference side are designed for the reader to be able to easily access certain parts in the book without having to read the whole thing; offering detailed tables of contents, indexes, thorough use of headings, bullet points, diagrams etc.

This book has a fairly thorough table of contents and a tiered heading system throughout it as well. However, these exist to help orientate the reader as the book's narrative is strung out. The book is designed as a learning continuum that builds on itself as it goes. So the reader who jumps around sections of it is likely to find themselves confused at certain points because they missed the prerequisite knowledge and references that were taught earlier in the book. The book is not intended for the reader who wishes to only glean a summary from the bullet points at a chapter's beginning and be done with it. It is for the reader who values the power of a full narrative, fine detail, and thorough explanation. I tell the attendees of my trainings beforehand, be ready to take notes because you are going to receive a lot of information and ideas, and it is best for you to write down your takeaways. The same is true for this book. There will be a lot you wish to take out of it. But by design, you will have to travel through the foundational knowledge that the main points and strategies are built upon. They will not be delivered to you in a bulleted sheet.

The effectiveness of strategies in education is dependent on treating underlying causes of the problem the strategy aims to fix, and having a thorough understanding of why the strategy is set the way it is. Too often, educators only look at the most cosmetic aspects of strategies and methods before implementing them, and then are frustrated when they fail to be effective; not realizing that they are falling into the building of a house without a foundation problem. This book is designed to mitigate against such haste. Any strategy needs to be tweaked, adjusted, and improvised with in order to be effective in any particular context. It is a solid footing in the reasons and knowledge that underpin the strategy's theory that enable this to occur.

Footnotes and Sourcing

It will become very apparent to you as you read this book that I like footnotes. In large part this affection developed in me through my experience in life reading Islamic texts, which make extensive use of them. The best part about footnotes is they allow for different levels of engagement with the text. Footnotes are often used in this book to provide more thorough detail and elaboration, as well as side elaboration that is interesting to include, but might be overly tangential to insert into the flow of the main narrative. In my experience conducting trainings through oral presentations, I have found that oftentimes the most interesting parts for some of the attendees are not the main parts of the presentation, but rather side points that are ancillary or brought up in response to a question. I think of the footnotes as serving this function within the book. So some readers will find that the most useful specific information and resources they take away will come from the footnotes. While others will deem that the main running narrative grips them enough that veering off of it would be overload, and they can opt to skip the annotations.

The other service of footnotes is to provide some source referencing. The research cited in this book from Western academia is done in APA format, and the reference list at the end of the book is alphabetical to the entire book and not divided by chapters. The in-text citations to these references are in the book's main text, not in the footnotes. However, there is some sourcing that I felt was best done utilizing the footnotes. Primarily, sourcing Islamic texts, because this is the common way it is done in Islamic writing, and the traditional mode of transcribing Islamic references simply does not lend itself well to the Western modes of citation. You will learn more about Islamic sources in chapter three.

In addition to that, there are just some other sources to be cited that I felt worked best being done in the footnotes. All Supreme Court cases that are cited, for example, I have put the citation in the footnotes, in addition to some other web resources that I thought putting in the reference list would make it too cumbersome.

About Generalizations

If you are not aware, Muslims are all individuals and not all Muslims are the same. Now if you had to be informed of that let me also inform you that the sun rises in the east and it sets in the west. To me, in today's world, the need to point out both of those is about the same. Nevertheless, be as it may for good reason, people are very sensitive about the idea of stating generalizations about a group of people. At the same time, the very same people often have a strong and sincere eagerness to get to know people from different backgrounds as individuals. I too share in both this sensitivity and eagerness, but I also know that in order to genuinely satisfy the second, I have to recognize that there can be pitfalls in going to extremes about the first.

Especially when it comes to Muslims, the fact is that when a non-Muslim lacks general understandings about Islam, history, and the Muslim community, many matters that are specific to an individual simply become too big of a burden to explain. This creates built-in roadblocks to the development of genuine connection and authentic understanding between people. In order for a Muslim to explain to a non-Muslim the particulars about an individual matter with due justice, it would typically involve informing them about a whole world of general background information that they do not have. Thus giving any explanation becomes overwhelming and burdensome. This relational dynamic comes up all the time with Muslims and their interactions with non-Muslims, and really it exists on scales from individual relationships to societal wide ones.

Our public schools are probably the place in American society where Muslims and non-Muslims come together and are placed into relationships with one another more than anywhere else. It is a central purpose of this book to fill in the necessary background information for the non-Muslim educators to take a step towards fostering deeper and more authentic relationships with the Muslim students and families they serve. The public education system has long held a place of ambivalence and consternation for the Muslim community. Like all other families, Muslims want their kids to be successful in school. At the same time there has always been active concern about how their children are influenced in these institutions. So the reader of this book will inure information and perspectives that the Muslim community desperately wants and needs public school educators to know, but has struggled to come together and articulate productively.

So while I am sensitive to making generalizations, and this shows up in the book with my frequent use of phrases such as "oftentimes" and "it might be the case" or "with some" in order to avoid making statements about people in absolute terms, it is still the case that there are times where I found it to be most appropriate to make declarative statements about Muslims as a whole, or about a Muslim individual as a generalized archetype; usually in an idealized abstract sense that relates to the teachings of Islam. I can make no apologies for that, and please consider this my adding the qualification that there are real world exceptions to every generalization, and some of the matters addressed in this book will apply more to a minority of students as opposed to the generality, but that ought to be apparent based on the learner characteristics described.

It is part of the basic cognitive architecture of humans that more specific understandings are built upon more general ones. Every educator should know this. A central aim of this book is to arm the non-Muslim educator with appropriate knowledge, insights, and considerations that can serve as a platform that will enable them to better know and engage as individuals the Muslim students and families they serve. I am hopeful and cautiously confident it will be found to serve that purpose.

Arabic Words and Diacritical Markings

This book makes use of many Arabic terms. The meanings of them will all be explained in the text, so there is no glossary. Terms that are used are ones that are generally used often when Muslims talk to one another whether they are Arabic speakers or not, or are using Arabic in their own conversation. Knowing these words as a non-Muslim can create the potential for you to have deeper engagement, and access culturally specific topics and information, in your dialogs with Muslims. These words will appear italicized in the text except for words that I believe are used so commonly that they essentially ought to be considered part of the English language lexicon, and many of them appear in standard English language dictionaries; words such as Islam, Muslim, Allah, Hajj etc.

Arabic phonetics have many direct corollaries to English but also several sounds that are not present in English at all. Historically, there have always been different methods employed for transliterating Arabic phonetics to the Roman alphabet. More and more what has become common amongst Muslim writers in the English-speaking world is employing the use of diacritical marks to indicate subtle differences in sound between one letter and another. In this book my goal with the Arabic wording is to show them in a way that will best accommodate a native English speaker pronouncing them a *little bit* better than they predictably would. The goal is not to have the native English speaker be able to enunciate them perfectly by reading them in this book, because that goal is not realistic and would take a lot more practice for them to execute properly.

Following that, I have only included diacritical marks for vowel sounds and to indicate the consonant *hamza*. I have not included the diacritical marks that differentiate between other consonants. So for example, Arabic has two sounds that can be represented by the letter "d" that are enunciated rather differently. In diacritical marking their difference is transliterated with the use of an underdot, one being "d" and the other being "ḍ". The same relationship exists in Arabic for "t","z", and "h". I have also opted to not include the right facing apostrophe that is used to indicate the consonant *'ayn*. Enunciating these differences quite simply would take extended work and practice for an anglophone. I do not want the non-Arabic speaking readers of this book to read words and be distracted by being prompted to think about how to enunciate these consonants when it would be difficult for them.

The vowel sounds are much easier to grasp. There are essentially six vowel sounds in Arabic consisting of a long and short version of the sounds "a" /e/, "i" /ɪ/, and "u" /ʊ/. The short versions are transliterated as you see in quotation marks in the previous sentence. The long versions employ the diacritical mark that is called the *macron*, which appears as a line above the letter. So the long vowels are transliterated as ā, ī, and ū. The long vowel sound in Arabic is different from what are called the long vowel sounds in English. In English, long vowel sounds render the letter sound to be the same as pronouncing the vowel's name. In Arabic, it is simply an extension of the short vowel sound, it is the same sound only held a little longer. These correlate to IPA symbolism as $\bar{a}$ = /æ/, $\bar{i}$ = /i:/, and $\bar{u}$ = /u:/. Note that I have opted not to include the macron in the words Allah (*Allāh*) Qur'an (*Qur'ān*), and hadith (*hadīth*), nor in the Arabic definite article, due to their already common use in English writing.

The left facing apostrophe (') is used to indicate the consonant *hamza*. While there is not a Roman alphabet corollary to this sound, the majority of American English speakers actually do make this sound when they pronounce words that have a double t (tt) that appears in between two vowels. Such as in the words "kitten" and "rotten". Most American English speakers will find that when they say these words they enunciate the middle consonant as neither a "t" or "d" sound, which are both executed by tapping the tongue to the roof of the mouth. But rather they make a slight stoppage of the air passing through the recess of their throat where their vocal cords reside, an area called the glottis. Thus linguists refer to this sound as a glottal stop. Both Arabic and American English use this sound, but Arabic assigns an alphabetic marking to it.

PROLOGUE

This book is a humble effort to put to text a training program that I designed for public school educators entitled by the same name. Parts of this training were originally done at educator conferences in the Twin Cities, and then as specialized presentations in a training program for in-service educators at Hamline University in St. Paul, Minnesota. After that it was conducted twice as a 24-hour training course for interested educators in Minneapolis Public Schools in the 2017-2018 school year, through a program sponsored by the teacher's union. That same year I began making a condensed-down six-hour version of the training available to any educator in the Twin Cities and offered it privately on selected Saturdays. To my surprise the demand for this training was enormous, and more than I could meet. After conducting the trainings, reception to it was overwhelmingly positive. The testimonials page on abrahameducation.com/testimonials can give you some idea of the sentiments that attendees took away from these training sessions.

Over the course of two years I conducted the training as much as I could, while remaining as a full-time teacher, and expanded it out to greater Minnesota as well as the states of Washington and Ohio. I also started receiving inquiries about the training from educators around North America and even as far away as Melbourne, Australia. Overall, I delivered this training at least in part to over one thousand educators representing more than 50 school districts and many more different schools and institutes from pre-K up to universities and adult basic education. Also during this time, my website became sort of a go-to place for educators who knew about it to shoot me questions about engaging with some students and families in their schools; and I would respond to inquiries and advise people via email or telephone.

What mostly made the training popular was the information that was given, which gave educators insights for which they were thirsty. Teachers are told so much about the importance of knowing the home culture of students, and practicing culturally-relevant pedagogy. But rarely do teachers feel that they are actually given an inside view into the home culture of their students and directly how it relates to teaching them and the way they show up in school. While many of the proponents of culturally-relevant teaching can reveal the need for it to educators rather seamlessly, most still struggle to put their finger on how it might actually manifest in the school and classroom.

I believe another aspect of the training's popularity was the efforts I made to create an environment that was truly open for questioning. In particular, I made sure that the training's attendees would have the opportunity to ask any questions that were pressing on their minds without fear of judgement, or being guilted and chastised. Key to doing this was that every attendee was provided an intake form to fill out before the day of the training where they could anonymously submit any question they had about Muslims, Muslim students and families, and Islam; and I encouraged them to not be bashful. In turn, I would answer these questions by stringing them into my presentations without anyone having to know who asked it, and the privacy of the inquirer was maintained. Also to maintain privacy and anonymity, I would not ask the attendees to share anything about themselves or even greet one another if they did not so choose. Anyone who wanted to could simply come and listen and do nothing more. If you know about educator professional development then you know that this type of approach is very rare. But to talk about religion and its real-world interplay on people's lives and psychology is an extraordinarily sensitive topic, perhaps more so than any other. So the benefit to an approach that maximizes the potential for people to maintain anonymity is that they feel safe in letting their guard down enough in order to ask the questions they genuinely have. That benefit transfers to this book in that every single matter that is brought up in it informs about something that relates to genuine questions and issues that have been brought up to me by real-world educators in public schools.

Many of these educators had questions that had been burning inside of them for a very long time, sometimes decades. After years of experience they knew patently that the role and influence of religion was central to the lives of their Muslim students and families, but they had never been offered the time, space, and opportunity to ask and learn. Attempting to gain an authentic understanding of Islam's influence on the lives of real world Muslims is simply not adequately served by internet searches or reading standard trade paperbacks on Islam; and certainly not by consuming news media and political propaganda. Like 99% of the people in public education, I found these educators to consider themselves to be in service to their students and their students' parents and families. They genuinely wanted to nurture the young people put under their care in a way that accorded to the desires of those young people's parents.[1] To give the public school educators of Muslim children the opportunity to break through the fog of media characterizations, political interests, and interpersonal sensitivities that corrupts our discourse and understanding of religion and how it interplays in peoples lives; and to instead access a real window, limited though it may be, into the inner lives of the students and families they serve was considered truly precious. I am humbled by all the gratitude and encouragement that my trainees have expressed to me over the past two years.

In the summer of 2019 I was exhausted from the work and travel of conducting the training continuously on the side to being a full-time teacher, which I had no desire to recede from

---

[1] And this book is written for an audience of these types of people. For those of you who have acquired this book to "hate" read it, consider this your trigger warning that you are not likely to get through this book without having a conniption.

doing. So I put the trainings on hiatus at that point and decided to devote my free time in the 2019–20 school year to putting the training into a book that could be used to reach demand for it that I could not do in person. That brings us to where we are right now.

If I could dedicate this book to anyone, it would be to the parents of Muslim youth in America. They have not elected me to be a spokesperson for them, and I am not. Rather I am indebted without end to the aid, guidance, and education that this community has given me, especially in my years as a young man. At the same time, I have absorbed and shared in enough of their anguish, trials, and stress over raising children in the West that the information and perspectives in this book are something that I have a personal and cathartic need to bring forth. I ask humbly of Muslim parents in America that they consider this book a sincere attempt to advocate on their behalf.

As is part of Islamic etiquette to observe, I thank God first and foremost for permitting me to complete this. Any good that comes from this book is attributable to God's greatness, and any wrong that comes from it is attributable to my own deficiencies. After God, the amount of people I have to thank is ever-numerous, but it certainly begins with my parents, wife, and family. Thank you to all of you for being by my side for so long. Also I would like to thank you, the reader, for acquiring this book and having a mind open enough to read it. Please know that, for me, in many ways this book is the culmination of a life's work, yet an effort that is feeble.

Michael Abraham
May 10th, 2020 CE
Ramadan 17th, 1441 AH

Chapter 1: NEED AND JUSTIFICATION IN EDUCATIONAL RESEARCH
A Brief Overview

If you are reading this book it is likely you already have a reason and understanding for why its topic should be studied. Nevertheless, as is part of the decorum of academic practice, one must honor what has been said in the field already that justifies and identifies the need for study of the topic set out to be taught. Discussions of research can lead to many different avenues and prompt for all sorts of side discussions and critical analysis of the research itself. While there is room to venture further into educational literature that relate to the topic of Muslim students in public schools in the West, this is only a very brief overview that is constructed to familiarize the reader with the basics and seminal studies that have been done on Muslim students in public schools. The goal is to demonstrate why this topic should be examined intentionally, and how educational research itself lends to justification for the reading of this book by educators.

Religious Diversity is Neglected in Preservice Training

Religious diversity is neglected in preservice teacher training. This point is obvious to most who experienced preservice training. It is common nowadays that states or licensure courses require that diversity, usually as an academic concept, be addressed in teacher education. This frequently manifests in mandates that teacher licensure programs offer at least one course that examine concepts that are typically dubbed as being courses on diversity, equity, inclusive practices, or multicultural education. This in turn results in courses that examine and introduce theoretical frameworks and academic jargon concerning educating students who are, basically, non-white, or non-heterosexual, or non-Christian, or some combination thereof. Students who do not fit these identity markers are commonly referred to as not being from the "dominant" culture, which I find can be useful terminology. Some courses will specifically look at student groups under certain categories that signify minority status in America, such as African-American, Hispanic, or Native-American etc.

However, courses that look specifically at religious diversity, or at a specific religious minority group, are exceedingly rare in teacher education. None exist that I have been able to locate. Rare also are academic studies that specifically examine the issue of preparing teacher candidates to engage with religiously diverse students in preservice training. There was one study done of preservice teachers at Ohio State University in 2006 that examined attitudes towards religious diversity of preservice teachers in Columbus, OH. Predictably, it found that it was a sensitive topic for the student-teachers to approach, and they were therefore hesitant to approach religious topics at all despite the fact that they actually had many questions about it they wanted to have answered. The study found that both these questions, and the reluctance of the study's subjects to approach them, increased when religious issues intersected with race and gender topics (Subedi, 2006).

Shortly after 9/11 there was one quantitive survey done of preservice teachers' knowledge about Muslims and Islam. It found that the majority of respondents lacked even a "rudimentary" knowledge about Islam or the "global reach" of Muslim populations. This is not exactly surprising and is really only consistent with broader trends in society, which have been indicated by Pew Research (2011) polls to show that most people simply do not know much about world religions aside from their own. It is a side note, but there have been interesting arguments made that assert that this lack of religious literacy on the part of the general public is in large part due to the fault of a public education system that fails to address and introduce to students, particularly at the secondary level, to religious ways of looking at the world and basics in religious literacy (Nord, 2010).

What results for Muslim students from this lack of knowledge about religion amongst educators? What results from the lack of it being addressed in settings where educators develop as professionals? One thing is that misunderstandings between Muslim students and non-Muslim educators become inevitable. It further follows that an increase in the background knowledge of the educator about Muslims and Islam could have acted as a remedy to these misunderstandings. When misunderstandings arise clashes can take place, and the students' schooling experiences fail to reach the lofty goals of respect, diversity, and inclusion that are set out by schools.

The second result that I point toward is that the hesitancy or incapacity to examine and learn about Islam on the part of educators results in the framing of the experiences of Muslim students' in the world of educators to necessarily be conceptualized using theories of understanding that were developed to address the experiences of other more-frequently examined minorities. In particular, framing their experiences through critical race theory, and other offshoots of critical theory in general. Not all aspects of this may be negative in and of themselves, however, what results is the pigeonholing of Muslim students into boxes of being a minority general, or boxes of race, gender, or ethnic status. All the while downplaying, if not outright suffocating, discussion and examination of the role of religion as a part of who they are and from where they come.

To illustrate both this pigeonholing and the pitfalls that are fallen into when well-meaning educators lack background knowledge about Islam, I will reference an anecdote from the book *Waking Up White* by Deborah Irving (2014). The book is about Irving's journey growing up as a privileged white female and learning the realities of race in the world, both historical and modern, while working as an educator in her adulthood. I have known of schools that focus on racial equity who have found it beneficial to have white teachers read this book in order to prompt them into having a sort of awakening to the realities of society's racial disparities. The hope is it will increase their sensitivities to their students. Irving's story may very well suit this purpose[2], however, I would like to use a part from it here to illustrate how a lack of background knowledge about Islam on the part of educators is 1.) an obvious cause of educators' inability to avoid missteps and anticipate cultural clashes with Muslim families, and 2.) perhaps only confounded by solely considering racial equity lenses, which can result in the pigeonholing of Muslims into boxes they likely did not choose for themselves.

In Irving's 25th chapter, entitled "Belonging", she recounts her experience as a parent in the public school district of Cambridge, MA where she served on the "Family Connections Committee" of her child's school. This committee was formed to reach out to the growing population of "Ethiopian, Somalian[3] (sic), and Haitian families". Irving describes how over the years it was observed that an increasing number of these families opted not to have their children participate in the school's long-loved annual tradition of having a Halloween parade. That the school failed to anticipate these families would not want their children to celebrate Halloween is one thing, but I want to focus on an excerpt where she talks about the school's principal confronting parents about why they would not allow their child to participate in the parade. She writes:

> At the first Family Connections meeting, the principal asked those who did not allow their children to participate in the parade to help the rest of us understand the experience from their perspective.
>   "Ahhhh," one woman shook her head and looked at the ceiling.
> "**It's so complicated**." (bold added)

What can be seen here is exactly the type of situation that Muslims in the West are repeatedly put into when they are around people who want to be respectful and understanding, but have not done any research on their own about the teachings of Islam and its practical applications in life by Muslim people. There are actually very precise reasons[4] why Muslims do not celebrate Halloween, as well as many other holidays. However, to explain the precise reasons, one would

---

[2] And I would not stop from recommending reading Irving's book to white teacher colleagues who have a very low level of racial awareness.

[3] The term "Somalian" is an anglicization of the term *Somali*, which is what people of Somali ethnicity ought to be referred to as; many Somalis find the use of the term "Somalian" to be offensive and ignorant. Irving, I am sure, had only innocuous intentions in her use of it.

[4] In Chapter 3 this will be explained.

first have to fill in the listener on a whole other load of general background information that would be exhaustive and emotionally tolling to articulate in the context of everyday interpersonal interactions. Especially one like this where a cultural conflict and disagreement have already been made apparent and serve as the basis for having the conversation in the first place. This inner emotional toll is precisely what is indicated in the exasperation of the woman in the excerpt. If this was a Muslim parent[5], which it likely was[6], and if the principal actually had background knowledge about Islam itself, much of this complication that is interpreted as a barrier to giving open explanations by the parent would be cut right through.

For Irving's part, while she is certainly innocuous in her own intent[7], any mention of Islam, or that a sizable portion of people in Cambridge are Muslims, escapes her exposé. This reinforces to the reader that making a religious distinction between peoples from Haiti, Ethiopia, and Somalia makes no appreciable difference. What is reinforced is that they are best understood as being under the umbrella of "people of color", which is what she refers to them as in this chapter. What results is her own explanation as to why these families do not participate in the Halloween parade is biased toward the way a Haitian would articulate it[8], who is likely to be closer to her own Christian religious background of understanding. All the while the pertinence of understanding religious distinctions between people and having background knowledge of world religions remains unrecognized as a concern in the entirety of the book. The lone times

[5] And while I suspect it was it is not confirmed either way in Irving's book as to whether or not the parent was Muslim, since Irving opts to only identify the parents by their ethnic backgrounds and also to generally identify them as "people of color".

[6] If you are not aware, Ethiopia is a 33% Muslim country and Somalia is 98.6% Muslim. So several of these parents are undoubtedly Muslim, it is also no secret that the city of Cambridge has a significant Muslim population.

[7] And I do want to emphasize that while I am making a critique here to illustrate a point this is not meant to be an attack on Deborah Irving, nor to give her a nefarious characterization.

[8] She says, "Through these meetings, I learned that in some cultures Halloween is experienced as an offensive and potentially spiritually harmful celebration of the dead." In essence, Muslim cultures do not experience Halloween at all, and whether or not one characterizes it as a celebration of the dead is immaterial to the reasons why Muslims do not celebrate it. Again, I will explain the Islamic understanding of holidays in chapter three.

that the word "Muslim[9]" does appear, it is only as part of a list that groups it under other umbrellas of minority characterization.

This is representative of a general pattern of patronization and disingenuousness that takes place in discussions on equity and multiculturalism in education (Jay, 1994; Parekh, 1995; Abu El-Haj, 2002). The result is that Muslims are typically missing the chance to articulate an understanding of themselves *as Muslims*, and the needs that emanate for their children in public schools *as Muslims*. Bridging this gap in understanding is a central purpose of the book you are reading.

Teacher Evaluation

Most states and districts in the country use the Standards of Effective Instruction rubric by Charlotte Danielson (2013) as a template for their teacher evaluation. There are two noticeable themes in the exemplary indicators of Danielson's rubric. One is student independence and ownership of learning. The second is honoring, sensitivity, and relevance to student culture.

Student ownership of learning runs through the exemplary indicators because it is not something that can be faked in a one-shot observation of a teacher. It indicates student motivation and mastery, which can only be built over time. The issue with student independence and ownership is that students need comfort in the classroom and confidence in the curriculum in order to take a hold of it. This is unlikely to happen when the classroom and curriculum are disjointed from the student's background knowledge, and when the student's home culture clashes with the classroom and school culture; thereby suffocating the student's sense of their home culture, or implicitly saying it's absence is necessary for the comfort and ease of others. Student independence, initiation, and assumption of responsibility is unlikely to take place when there is a wide gap between the content learning and the student's own background knowledge. One of the major factors of one's background knowledge is their

---

[9] At the end of one chapter Irving lists "Muslim" along with other minority groups in a prompt for her readers to write down stereotypes that they have about each group. The prompt in her text says, "Create a column that contains these labels: African Americans, Asian Americans, Native Americans, Jews, Latinos, Muslims, Whites. Next to each, quickly write at least five stereotypes that come to mind for each." This type of listing may be innocuous in and of itself but the implicit message it gets across is that being Muslim, a religious identity, is just another identity-marker along the list of other minority *ethnic* identities (and while 'Jew' is a religious identity, it is also an ethnic identity and in today's world it is at least as likely to be used as an ethnic marker of identity as it is a religious one [Pew Research, 2013]). This is one of only two uses of the word Muslim in the book even though she is telling the story of being an educator in a city with a significant Muslim population, and it illustrates a pattern of deemphasizing the importance of religious identity and prompting the reader to see being Muslim as something that is merely syncretic to any other minority indicator.

academically-oriented experiential base garnered from their home cultural experience (Marzano, 2004). For Muslim students, this is entirely rooted in religious education.

Danielson's rubric explicitly states in the exemplary indicators, "Planning includes opportunities for students to explain language and cultural context to their classroom community" and "the teacher is well informed about students' cultural heritages and incorporates this knowledge in lesson planning." Therefore, if mandates of teacher evaluation are to be taken seriously, the students' home culture needs to be studied and known about by the teacher. For Muslim students, it is impossible to extract this learning from learning about Islam and the realities of Islam's application and interplay in everyday life for Muslims.

Child Development

The depth of understanding that a teacher has about the learner has been recognized by some as the most important aspect of teaching. Research has consistently told us that teacher knowledge of the learner's background is the most important factor of instruction (Hollins, 2011), and that a student's prior understandings form the basis for new learning (National Research Council [NRC], 2005). Student's live within an immediate social context of learning, family, and community. It is here that initial experiences for formal learning are developed along with mental frames and processes that provide the basis of cognitive structure for formal learning throughout childhood and adolescence. The efficacy of the teacher increases with the extent to which these funds of the student can be drawn upon (Bornstein, 1995; Cole, 1995; Hollins, 2011; Jordan, 2010; Stinson, 2006). Hollins (2011) points out that while linking new learning to prior knowledge is tacitly recognized in many teacher training programs, there is rarely practice in direct application of it. This leaves teachers unprepared to utilize the cultural funds of students. So this book will give insight into mental processes, habits of mind, and initial experiences of formal learning that Muslim students are likely to have.

Experience of Muslims Students in Public Schools

The examinations in educational research of the experiences of Muslim students are not as cumbersome as other minority groups, such as African Americans, Native Americans, and Latinos, who have a longer and more visible history in the public education system. Nevertheless, there is plenty of literature to draw on. Within these analyses and case studies some literature focuses solely on ethnic identity and renders the Muslim identity of students as either tacit or non-explicit altogether. The discussion below is limited to studies that specifically identify the subjects as Muslims.

The earliest case study that examines the experience of Muslim students in North America was done by Lila Fahlman in Ontario in 1984. There were some studies done in the 1970s on attitudes of Arab immigrant college students and their attitudes towards America and their likeliness to stay in the country (Pulcini, 1993), but these were surveys and quantitative in nature and more geared towards assessing that population's trends of assimilation. None of those studies explicitly identified its subjects as Muslim either, and likely looked at mixed-religious populations of Arabs.

Case studies of Muslim students in Western countries increased significantly after September, 11th, 2001. From these, the theme of students having detrimental experiences in school is common, and the lack of knowledge on the part of educators about Islam and practices both cultural and religious are frequently pointed at as root causes of these issues. It can be further said that this phenomena is found in case studies of Muslim students across differing ethnic backgrounds as well as Western continents and countries.[10]

Still, the narrative of detrimental schooling experience for Muslim students is not universally held. The argument has been made that the prevailing narratives of studies on Muslim students takes on an overly-dubious tenor of victimization on the part of the students, and incrimination on the part of the educators. In particular this refers to the work done by Toronto-based researcher Sarafoz Niyozov in 2009, who examined the perspectives of teachers of Muslim students (Niyozov, 2010). There could be some merit to this point, issues of bias on the parts of the researchers could very well exist. Some of the key case studies that have been done on Muslim students that form a detrimental treatment narrative were done by Muslim researchers who were more or less explicit about the fact that they were attempting to bring to the light of educational research phenomenon that they knew to exist from their own school experience or their experience as residents in a non-Muslim country (Falhman, 1984; Zine, 2001; Ahmad, 2003).

In what is perhaps the largest quantitative survey of Muslim students ever done, by New York City Public Schools, it was found that most Muslim students identify themselves as having a satisfying school experience (Cristillo, 2008). Still, while Niyozov's critique had some merit to it, a closer scrutiny reveals its errors, and this will be touched upon in chapter six. That a gap of understanding exists between Muslim students and non-Muslim educators is demonstrable in the case studies, and it is actually *affirmed* by a critical analysis of Niyozov's cross-referencing with teachers, despite his own assertions to the contrary (Abraham, 2019).

---

[10] For example, Fahlman (1983) and Zine (2000 & 2001) in Canada, De Voe (2002) and Ahmad (2003) in the United States, Gilbert (2004) and Abbas (2003) in the UK and Alitialaopp (2004) in Finland. These are only samplings that are limited to what is available in English as well.

I am not one to indict teachers or anyone else for issues that arise or are latent due to misunderstandings; and I believe that the need for educators (not to mention the broader society) to know more about Muslim students' cultural and religious backgrounds is obvious to most. Yet, to the extent that this need warrants justification from within the archives of educational research one should rest assured that it exists. However, I reemphasize the point, that case study examinations of Muslim students and the framing of their experience along patterns of victimology, and using analytical frameworks from critical theory, can also result in a pigeonholing of Muslim students into boxes in which they or their community may have never asked to be put.

If Muslim students are viewed through lenses that downplay the importance of religion in their lives, a key piece of the equation of engaging them in public schools is amiss. Researchers of Muslim students and their families almost without exception acknowledge the importance of religion and Islam in their lives. Research also confirms that families view the development of a positive Muslim identity as carrying numerous secular-world benefits along with it (Guo, 2011; Ahmed, 2015). It has been observed by some that a sense of religious priority, identity, and communal solidarity is heightened within a diaspora experience, and/or following refugee or distressed immigration experiences (Berns-McGown, 1999; De Voe, 2002; Farid & McMahan, 2004; Bigelow, 2010). According to Cristillo (2008), Muslim students are more likely to cite religion as being "very important" in their lives compared to non-Muslim students by a factor of three to one, and 98% of Muslim students in his survey said religion was important in their lives. In short, educational research overwhelmingly confirms that there is a need to examine and understand Muslim students *as Muslims*.

Chapter 2: HISTORY OF MUSLIMS IN AMERICA AND ITS LOCALITIES
A broad overview to understand diversity

Understanding the history of Muslims in America and how Muslim communities have come into being in America is a key way to understanding the diversity that exists amongst them and, to another extent, diversity that is exhibited in the way that students show up at school and in the classroom. There are of course a million different stories that could be told, and each student is an individual. However, with Muslims (and others) it is often the case that non-Muslims in their lives do not even have enough general understanding of their backgrounds to even be able to access understandings that are specific to individuals. The experiences of individuals are not divorced from broader historical trends and patterns, and understanding broader trends is the beginning point to understanding more individualized phenomena. Aspects of both will be taught and pointed to in this chapter. What is taught in this chapter is also crucial information for teachers to know so they can help Muslim students in their classrooms better understand themselves and locate their own place in historical, economic, and geographic timelines. Muslim students of K-12 ages usually have yet to learn themselves about the broad range of detail absorbed in the Muslim community in the United States and its demographics. But usually they are earnestly curious about it. Certainly this topic could be written into its own book, so I have narrowed the information and discussion here to that which I think is most pertinent to educators for inclusion in curricula, and that can help prepare teacher background knowledge to better use the resources that are offered in chapter six.

Islam and African Americans

The general population in America is often woefully unaware of the strong and deep relationship that African Americans have had with the religion of Islam throughout American history. There is much that students learn in public education about the plight, struggle, and advancement of African Americans in American history; but the role that the religion of Islam and Muslim identities has served in that history, and in the general stabilization of African American communities, is a topic that often does not get the attention it merits.

Amongst the five northernmost countries covering the territory in West Africa that had slaves taken from it by America and Western European countries, the three largest were what are today named Senegal, Sierra Leone, and Guinea. Senegal is a 90% Muslim country, Sierra Leone is 78% Muslim, and Guinea is 85% Muslim. So many of the slaves taken from those regions were undoubtedly Muslims. Most of them would lose their religion or be directly forbidden from practicing it while they were slaves in the Americas, but there are still some surviving stories of slaves who practiced Islam. It is estimated that between 15 and 30 percent of the slaves brought to the Americas from West and Central Africa were Muslims (Hill & Wilson, 2005).

There is a well known story of a man named Abdulrahman Ibrahim ibn Sori. He was a West African prince that was captured by slave traders in 1788. He was a slave for 40 years in America and his slave master would call him "prince". Since he had an advanced education in Africa he was seen as a very valuable slave who was used as a sort of supervisor over others. He spoke six different languages, including English and Arabic, and was educated in Islamic sciences as well. In 1828 he was freed from slavery by the order of president John Quincy Adams after the Sultan of Morocco learned about his encapture and presence in America and requested that he be released (Higgins, 2019).[11]

Converts and Community in the 20th Century

The end of slavery after the civil war left African Americans looking for direction with a newfound freedom, limited as it was, after having their cultural history destroyed and stolen from them. In the 20th century many African Americans began looking at traditions from Africa and the Eastern world in order to find meaning in life, and ways for themselves to assert an identity and sense of community that was distinct from the influence of whites and Christianity.

Timothy Drew and The Moorish Temple of America

One of the first of these was a man named Timothy Drew (later in life known as Drew Ali) who founded what was called *The Moorish Temple of America* in 1913 in Newark, New Jersey. The word *moor* was the name that Europeans in Spain, France, and Italy gave to Muslims living in Spain under Christian rule and in Morocco. It originates from the Greek word "mavro" and means "blackened". Drew taught that African Americans were originally of "moorish" descent as a way for them to rediscover their African roots and have racial pride in being black. This also meant, according to Drew, that the original faith of African Americans was Islamic.[12] In the

---

[11] The University of North Carolina at Chapel has a database of American slave narratives where the stories and documentation of other Muslim slaves in America can be found. The best landing point to access those is here https://docsouth.unc.edu/highlights/omarsaid.html

[12] See the document authored by Timothy Drew and entitled *The Holy Koran of the Moorish Science Temple of America: Chapter XLVIII The End of Time and the Fulfilling of the Prophesies* where Drew states, "While we, the Moorish Americans are returning to Islam, which was founded by our forefathers for our earthly and divine salvation". Please note that while Drew dubbed this document as "The Holy Koran" it is his own writings and distinct from the actual divine scripture of Islam. Drew's text is retrievable online at https://hermetic.com/moorish/7koran

1920s Drew moved the Temple[13] to Chicago where it expanded greatly. Congregations of the group would also start in the cities of Detroit, Philadelphia, and Washington DC. During this time these cities had a greatly increasing number of African Americans as many of them were migrating from southern states. Drew's movement had an appeal to some who were searching for a unique identity. Drew also had a positive message. Encouraging blacks to build themselves up to be respected and active citizens who contributed positively to society.

Members of Drew's movement adopted some practices that would be familiar to people from Muslim countries. They wore head coverings such as *keffiyehs*[14] with an *igal*[15], or a *fez* that is commonly worn by Islamic scholars in Egypt and Turkey, as well as robes that are similar to a *thobe*[16] or *kamis*.[17] They would also change their names to Arabic and Islamic names, as Drew changed his last name to Ali.

However, the core of their practices people from the Muslim world would find to be heretical. For example, Drew gave himself the title of "prophet" and proclaimed himself to be one. Drew claimed that an Egyptian magician had given him a "lost" section of the Qur'an that only he had. This text came to be known as the "Circle Seven Koran" and really it was a combination of writings taken from a Christian preacher in Ohio, another European book from the 17th century, and then some writings by Drew himself (Spalding, 2010).

The idea of adding a section to the Qur'an would seem shocking to orthodox Muslims as it goes against core tenets of Islamic belief. It is important to remember that in America in the early 20th century there was only a relatively small number of Islamic books that were translated into English. Even the English translations of the Qur'an that are most commonly accepted today had not been done yet; and the large English translations of *hadith*[18] collections were far from being

---

[13] The word "temple" itself is not native to Islam. The house of worship in Islam is called a *masjid*, which in English is referred to as a mosque.

[14] *Keffiyeh* is a general Arabic word that can be translated as "scarf" that refers to towel-like head coverings worn by men. Some of these have more specific names depending on its style.

[15] An *igal* is an accessory chord, usually black, that is worn on top of the scarf head covering to keep it in place. They are common in the Arabian Peninsula.

[16] A *thobe* is a long robe-like dress commonly worn by men in the Muslim world.

[17] While the word *kamis* generally means "shirt" in Arabic, and yes the Spanish word *camiseta* comes from it, Somalis refer to longer male dresses as a *kamis*, while Arabs would call them *thobes*.

[18] *Hadith* is the name of a certain type of source text in Islam, this is explained in chapter three.

done.[19] So I believe it might be accurate to say that Drew was very limited in the actual extent to which he could learn about orthodox Islam.

Drew's methods of taking concepts from Islam and mixing it with ideas from Christianity, African racial pride, and other philosophies would set a tone for other African American groups that asserted a Muslim identity and were progenated from his movement.

The Nation of Islam (NOI)

Drew Ali died in 1929 at the age of 43. After that the Moorish Temple split into many different groups, with many different members claiming the right to be the Temple's next leader. One group that split off was started by a man who is today known as Wallace Fard Muhammad, he had been known within the temple as David Ford El. Fard Muhammad, at first, claimed that he was the reincarnation of Drew Ali (Ahlstrom, 2004). This claim was rejected by the vast majority of the temple members, so Fard Muhammad moved from Chicago to Detroit where he started his own group that he named "The Nation of Islam" (NOI) in 1930. At the time sociologists estimated that within 3 years Fard had a following of about 8,000 people in Detroit (Beynon, 1938). He preached a message that encouraged absolute separation from whites and direct hate of them. He claimed that blacks were the "chosen people" of God and that the whites were devils. Again, these are ideas that are completely antithetical and heretical to authentic Islamic teaching.

In 1933 Fard Muhammad mysteriously disappeared. To this day it is unknown what happened to him, but he is said to have been last seen by his closest student, Elijah Muhammad, who would take over leadership of the NOI after him. Elijah Muhammad was born in Georgia in 1897 and had moved north to Detroit in his twenties to escape the racism and poor conditions of the South. He later said that he had seen black men hung by whites in Georgia three different times before he was twenty (Clegg, 1997).

Elijah Muhammad and the NOI's movement was stalled for a period in the 1940s when Elijah was arrested for dodging the draft. But by the 1960s the NOI had temples in most major

---

[19] Hadith translations that would have been done at this time would have only been found in the libraries of Universities that had orientalist studies departments to which access would have been exclusive. Though in America even these departments did not develop until later than ones in Europe. Princeton had one of the first ones but it was not founded until 1927 https://eas.princeton.edu/about-us/history-department, just two years after Drew's death. Muhammad Muhsin Khan did not do the commonly used translation of Bukhari's hadith collection until 1971. The University of Southern California had not catalogued that collection digitally in a database that is commonly used today until 2005 http://www.cmje.org/about/history/.

northern cities and had an active role in the civil rights movement. Elijah preached that blacks should separate from whites and have their own businesses, security force, agriculture, and infrastructure. Elijah mentored converts to the NOI such as Malcolm X and Muhammad Ali who brought greater national fame to the organization. Muhammad Ali was well known as a star boxer, and many other famous black athletes joined the NOI movement. Malcolm X became known as a prominent preacher for the NOI and made more appearances on television and in front of media than Elijah Muhammad did.

Transition to Sunni Islam

Malcom X

The number of members of the NOI reached at least 50,000 in the 1960s. Beginning around that time some key occurrences would provide the impetus for the vast majority of NOI members to shift away from the group and towards Sunni, or orthodox, Islam.

First was the conversion of Malcom X to Sunni Islam in 1964. In March of that year he publicly announced that he was leaving the NOI saying he believed it had "gone as far as it can go" and embraced a more inclusive idea of progress for blacks in the civil rights movement. Outside observers had considered Malcolm X a more extreme figure in the Civil Rights movement than Martin Luther King Jr because of the NOI's message that blacks should separate from whites completely.

After leaving the NOI, Sunni Muslims began encouraging Malcom X to accept orthodox Islam, which he quickly did. In April of 1964 Malcom X went on *Hajj*, the pilgrimage to Mecca, which is one of the five pillars of Islam that all able-to-do-so Muslims are obligated to perform once in their lives, this is discussed in chapter three. A letter that Malcom X wrote from Mecca about his experience in Hajj shows the power of his experience and seeing Islam as something that encouraged and provided for harmony amongst all races and peoples. He wrote in it:

> *"Never have I witnessed such sincere hospitality and overwhelming spirit of true brotherhood as is practiced by people of all colors and races here in this ancient Holy Land, the home of Abraham, Muhammad and all the other Prophets of the Holy Scriptures. For the past week, I have been utterly speechless and spellbound by the graciousness I see displayed all around me by people of all colors."[20]*

---

[20] His full letter is retrievable at http://islam.uga.edu/malcomx.html, it can also be referenced in his autobiography: *The Autobiography of Malcom X as told to Alex Haley*. New York: Grove Press, 1965. Pages 388-393.

Malcolm X returned to America impassioned and in the middle of developing a new philosophy of empowerment for black people. But his activist efforts would be cut short in 1965 when he was murdered.[21] Many other African Americans were inspired to convert to Sunni Islam following his example, and people of all stripes continue to be inspired by his autobiography which was published after his death.

Warith Deen Mohammed

Warith Deen Mohammed was the son of Elijah Mohammed. Elijah Muhammad had anointed and planned for his son to take over leadership of the NOI after his death (the name Warith Deen actually means *inheritor of the religion*), which he did in 1975. Almost immediately he began disbanding the NOI and urging its followers to accept Sunni Islam. He renamed the organization the World Community of Al-Islam in the West and later renamed it to what it is called today, the American Society of Muslims.

Warith Deen used the NOI's newspaper to explain the many changes he was starting. This included introducing his followers to the five pillars of orthodox Islam and denouncing many of the teachings of his father and Wallace Fard Mohammed. He denounced the idea that white people were devils, as well as the idea that his father or Wallace Fard were Prophets. Warith Deen greatly encouraged African Americans to live in harmony with other communities. He would read as much as he could from Sunni Islamic books and write about his interpretations[22] of them for his followers in the former NOI publications, *Muhammad Speaks* and *The Bilalian*, which he later renamed to *The Muslim Journal*. The Nation of Islam does still exist today because it was revived in 1977 by Louis Farrakhan[23], a follower of Elijah Muhammad who did not agree with Warith Deen's reforms. However, their following today is very small compared to what it was before 1975.

---

[21] Ostensibly, Malcolm X was killed by members of the NOI who considered him a trader. The NOI itself claimed, and continues to claim, that the FBI was the instigator of his assassination. There is dispute about where responsibility lies for his assassination to this day.

[22] While Warith Deen renounced many of the NOI's previous teachings it has been noted by Sunni Muslim observers that Warith Deen had *some* more liberal teachings and approaches to understanding of Islamic texts that would rightly still be described as antithetical to Sunni Islam.

[23] Farrakhan has had various instances of national prominence in his career. Most notably when Barack Obama was linked to him through mutual associates they had in Chicago, where Farrakhan and the current-day NOI are based, from the National Black Caucus. Farrakhan is roundly recognized and condemned as an anti-semite, so this connection was used by adversaries of Obama as a means to criticize him. Farrakhan is considered both a pariah and a heretic by the orthodox Muslim community in America, who also roundly condemn him.

The conversions of Malcom X and Warith Deen Mohammed and his followers led to mass numbers of African Americans converting to Sunni Islam in the 1970s and after. This caught the attention of Islamic scholars in the Muslim world. When Malcom X first went on Hajj in 1964 the government of Saudi Arabia put him through a vetting process to verify he was a Muslim because he had an American passport and did not know Arabic. Now, they were seeing that large numbers of African Americans were becoming Muslim in America's big cities.

Scholars in the Muslim world wanted to make sure that there were people well educated in Islam to lead and teach the newfound urban communities of Muslims in the United States. Therefore, beginning in the late 1970s many young African Americans from these communities were given, and still are given, opportunities by Muslim governments and philanthropists overseas to travel to learning institutes in the Muslim world. Many would make this learning journey of their own expense as well. They would especially go to the countries of Saudi Arabia, Yemen, and Egypt. At these institutes they learn the Arabic language and religious jurisprudence directly from Islamic scholars.

Probably the most well-known of these students is Jeffrey Kearse, who would rename himself to Siraj Wahaj. Wahaj was born in Brooklyn and joined the nation of Islam in 1969 at the age of 19. He was one of the many members to renounce the teachings of Elijah Muhammad and convert to Sunni Islam under the encouragement of Warith Deen Mohammed (Barrett, 2007). In 1978 he was given the chance from the government of Saudi Arabia to study Islam and Arabic at Umm al-Qura University in the city of Mecca. After returning from his studies Wahaj became an Imam in Brooklyn and would record his lectures on audio cassette tape, and his students would make copies of them and distribute them to mosques[24] in America. This gave many young American Muslims their first chance to hear a native English speaker who had studied at an Islamic University in the Muslim world lecture about Islam. Today he is still the Imam of Masjid al-Taqwa in Brooklyn (Dulong, 2005).

Another more recent example of the many African Americans who have gone overseas to study Islam is Tahir Wyatt, a native Philadelphian. Wyatt was born after the movement of Warith Deen Mohammed had begun, so he grew up in a Philadelphia where African American Muslims had become commonplace in the city. In high school in the 1990s Wyatt was signed to a record deal as a rap musician by Troy Carter, who is known today as being the manager of Lady Gaga. As big a deal as it was to be signed to a record deal at age fourteen, Wyatt decided instead to accept Islam and leave his ambitions for a career in music. Shortly after high school he took the

---

[24] *Mosque* is the English name of a house of worship in Islam. Muslims generally do not use the word "mosque" they use the Arabic word *masjid*, these two words will be used interchangeably in this book.

opportunity to attend the Islamic University of Madina on a scholarship. He would end up staying in Madina for almost 20 years and earning his PhD from the University. In 2012 Wyatt was assigned by a decree of King Abdullah of Saudi Arabia to become the first American teacher at the Mosque of The Prophet Muhammad ﷺ[25] in Medina, where many renowned Islamic scholars from around the world teach.[26]

Conclusion

The post-slavery eras in America have left African Americans searching for their own unique identity and place in the world. This has led to many different paths for what it means to be African American. They are a people that are still subject to mistreatment, abuse, and manipulation by the machinations of many outside forces. Amidst this many have found Islam and a Muslim identity as a place for their unique personal and communal expression as African Americans to such an extent that today, in a time in the 21st century where there are more Muslims in America than ever before, it is often not recognized that up until 2011 the most common ethnic group to which Muslims in America belong to is that of native-born African Americans. Still today native-born African Americans make up 30% of the Muslim population in America. The most organized, well-integrated, civically-involved, and long-standing Muslim communities in America are communities that are primarily comprised of and led by African Americans; especially in the cities where the NOI had a strong presence .

The time period since the Civil Rights Act has seen immigrants from all over the Muslim world come into America. Many of these immigrant communities have a distinct and well-known presence in certain places, but despite the ever-increasing visibility of immigrant and recent-generation Muslim communities, the places in America where one is likely to see the most mosques are in the cities where African American Muslim communities formed in previous generations.

Earliest Immigrant Waves

The immigration patterns of the late 19th century and early 20th century in America witnessed the first identifiable numbers of Muslim immigrants coming to America. At this time the United States had opened its doors to immigrants from new places in eastern Europe, Russia, and Western Asia. Muslim immigrants in this time period came in particular from the area that is referred to as the Levant or the Fertile Crescent in English terminology, which is today the Arab

---

[25] It is part of Islamic etiquette to say "peace be upon him" after the Prophet Muhammad ﷺ is mentioned, and likewise to write it out after he is referred to in written text. The symbol that is annotated here is Arabic calligraphy that writes this out.

[26] Tahir Wyatt's autobiography can be found here: https://www.youtube.com/watch?v=Gx6JhmTxk38

countries of Lebanon, Syria, Jordan, and the Palestinian territories.[27] Muslims also came from Turkey at this time as well. There are not exact figures on the amount of Muslim immigrants to come at this time but they were by far the minority of immigrants from these lands. Estimates are that at least 90% of Arab immigrants to come to America at that time were Christian. Researchers have stated that the Muslim migrants from the Levant at this time were predominantly male, with few female arrivals. It was also not uncommon that married Muslim male immigrants came with the expectation that they would return to their left-behind families in their homeland after only a few years (Naff, 1985). Though this did not occur universally.

One of the most significant pockets of Muslim immigrants were Arabs who came to the state of Michigan from Palestine, Lebanon, and Yemen to work at Henry Ford's Model-T plant (Abraham & Abraham, 1983). A result of this today is that Wayne County, Michigan is a significant hub of the Arab-American community in the United States. In the city of Dearborn over thirty percent of the 98,000 residents are Arab Americans, and they are predominantly Shia Muslims (Roberts, 2004; Hosseni, 2018). The only Arab-American museum in America is in Detroit, having been founded in 1971, and Michigan is the only state that lists Arab Americans as having their own racial category in demographic tracking (Michigan Department of Community Health [MDCH], 2008). The early Arab immigrants to Michigan were religiously diverse, but a significant number of them were Shia Muslims. That Shias were a minority under Ottoman rule in the early 20th century could have given them more of an impetus to immigrate to America in the early 20th century.

Some of the Muslim Arab immigrants to Michigan spread out to other places and other Arab Muslim immigrants went directly to other locales. Being that many were from agrarian backgrounds they actually migrated towards more rural places, and in particular the Dakotas and Iowa. An account from a newspaper in 1967 cites Syrian Muslims as having settled in the city of Crookston, MN in 1902. The first building ever built to be a mosque in the United States was in the tiny town of Ross, North Dakota in 1929 (Naff, 1985).[28] The longest still-standing mosque was built in Cedar Rapids, Iowa in 1934, which is now registered with The National Registry of Historical Places.

There were also some Muslim immigrants to the Pacific coast in the early 20th century from South Asia, and in particular from the Punjab region of India. These immigrants mostly worked

---

[27] This region is referred to as *Ash-Sham* in Arabic and by people native to it.

[28] Arabs in Michigan lay claim to have the first established mosque in the United states in the second decade of the twentieth century (Abraham & Abraham, 1983). But it was in a building built for a previous purpose.

as farmers or lumberers. It was also common with this group that only men would come with the expectation that they might soon return home (Frederking, 2007).

Racial Classification of Arabs and South Asians

From the time of their first arrival, Arabs and South Asians have had an interesting and complicated relationship with the United States pertaining to how they have been identified, treated, and categorized racially. The need to have racial categories is somewhat of an American phenomenon in itself that immigrants from these lands had generally not dealt with in their home countries. These countries were more likely to organize society by religious adherence (in the Arab world[29]), or caste system (in India[30]), or some combination of both (India).

There was much initial confusion, arguing, and differing between these groups and European-heritage whites over how they would be categorized racially in American society. In the first decade of the 20th century the Bureau of Immigration and Naturalization was ordered to restrict citizenship eligibility for certain ethnic groups of recently arrived immigrants. A debate in society ensued about how to class Syrian-Arab immigrants in particular, and as to whether or not they should be categorized as white or Asian. Syrians at that time argued vigorously in courts, the press, and society in general that their ethnic stock originated from caucasian semitics and they were therefore white (Arab American Institute [AAI], 1997).

South Asians had been classed as "Hindus" from 1920-1940 and then later as "white" with the reformation of immigration laws in the 1950s, until being classed as "Asian" under the racial categories used today by the federal government for the census, which were essentially established in 1978.[31] Those same racial categories place Arabs under the category of "white". This has caused almost all Arabs, Muslim or otherwise, since the 1970s to consistently have an experience of being classed as white on official documentation while not infrequently having an experience in the society of being ostensibly classed as "people of color". This is likely even more true for Arabs who solidly identify as Muslim, and especially those who express that identity in their external appearance. The early 20th century Arab immigrants, who were overwhelmingly Christian, advocated for their own whiteness in the society so they could reap

---

[29] In the Arab world identifying by religion is so common that governments usually put a person's religion on their identification card. Human Rights Watch has many reports on this https://www.hrw.org/

[30] The caste system in India is called *Jati* and comes from Hinduism and Hindu culture. There is nothing about castes that are integral to Islam, but some Muslims cultures in South Asia have practiced a caste system inherited from their pre-Islamic eras (Ansari, 1960).

[31] United States Census Bureau history of racial classification https://www.census.gov/data-tools/demo/race/MREAD_1790_2010.html

the numerous social and economic benefits of being white; and they did this successfully. Generally, they were also fervent to assimilate civically into their communities in order to avoid discrimination and stigmatization.

As more Muslim immigrants came from the Arab world and South Asia following the Immigration Act of 1965, viewing people from these groups as primarily an ethnic-racial group becomes complex. Their external complexions might indicate sameness to the typical racial lenses that American society and the Western world has put onto its categorization of people. Yet they come from societies where religion is frequently the distinguishing marker amongst people. Since Muslim immigrants would find themselves as a religious minority in the society, assimilation is much less seamless for them compared to a Christian immigrant from the same homeland.

This is one reason why the early 20th century saw Arabs advocating for themselves in court cases to be classed as white, while the end of the 20th century sees them petitioning the federal government to be given their own classification under the census so as to not be classed as white (AAI, 1997; 2019). The influx of newer immigrant Muslims that came into these ethnic populations by the late 1990s changed the way the ethnic terms, as racial identity markers in American society, related to the society at large. Interestingly, in 1997 the federal government denied the Arab American community's petition to be classed as a racial minority (and again in 2017) due to their findings that Arabs were on average of a higher socio-economic status than ethnic European whites, and concluding that classing them as racial minorities would open them up to undue benefits under affirmative action laws (Brittingham & de la Cruz, 2005).

For most of the history of Arabs in America they have had what academics have described as an "on and off" racial visibility in society (Jamal & Naber, 2008). Meaning that they frequently have been capable of blending in as white but oftentimes will not. Religion is a key factor that contributes to this degree of visibility, as well as one's own choice and degree of comfort with external expression of religious identity. A Muslim wearing garb that indicates religiosity is not likely to see themselves as racially invisible in American society. The risks associated with this visibility can also impact a Muslim's decision-making process as to whether or not they do externalize themselves cosmetically as religious. Wanting to avoid stigmatization can heavily influence the decisions of individuals as to whether or not they wear gowns, head coverings, or grow a beard, in spite of the religiosity they might feel internally. Specifics of racial complexion play into this as well, as both Arabs and South Asians can cover a wide spectrum of skin tone shades, some more readily to be interpreted as "brown", "dark", or "colored" than others.

Another significant factor is the political climate of a given time in American society. Political events of the 1960s and 1970s[32] that positioned the United States to be in conflict with Middle Eastern[33] countries had the effect of putting images of Arab and South Asian people in the news media. Images that were not flattering to American sensibilities. During these times, the racial complexions and facial features of Arabs and South Asians would become subject to patterns of stereotyping[34], and thus receive a negative association in the society's collective consciousness. The events of September 11th, 2001 have served to change the racial visibility of Arabs and South Asians from an "on and off" dynamic to one that is fully on.

Professional Class of Muslim Immigrants

It is impossible to know exactly how many Muslims have immigrated to the United States or what the exact Muslim population in the country is since the United States government does not track residents and citizens by religion. However, taking into consideration federally reported issuances of regular green cards, the most-recent country of residency stated by immigrants coming from countries of high Muslim populations, and geopolitical and economic factors that have driven immigration and effected the causes of migration from within certain Muslim countries; some estimates can be arrived at and general trends can be ascertained.

The United States instituted racial quotas in immigration in 1923 that severely limited the number of non-Western Europeans who could immigrate to the country. Therefore the succeeding decades saw limited immigration to the United States from Muslim lands. But the 1965 Immigration Act ended those quotas in the context of the Civil Rights era, and this opened the door for immigration from Muslim countries once again. Immigration reform following the 1920s had also seen new restrictions put in place on immigrants based on provable income and professional qualifications. Preferences for relatives and near family members were also put into the immigration codes. As a result, Muslims who came to the United States after 1965 were mostly professional or upper-class citizens in their home countries who were immigrating for

---

[32] Such as ongoing conflicts between Arab countries and Israel, the Israeli oil embargo of 1973, and the Iranian revolution of 1979.

[33] I use the term "Middle Eastern" here because it has been the terminology typically used by the news media. As a term it is at best, nebulous, and oftentimes counterproductive. This has been acknowledged in academia as far back as the 1960s (Davison, 1960). In my opinion it ought to become an archaic term in favor of simply designating specific countries, or referring to the Muslim World.

[34] To understand more about historical patterns of the Western world stereotyping the Arab and Muslim world please read the book *Orientalism* by Edward Said from 1978, which was profoundly influential upon critical theory in the humanities. To learn about how these patterns of stereotyping have played out in American cinema in concert with American political interests please look into the book and documentary *Reel Bad Arabs* by Jack Sheehan. These resources offer valuable insights into critical lenses that can be passed onto students as well.

professional, business, or educational purposes. In particular, these immigrants came from Muslim countries that had experienced long periods of colonization from the French and the British, where colonial reform of their educational systems had prepared the upper-class citizenry to travel abroad to Western countries in order to advance their professional expertise in the hopes of one day returning home to help develop the third world or developing countries from which they hailed. According to the federal government's annual publishing of immigration statistics[35], an annual average of 1,803 Arab immigrants came to the United States from the countries of Jordan, Syria, Lebanon, Egypt, and Iraq[36] from mid-year 1963 to mid-year 1966.[37]

A significant rise happens when the Immigration Act takes full force with the reported number of immigrants from these countries going from 1,406 in 1966 to 5,685 in 1967. Also, interestingly, while the number of family relation visas issued to Arab immigrants from 1964-66 is almost three times the amount of occupational visas (2.87:1), in 1967 the amount of occupational visas became more than twice that of family relation visas (2.12:1). The 1964-66 visas are likely being issued to relatives of previous ethnic Arab American citizens whose families had been in the country for a generation or more, and as such would be of a religious makeup similar to that of previous generations; i.e. predominantly Christian.

Overall, the decade following full enactment of the 1965 immigration law sees immigrants from Arab countries listed in the federal government's annual reporting average around 7,000 per year; with twice as many occupational visas being issued as family relation ones. However, there is an ebb and flow in approximately three year chunks between which visa category is issued in higher amounts. Suggesting waves of professional visas being issued were then

---

[35] All discussion on immigration statistics in this book are taken from my own analysis of raw data tables from the Department of Homeland Security's (DHS) annual *Yearbook of Immigration Statistics*. Available here https://www.dhs.gov/immigration-statistics/yearbook for years after 1996. For years prior to 1996 the yearbook was published under the title the *Statistical Yearbook of the Immigration and Naturalization Service*. All yearbooks and statistics were published by the Department of State prior to the DHS's founding in 2002. Yearbooks prior to 1996 were accessed through the Center for Immigration Studies. I opted to do my own analysis of the raw immigration statistics because many claims are made by secondary sources about immigration numbers of Muslim peoples to America, but I have found in my research that these claims, which come from a variety of different parties, commonly do not cross-reference well with the actual data from the federal government. Since immigrants are not tracked by religion there is always a subjective element to any analysis like this, so the methods I used to arrive at estimates are explained in the discussion here and I prefer to simply use raw numbers to illustrate the explained phenomena.

[36] These are the specific Arab countries for whom the federal government published numbers, immigrants from other Arab countries during this time would have been classed in federal reports as "other Asian" or "other African"

[37] The government's annual reporting of immigration statistics lists the previous year's numbers as beginning and ending in June.

followed by waves of family-relation visas being issued. This likely shows a pattern where professionals had to arrive and establish themselves ahead of time, while their family stayed in the home country for a few years before immigrating to reunite in America. The government reported immigrant numbers from Pakistan (a non-Arab 98% Muslim country) from 1966-1973 were just over 900 arrivals per year on average, with the ratio of occupational to family relation visas being just under 2:1. Subsequent to that Pakistani immigrants would be listed under "other asian" until 1986 and their numbers are therefore indiscernible.

In 1986 the federal government began reporting much more detailed immigration numbers by country. Taking countries with a vast majority Muslim population and norming[38] their immigration totals by the country's actual percent Muslim population indicates that around 49,000 Muslim immigrants arrived in the United States annually from 1986-1990. A significant portion of this number belongs to immigrants from Iran and Iraq. The political circumstances by which these immigrants came in the 1980s is such that non-Muslims from Iraq[39], and less-religious or fully-secular Muslims from Iran[40], were more likely to immigrate to the United States during this time (and before and after as well to a fair degree, which will be discussed shortly). If these two countries are excluded from the numbers it drops to approximately 27,500 annual Muslim arrivals. If we look at just the Arab countries that were tracked in the 1970s *and* norm each country by its Muslim percentage, the annual arrivals are approximately 6,500, which was an increase of over 40% from the 1970s to 1980s.

What emerges from this analysis of immigration patterns and visa issuance from 1965-1990 is that, overall, it is a professional class of immigrants with most immigrants coming because they meet occupational qualifications requirements. While the initial waves of immigrants in the 1970s would often see several years where immigrants coming on professional visas outnumbered those being brought on family-relation visas, over time immigrants coming on

---

[38] Norming here means taking the total number of immigrants from a country with a high Muslim population but only including a percentage equal to the percent that that country's population is Muslim.

[39] A large amount of these immigrants came as refugees who were under persecution from Saddam Huessein during the Iraq-Iran war of the 1980s. Hussein explicitly targeted non-Muslim populations such as the Kurds and Chaldean Christians as a wartime tactic. The United States welcomed refugees from these populations with open arms.

[40] A large number of immigrants from Iran in the 1980s were refugees who were fleeing from their war with Iraq as well, but also fleeing from the regime of Ayatollah Khomeini that had taken over in 1979. These immigrants were largely secular and opposed to the religious authoritarianism imposed by Khomeini. Due to this, and other reasons, Iranian immigrants to the West are often less-likely to be religious than Muslim immigrants from other countries. According to Pew Research (2018) more than one in five Iranian ethnics in the United States that were born to a Muslim family no longer identify as Muslim when they are adults.

family-relation visas began to outnumber those coming on occupational visas by about a 2:1 ratio on an annual basis.

Estimated Muslim Immigrant Arrivals from Selected Countries

Decade	Annual Average
1970s	6,500
1980s	31,000
1990s	55,000
2000s	85,000
2010s	44,000

While there was a gradual increase since the 1965 Immigration Act in the number of immigrants coming to the USA from Muslim countries, the largest amount come after the turn of the century in the first decade of the 2000s. This trend suggests an increasing amount of Muslim students attending American public schools in the 21st century. An amount that will not likely decrease in the future as the immigrant populations themselves are on average young, many still of child rearing ages, while those who immigrated as children in the 90s and early 2000s are now coming to the ages of child rearing and family settlement.

Important to Understand about Professional Class Immigrants

Muslim immigrants from South Asia and Arab countries have by and large come as a professional working class. Immigration regulations dictate that immigrants coming under occupational visas will have to meet requirements whereby they are at least one of the following:

- Highly qualified to practice their profession[41]
- Highly wealthy[42]
- Willing to work in an area of need[43]

Many professional class immigrants first came to the United States with the idea that they would come temporarily to acquire qualifications and skills to enhance their professional expertise that they could then bring back to their home country, which would have been in earlier stages of industrial development. But the reality was typically that both comfort and upward mobility was found in life in America and they ended up opting to stay, and oftentimes opting to earn citizenship after a while, which would thereby enable them to sponsor more family members to also immigrate.[44]

This results in these immigrant populations building communities up overtime in certain locales as opposed to replanting en masse. Predictably, this also means these populations exist in their largest numbers in the American cities that have the largest populations, such as New York and Los Angeles. But it also results in significant populations in metro areas that have had burgeoning economies since the 1970s alongside several colleges and universities. So while Pakistanis, for example, are most populous in New York City, and have a large population in other cities with over 2 million people, the metro area with the second largest percentage of Pakistanis as part of the total population is the Washington DC & Arlington/Alexandria, VA area. The same area is the third most populous (after NYC and LA) for Egyptians.

---

[41] This usually means that in their home country they were the best of the best and the needed qualifications that they do have can not be met by the labor pool of American citizenry https://www.uscis.gov/working-united-states/permanent-workers.

[42] Those who get EB-5 visas as foreign business investors certainly apply here, but it is also typically the case that those coming as students on F1 visas (not a permanent Green Card visa) have an easier time doing so when their families can prove a substantial amount of wealth. The federal government requires that people coming on student visas "must have the financial resources to live and study in the United States" https://studyinthestates.dhs.gov/financial-ability. Student visas are not included in the numbers I showed because an F1 visas does not grant permanent residence, however, being hired for a job after finishing school is often a route for foreign students to obtain permanent residency, or, by being sponsored by a family member who is already in the country.

[43] This may or may not mean having an upper-class occupation. For example, throughout the 1970s and 80s Arab immigrants often acquired visas to work as taxi drivers in New York City. Since the 1990s, many immigrants from India and Pakistan, as well as some from the Arab countries, have come on occupational visas to work in the tech industry due to a lack of qualified candidates within the United States. There was also another spurt of Arab immigrants brought to work in automotive plants in Michigan in the 1960s. American enterprise directing the development of the petroleum industry in the Arab world also brought many professional immigrants in engineering in the 1970s

[44] This in turn creates a side phenomenon where immigration to the United States is often a source of developing countries losing the residency of their top professionals, inhibiting the potential for the native population of their countries to build it up.

While New York and LA almost certainly have the largest number of Muslims due to their size, other cities have significant Muslim populations that represent a higher portion of the cities' and metro areas' populations in general. According to one metric,[45] the metro areas with the largest percentage of Muslim immigrant populations are Washington DC, San Bernardino, Minneapolis, Atlanta, and Providence, in that order. Educators in metro areas such as these may experience that Muslim immigrant communities have a stronger "presence" in their school systems compared to larger metro areas.

Assimilation

One thing I enjoy about illustrating this immigration pattern that stretched back to the sixties and seventies is that it makes apparent to people that there is a longer history than is often perceived of Muslims being spread out throughout the country. Educators nowadays might have grown up in the 1970s-90s, and done so without the impression that they grew up around any Muslims at all. In the pre-9/11 era what Muslims and Islam even were may have been something of which they were wholly unaware.

What is often not considered by people is that they might have known neighbors, acquaintances, colleagues, or classmates who *were* Muslim, but they were not aware of it. The reason for this being that it was typically the case amongst professional immigrants who came from the Muslim world in the 1970s and 80s that they were explicit and intentional about assimilating into a professional culture where they would not externalize their Muslim identity. What does this mean? It means that if you were a Muslim man coming to work at a professional company in America, there would be no way that you would do so with the expectation of showing up to work with a beard or in a long gown.[46] Likewise, a woman would not plan to show up to her office job wearing a *hijab*. Rather, they would come to the country with full expectation and readiness to assimilate into professional culture.

Why? One of the main reasons is that since these professional immigrants were coming from countries that had experienced long periods of colonization from the British or the French (or both) the education systems in those countries, especially those available to upper-class people, had been reformed in order to prepare people for the possibility to live and work in the West (Kinsey, 1971; Mazawi, 2002). Many people in their home countries would have already done this when migrating to European countries, the 1965 Immigration Act simply opened the door

---

[45] The amount of immigrants who state they intend to live in that area upon arrival.

[46] The wearing of long gowns is a common form of dress for men in the Muslim world. and wearing one (while not mandatory to do) is a part of religious practice. These gowns can vary in length, style, and name from culture to culture.

for America to be an option for assimilatory professional migration as well.[47] This is something of a key point to understand, that immigrants who came to America as professionals from Muslim communities typically have a fair extent of formal education, as well language attainment, that amounts to being effectively conditioned to functionally operate in the Western world on a professional level in such a way that their "Muslimness" would be masked or unapparent.

It is also important to understand that children of professional-class immigrants who come either at young ages or are born in America will have a very different experience than their parents growing up. Their parents had the benefit of growing up in the home culture and had received, to an extent, an explicit preparation for how they would conduct themselves living in the West, and how they would balance assimilation with their home cultural identity and values. The younger generation, on the other hand, does not get a fully immersed inculturation into the home-country culture. By growing up in America they will experience being a religious and (most likely) racial minority. They will also grow up in a society that is not structured to accommodate the practice of Islam, which has profound familial and psychological implications for how these families operate. Their parents are also likely to have grown up in a culture with a very different concept of adolescence and the role and expectations of youth.[48] On top of all this they will likely have a family background and tradition that places a high value on education and professional attainment, and strong familial pressure to do well in school and even to strive for attaining particular occupations[49] regardless of personal taste. Thus they incur a complex set of compound pressures, and in one manner or another this is the case for virtually all Muslim youth in the West as the ensuing chapters of this book will illuminate.

---

[47] Albeit with America having more difficult criteria to meet in order to be granted visas than other countries, particularly Britain and Canada. Due to this some of the ethnic immigrant communities from Muslim countries that have formed in in America have corollary communities in Canada, Britain, or other Western countries that may have a longer history of being there. These transnational communities are what is dubbed a "diaspora" and often they stay connected to one another, made easier in the modern day due to social media.

[48] It is extraordinarily common for immigrant Muslim parents to interpret their children who grow up in America as being "spoiled" due to the amount of autonomy that American children assert and come to expect, as well as the extent to which they will hold onto petulant behaviors in latter ages past puberty relative to the expectations in their home country.

[49] The medical and engineering fields generally have a very high status in both Arab and South Asian culture. It is not uncommon that children are told from a young age to specifically strive for those professions. As an example to illustrate this, studies have found that over half of undergraduate students in a major university in Egypt pursue degrees in engineering fields (El-Sayed, 2004); more than twice the rate in American universities (Yoder, n.d). These professional priorities can be a factor, albeit with some different dynamics, amongst other Muslim cultures as well.

Commonly, the children of Muslim immigrants usually face the need to have an explicit internal confrontation with their own identity when growing up in America at some point in their life. In contrast to their parents who would have grown up in an environment where the religious and cultural values were reinforced throughout all reaches of the society, these children find themselves growing up with their parents being the main, if not lone, source of reinforcement of the values and traditions of their religion and native ethnic culture. Part of how parents do this is by desperately trying to create an enclave community that reflects those values, but in doing so they have to battle upstream against American society's cultural currents by always remaining isolated and unbeknownst to some degree to the rest of society.

For Muslim communities the pain of these battles manifest especially in the lives of young people. Where pressures from peers and the society in general reinforce attitudes, behaviors, and dispositions that come into conflict with home-cultural and religious teaching. Especially at ages when youth are susceptible to peer pressure and being enchanted by American pop culture. The adoption of behaviors that earn appraisal from peers are likely to be found as unbecoming by parents who come from cultures where admonition, and reprimand of nonconformist young people is honored and expected; and the place of religious guilt has no small part in this. Therefore internal conflicts arise from the need to reconcile questions of personal identity, life pathways, and competing social, familial, and interpersonal pressures. These conflicts often stretch into early adulthood and may even be a lifelong process of sorting out an assured self-identity.

In this sense, the home culture becomes a hidden baggage that Muslim kids always carry with them when they are in spaces outside of the Muslim community. A primary factor that compounds the weight of this baggage is the pure lack of knowledge that non-Muslims have about Islam and Muslim culture. Especially, when those non-Muslims are adults who are charged with facilitating these young people's growth, education, and development (i.e. their educators in public schools). This book is a humble attempt to bridge this gap to some degree, and arm non-Muslim educators with at least a beginning step towards having the actual knowledge needed in order to at least consider assisting Muslim families in raising kids according to the values they hold dear.

Educators in public schools have to understand that there is perhaps no more of a square example of what researchers have called the "immigrant paradox" in America (García Coll & Kerivan Marks, 2012), than the case of Muslim children. The "immigrant paradox" refers to the fact that immigrants and their children are, and have always been, under extraordinary pressure to assimilate into American society. Yet, it is shown overwhelmingly by research that the closer immigrants stay to their home culture, the *less likely* they are to experience a virtually full array of impairments to personal health and mental well-being that dominate concerns over youth and adolescents.[50] Educators in public schools also need to accept and acknowledge that the research that undergirds the immigrant paradox lends near indisputable support to the argument that reinforcing the values of their Muslim students' families in the schooling context is consistent with producing healthy and productive life outcomes for their students.

Refugees

Just as the Immigration Act of 1965 created new openings for professional migration to America, the same is true of the Refugee Act of 1980 for the resettlement of refugees. Prior to 1980, refugees and asylum seekers had to have been fleeing communist regimes in order to be admitted into the country (Felter & McBride, 2018). Due to this, the first Muslim group of people to relocate to America via the refugee process were members of the Cham community of Southeast Asia[51] who relocated to the Seattle metropolitan area in the 1970s (Douglas, 2005). While Muslim immigrants coming from anywhere and anyway to America brings about similar concerns and dynamics, the refugee experience carries some different factors and considerations for educators to know about in contrast to professional class migration. In some cases it has made it so the refugee migration of people has happened on a larger scale with people resettling in a more group-like fashion and developing diaspora communities with a heightened sense of immediacy, urgency, and dependency on one another. As opposed to coming in a parsed out manner and forming cultural communities over time and even generations succeeding one's arrival. Adjustment and resettlement of refugees is typically aided by non-profit organizations that receive some measure of government funding from the State Department. In turn, refugee communities usually end up in states and metro areas where such organizations have a strong presence, and the dynamics of the local economy creates a political desire for them to come.

---

[50] The psychologist Leonard Sax has aggregated this research, which shows girls and boys whose families have recently immigrated to North America when compared to girls and boys born and raised in North America are less likely to be anxious or depressed (Takeuchi et al, 2007; Alegría et al, 2008; Suárez et al, 2009; Nguyen, 2011), less likely to engage in binge drinking or other forms of alcohol abuse, and/or substance abuse (Vega et al, 1998; Allen et al, 2008; Prado et al, 2009; Hernandez et al, 2012); and less likely to make unhealthy choices regarding adolescent sexuality, such as having intercourse before 15 years of age (Guarini, 2011; Raffaelli et al, 2012). Summaries of these studies findings and more is available here https://www.ashmi.org/uploaded/parents/ash.pdf

[51] Primarily Vietnam and Cambodia as far as from where refugees came to America, but the Cham community is spread throughout Austronesia.

Education levels of refugees can vary greatly depending on country, regional place of origin[52], and class status in their home country. However, something that is common to people who go through the refugee process with a background of being educated and having professional expertise is finding that their qualifications do not transfer, or are unable to be transferred, to their new homeland. This is almost certain to be the case in America if their professional training and credentials were not earned in the English language[53] (Yildiz, 2009). This can result in people who had professional class status in their home country being forced to settle on working lower-class menial occupations in America.

The refugee process is in no way smooth, people can spend any number of years in refugee camps awaiting resettlement, and refugees have only limited say, if any at all, as to the country in which they will be assigned to resettle.[54] In this light, America is often seen as an idyllic and hoped-for destination amongst Muslim refugees, however, this idealization frequently leads to a let down once arrived when the lived experience is found to not match fantasized expectations (Abdi, 2015).

The experience of trauma is another factor typically experienced by refugees and it comes along with a myriad of implications for students and families in the school system. This is discussed in more detail further down.

Iraqis

Iraqis have made up the second largest national grouping of refugees to come to the United States since the turn of the 21st century.[55] This is in addition to large numbers of Iraqi refugees coming during the Iraq-Iran war of the 1980s. The first thing to know about the Iraqi refugee population is that it is very diverse, proportionately more diverse than Iraq itself. While Iraq is

---

[52] Educational attainment is generally higher amongst people from urban vs. rural locales in the Muslim world, and better part of the developing world as well (Winthrop & McGivney, 2015).

[53] As will be discussed, the two countries where the vast majority of Muslim refugees in America come from are Iraq and Somalia. Iraq's education system is primarily in Arabic but the fields of medicine and engineering are done in English and educational record keeping is done in both English and Arabic (NAFSA: Association of International Educators, n.d.). Somalia's formal education system was developed historically while under colonial rule of Italy, resulting in some secondary school options being geared to prepare students for study in Italian universities.

[54] According to reports from the United States Congress, refugees are passive in the selection process regarding their country of resettlement. Though it could be that some expression of preferences takes place as part of the vetting process in determining eligibility (Congressional Research Service [CRS], 2020).

[55] The highest is Burmese refugees. While Burma is not a majority Muslim country, a fair number of the refugees who have come from Burma/Mayanmar are estimated to be Muslim as Muslim ethnic groups there have been subject to persecution. The largest ethnic group, however, to come from Burma are the Karen people who are predominantly Christian.

98% Muslim, US State Department policy has favored taking in refugees of non-Muslim ethnic minorities from Iraq, especially during the 1980s; primarily Chaldean Christians. The same is true of Iraqi Kurds, who were explicitly targeted for persecution by Saddam Hussein in the 1980s in what was classified as a genocide by international agencies (Human Rights Watch [HRW], 1995). Kurds are nominally Sunni Muslims, however, throughout their history they, unlike most Sunni Muslims[56], have maintained a religious understanding that gives prominence to ethnic identity over a religious one. As such, researchers have noted that Kurds tend to be overwhelmingly secular and less religiously observant compared to other, especially Sunni, Muslim societies (Aziz, 2011). Kurds have long fought for national autonomy and self governance in the northern region of Iraq, having created their own government in the northern region they inhabit that is called Iraqi Kurdistan. The deposition of Saddam Hussein in 2003 greatly helped to advance that cause, nevertheless, Iraqi Kurds still find themselves at the center of political and militant turmoil and persecution. In the recent decade they have been targeted for persecution by ISIS[57], creating a whole new round of Kurdish refugees fleeing into Turkey.

While the exact religious demographics of Iraqi refugees in America cannot be quantified, a significant portion is Chaldean and non-Muslim. Enough non-Muslims refugees have fled out of Iraq during these times that the CIA World Factbook reports that the total percentage of Iraq that is Muslim increased as a result (Central Intelligence Agency [CIA], 2015). In Michigan, the state with the largest percentage of Arabs and the only one to track Arabs demographically, the state formerly used the appellation "Arab/Chaldean" as a racial category due to the presumption that such a high portion of Arabs in the state were Iraqi Chaldeans (MDCH, 2008).

Iraq is also one of two Muslim countries, along with Iran, whose population is majority Shia Muslim[58], with numbers typically cited as 66% of the Muslim population being Shia (CIA, 2015). Iraqis who emanate from the major cities and provinces east of Baghdad[59] are much more likely to be Shia than those from the western part of the country.

I am sometimes asked about the differences between Sunni and Shia Muslims. While there are definitely differences between them that have importance, the religious differences generally pertain to matters that, for outsiders, are esoteric to enough of a degree that it will rarely make a

---

[56] More on the place of religion in identity construction is discussed further down and in Chapter three.

[57] ISIS is a corrupt and evil group of renegades and criminals whose actions and espoused ideology are an absolute and undeniable corruption of the religion of Islam. More can be read about this at abrahameducation.com.

[58] Shia Muslims have the plurality of religious populations in Lebanon, but not an overall majority.

[59] Namely the cities and surrounding areas of Najaf, Karbala, and Basra.

difference with the way Muslim students show up in school to the view of the average non-Muslim educator. This might be excepted for in cases where students are noticed to have inter-religious disputes with one another, which is perhaps more likely to take place in Social Studies classes where world religions are taught about and some kids may feel pressure to want certain historical narratives to prevail over others when overviews of Islam are taught. One way or the other, if one wants to understand the difference between the two it necessitates understanding the basics of Islam generally, how the religion is sourced, and how its fundamentals are structured, in order to know how and why differences follow thereafter.[60]

The core teachings and practices of the religion are essentially universal to all Muslims. Sunni Muslims make up 87-90% of the Muslim world (Pew Research, 2009) and the term "Sunni", in this context, is rightly synonymous with what is frequently termed "orthodox" in Western study of religion. How the minority sects that exist amongst that 10-13% are defined is part and parcel with how they choose to distinguish themselves from orthodox tradition, and the histories that have brought about the phenomena of such distinction.

While it is a generalization to be sure, there is evidence that suggests Shia Muslims are more likely to be secular than Sunni Muslims, and perhaps even more so those who have migrated to the West. Per my experience with people, I would also say that Shia Muslims are more likely to adopt a religious understanding that accommodates secularist views on religion's role in life. Surveying done by Pew Research has backed up this idea in more than one study (Pew Research, 2006; 2018). Iranian[61] Americans have been regularly found in studies to be the most likely Muslim group by national origin to favor secular world views as well as to de-emphasize being Muslim in one's personal identity. One large scale survey study touted by the Public Affairs Alliance of Iranian Americans (PAAIA) demonstrates that Iranian Americans are actually less likely to identify as being religious than the average American by a factor of almost

---

[60] The matters listed here, and how they directly connect to students and families, will be addressed in chapter three.

[61] Iran is 89% Shia Muslim, making the vast majority of people who come from there of a Shia family background. Since the 1979 Iranian Revolution was a theocratic takeover the result is that many who fled the country at the time and in subsequent years had more proclivity to be secular, and the revolution itself was a reaction to increasing secularism that had gone on in the country in decades prior, leading many Iranian families to have adopted such a world view. A 2018 survey by Pew Research found that one in four people who had been raised in a family that identified as Muslim, but no longer did so themselves in adulthood. The survey attributes this phenomena to the high amount of Iran refugees who migrated in the 1980s following the Iranian revolution, and the high amount of Iranian respondents in the survey. It should be noted also that Shiism itself has many different strands and there are religious differences between Iranian and Iraqi Shias despite being adjacent to one another geographically. Iranians, as non-Arabs, generally follow a brand of Shiism that is quite syncretic with concepts of pre-Islamic Iranian thought and Zoroastrianism, the traditional religion of Persians prior to Islam (Cottrell, 1980). Again, these matters are esoteric to the average non-Muslim but I want to give you a broad understanding of these differences.

four to one. The same study found that Iranians are more likely than the average American to identify as atheist, and that only one in three Iranian Americans identify as Muslim[62] (Public Affairs Alliance of Iranian Americans [PAAIA], 2013). Pew Research (2006) found in a survey of six Muslim countries that respondents in the Shia-pluarity country of Lebanon were the most likely to downplay the importance of religion in their lives by a wide margin.[63] This stands in large contrast to findings about Muslim Americans generally, and even more so concerning surveys that have been done specifically on Muslim students (Cristillo, 2008).[64]

The eastern province of Iraq is the center of pilgrimage sites that are specific to Shias and not followed by Sunnis.[65] This creates the possibility that there is more fervency for Shia Islam amongst Shia Iraqis than others. There have been some surveys done that suggest Iraqi Shias are more open to religious governance within Iraq than Iraqi Sunnis (Moaddel, 2014). However, these numbers cannot be looked at without consideration for particular political circumstances within Iraq. Also, these surveys ask specifically about the respondent's desire for the orientation of the Iraqi government and political system, as opposed to asking about the importance of religion in one's personal life (as the Pew Research and PAAIA studies do). These surveys also have volatile numbers over the course of different years and decades, and there certainly seems to be a correlation between respondent trends and changes in Iraqi political climate, including who governs Iraq itself.[66]

The Iraqi people most likely to come to the United States as refugees has also changed with the political times of Iraq. During the 1980s this meant that Kurds, Chaldean Christians, and Shia Muslims were far more likely than Sunni Muslims to emigrate as refugees. This is why today

---

[62] It should also be noted that there can be some complicating factors of saying you "identify" as Muslim when taking a survey. Even in an anonymous context, social stigmas can lead to preference falsification (i.e. expressing externally something different than what one actually feels internally due to social pressure), which Timur Kuran, Professor of Economics and Political Science at Duke University, has found to take place specifically in the context of Muslims concealing public expression of religiosity in a society with prevailing pressures towards conformity with secularization (see his book *Private Truths, Public Lies*). It could also be that one might respond based on what they actually say to other people about their identity in social situations, which biases towards ethnic and racial identity in the West, more so than what one might internalize.

[63] When respondents from six Muslim majority countries were asked whether or not religion was very important in one's life, answering in the affirmative was found as follows: Morocco 96%, Pakistan 96%, Indonesia 93%, Jordan 86%, Turkey 69%, and Lebanon 54%.

[64] Specific findings from this survey were reviewed in chapter one.

[65] Most famously and widely attended is the Arba'een Pilgrimage to the city of Karbala that takes place in the first month of Islamic calendar that is done to mourn the death of the Prophet Muhammad's ﷺ grandson's. More on pilgrimage practices and its place in Islam will be explained in chapter three.

[66] For example, support amongst Shia Muslims for religious governance in Iraq increases sharply in years where surveys were conducted *after* Shias took over the government.

amongst the minimally estimated 150,000 people of Arab ancestry in Michigan[67] there are at least 64,000 Iraqis and 38,000 of them are Chaldean Christians (MDCH, 2008; Warikoo, 2013).

The toppling of Saddam Huessein in 2003 and his replacement with Shia heads of state in the government resulted in more favoritism towards the national government by Shias, and the conflicts that have taken place since then have more commonly been in the Sunni-majority regions of the North and South. This opens up the possibility that a fair amount of the Iraqi refugees that came in the first decade of the 2000s were Sunni (yet this is hard to determine statistically and does not appear to have been closely looked at). The advent of ISIS and its spread to the northern region brought back the persecution of Kurds, whose presence in Iraq have dwindled in significant numbers in the most recent decade (CIA, 2015).

Conclusion

A clear takeaway is that Iraqis in America are a very diverse group. Definitely, one cannot meet an Iraqi student or an Iraqi family and make assumptions about their religious background.[68] This broad overview of recent political history is worth knowing for the implications that it may have for the way people have migrated. However, it should not be taken to mean that Iraqis (or anyone else for that matter) should be primarily viewed through a lens where they are related to by the geopolitics of Iraq. To the contrary, for many who flee places of conflict the distance from such situations may be a source of great reprieve, and the opportunity to live in different political circumstances seen as a welcome opportunity, while reminders of, and certainly pressures to be "representative of"[69], the associated conflicts from their native region are unwelcome.

Furthermore, despite the large number of Iraqi refugees who have come to America there are still significant numbers who have come as part of the professional class as well; and coming as

---

[67] This is the figure reported by the government of Michigan, but they also note that while Michigan does more explicit tracking of its Arab population than any other place in America, the figure of the total number is debated. The Arab American Institute (AAI) estimates Michigan to have almost half a million people of Arab ancestry.

[68] One way that this *is* done amongst Arabs and other Muslim populations is through an understanding of naming patterns. Muslims tend to have fairly distinct naming patterns; such that one with the appropriate background knowledge can meet someone and know simply by their name that they are Muslim. Some examples of naming patterns practiced by Muslims will be discussed in Chapter three.

[69] It is generally never a good idea to put kids on the spot in class and ask them "what they think" about political conflicts relative to their ethnic or religious identity. This is not to say these topics cannot be brought up in school, but it is important that a good relationship is established in the first place, and that the context of political conflict is not the first place where their identity, religious or ethnic, is brought up in the classroom. The information and resources that follow in this book are designed to provide for this regarding Muslim students.

a refugee certainly does not preclude one from being a professional either. The immigration numbers published by the federal government prior to 1986 only found significant enough numbers of five Arab countries to list them individually and Iraq was one of them, so we can analyze the statistics of the professional class's immigration patterns exclusive to Iraqis. Over 20% of the immigrants who came from Arab countries in the 1970s were from Iraq. Iraq's oil resources are vast and many of the professional class immigrants that began coming in the 1970s were part of the oil industry or striving to participate in that emerging part of their home country's economy.[70]

Iraq also has a long history of formal education. Deeper in history the Abbasid empire that was based in Baghdad was a center of formal learning that led the world in its time in civilizational advancement. This part of history may be less relevant to Iraqis in the immediate term, but can be a source of ethnic pride, as well as a source of learning and reference in public schools. Some of the book recommendations that are made in chapter six can be used to serve this purpose.

In more recent history, the British instituted educational reforms in Iraq in the early 20th century, giving it a long term confluence with Western education systems. Education has long been compulsory in Iraq, though its actual delivery to the populace has often been interrupted due to political turmoil.

Somalis

After the Burmese and Iraqis the third largest group of refugees to come to America after the turn of the century is Somalis. The Somali refugee crisis was spurned by the outbreak of civil war in the country in the early 1990s. Refugees from Somalia began coming to America in significant numbers in the 1990s, however, nearly five times as many arrived in the following decade.[71] Egyptian and Pakistani immigrants were most numerous in naming New York and Los Angeles as their most-likely place of destination, while other smaller metro areas became home to less immigrants from these countries in pure numbers but as a larger percentage of the population relative to New York and LA. Iraqi refugees ended up in Michigan and the Detroit metro area due to the deeper history that the area had of welcoming Arab immigrants since the early 20th century.

---

[70] The positive relationship the US government had with the Baathist regime, Saddam Hussein's party, at that time might have helped create the impetus and structure to have the field of engineering be done in English within Iraq.

[71] A few more than 16,000 arrived in the 1990s and over 55,000 in the first decade of the 2000s.

Different from all these groups, Somalis have had their own distinct migration patterns in diaspora and within the United States. While San Diego was the first city that Somali refugees resettled to (Yusuf, 2012), the largest number of them by far and away have ended up in the Twin Cities. After that Columbus, Seattle, and Washington DC have the largest numbers of Somalis. Yet, there are still significant numbers of Somalis in several other metro areas,[72] as well as several rural cities. Toronto also has a sizable Somali population, second to the Twin Cities in North America; and there is in the current day a far reaching Somali diaspora throughout the world. London and Birmingham in the UK as well as Melbourne, Australia are other major cities in the anglosphere with large populations of Somalis.

Numerous Youth

A significant impact (of many) upon both the Muslim community and the school systems of the areas that Somalis have migrated to is the significant amount of youth the community has. Children under 18 comprise roughly 15% of all immigrants in any given year, but the DHS does not list immigrant totals by age filtered by home country. While the precise numbers of Somali immigrants that have arrived as children might be difficult to pin down, it can be assumed to be more numerous than others because the median age of Somalis is 18.1 years; younger than all but 14 other countries in the world. Furthermore, Somalia has a higher birth rate (6.123 children per woman) than every other country in the world except Niger.[73] I believe it is fair to assume to some degree that birth rates from developing countries would decrease in ethnic populations once arrived in America; yet it is also wrong to assume that these rates are entirely divorced from cultural factors, solely determined by environmental conditions, and that they would regress to the mean of American averages within only a generation of arriving to the United States. As such, if one were to average the birth rate of the home Muslim countries we have discussed with the (almost always) lower birth rate of Americans in general, and multiply the number by half[74] of the arrived immigrants who have gained legal permanent status; it becomes the case that over the course of one generation from the first decade of the 2000s Somalis would become the second largest ethnic population of Muslims in the country after Pakistanis.[75]

---

[72] Including but not limited to both Portlands, Boston/Cambridge, Houston, Atlanta, Louisville, Nashville, and Fargo.

[73] These statistics are all from worldometer.info, which is part of the *Real Time Statistics Project* and managed by a global consortium of researchers and staticians in academia. More can be read about it here https://natlib.govt.nz/blog/posts/worldometers-real-time-statistics. Numbers are current as of Winter 2019.

[74] Accounting for the fact that approximately half the immigrants would be women and birth rate statistics are calculated on a per woman basis.

[75] This does not take into account African American Muslims, it is a statement restricted to the discussion here under the headings of originally-immigrant populations.

All that is to say that there are many Somali young people in America, and where Somali communities exist they tend to encompass an outsized proportion of the youth in both the Muslim community and the public school system relative to the amount of Somali adults that the community has. My experience talking to educators in the Twin Cities, Seattle, and Columbus is that teachers are often surprised at the impact and numbers that Somali children seem to have in the school system relative to the extent that they feel the community's impact outside of it. Likewise, I have known from people within Muslim communities in those same cities as well as Houston, Atlanta, Cambridge, Birmingham, UK and Melbourne, AU who also observed that Somali youth comprise an outsized portion of participants in Muslim youth activities relative to the commonly perceived size of the community in general. This means that the impact of these young people on the futures of these communities a generation from now will be larger than the current influence that Somali communities have. An influence that is increasing with each passing year.

Dispersion

San Diego and the Washington DC area of Virginia were the first places to which Somalis were resettled in the early nineties (Yusuf, 2012). Somalis were quick to be active in secondary migration and their beginnings in the cities where they are now in the largest numbers started with that. In the case of Minnesota, it is not actually the Twin Cities where Somalis first migrated to, but rather the much smaller town of Marshall in western Minnesota, and shortly thereafter to the town of Willmar, also in western Minnesota. It is from there that migration to the Twin Cities occurred and the Minnesota Somali population boomed.

The city of Willmar exhibits a sort of microcosm of the phenomenon of the high population of youth that the Somali community has on the greater community. The total population of Willmar is just over 19,000 and Somalis account for seven percent of that. But in the local school district Somali children account for about 20% of the student population.[76] The same is the case for the larger college town in central Minnesota of St. Cloud, where approximately 10-12% of the total population is Somali, but the percent in the public school district is nearly three times that.

---

[76] The population figures in this paragraph are gathered from city-data.com and the student figures are gathered from the Minnesota Department of Education's school report card, available on the department's website. These data report by race, so what I have reported here is the percentage of blacks that are reported for the city and school district. It is well known in Minnesota that very few non-Somali blacks live in the city of Willmar.

How do Somali refugees end up coming to small rural cities like Marshall and Willmar? In the case of both these cities the answer lies largely in the fact that these towns are homes to meat processing plants that are central parts of the local economies. The same happens to be true for the cities of Liberal and Dodge City, Kansas as well as Shelbyville, Tennessee; all of which are small towns that have a large Somali population.

It is not only the meat industry that has attracted and benefited from the arrival of refugees to areas they are located, but these smaller towns illustrate in a clear cut way the economic benefit and necessity in many areas of having refugees arrive. All of these small towns would have gone through population reductions in the nineties and early 2000s as the millennial generation graduated high school and left town for more urban areas; a phenomenon that has hollowed out the economies in many small towns. When such trends begin, or are projected to take place in the future, it becomes apparent to local businesses and politicians that the local economy will not be able to be maintained at status quo if the town cannot provide workers for local factories, not to mention students for the local school district. In more urban areas the phenomenon may not be so starkly linked to just one industry, but what is seen there is an influx of refugee and immigrant populations settle into neighborhoods that would otherwise have been victimized by urban sprawl. Therefore, properties that would have potentially been left vacant due to population decreases are used, maintained, and often commercialized, due to the arrival of immigrants and refugees. This causes property values in general to stay up as well as the base of taxpayers. In the urban areas, refugee immigrants fill a variety of worker niches in the economy.

The potential harm that population decrease could do to the economy as the baby boom generation grew older without having spawned a generation numerous enough to replace them was long projected by economists and of concern to politicians. This is part of the reason why laws like the 1980 Refugee Act were passed. It also spurred the development of State Department programs that gave funds to non-profit organizations who were willing to do the leg work of providing services for refugee resettlement. These are often Christian organizations such as Lutheran Social Services and Catholic Charities.[77]

---

[77] Religious organizations play a large role in refugee resettlement. The United Nations High Commission on Human Rights lists nine resettlement agencies that it works with (via the State Department) for refugee resettlement in the United States. Five of them are Christian organizations and one is Jewish https://www.unhcr.org/en-us/resettlement-in-the-united-states.html. These organizations usually have more local subsidiaries and partner organizations they work with as well. Forming an Islamic-based non-profit organization that works with refugee resettlement might be an interesting career path that we could prompt our Muslim students to think about.

The maintenance and growth of the size of public school districts is no negligible beneficiary in this phenomenon either. In many localities that have experienced an influx of refugee immigrants over the past two decades or more, the school systems have not changed too much in terms of overall numbers, but the demographics of the student body has changed.[78] This means that many teachers and other educational professionals would have been out of jobs had the refugee children, and the children of refugees, not entered their systems.

There is an extent to which these economic contributions of refuge arrivals are important to teach about in school. The kids from these communities do not always know about them and they have a right to understand the dependence that the cities and local communities they live in have on them and their community. At the same time, these underpinnings of economic interests behind the refugee resettlement process also illuminate that these resettlement projects are not entirely rooted in acts of benevolence; as they are often portrayed to be by the politicians and organizations involved with them. There are economic interests at play the whole way through, and there is an extent to which one could interpret this as dehumanizing to the people who are upended and relocated in the process. All in order to end up serving the economic interests of others.

Assimilation

I would argue that there has never been anything quite like Somalis coming to the United States given the following aspects of their migration, taken as a whole:

- They came en masse, and came relatively sudden.
- They came mostly of low socioeconomic status.[79]
- They originated from a Muslim country.
- They had not undergone Westernization. Unlike others from Muslim countries who had come before them for professional reasons.[80]

---

[78] Using Willmar as an example, in 1999 the district had 4,590 students but only 64 (1.39%) were black. In 2019 they only had 99 less students overall (4,491) but now 831(18.5%) were black, again the vast majority of those being Somali.

[79] As stated before, those who did have professional status back home would have been very unlikely to have had their expertise able to be transferred to the United States when undergoing the refugee process and the turmoil that comes along with the fleeing of conflict.

[80] Somalis immigrating to the US on occupational visas are rare, from 2001-2010 out of 64,150 Somali immigrants given legal permanent status only 112 came on occupational visas.

I do not believe that these four attributes apply as a whole to any other immigrant group that has resettled in the United States, and maybe even the Western world.[81] These unique aspects, along with simply the culture of Somalis in general, bring certain factors into play that must be understood and considered.

Firstly, as a community Somalis tend to stick together very strongly. This results in a high amount of secondary migration to the areas where there are already an appreciable number of Somalis. Within those areas it can often result in the community concentrating into certain neighborhoods or immediate suburbs. This is seen in South Minneapolis and the Cedar-Riverside neighborhood, the Northland neighborhood of Columbus, and in the Seattle suburb of Tukwila, WA as well. Oftentimes the same tendency exists in patterns of school choice, whereby Somali families will tend to send their kids to schools where they know there are large groups of Somalis; and often where the children of relatives or friends also attend. In Minnesota and Columbus this partly manifests in their being several charter schools that are almost 100% Somali students (Hussein, 2012).[82]

One of the great strengths that Somali communities, and the Somali diaspora generally, have is their togetherness, and social capital. This is true of other immigrant and Muslim communities as well, but with other factors effecting Somalis as immigrant communities that have formed under duress and without prior westernization before arrival, this togetherness might manifest in a way that is perceived as insular to those outside the community. There are numerous factors that play into this and educators ought to find insights from this book as helpful in this regard.

I believe it is the case that virtually all Muslim parents have anxiety over how their children will grow up and assimilate into American culture. This is not to say that parents do not have an understanding that their American-raised children will turn out differently than themselves, or that children will hold onto the home culture entirely. However, with a community that has migrated under duress and that did not have a process of prior reconciliation over their own role in Western society before their arrival, there can be an uptick in this anxiety over the idea of what it is going to mean for their child to grow up in the West and be a Muslim.

---

[81] There were a considerable number of South Asian Muslims who resettled to England in the 1950s during the disputes over the Kashmir region following India's partition in 1947, but they were coming from a place that had experienced a century of British colonization and were likely to at least know basic English (Peach, 2006).

[82] Charter schools have been much harder to start in Washington due to state regulations, where there has been some debate in the court system as to whether or not it is even legal for charter schools to receive public funding. The state supreme court ruled that it was legal in fall of 2018.

This anxiety can often be realized in a strong need to want to have protection over the children, and this results in certain patterns over how children are managed socially within the community. At a base level, that means Somalis make strong efforts to keep their kids together with one another physically; living in the same cities and neighborhoods (even building complexes), attending the same schools, attending the same recreational activities, and attending the same mosques and weekend religious schools. This collecting of the kids into the same places that the community has some familiarity and comfort with provides a baseline feeling of safety and a modicum of control over the many social influences that will shape their children as they grow up.

It is well known and apparent to both researchers as well as anyone who is close to a Somali community that the importance of tradition and religion is usually preeminent to how they understand themselves. A survey from Concordia College's School of Business in St. Paul found that Somalis value preservation of their own cultural language[83], adherence to religious rituals, and the maintaining of religious and cultural traditions within America as not only high, but higher when compared to other African immigrant groups (Corrie, 2015). Academics who research Somali communities almost always cite the importance of religion within the community and find that leaders and elders within the community cite the importance of religious observation and identity in fostering a healthy development of the community's youth (Berns-McGown, 1999; De Voe, 2002; Farid & McMahan, 2004; Bigelow, 2010).

Something I tell teachers that they have found useful is to understand that with Somali students (and families as well) there can frequently be a trust deficit at the outset of the relationship relative to what the average educator might expect with mainstream students. There are compounding factors that contribute to this, and some of the community's tendencies towards insularity certainly are a part of that. But another critical aspect for educators to consider is trauma, as mistrust at the outset of new relationships and the testing of trust boundaries are common features of traumatized people (Matsakis, 1998; Ratcliffe et al, 2014).

Trauma and Trust

In the case of Somalis, it is certainly factual that students currently in K-12 education were not in Somalia during the conflicts of the 1990s. I have spoken to some educators who have told me

---

[83] This can mean both Somali and Arabic to Somali people. While Somali is an ancient oral language that historically took on written forms using Arabic and local alphabets, it did not have an official written form until the 1970s when the government of Siad Barre opted to use roman script. Arabic, meanwhile, is commonly a language that Somalis may be more likely to have literary capacity in due to the religious tradition of reading and memorizing the Qur'an. Arabic is also, and has always been, an official language of the Somali government.

that staff at their school dismiss the idea of trauma playing a role with these students because of this. Such thinking is short-sighted and incorrect. In one matter, it fails to acknowledge that many students who have come to the country in succeeding decades would be coming from refugee camps where a type of trauma could have been experienced. It also dismisses the fact that the parents of many students were not only in Somalia during the times of conflict, but many of them were at younger developing ages when these events occurred. It is not uncommon at all that immigrant parents of Somali children in public schools today might have experienced conflict firsthand in their youth and gone on to spend years, if not decades, in refugee camps before coming to America. This creates an experience of not only having suffered through the after effects of trauma due to exposure to violence, but also then having it compounded by the trauma of losing the cultural life and heritage from where their family emanates; or never having fully known it in the first place.

But a major factor that needs to be considered in any discussion about trauma is that research is finding that trauma is passed down through generations, to such an extent that it may even affect DNA. This has been looked at closely in the case of succeeding generations of holocaust survivors by the Icahn School of Medicine's Traumatic Stress Division at Mount Sinai in New York City. Studies from there have found similar genetic variations from the norm in succeeding generations of survivors for the gene associated with depression and anxiety disorders. The researchers said that the findings imply that children of individuals who experience profound stress in life may be more likely to develop stress or anxiety disorders themselves at a genetic level (Yehuda et al, 2014).

What has been dubbed "implicit racial bias" in academia is also a factor to be considered as a challenge in building trust with students. Some foundational tools used to attempt to measure implicit racial bias are studies where subjects are shown pictures of facial expressions being made by individuals from both the same race as them and others from people of different races. When shown those images participants are asked to name the emotion that they see and then rate on a scale the intensity with which they believe the pictured individual is portraying that emotion. These studies were initially done between whites and Asians, and they find that participants consistently rate their perceived intensity of negative emotions in people of different races, such as sadness, anger, and fear, with a higher intensity than was intended to be put off; but the same skewing does not take place for interpretations of positive emotions or when looking at same-race facial expressions (Wang et al., 2014). In theory, this means that a person is more likely to perceive negative emotions of someone from their racial outgroup with a higher intensity than is intended to be put off.

Generally, I believe that these studies, as well as several others within the social sciences, are only trying to academize phenomena that are sensed as taking place by common people in the real world. Nevertheless, it brings an important point to teachers that they need to be aware and sensitive to the fact that they may misinterpret kids, and kids may misinterpret them, through subtle matters of body language, facial expression, and tone of voice. I have witnessed this phenomenon take place often between Somali students and white teachers, and especially between Somali male students and white female teachers; and it is important to emphasize *that it works both ways.* Not only can there be a tendency on the part of the teacher to interpret the student as more hostile, angry, aggressive, and obstinate than the child is meaning to project, but likewise the child might interpret the teacher as more angry, rigid and stressed out than the teacher means to put off. These dynamics can only serve to compound issues of mistrust in building relationships when they are not tended to intentionally by the teacher. Of course these dynamics are not exclusive to student-teacher relationships with Somalis but affect students from many other racial groups as well.

A major takeaway from these factors is that having a *calm disposition and demeanor* is of essential importance when working with students who may have issues working against them in developing trust with their teachers. Being calm in the classroom is one and the same with being calm inside one's own heart and mind. Fred Jones[84] had a saying for teachers: *calmness is strength, upset is weakness.* How one interprets stress in another individual often comes down to how subtilties in body language, facial expression, and tone of voice are read (Todorov et al, 2008; Foley & Gentile, 2010; Kurien, 2010). When considering classroom management teachers should not neglect studying the experts who have looked at it from the perspective of body language and non-verbal cues. The works of Fred Jones and Michael Grinder[85] are paramount in this area. Personal reflection can be one of the most important tools in attaining a higher level of self control, and reading what follows in this book can be a vehicle for that as well.

The book *A Long Way Gone* by Ishmael Beah offers valuable insight for teachers to consider when teaching students whose families have experienced the effects of trauma. Beah was a child soldier during the Sierra Leone civil war of the early 1990s. His book tells his story of being entrapped by the defunct republican army and coerced into fighting in the conflict at age 12. There are two main things that teachers can glean from this book. First is the chance to get a

---

[84] Fred Jones was a clinical psychologist and PhD from UCLA. He spent decades observing high needs schools in Los Angeles Public School district and catalogued strategies that effective teachers used with those students. His book *Tools for Teaching* (2000) is the magnum opus of his findings. I recommend it for teachers who wish to up their game in classroom management.

[85] Grinder is the author and founder of the behavior management system EnVoy. More can be learned about him at www.michaelgrinder.com

window into the nature and brutal extent of trauma[86] that people went through in African wars in the 20th century. These wars were essentially instigated by proxy factions of the competing powers in the Cold War. These conflicts exhibited a mix of old world modes of tribal conflict clashing together with modern-age weaponry and drugs that were provided to differing factions by Western countries and the Soviet Union; creating an especially brutal experience for the unfortunate souls who were caught in the middle of it. This manipulation by colonial powers made native modes of peaceful resolution that these societies traditionally had impossible to attain (Salih, 1989).

I have talked to teachers who have suspected that trauma plays a significant role in how their students show up in the classroom, but who also complain that others in their school staff dismiss such concerns. The narrations in *A Long Way Gone* are graphic and not for the faint of heart, and they cannot be read without heightening one's appreciation for the background experiences that people in traumatized communities have had. Beah's story also gives a clear illustration of the phenomenon of post-trauma mistrust when he and his peers were taken out of the republican army by UNICEF. In their interactions with the nurses tasked with providing them therapy, the boys immediately challenge the boundaries of trust in the relationship. This involves them committing actions that are much worse than what students do in the classroom (most classrooms at least), such as throwing objects, cursing and threatening the nurses, and even endangering them physically to the point that the nurses would have to retreat to a locked safety room.

---

[86] The use of the word "trauma" has undergone an evolution of sorts in American psychology that has caused its definition to alter over the last four decades. In this discussion trauma refers to what is defined as Post Traumatic Stress Syndrome (PTSD) by the *Diagnostic and Statistical Manual of Mental Disorders* (DSM) published by the American Psychiatric Association prior to 1994. That definition referred to trauma as occurring when "the person *has experienced* an event that is outside the range of usual human experience and *that would be markedly distressing to almost anyone*" (emphasis added). Alterations to the definition of PTSD in the DSM beginning in 1994 cover a range of detail, but included in that was a broadening of the definition of trauma concerning the points I have emphasized here. The 1994 definition changed "has experienced" to "has been exposed to…experienced, witnessed or was confronted with…" and the criterion of "markedly distressing to almost anyone" was changed to "the person's response involved intense fear, helplessness or horror" and revisions in the years 2000 and 2013 only saw the definition broaden further (see *A Treatment Improvement Protocol Trauma-Informed Care in Behavioral Health Services Part 3: A Review of the Literature* published by the US Department of Health and Human Services (HHS) Substance Abuse and Mental Health Services Administration (SAMHSA) available here https://store.samhsa.gov/sites/default/files/d7/priv/sma14-4816_litreview.pdf (see Exhibit L-1 on page 9 of the pdf). While not questioning the full range of considerations of the APA in choosing to change these definitions, an effect that I believe has taken place from this is that the definition of "trauma" in some contexts has become subjective to such an extent that almost anyone could categorize themselves as traumatized, and also define normal experiences of stress as traumatic. The field of education has been affected by this, and I feel it can be wrongly belittling to people who have experienced trauma in serious ways and its effects; which is what is being discussed here.

But what Beah also recounts is the ways in which the nurses were able to treat and rehabilitate the boys from their trauma. At the core of this was that the nurses always remained calm with them and did not attribute their challenging behavior to themselves as boys or individuals, but rather they attributed it to the trauma that they experienced. This mental disposition that disentangles the child's personhood from the misbehavior they exhibit provided the inner emotional foundation the nurses needed in order to remain calm with their patients even when times were challenging, and thereby earning their trust and respect over time.

In his book *Accommodating and Educating Somali Students in Minnesota Schools* Mohamed Farid (2001), a former Somali school teacher in Minnesota, expounds on the effect of trauma and the refugee experience on Somali children. It is worth quoting at length:

> Most refugee children who come to our school system adjust very quickly and remarkably well, considering gaps in education and hardships they have experienced. Unfortunately, many Somali children have not adapted well. From our own [the authors'] experiences and through our conversations with other teachers who work with Somali students, inappropriate behavior is an overriding concern. For example, students engage in fights and teachers complain that Somali boys do not show respect for female authority figures…This misbehavior that we see exhibited by Somali students in school was unheard of in Somalia before the war. **Somali parents expect their children to respect and obey their teachers completely.** When teachers report that their children are not showing that respect, they are deeply dismayed and embarrassed…Somali adults perceive persistent misbehavior as stemming from two sources. The first source is that the *misbehavior is learned by example from American kids*. In Somalia it is unheard of for a student to refuse to follow directions or talk back to a teacher, but in urban American schools, defiant behavior is common….The second source of misbehavior is perceived as being the destruction of the family and *the erosion of Islamic values* through war and refugee experience…[In refugee camps] children spent their days almost unsupervised, [sometimes] without even the benefit of basic schooling. Refugee communities were shattered by war, and so were the traditional values of Somali and Islamic culture…There is a common perception among Somali adults that the weakening of the family structure has resulted in a lack of proper Islamic training and discipline on the part of the young generation. This is a concern because Islamic values hold Muslim cultures together. To Somali people the lack of order in society is directly attributed

to the erosion of those values. The restoration of Islam in the minds and hearts of Somali young people is viewed as essential to the success of children and to the survival of a healthy Somali community in Minnesota. (Farid & McMahan, 2004, pg. 47-49). (emphasis added)

Conclusion

Farid's words offer some key takeaways. Firstly, it reinforces the connection between misbehavior and trauma and that trauma can take place in many different places. While the reference here is particular to Somali students, and perhaps even more so specific to Somali boys, the same phenomenon has been found in studies of other Muslim student populations in the Western world. Sarroub (2005) found it with Yemeni refugee boys in Michigan, Iqbal (2017) found it with South Asian[87] boys in the UK, and Merry (2005) found it with Morrocan boys in Flemish schools. Bigelow (2008) has found that Somali boys being misbehaved is a common stereotype amongst educators in Minnesota. In the first year and a half of my own surveying[88] of training attendees I found that in over 267 queries issued to me by educators of Muslim students, misbehavior or disengagement of boys was the second-most inquired about concern, amounting to 9.7% of all questions asked. I will note that De Voe (2002) and Zine (2001) both found attitudes of defiance amongst Somali and Pakistani girls respectively.

All of these researchers agree, and I believe it is well understood to educators, that the root causes of misbehavior and disengagement in school are complex. What is also found in these case studies, and reinforced to me by my interactions with teachers of Muslim students, is that when misbehavior is an "overriding concern" it is in the form of lower tier misbehaviors happening frequently. What you might call "nuisance behaviors", as opposed to higher tier behaviors that verge on threatening an environment of safety. That is to say, it is more likely the case that concerns are over behaviors such as constant talking during instructional time, petty defiance and backtalk to small redirections, or students assisting one another with work in a way that teachers interpret as cheating.

I have emboldened the part where Farid emphasizes the high expectations of parents for a particular reason. While there is no doubt that schools need to do better in building

---

[87] While the South Asian community in the UK is economically diverse, on the whole it is of a lower class than that of the United States South Asian community. This is due to the fact that Britain has had many more South Asians come as refugees, or with a lower bar of socio-economic status accepted for admittance going back to the 1950s (Peach, 2006).

[88] Before I do trainings I ask participants to fill out an intake form where they have the opportunity to remit questions that they have about teaching Muslim students beforehand. In analyzing these questions I determined they could fall into roughly thirty-five different categories.

environments that feel welcoming to students that are racial minorities in America, I have some concern about the current state of equity and multicultural education. Its attempted implementations in classrooms have left some educators concluding that misbehavior and defiance by non-white students ought to be interpreted as something that simply emanates from differing cultural dispositions and should therefore be excused, permitted, and not subject to redirection, reprimand, or consequence. This may be the case even more so when the defiance takes on a form of verbal altercation, due to an understanding that students may come from an oral culture and the teacher or educator from outside that culture might suppose that such defiance and verbal altercation is simply normal; and it is therefore concluded that we should "let it go" under the guise of being "culturally responsive". Stated clearly, *this is a mistaken viewpoint when it comes to Muslim students.*

Yes, it is the case that many Muslim students come from cultures with strong oral traditions, and it may be the case that social interaction within their home culture could be characterized as more boisterous than that of anglo-northern European social interaction. Nevertheless, disrespect and defiance of teachers and people in authority is *not from Islamic or Muslim culture at all.*[89] It is widely found amongst researchers of the parents of Muslim students of all ethnicities that respect and obedience of teachers in a near-absolute sense is the common expectation of families. This is common knowledge to anyone who has firsthand familiarity with Muslim communities. Therefore the question of what to do about misbehavior and defiance when it arrives is not one of permissibility, but rather one of the proper approaches, strategies, and understandings needed to cause remediation in a way that preserves student-teacher relationships, honors student background, and effectively nurtures positive life habits and skills.

In this vein, what researchers also agree upon is the essential importance for teachers of these students to explicitly learn about their cultural backgrounds, and for Muslim students this *cannot* be extracted from learning about Islam itself. As has been said and well-accepted by educational psychologists, "when subtle cultural differences meet, conflicts arise" (Hoy, 2010). However, when the subtle difference can be properly revealed to the educator it generates what ethnographers have dubbed the "a-ha!" moment, where the educator is emotionally empowered by new-found knowledge to attempt changes in practice (Willis & Trondman, 2000). Providing these is a key benefit of the succeeding chapters of this book.

Another takeaway from Farid's excerpt is that there is a degree to which Muslim families see themselves in contrast to "American" culture. The firsthand experience for Somali parents of the immigrant paradox is writ large here. Behavior in urban American culture is what Farid

---

[89] Qur'an 4:59 https://quran.com/4/59, Sahīh Muslim Book 33 Hadith 53 https://sunnah.com/muslim/33/53, Sahīh Muslim Book 33 Hadith 61 https://sunnah.com/muslim/33/61

mentions, but this can be extended to many different aspects of American pop culture, whose availability and exposure to by youth of immigrant communities has skyrocketed in the last decade with the advance of smartphones and social media, adding another stressor to the sentiment of lacking control that parents already have.

What is important to understand is that since Islam forms the basis of values for Muslims, the way other cultures, philosophies, or ideologies tend to be viewed by Muslims is through a lens where Islam sets the criteria[90] by which such things are to be judged. Therefore when viewing any other culture or ideology through a lens that is influenced by Islam there is likely to be some aspects of it that a Muslim can agree with, while others that the Muslim feels prompted to reject and stay away from. Since Muslim children in the West are growing up influenced by a culture alien to Islam, while also not yet having the capacity to dispense what does and does not correlate to religious teachings, anxiety is induced upon Muslim parents concerning their children's own ability to make healthy life choices. Likewise stages of confusion and unsurety in oneself are to be expected in the lives of Muslim youth.

In the pages that follow a unique journey is offered whereby the religion of Islam is taught in a prose that is specifically written for the public school educator with the goal of not only offering new and practical insights, but also ideas and consideration for practice that would take culturally-relevant pedagogy of Muslim students out of the nominal and superficial and into the authentic.

---

[90] One of the appellations given to Islam's holy book, the Qu'ran, is *al-furqan*, which literally means "criterion" and the application of that word into a Muslim's understanding of the Qur'an in their worldview is meant as is described here, it is meant to be the criteria by which a Muslim judges everything in life. Qur'an 25:1 https://quran.com/25/1.

Chapter 3: ISLAMIC BELIEF AND CONNECTIONS TO STUDENTS & FAMILIES

Sources of Islam

How does one know what Islam is? Islam is a highly sensitive topic for people, both Muslims and non-Muslims. Part of this has to do with the fact that Islam is a topic that many people in society make claims about, but there is confusion as to the motivations behind much of these discussions and how to verify claims that are made.

The answer to this comes in knowing that Islam is understood by referral to its appropriate sources. Islam does not have a governing hierarchy, like the Catholic Church, that makes theological decisions that are then taken as immutable and dogmatic. Rather, all matters that pertain to the question of what Islam is necessitate referral to Islam's source *texts*.

Essentially, there are two words by which the textual sources of Islam can be known: *Qu'ran* and *Hadīth*. Any discussion about what Islam is that does not have a thorough and comprehensive referral and basis in these sources is not an authentic conversation about Islam and will inevitably fall into errancy; intentionally or otherwise. Furthermore, the religion itself actually dictates that an understanding of it is only transmitted properly through these sources. So it is necessary to explain what these are before using them to explain the religion and how it connects to our interactions with students and families.

The Qur'an

Most people have heard of this text, and its name is properly transliterated from Arabic to English as it is written in the heading above.[91] The Islamic teaching is that the Qur'an is a divine revelation. It is the literal spoken word of God transmitted to a man that lived in the 7th century who is referred to as The Prophet Muhammad ﷺ[92] through the supernatural being that is referred to in Christian and Jewish theology as the archangel Gabriel.[93] The word Qur'an in Arabic is a nominalization of the verb قَـرَأَ (qar'a), which means "to read" or "to recite", so the literal linguistic meaning of the word Qur'an is "the reading" or "the recitation" because it is a book that is meant to be read and meant to be recited, and doing so is an act of worship for Muslims.

---

[91] Many western books and articles transliterate this word as "Koran", while this may be familiar to people and can function well enough, it does not indicate the proper correlation to Arabic letters.

[92] It is part of Islamic etiquette to say "peace be upon him" after the Prophet Muhammad ﷺ is mentioned, and likewise to write it out after he is referred to in written text. The symbol that is annotated here is Arabic calligraphy that writes this out.

[93] Gabriel is referred to in Islamic sources simply by the Arabic name for Gabriel, *Jibrīl*

The second source of Islam is the life and example of The Prophet Muhammad 🕌. This is called the *Sunnah*. It is beyond the scope of this book to go into a detailed account of his biography, but what is important to understand is that The Prophet Muhammad 🕌 is considered the most perfect example of human behavior in Islam and the living embodiment of behavior that a Muslim is to strive to achieve.[94] Therefore he is meant to be followed by a Muslim in a quite literal sense. The word Islam[95] means "submission", as in submission to God, and the word Muslim means "one who submits to God". This submission is done by following The Prophet Muhammad 🕌, especially in terms of doing what he commanded and staying away from what he forbade. So the The Prophet Muhammad's 🕌 life, actions, and teachings are essential for understanding Islam and for a Muslim to understand their religion. Thus these were recorded by those who lived around him and are known through a body of text that is referred to as *Hadith*.

Hadith & Sunnah

Hadith is a textual collection of written traditions that record Islam's second source, the *Sunnah*, or the life and practices of The Prophet Muhammad 🕌. Hadith literature contains his sayings, accounts of his daily practices, things he approved of, disapproved of, and so on. *Ahadith*[96] constitute the major source of Islamic jurisprudence and work in concert with the Qur'an as a religious guide. The word *hadith* itself means "narration" or "something that happened; originated; or came into existence".[97]

While most non-Muslims have at least heard of the Qur'an, the word *hadith* is usually much less familiar and known. However, I promise you it is a word your Muslim students know, even the very young ones. While the Qur'an as a book is about 600 fifteen-line pages containing 6,236 verses, Hadith exist in various collections that would be larger than the average library. The Qur'an itself cannot be fully understood without reference to Hadith, because the verses of the Qur'an are contextualized and explained by it.

---

[94] Qur'an 33:21 https://quran.com/33/21, Jami' at-Tirmidhī Book 27 Hadith 121 https://sunnah.com/tirmidhi/27/121

[95] The proper pronunciation of the word Islam enunciates the letter "s" as an /s/ sound, like in the English word *slam*. Pronouncing it with the letter "s" enunciated as a /z/ is an anglicization of the word and is not the pronunciation Muslims use themselves. The same is true in the pronunciation of the word Muslim.

[96] This is the plural form of the word *hadith*.

[97] Refer to the definition of حَـدَثَ in the Arabic-English Lexicon of Edward William Lane http://arabiclexicon.hawramani.com/حدث/?book=50#2a4579

In this book I basically take the approach of trying to support every assertion I make about Islam with reference to the Qur'an and Hadith as sources. In this chapter especially, that will entail me showing you the wording of some verses of the Qur'an and some specific *ahadith*. However, in most parts it will involve footnoting the reference to the specific verse from the Qur'an or Hadith that serves as textual evidence for the assertion that I make about Islam. This provides for more efficiency in written explanations.[98] In this chapter I want the reader to get some feel for what it is like to actually read verses of the Qur'an and Hadith, or English translations of them anyway, because this is such a common experience and staple part of the lives of Muslim students and their families. As the book goes on it becomes more efficient to rely on the footnote sourcing. You will notice in the sourcing that I provide links to the actual text of the verses of the Qur'an and book source of the Hadith from online databases or digital libraries, and I have erred towards linking to English language translations wherever possible.[99]

Importance of The Prophet's ﷺ Companions and Early Followers

What further explains and contextualizes both the Qur'an and Hadith is the explanations and rulings of the Prophet Muhammad's ﷺ companions and the first three generations of Muslims.[100] This is because the The Prophet Muhammad ﷺ gave authoritative weight, in a prophetic manner, to these generations when he said:

---

[98] It is important to note that everything that is covered in this book is rather basic knowledge to Muslims and a specific verse or hadith that I cite may only be one component of the overall ruling that has come out of Islamic scholarship.

[99] If you are reading the book in print, Google searching the written citation ought to bring up the associated link in most cases. The vast majority of the Hadith links are from the database sunnah.com. However there are still canonical Hadith collections and books that are not on sunnah.com, in those cases I have usually linked to the actual text from archive.org, but substituted that link with a tiny URL. I want the reader to have easy access to the actual text if they choose to explore it.
Note to the Muslim readers: I have used sunnah.com's own numbering system because it correlates best to the URLs of the Hadith and makes the citation more searchable on Google. Hadith collections do not always have consistent numbering systems from one publisher or database to the next. Especially when what is being referenced is an abridged English translation of the Hadith collection. Per my investigations, those usually do not have the same numbering system as the original Arabic. The USC collection which is so commonly referenced does not have the same numbering system for Bukhari and Muslim as the original Arabic, yet people cite numbers to Hadith using its system all the time without specifying where the numbering system actually comes from. So a problem occurs, especially online, where people frequently cite a hadith from a collection and follow it by a number, but that number does not necessarily make the actual text accessible to the reader from a source text if it is not specified what numbering system and from what publisher the citation comes.

[100] These generations begin in the 7th century and end in the 9th century. A companion of the Prophet ﷺ is defined as any one of his followers who had personal contact with him in his lifetime.

> **The best people are those of my generation, and then those who will follow them (the second generation), and then those who will follow them (the third generation).**[101]

I ask people in my trainings if anyone would like to venture a guess as to how many companions The Prophet Muhammad ﷺ had. People are usually hesitant to answer, but of those brave enough to offer a guess the most frequent answer I receive is twelve. The Prophet Muhammad ﷺ had at least 8,000 companions, and when the first three generations are taken together there is at least 40,000 people who transmitted Hadith, commented on them, and explained rulings on them.[102]

Progression of Islamic Sourcing

Qur'an & Hadith

↓

Explanation of first three Muslim generations (salaf)

↓

Consensus of previous Islamic Scholars ('ijma)

↓

Analogical deduction (qiyas)

Islam has no real concept of separation between religion and any other area of a person's life. It is from this body of texts that a Muslim is informed on how to live a life that achieves the goal of submitting to God. Islamic scholarship is built upon these texts, and it is part of Islamic jurisprudence that literally any act a human being can do will take on one of five rulings according to Islam's teachings. An act can be obligatory (*wājib*)[103] to do on one end or forbidden (*harām*)[104] to do on the other. Within that spectrum an act can be *encouraged*[105] (aka

---

[101] This is a hadith, it is part of Islamic written discourse to always cite the book source and reference number of a hadith, these references will appear throughout this book in the footnotes as opposed to being part of the references page: Sahīh al-Bukhārī Book 81 Hadith 18 https://sunnah.com/bukhari/81/18

[102] To Muslim readers, these counts are taken from http://muslimscholars.info/ where the primary sources used are *Tahzeeb al-Tahzeeb and Taqrib al-Tahzeeb* by Ibn Hajar for scholars who are hadith narrators (including companions, followers (Tabi'een), successors (Taba' Tabi'een) and students of successors). The information is linked and cross-referenced with other resources such as *at-Thiqat, Tarikhul Kabir, Tabaqat* and others. As *Tahzeeb al-Tahzeeb* and *Taqrib al-Tahzeeb* contain only narrators of 6 hadith books, *At-Thaqat* and *al-Tarikh-ul-Kabir* are used as primary sources for other narrators. I understand there are sources that state the numbers as being much higher, but I wanted to stick to something countable, this is why I have qualified the statements with "at least". If there are any errors with these counts that can be made more exact please contact me and I will update the second edition.

[103] Meaning the act reaps reward for doing it and incurs sin if not done.

[104] Meaning the act is a sin if one does do it.

[105] Meaning the act reaps reward for doing it but does not incur sin if not done.

Islamic Rulings' Spectrum of Permissibility for Human Actions

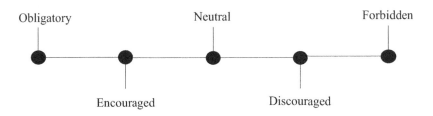

supererogatory), but not obligatory, or *discouraged*[106], but not forbidden; or an act can take on a ruling of neutral.[107]

When an Islamic scholar is to make a ruling on something they first look to the Qur'an and hadith and ask if there is a clear text that dictates what a ruling should be, and the understanding that the companions and early generations of Muslims had of those texts is what informs the scholar's understanding. If a text is not found in the Qur'an and hadith to apply a ruling, then the words of the Prophet's ﷺ companions and early Muslims are referenced. If still these sources cannot inform a ruling the scholars can go to what is called *qiyas*, which means "analogical deduction", and even in this the scholars are to err on the side of the *ijmā* (consensus) that previous generations of scholars had on issues. *Ijmā* is not unlike the traditional concept of precedent in Western law. Islamic scholarship is a legislative science that was drawn out by the early Muslims themselves.

Music, Capitulation, and Insight from Understanding Islamic Sources

In my trainings I almost always have at least one music teacher who attends. Islam's teaching about music may not be the most preeminent issue to talk about, but I begin with it because it illustrates an example as to why this matter of sourcing and a basic understanding of Islamic scholarship is important for people to know in order to have a true grasp of beneath-the-surface issues that can take place with Muslim families.

---

[106] Meaning the act does not have the necessary textual evidence to be categorized as forbidden, but is nevertheless not in accord with good acts and endanger the Muslim of being led into that which is forbidden.

[107] Meaning there is not enough textual evidence to make a decisive ruling, and while there may be many things that can be ruled as neutral, Islamic texts also warn Muslims to be cautious of filling their time with things that have no benefit, or are vain, even if they are permissible to do. Sunan ibn Mājah Book 37 Hadith 4309 https://sunnah.com/urn/1292720, http://sunnah.com/adab/33/3

Music teachers have typically had the experience of having some Muslim students who participate in class and some who refuse, and also having some families who say they do not want their child in music class and who tell them that it is something not allowed in their religion. For the teacher's part, they are often confused as to why families and kids take these differing actions on the same issue.

So does Islam forbid a Muslim from partaking in music? Basically, the correct answer to this question is *yes*. However, if one were to only look at the verses of the Qur'an they would not know this, as there is no verse that explicitly prohibits music. There is a verse that says:

And of mankind is he who purchases <u>idle talks</u>
to mislead mankind from the path of God without knowledge
and who takes it in ridicule. Those will have a humiliating
punishment
[31:6][108]

The word in this verse that is translated as "idle talks" (لَهْوَ - *lahu*) does not mean music in and of itself[109], so reading and knowing this verse alone would not indicate to someone that music is forbidden in Islam. But if one looks to the explanation of this verse by the Prophet Muhammad's ﷺ companions, they would find it explained that this word refers specifically to music, singing, and the playing of musical instruments.[110] The word also refers to other forms of vanity such as useless conjecture and falsehood, but the specification about music was made explicit by the Prophet's ﷺ companions. Also, if one looks at the Hadith literature they would find the Prophet Muhammad ﷺ issuing a warning in the following hadith:

---

108 This is the chapter and verse citation from the Qur'an. A chapter from the Qur'an is called a *sūrah*. Each *sūrah* has a name that it is referred to by as well, but in this book I will only cite the numbers. Note that the actual Qur'an only exists in the Arabic language. in this book you will only see translations, which are used to illustrate the meanings of its verses and can often fall short of illustrating the verse's richness and full depth of meaning.

109 See لهو in the Arabic-English Lexicon of Edward William Lane http://arabiclexicon.hawramani.com/لهو/#9de600

110 The companion Abdullah Ibn Abbas رضــي الله عـنه (d.687 CE) said, "this means singing" in reference to the verse, this is recorded in the famous exegesis of the Qur'an by Muhammad ibn Jarir at-Tabri (d.923 CE) as well as Al-'Ādab al-Mufrad by Bukhari Book 33 Hadith 33 see https://sunnah.com/adab/33/33. The companion Abu Umamah رضــي الله عـنه said it refers to purchasing singers for entertainment in Jami` at-Tirmidhi Book 47 Hadith 3499 https://sunnah.com/urn/642250. The companion Abdullah ibn Masūd رضــي الله عـنه (d. 653 CE) said this verse was revealed concerning "singing and musical instruments", as is recorded in the famous exegesis of the Qur'an by Ismail ibn Kathir (d.1373 CE) see pg. 571 of volume 1 of the abridged English translation published by Darussalam https://tinyurl.com/y9gela7j

> **People among my ummah[111] will drink wine, calling it by another name, and musical instruments will be played for them as well as singing girls. God will cause the earth to swallow them up, and will turn them into monkeys and pigs.[112]**

In other *ahadith* the Prophet ﷺ warns that the one who partakes in music should expect to be punished in hell.[113] Others link music with being a cause of hypocrisy[114] in the heart as well as being a precursor of using intoxicants[115] and committing illicit fornication[116]; all of which are severe sins and vices in Islam that are forbidden.[117]

What this illustrates is that understanding details of rules pertaining to Islamic teachings, as well as foundational purposes behind those teachings, cannot really be understood without knowledge of Islam's sourcing. While on the other hand knowledge of Islam's sourcing reveals underlying impetuses to actions that educators see with their Muslim families. For a non-Muslim from the West who has had a positive experience and association in their life with music, it might seem odd for a family to prohibit their child's participation in it. Yet, it is not unreasonable to look at these teachings on one hand and consider the vice-promoting culture of popular music in the West on the other, and from there be able to ascertain how a Muslim family might see their religious beliefs about music being totally reaffirmed by what the culture of Western popular music promotes.

Even for music that does not promote vice, the rhythms, beats, and harmonies that are most-commonly used and taught in music are those that are likely to make the music "stick" in a person's head in an involuntary fashion (Jakubowski et al, 2017). This is something people experience whether they want to or not just by absorbing music that is part of the ambiance of the general public and media. For a Muslim, music being "stuck in one's head" can be interpreted as blocking their mind (and by extension their heart) from reciting the Qur'an, and and having their heart and mind entrapped by nefarious forces. When this takes place it is a

---

111 The word "ummah" is the Arabic word for "community" or "nation" - linguistically it comes from the word "umm" which means mother. The word is used to refer to the Muslim community at large, and its linguistic connotation signifies the idea of Muslims belonging to one family of faith.

112 Sunan ibn Mājah Book 36 Hadith 95 https://sunnah.com/ibnmajah/36/95

113 Sahīh al-Bukhārī Book 74 Hadith 16 https://sunnah.com/bukhari/74/16

114 Sunan Abī Dawūd Book 43 Hadith 155 http://sunnah.com/abudawud/43/155

115 Jami` at-Tirmidhī Book 33 Hadith 55 https://sunnah.com/tirmidhi/33/55, Tafsīr Ibn Kathīr 5:90-93, see pg. 261 of abridged volume 1 published by Darussalam https://tinyurl.com/yb5e9y9f

116 Sahīh al-Bukhārī Book 74 Hadith 16 https://sunnah.com/bukhari/74/16

117 Qur'an 25:68-69 https://quran.com/25/68, Qur'an 2:219 https://quran.com/2/219

reaffirmation of what was said by one of the most prominent scholars in Islamic history, **"The Qur'an and music cannot coexist in the heart of a person because they are opposite of one another."**[118] Some families might have their children spending hours outside of school learning to recite the Qur'an. If we know these religious teachings it becomes pertinent to ask: Why would they not see their children attending music class as counterproductive to the work they put in learning the Qur'an outside of school?

So why do some Muslim families request their child to not be in music class while others do not say anything about it? When Muslims have to choose between going against the general societal grain and following Islam they will fall into one of three general categories relative to the Islamic ruling:

1. Ignorance
2. Capitulation
3. Reconciled Interpretation

I will explain each one of these, but first I wish to emphasize that my experience lends me to believe the majority of families who do not advocate for their child to be excused from music class (as well as many other matters that would relate to issues of religious accommodations to students) are in the *second* category: *capitulation*.

The first category, ignorance, means that the families themselves do not have enough knowledge about the issue to fully know and understand that Islam does forbid music.

The second category are those who know well enough that Islam forbids music, but they do not want to be a bother to the school, or to be misunderstood, or to be stigmatized within the school community, or to be burdened with giving people complicated explanations about various matters that are both sensitive and unfamiliar to the non-Muslim school employees and stakeholders. Thus, they capitulate to the standard societal expectations and allow their children to go to music class despite having misgivings about it. It is actually a persistent problem that when a Muslim's need for non-Muslims in their life to understand Islam arises, it is typically in the context of issues like this that are conflictual. The difficulty that brings for the Muslim is that in order for the non-Muslim to really understand the issue at hand, they would need to have a broader understand of Islam, how it operates in an individual's life, and how it is sourced. So broaching a specific issue might seem as small as simply saying something like, "well our

---

[118] *Ighāthah al-lahfān* (Supporting the Distressed...) by Ibn al-Qayyim (d.1350 CE), see pg. 131 of the English translation published by Darussalam.

religion forbids my child from attending music class". But in reality, saying something like this opens up a whole chasm of explanation that is needed in order to give the issue the breadth it deserves and to ensure confusion is not caused on the part of the non-Muslim. This is an intimidating undertaking for most people. There can be ever-numerous other issues that compound that intimidation, but not least of those is simply not wanting to seem like you are being difficult or unkind. Muslims are also sensitive in these situations to not wanting smaller issue to give off a negative impression to people about Islam. Impressions that might be waned if the non-Muslim had a more comprehensive understanding of it. All this amounts to Muslims choosing a route of least resistance that is realized as a constant capitulation in their religious observance to the ignorance of non-Muslims about Islam.

The third category are families who have adopted an interpretation of Islamic sources in which they reconcile that music is actually permissible. This can take on a few different shades, but overall there are only a minimal amount of Islamic scholars in history who have adopted this view; and with all of them it takes a fair amount of negligence towards Islamic text and tradition in order to do so. It can also be the case with Muslims in this category that their reconciled interpretation is due to a degree of ignorance about the Islamic texts, and therefore they might move into the second category in a future day after acquiring more learning.

Implications and Caveats

Educators I train usually find information such as this about Islam and music to be latent with the families in their school community but unbeknownst to themselves prior to me pointing it out to them. Consequently, this new learning for the prior-to-unaware educator is accompanied by an anxiety as to what should be done with these newfound insights alongside a genuine desire to serve the true needs and wants of families. So throughout this book I will do my best to discuss implications for practice at the ground-level of teachers and schools with each issue that is brought up. Firstly, I advise a general rule for educators to think in terms of incremental small steps when it comes to altering practice. Larger-scale changes can often be shocking to a school community and are typically not set up to be successful and sustainable if implementation is not done in a sequence that is incremental, logical, and sensitive to all stakeholders. Remember that simply acquiring new understandings yourself is a significant first step. With any matter, having appropriate knowledge is an essential step to building a foundation that will best inform your actions in your own context.

Having an understanding and using new found learning as a basis to gather targeted information and feedback from families and to expand learning of both families and staff can be a very positive first step. Perhaps reading this book chapter has already given you newfound insights into beneath-the-surface issues that may be at play with your Muslim students and families. This is positive, yet it would be an overly dramatic action step, and overly presumptuous, to do something like taking all of the Muslim kids in your school out of music class tomorrow and having them read books quietly in a separate room instead while you call their parents groveling to apologize for being so culturally insensitive. Rather, forms of information gathering and sharing can be a more incremental step that carry the potential to yield positive outcomes in and of themselves, as well as the potential to offer guidance for further steps to be taken.

❖ *Sharing information*

A natural step to take with colleagues is sharing the newfound information one has learned and engaging in a reflective discussion on it and its implications for the school site and individual practice. It might be a more incremental step to first use your newfound knowledge with colleagues before families and students. This might mean referring them to read this book, or putting aside a specialized time to read parts of it during professional development.

Information that pertains to religious rights in the public education system is crucial information that ought to be shared with families in a proactive manner. It is my experience that Muslim families are frequently unaware of the full degree of religious rights that they and their children have within the school system. The default disposition that families generally have is one of ambivalent passivity. This can be due to a lack of awareness of their own religious rights and rights of advocacy, but more frequently results from an anxiety of being stigmatized if they single themselves out for special treatment. Therefore, action steps taken by schools that signify an advanced awareness of religious needs and preferences can be taken as very endearing to Muslim families.

Another important issue pertaining to this is the fact that school staff in public education institutions are often very unaware and confused themselves about the religious rights of students and families; as well as the proper place of religious discussion in the education curriculum, instructional practice, and religious accommodation within the school's structure. Educators are not properly prepared for this in preservice training, and this typically results in teachers having a disposition where concerns about church-state violations are overly inflated. Consequently, in-school practices are often directly suppressive of religious rights at worst, and avoidant at best; such trends have their own implications for violations of the First Amendment and servicing a liberal education (Nord, 2010). Specific references to religious rights will be made throughout this book, and a good starting resource for knowing religious rights is the *Guidance on Constitutionally Protected Prayer and Religious Expression in Public Elementary and Secondary Schools*[119] that was released by the federal Department of Education in January of 2020. This memo should be read and known to school staff, and its information should be communicated to parents in a proactive manner as well. Translation and different modes of communication should be used in doing this to ensure families understand. It is my plan in the future to have translations of the federal guidance posted in Somali and Arabic on abrahameducation.com. It is important for educators to know that within a school site the educators themselves do have a responsibility to know what the religious rights of students and families are for the sake of the dual responsibilities of adhering to the dictates of the establishment clause, while also honoring the individual rights of religious practice granted by the freedom of expression clause. It is the administration, and specifically the principal's responsibility to be the school's guardsafe in deliberating proper adjudication on these matters, and all schools and districts have lawyers and counsels that are either employed or contracted by them who can provide necessary training on such matters as well as advise on specific situations. But school's need to be proactive in seeking this counsel out.[120]

❖ *Information Gathering*

There are many ways schools can gather information from families. Schools can use surveys, phone calls, in-person gatherings, or hold their own public awareness seminars where feedback is sought by attendees. Simply asking families whether or not there are any classes or subjects of study at school from which they would prefer their child to be excused can be a positive first step. This can be done with a caveat provided that explains that parents are being surveyed as

---

[119] This is available at https://www2.ed.gov/policy/gen/guid/religionandschools/prayer_guidance.html, I am hoping to provide translations of this in Arabic and Somali through my website abrahameducation.com in the near future.

[120] I have done my best to be judicious and fair in this book and not make any recommendations that go against the first amendment. Nevertheless schools must seek out their own counsel always. Generally, school's, like legislatures, are bound to follow what is referred to in case law as the "Lemon test" which dictates that their actions must have a primary secular purpose, that the primary purpose can neither advance nor prohibit religion, and must not result in an "excessive government entanglement" with religion. Factors used to evaluate this are the character and purpose of the institution, the nature of aid the state provides, and the resulting relationship between government and religious authority (*Lemon v. Kurtzman*, 403 U. S. 602 [1971]). At the same time, there are still many grey areas in the law pertaining to religion in the schools, and it may be that the increasing presence of Muslim students and families in public schools properly provides an impetus for schools and districts across the country to mete out some of these issues by seeking counsel. The Lemon test itself is under scrutiny in the court system. Even after the Lemon Test, the Supreme Court confirmed that when a governmental action or policy ostensibly promotes a secular interest while having an incidental or even a primary effect of helping a sectarian belief or practice it is **not** invalid under the establishment clause (*Wallace v. Jaffree, 466 U.S. 924* [1984]).The Supreme Court has acknowledged that *"the Court has struggled to find a neutral course between the two Religion Clauses, both of which are cast in absolute terms, and either of which, if expanded to a logical extreme, would tend to clash with the other." (Walz v. Tax Commission of the City of New York*, 397 U.S. 668–69 [1970]).

part of an information gathering process for the school, especially if the school does not feel it is structurally ready to provide accommodations. However, it could be the case that information gathered from surveying provides the impetus for longer-term structural changes that are implemented incrementally. For Muslim families, asking specifically about music class can signify that the school has a deeper level of awareness than most parents would expect. Therefore, simply asking the question is an action step that Muslim families could find endearing, respectful, and appreciable. This is a benefit that is derived even if families still choose to capitulate. There is always an internal barrier that exists between the passive disposition of capitulation and the assertive disposition of self-advocacy. Asking a culturally-relevant question to families in and of itself may not be enough for families to be comfortable passing through that barrier; but it can signify to them that doing so may actually be a possibility within their child's school community, which can be very encouraging and create positive sentiments about cross-cultural relations. It should also be taken from this that such questions should be asked on an ongoing, perhaps annual, basis. As families may not feel comfortable advocating for themselves at first, but could be over time after the sentiment has settled in that the school is ready to take such concerns seriously.

Keep in mind that there are practical considerations to surveying parents. Many schools send out Google forms and emails to intake information from families at the beginning of the school year. This is a fine practice but it is also not suitable and effective for all families, especially those where the parents lack literacy in English. It is also true for families who are from highly oral cultures. With these families it is generally best to rely on verbal communication, either via the phone or in person, and of course with effective translators when needed. Telelinks and some of the live streaming methods available in social media I have known to be used for a variety of purposes within Muslim diaspora communities. Even people with low-levels of formal education are familiar with using these mediums. Schools could use them also as a way to engage families remotely.

I think it would be a great idea for schools and districts to hold an annual informational seminar available for all families on religious rights in the public schools. Again, the content of the federal government's guidance can be gone over in these seminars, and the gatherings themselves can create an excellent opportunity to garner feedback from families. The primary secular purpose for the school can be informing families on their rights and working to ensure an inclusive school environment from parental feedback. Schools can always provide disclaimers that it does not endorse, advance, nor hinder any particular religious belief in accordance with the Constitution; and that it also abides to accommodate religious rights that are asserted by students and families also in accordance with the Constitution. The Supreme Court has ruled that if a governmental body claims or disclaims a certain intent then the court should defer to accepting that intent as the basis for the action, which matters significantly in establishment clause issues.[121]

❖ *Other Considerations with Music*
Music in school is, of course, not restricted to music class. I am frequently asked about using music as an instructional tool in class, especially in the younger grade levels. This is an area where some insights into the caveats of Islamic rulings have some benefits, as well as to how religion intertwines, and not always accords, with specific cultures to which Muslims belong. Generally, the prohibition of music in Islam does not include chanting[122], and there is some religious pretext to claim that use of instrumentation is much worse than singing[123], since singing is allowed under some circumstances.[124] Using songs in an acapella-like fashion in classrooms for the purpose of memorizing learning material is generally okay. If this errs on the side of being more chanting-like as opposed to signing-like, I believe it is safe to say that it is something not only permissible in Islam but even something that is not unlike some modes of memorization learning that is done in Muslim educational settings. Besides this, I would also say that sensitivities about the use of music for learning with younger children in preschool and the early elementary grades is not something that families are too caught up about. I have even known this type of learning to be used with these age groups in conservative Muslim countries. At the same time, these are situations without instrumentation and where learning content is the primary purpose, and not learning music. If you wish to ask families whether or not they mind you using music as an instructional tool that is fine, but I would not say it is of preeminent concern at early ages. Especially if it is used as a tool for non-music subject-area learning or to aid in the performance of physical tasks.

---

[121] See (*Wallace v. Jaffree, 466 U.S. 924* [1984]). In the concurring opinion of Justice Sandra Day O'Connor: *"If a legislature expresses a plausible secular purpose for a moment of silence statute in either the text or the legislative history, or if the statute disclaims an intent to encourage prayer over alternatives during a moment of silence, then courts should generally defer to that stated intent...Even if the text and official history of a statute express no secular purpose, the statute should be held to have an improper purpose only if it is beyond purview that endorsement of religion or a religious belief 'was and is the law's reason for existence.'"*

[122] Saḥīḥ al-Bukhārī Book 78 Hadith 234 https://sunnah.com/bukhari/78/234

[123] Sunan an-Nasā'i Book 26 Hadith 174 https://sunnah.com/nasai/26/174

[124] Singing and percussion is allowed for females at weddings and Islamic holidays. Sunan an-Nasā'i Book 26 Hadith 174 & 188 https://sunnah.com/nasai/26/174, https://sunnah.com/nasai/26/188, Sunan ibn Majah Book 9 Hadith 1973 https://sunnah.com/urn/1262170
Chanting and singing can be used to move along with tasks of physical exertion. Saḥīḥ al-Bukhārī Book 78 Hadith 234 https://sunnah.com/bukhari/78/234, Saḥīḥ al-Bukhārī Book 87 Hadith 29 https://sunnah.com/bukhari/87/29, Saḥīḥ Muslim Book 5 Hadith 13 https://sunnah.com/muslim/5/13

Furthermore, there is also religious text to ascertain that the use of percussion is not fully included in the prohibition of using musical instruments.[125] The use of beat-based chants in the classroom as a tool for subject-area learning and memorization is something that I believe one would be hard pressed to find a family taking issue with, especially in the case of its use with young children. Nevertheless, I have known educators of young children who have had families request them to not use music as a learning tool in the classroom, but this was in specific reference to playing music that involved instrumentation.

Religiously, there is no sin on a Muslim for being in the presence of music whose audibility they did not initiate. There is religious evidence to justify for avoiding circumstances where music is played[126], but this is not at the cost of other needs. So, for example, there is no issue with a Muslim going into a retail store where music is played on the overhead audio system in order to buy something of their basic necessities. There is an extent to which this could be extrapolated to a classroom where the teacher regularly plays music in order to soothe, energize, or teach the class. Theoretically, if a Muslim student is in such a classroom they need not distress over the idea of incurring sin by being in the presence of the classroom because they did not initiate it being played, and they are not given a choice to be elsewhere.[127] Still, it is a recommended practice that teachers gauge the class sentiment about the idea of playing music in it, and this is best done in a way where students can submit their preferences anonymously. This means that if a teacher says to a class, "do you guys mind if I play some music while you work?", to the whole class at once, the few Muslim students in the class may not say anything for fear of being ostracized by the social pressures of others. Generally, in classrooms that have large percentages of Muslim students, I feel it is tone-deaf (no pun intended) to presumptively play music in the classroom. The default presumption ought to be that music should not be played except for the caveats already discussed. Even if the students are gauged for their preferences and grant consent for music to be played, the question remains as to whether or not the preference of their parents has been gauged. While many teachers find there is a benefit to playing classical or ambient music in a classroom for the sake of calming kids down, there is no reason why alternatives cannot be sought, such as the playing of nature sounds to relax, or percussion-only options if intended to energize.

❖ Curriculum Considerations with Music

As stated above, there is religious text that lends to concluding that the use of percussion instruments is okay. One music teacher who attended my training was from St. Cloud, MN

---

[125] Sunan an-Nasā'i Book 26 Hadith 174 https://sunnah.com/nasai/26/174
[126] Sunan Abī Dawūd Book 43 Hadith 152 https://sunnah.com/abudawud/43/152
[127] Islam lays no sin or fault upon one who is compelled to do something outside their control. Qur'an 24:33 https://quran.com/24/33

where the demographics are drastically shifting towards a majority of students in many of their elementary schools being Muslim. This teacher had constantly dealt with families who wanted to remove their child from music class at an ever-increasing rate each year. Naturally, she looked at the population changes taking place in her hometown and recognized that if she did not take action she could potentially be looking at being out of a job in the future. Canceling music class ought not to be out of the realm of consideration for many schools who are undergoing and projecting a major demographic shift such as this in their student population. Based on my conversations with both educators as well as Muslim parents, I would say that wanting to avoid music class is one of the major drivers of the spurt of charter schools in the Twin Cities that are almost 100% Somali; those schools *do not* have music class at all and find alternative elective classes to offer.

This teacher in St. Cloud was a very pro-active and intelligent young lady and she was well aware of these sensitivities surrounding music before attending my training. So she was in the middle of a project of authoring a complete K-12 world percussion curriculum that she was going to propose as an alternative track for the school to offer to students who did not want to take traditional music class. This is a type of proactive step that I feel is very appreciable. Not only is it explicitly aware of the religious and cultural sensitivities and takes them into account, but it also examines student engagement at the level of curricula content and takes into consideration the longer-term direction and purpose of the school in regards to it undergoing a demographic shift. This is not a mere band-aid nor reactionary solution to a cultural conflict taking place, it is a holistic and proactive approach.

Implementing a world percussion curriculum is something that schools and districts might consider exploring to meet the needs of Muslim families and students. Likewise, being intentional about not forcing students into classes and activities that involve partaking in other kinds of instrumentation ought to be considered at a minimum. This means when schedules for high school students are generated, it is culturally insensitive to automatically place students in guitar class (I know *many* students in Minneapolis for whom this happened). Likewise, the units where students are given recorders and learn to use them, commonly done in fourth grade, are perhaps something that is best opted into as opposed to assumed and mandated. Islam is explicit in condemning the playing of stringed and woodwind instruments.[128]

---

[128] Sunan Abī Dawūd Book 43 Hadith 152 https://sunnah.com/abudawud/43/152, Tafsīr Ibn Kathīr 5:90-93, see pg. 261 of abridged volume 1 published by Darussalam https://tinyurl.com/yb5e9y9f

❖ *Muslim Cultures and Music*

It is correct that the Muslim world has a complex relationship with music. While Islam does forbid music, pretty much every Muslim culture still has a tradition of music of one type or another. It can be a perfectly secular objective to teach about and explore these types of music in a public education music class, and there could very well be Muslim families who are delighted to have their children taught about that. Still, the insight I would like for educators to take away is that just because a music tradition belongs to a certain Muslim culture, it does not mean that there is not controversy about that music within that culture. Too often it is blindly assumed that if something carries the label of Arab, Somali, or Persian music etc. it must be a culturally-relevant thing to introduce into class. It may very well be, but lacking the insight of the religious teachings deprives teachers of the opportunity to have a more in-depth view as to how these matters can be related to by families.

Furthermore, the perception that Muslim families might generally have of Western music is greatly influenced by the perceived negative, degenerate, and vice-encouraging aspects of popular music into which the profiteers of the world are constantly trying to hook children and adolescents. The music traditions in the Muslim world that do exist tend to be rather consistent in still abiding by wholesome themes in their songs, in stark contrast to the themes of violence, drug use, and sexual promiscuity that permeate popular music in the West. So I have certainly known families who listened to music from their home culture at festive affairs, but viewed that as being something very different from the musical culture of the West, and therefore still wanted to encourage their kids to not listen to music.

Something that music classes could do as alternative assignments is to give students the opportunity to learn about and articulate a critical analysis of the negative effects of popular music that exist in academia. The American Psychological Association (APA) has acknowledged since 2003 that listening to violent lyrics in rap and heavy metal music increases thoughts of aggression and violence in the listener[129] (Anderson et al, 2003). Surely, music class usually does not encourage partaking in this type of music[130], however, schools could do a favor to Muslim families and reinforce their values by having students take on this type of critical analysis, and providing them the information and explanation of studies that have shown its negative effects on a scientific level. Such learning can be a powerful experience for students because it offers the opportunity for them to have the rightness of lessons that their parents teach them reinforced through a different lens. Many students may need to be guided through reading and comprehending a report of a clinical study. But often the key to engaging students

---

[129] The full study can be retrieved from the APA's website here: https://www.apa.org/pubs/journals/releases/psp-845960.pdf

[130] Although having units on rap and hip-hop is something that is on the rise in many school districts.

at a deeper level involves selecting the appropriate work from higher academia and finding a way to scaffold comprehension of it down to K-12 levels.

There is feverish concern amongst Muslim communities and families across the country over the listening and participation of youth in rap music. Unfortunately, many public schools have been either incapable or oblivious to the idea of reinforcing and supporting family concerns such as these. Too often, schools or after school programs have been the places where students have been given the opportunity to create rap music, and this is done under the guise of cheap notions of supposedly engaging students based on their interests, or providing them with outlets for their creative expression. In addition to the negative effects that the APA has found about listening to rap music, the National Institutes of Health found in a study that, "Listening to rap music was significantly and positively associated with alcohol use, problematic alcohol use, illicit-drug use, and aggressive behaviors when all other variables were controlled" (Chen et al, 2006). The results and science behind these studies are more appropriate to be shared with and inculcated upon young students than encouragement to partake in activities that their parents are likely to be against, and medical authorities have apprised as detrimental to public health. The American Association of Pediatrics has made formal recommendations to pediatricians to be active in informing the public on the negative effects of listening to explicit music.[131] Why should the role of educators in the public school system be any different? Reading these studies, or other critiques like them, and analyzing those readings, could be a route of alternative assignments that students could undertake in music class that ought to spur interesting discussions that open the door for home cultural-religious values to be brought into the classroom by students where they might not otherwise have the opportunity. It can also provide an interesting route to show the scientific process and methods of research in a light that is of immediate relevance to youth. This can be an opportunity for students to learn about factors of research, such as controlled experimentation, or the difference between causation and association, and have discussions on them.[132]

---

[131] See: Impact of music lyrics and music videos on children and youth (RE9144). (American Academy of Pediatrics Committee on Communications). (1996). *Pediatrics, 98*(6), 1219-1221. Retrievable here: https://pediatrics.aappublications.org/content/124/5/1488

[132] There is a synopsis of the particular study cited here done by MTV that might be more accessible to student reading levels. It can be found here: http://www.mtv.com/news/1528932/study-says-hip-hop-listeners-more-prone-to-drug-use-aggression/ Another report that summarizes findings of studies with similar results can be found here: https://www.drugfoundation.org.nz/matters-of-substance/august-2010/when-drugs-and-music-overlap/

Conclusion

The sources of Islam go beyond the Qur'an and into other textual sources that are not commonly known about to non-Muslims. Understanding the framework of these sources and how they relate to one another is necessary in order to enter an in-depth dialogue or understanding of the reasons why Islamic practices are what they are. This has direct real-world implications in both public schools and any context where Muslims and non-Muslims come together; as is illustrated by the example of how Muslims relate to music and the depth to which the discussion on it can go.

Once pertinent newfound knowledge about Islam is acquired by educators an array of considerations and opportunities arise towards changing practice in order to engage students and families in a way that is honoring, respectful, and culturally-relevant. Nevertheless, because Islamic knowledge is esoteric in non-Muslims societies, Muslims have generally resigned themselves to varying degrees of capitulation regarding religious beliefs and practices; and how they relate to what their children are exposed to or forced to do in public education. This capitulation is a major underlying phenomenon that is latent in virtually all school communities with Muslim students and families. Consequently, it will typically not be expected from Muslim students and families to be engaged with the school community in a manner that is rooted on the non-Muslim school members having knowledge about Islamic belief and practice. Therefore change in educator practice is appropriately done in an incremental fashion.

The following pages will go over the core teachings and practices of Islam, that which is known and universal to virtually all Muslims. This will be taught through Islamic sources and followed by explanation and reflection as to direct ways in which these teachings effect our students and families, and also very practical ways they show up that non-Muslim educators heretofore might have not realized. Further, suggestions and ideas will be offered as to how this knowledge can be used in schools to engage students and families in a more culturally-relevant manner and positively support the ambitions of families and academic prowess of students.

The Core of Islam

The starting point of knowing the core teachings of Islam necessitates knowing and breaking down a single hadith that will be presented here in gradual chunks. The hadith begins:

On the authority of Abu Abdirahmān 'Abdullaah[133], the son of Umar ibn al-Khattab[134], who said: I heard the Messenger of Allah[135](Muhammad) say:

Islam has been built on five pillars...[136]

It is common enough for people to have heard of the five pillars of Islam, but an initial take away here is that this is a teaching and conceptualization that is native to the religion itself. It is not some sort of categorization that was put together by Muslims or anyone else who examined the religious practices within them in an academic manner, it is a direct teaching of the Prophet Muhammad 🌸. The term *rukun* in Arabic is translated into "pillar" and also means "corner", but pillar is the more appropriate word because it does not carry the connotation of being limited to four, a *rukun* is something that is literally needed to hold something up and make it firm.[137] What this means is that the five pillars are necessary for a Muslim to observe in order for their Islam to be complete.

The concept of completion via the fulfillment of pillars also exists in Islam within its individual practices; meaning that within Islamic legalese individual practices have pillars and conditions that need to be observed in order for the act to be considered complete and valid. It is important to understand that Islam very strongly has this concept of specific requirements needing to be fulfilled within its acts in order for the act to be "valid" or accepted by God as legitimate[138]; more specific references to this will be made in chapter four. The hadith continues to list the five pillars and here I will explain them with connections to students and families one by one.

---

[133] The way a hadith is written out is by beginning with listing the chain of people who orally narrated the hadith throughout the generations before it was catalogued into a written text. Abu Abdirahmān 'Abdullaah رضي الله عنه was a member of the second generation of Muslims, he was a child in the lifetime of the Prophet Muhammad 🌸. He is commonly referred to as Ibn Umar as well.

[134] Umar ibn al-Khattab رضي الله عنه was a famous companion of the Prophet Muhammad 🌸 and the second leader of the Muslims after the Prophet's 🌸 death. Many Muslim boys are named after Umar though the spelling may also be Omar as *o* and *u* are interchangeable when transliterating Arabic into English letters.

[135] "The Messenger of God" is an appellation of the Prophet Muhammad 🌸 given to him in the Qur'an (33:21 https://quran.com/33/21) and used to refer to him by Muslims. The meaning of it being a reinforcement that he literally brought to people God's message.

[136] Sahīh Muslim Book 1 Hadith 21 https://sunnah.com/muslim/1/21, Sahīh al-Bukhari Book 2 Hadith 1 http://sunnah.com/bukhari/2/1

[137] See ركن in the Arabic-English Lexicon of Edward William Lane http://arabiclexicon.hawramani.com/ركن/#9a8f7f

[138] Sunan Abī Dawūd Book 1 Hadith 101 https://sunnah.com/abudawud/1/101

The First Pillar - Monotheism

Below the first part of the first pillar has been added and is discussed thereafter:

> ### Islam has been built on five pillars...
> - ### To bear witness that there is none worthy of worship except Allāh...

This is the first part of the first pillar. There is a sound comparison to be made between this pillar and the first commandment given to Moses in the Old Testament.[139] Some examination of the word *Allāh* offers opportunities for insight and lessons that connect directly to students.

The word *Allāh* الله in Arabic means "God", it is the word used for God by non-Muslim speakers of Arabic as well. However, the letters *alif* ا and *lam* ل that are signified by "A" and "l" in the beginning of the English transliteration are actually the definite article in Arabic, and the word *lāh* means "God". As such, the most accurate linguistic translation of *Allāh* is "The God". What is signified by this is the Islamic concept, belief, and teaching of absolute, uncompromising, and unadulterated MONOTHEISM. This is the preeminent principle that Islam is about.[140]

Understanding the word *Allāh* and other names that are used to describe God in the Qur'an illuminates a certain naming pattern that is common amongst Muslim boys. The Arabic word and name *abd*[141] عـبـد means "worshipper"[142], when this word is conjoined with one of the Qur'anic names of God it creates a type of Muslim name. At its most basic level, if you take *abd* and conjoin it with the word *Allāh* it produces the name *Abdallah*[143], this name means "worshipper of God".

In the Qur'an, a way by which God is explained is through words that are referred to in Islamic terminology as His Names and Attributes, of which there are more than ninety-nine. If one looks at these names and then puts them in conjunction with this word *abd* the names and meanings of many Muslim boys are revealed. For example, one of the most frequently occurring names of

---

[139] Exodus Chapter 20 Verses 2-4

[140] Qur'an 21:108 https://quran.com/21/108, Qur'an 2:255 https://quran.com/2/255

[141] Somalis typically articulate this name as "Abdi"

[142] This word can also mean "slave" or "servant" and many students may know it by that meaning. I consider "worshipper" a more precise translation as the word comes from the Arabic verb *'ibada* which means "to worship". It does carry the meaning of "slave" or "servant" as in being a slave to God, however, due to the strong connotations that the word slave carries in English I do not consider it the best single word to use as a translation. See عبد in Lane's lexicon arabiclexicon.hawramani.com/عبد/#3426db

[143] There can be variant spellings on this name such as Abdullah or, common amongst Somalis, Abdullahi.

God in the Qur'an is the name *ar-Rahmān*.[144] These names are a sort of intensive adjective in Arabic and they are difficult to translate perfectly into English, but the best way is to use the superlative form. This means *ar-Rahmān* is best translated as "The Most Merciful".[145] So if *abd* is conjoined with *ar-Rahmān*, what is produced is the name *Abdirahman*, which means "worshipper of The Most Merciful".

The reason I draw this example out is to illustrate the general fact that the names of Muslim children, whether it follows this naming pattern or not, almost always have a deep meaning attached to them. It is typically the case that parents were purposeful in giving their child a name with its attached meaning. There is much discussion in equity circles of education about the mispronunciation of non-anglo student names, and how students lose something of themselves, and have it inferred upon them that they have an inferior status as minorities, when they go to school and have their names mispronounced (Kohli & Solórzano, 2012). It is certainly true that something is lost for students when this happens. At the same time, it is also the case that no single individual on planet earth can pronounce every name that exists outside of their own native tongue correctly. If a monolingual anglophone wished to pronounce names rooted in Arabic correctly, the fact of the matter is they would have to spend a fair amount of time, perhaps months or even years, training the fine muscles in their mouth's articulation cavities to execute the pronunciation of phonemes that do not exist in their native linguistic bank. Sure, they can ask students the correct way to pronounce their name, but typically students do not want to bother to be the ones to do that. Accepting that your name will simply not be pronounced correctly in school is a common area of capitulation on the part of students; to such an extent that they will become habitualized into giving a mispronunciation of their name as their real name to teachers in anticipation that it will be easier for them to pronounce. After enough time attending school, students even begin to call one another, or even their own self, by the mispronunciation of their name.

While effort in pronouncing names is valuable and I do not encourage neglect of it by teachers, I firstly advise that if one wishes to fret about proper pronunciation of student names, they should bear the burden of work, study, and practice that it takes to pronounce those names on their own shoulders and not attempt to burden students with having to teach them. Secondly, in the case of Muslim students, where I see a greater area of benefit for teachers to draw on is in

---

[144] The "l" in the definite article in this construction is silent.

[145] Even the superlative form in English suggests something of comparison to something else. However, the names of Allah carry the connotation of not being comparable to anything else, they also carry the connotation and meaning of being the originating source. So God is not only the Most Merciful, but He is also the ultimate source of all mercy that exists. Jami' at-Tirmidhī Book 48 Hadith 172 https://sunnah.com/ tirmidhi/48/172

connecting with students over the *meaning* of their names. Students can be asked to do an assignment where they research the meaning of their name and how to translate it properly into English, and they can inquire with family and community members about the meaning of the name and maybe why it was chosen for them. Then they could share with their class in a way in which they are set up for success. Again, it may be that students are sensitive at first about relating personal information like this, and perhaps even more so the case if their name has a religious meaning due to the always latent implication in public schools that religion is unwelcome and taboo to bring up. This is where the teacher having their own background knowledge about student culture and religion is beneficial. For a Muslim student to explain the full context of their name's meaning to a class might have to entail some rudimentary teaching about Islam as well. Students often do not know how to do this, are afraid of being stigmatized, and are lacking for models in their personal background as to how one effectively communicates about Islam to non-Muslims. The teacher who has the appropriate background knowledge his or herself can aid in this process.

The names of the Prophet's family members 🕌 and companions are often sources of names as well, both male and female. The names of the other prophets whose stories are told in the Qur'an are also sources of male names and many people are surprised to learn that these names are simply the Arabic versions of common English names.[146] Female names are often adjectives and nouns with associations of grace, gratitude, beauty, piety, or tenderness; and these names will have male corollaries as well.

The First Pillar cont'd - Uniqueness, Omnipotence, and Metaphysical Cause

The following is a short four-verse chapter[147] from the Qur'an, and one of the first that Muslim children learn:

Say[148]: He is Allah, the One!
Allah, The Eternal on whom all depend
He begets not, nor is He begotten
And there is nothing comparable unto Him
[112:1-4]

---

[146] These names are charted out in the section further down on Prophets and Messengers.

[147] The Qur'an is loosely organized by having longer chapters in the beginning and shorter chapters at the end, though this is not exact. An exception is the very first chapter, which is only seven verses and is recited in every prayer.

[148] The command "say" (*qul*) appears frequently in the Qur'an, and it is like a literal command to the Muslims to say this to people and amongst themselves.

That there is nothing comparable to Allah is expressed multiple times[149] in the Qur'an, as well as in Hadith.[150] Exhibited in this verse is the strict separation that Islam observes between *The Creator*, Allah, and the creation, which is everything in the realm of human existence.

Observance of this strict separation means that it is a sin, a serious sin, and a violation of this most important first pillar for a Muslim to attribute to *The Creator* any attribute of the creation. Likewise, it is a sin for a Muslim to attribute to the creation any attribute of *The Creator*.[151] This means that a Muslim is forbidden from ascribing any metaphysical or cosmological cause to anything other than Allah.

What does this mean in practical terms for educators? It means, for example, that a Muslim child is not suppose to speak about their mother's back breaking as a consequence of stepping on a crack in the sidewalk pavement. It means that a Muslim is not suppose to knock on wood, cross their fingers, or wish upon a star in hopes of bringing future beneficence upon themselves. The same is true of finding a four leaf clover, or a penny that is heads up, or really anything that has to do with the concept of luck, insofar as it connotes random chance as English use of the word does. It is part of Islamic belief that everything that takes place only happens by the will, decree, and permission of Allah. So any concept of randomized haphazard fortune that is implicit in the idea of luck is something that Islam rejects, and uttering phrases that pertain to luck is a minor violation of this first pillar.[152] It can even be the case that Muslim children are taught that it is good to have sensitive external reactions, such as invoking for protection from God out loud, while in the presences of such things. Belief in God's omnipotence and in predestination by God's decree are integral to Islam. However, this belief is not to be equated with fatalism and despair, which are not allowed in Islam.[153]

A long list could be generated of commonly-used tropes and conjurations in the West that violate this Islamic principle, and whose use end up being socialized into children in school. When Muslim children absorb these un-Islamic habits in the social environment of school and bring them home, it is distressing and alienating to Muslim families. It may be the case that these things are generally learned from media as well as non-Muslim peers, however, it should

---

[149] See also 42:11 https://quran.com/42/11
[150] Jami' at-Tirmidhī Book 47 Hadith 3690 https://sunnah.com/urn/680750
[151] Even when Allah is referred to by masculine pronouns in the Qur'an. This does not mean that He has gender like biological entities on earth have gender. The masculine pronouns, as well as the plural first person pronoun, are used because the syntactic forms of strength, dominance, generality, and authority use them. Arabic, like all Semitic languages, has no gender-neutral noun forms at all.
[152] Qur'an 9:51 https://quran.com/9/51, Qur'an 16:53 https://quran.com/16/53
[153] Qur'an 12:87 https://quran.com/12/87

not be neglected that it can often be teachers themselves who teach and prompt for these sorts of practices without knowledge of this underlying cultural clash that children are usually unable to protect themselves against. I personally have witnessed teachers tell Muslim children, ad hoc, to knock on wood, cross their fingers, or beseech "the basketball gods" for various reasons. Not to mention telling them that they can make wishes for snow to come by requesting it to cut-out drawings of snowmen that they made while rubbing them (this is a real example).

Teachers often express to me that learning about this is difficult because there are so many of these things that are taken for granted in Western culture and said out of second nature. This is true, so there are a few lessons to take away from it. One, as with all things regarding educator practice, the teacher ought to reflect on this point first and foremost. Again, the knowledge and understanding of how the Islamic perspective differs is the first action step in and of itself. If it prompts the teacher to think more explicitly about what they talk about and how they interact with kids, that is another positive action step. Beyond that, a teacher ought to make sure they do not inculcate upon Muslim kids a casual acceptance of these types of practices and concepts, and certainly not tell them to do it. As far as managing the interactions between kids. This is a more involved issue that will always relate to specifics of context, and is therefore difficult to draw a general rule or principle about. While overly managing kids interactions and banning kids from saying certain things is most likely an overreach, conversations that broaden perspectives in an age-appropriate manner can still be had. If kids have taken to doing some sort of practice that involves, or implies, metaphysical attributes to inanimate things, there is no reason why a reflective conversation that acknowledges there are differing points of view cannot take place, even with kids of young ages.

For example, many elementary school children enjoy creating a type of contraption out of folded paper with numbers and writing on it in certain sections that is typically called a *fortune teller*. The kids play a small game with it where one child opens and closes the fortune teller in their hand and another student chooses words and letters on it to reveal a written fortune underneath the folds at random choice. Of course, kids vary in the extent to which they actually believe this practice has the possibility of dictating or predicting their true fortunes, but sometimes there are kids who take to actually believing in it. There is no reason kids cannot be led in a conversation over whether or not the fortune-teller paper has the power to affect their future, and kids might be prompted and provided the space to express their own beliefs about it; and most importantly, the kids can be prompted to ask their parents what they think about it. These types of situations might be good entry points to introduce kids to the concept and terminology of metaphysics and then talk about how people can have very different beliefs about metaphysical cause. In a diverse classroom, students should be taught to not assume that their peers automatically have the same beliefs about metaphysical cause as their own. The teacher could mention that some people might believe in things like tricks, charms, and omens but there are others who believe it is *wrong* to believe in those. It is even okay and positive to express that there are children, families, and people in the world who believe such things are wrong because of their religious beliefs. If we cannot introduce students to religious ways of looking at the world in an objective manner, we cannot truly give them a liberal education (Nord, 2010).

So what do Muslims do instead of saying "good luck" to one another? Muslims do have substitutes for this and many other phrases that are used in everyday pleasantries.[154] If you hear Muslim students using this phrase and speaking about luck it is not because they have a belief that is variant to Islamic orthodoxy wherein the concept of luck is accepted. It is because they have been socialized into adopting the vernacular of the West as a way of meeting expectations of conformity. Many of them, perhaps even most of them at young ages, may be socialized into using such terminology before they even get the chance to learn, know, and understand that it violates their Islamic beliefs. In Islam, when a person wants to wish beneficence upon another for the future they will say "May Allah help you" or "May Allah make it easy for you". These are based on phrases that come directly from the Qur'an[155] and the Sunnah and that Muslims are taught to use. Sometimes a Muslim might tell another Muslim "I will make *duā*[156] for you", or they might ask another Muslim to make *duā'* for themselves.

Islam actually gives Muslims a whole host of phrases to use in everyday interactions that form the basis for the way Muslims exchange pleasantries. Some of these are directly commanded to

---

[154] There is an Arabic phrase "حـــظ طـــيبا" which some translate to mean "good luck". However, this is a limited translation that is problematic. It might be used at times situationally the same as English speakers use "good luck", and in that sense is a functional translation by context only. However, translating it as this ignores the meanings connoted in the word "luck" that is not carried by "حـظ". A better translation accurate to the meaning might be "May your share be good". Like how the Prophet ﷺ uses "حـــظ" in Sunan an-Nasa'i Book 22 Hadith 312 https://sunnah.com/nasai/22/312. Translators with a strong understanding of English do not use "luck" as a translation for "حـظ". See حـظو in the Arabic-English Lexicon of Edward William Lane. http://arabiclexicon.hawramani.com/حظو/#7a3b78

[155] Qur'an 12:18 https://quran.com/12/18

[156] *Duā'*, is a word that means "calling out" in Arabic, and it is the term used to define the type of praying that one does when they call out to God, either with their voice or perhaps just in their mind, and asks God for any type of blessings, forgiveness, and beneficence. *Duā'* in Islam can be done at anytime. However, this type of praying is different from the prescribed five daily prayers, which are much more exact as to how, when, and where they can be done and have their own term (*salāh*) to be called by. So the term "prayer" as an English word can be translated into more than one thing in Arabic and mean more than one thing in Islam.

be used in the Qur'an.[157] These phrases, of course, stay consistent with and promote remembrance of Islamic belief. Their counterparts in situational use of the anglosphere may or may not come into conflict with Islamic belief, as "good luck" does. An advanced level of engagement and connection with Muslim students would be creating opportunities and ways for them to learn how to interact with non-Muslims in these situations while using phrases that can be commonly accepted in secular fashion without violating Islamic belief. For example, instead of saying "good luck" I will say "I hope that goes well for you" or "I wish you all the best" to my non-Muslim friends and colleagues. This is a soft but important social skill that is quite complex for young people to navigate, and often might require a degree of linguistic competency that students may not have without explicit instruction. For students with immigrant parents who have a low level of English themselves it is not likely to be a skill their parents can teach.

Muslims are taught to not only avoid these types of attributions, but they are also taught to have a sensitive reaction when they are mentioned or used by others.[158] Children are not typically attuned to these violable attributions when they occur in the more subtle forms, but they can be very aware when they occur in an overtly explicit manner. This is the underlying reason for an issue that some teachers see where Muslim kids are worked up or reactionary when studying topics such as Greek mythology, Native-American origin stories, or Ancient Egyptian[159] customs, which make reference to concepts such as multiplicity of Gods, pantheons, or anthropomorphism.

---

[157] Such as the phrase "insha'Allah" which means "God willing", the Qur'an actually commands Muslims to not speak about anything happening in the future without saying this phrase. Qur'an 18:23-24 https://quran.com/18/23-24

[158] Commonly, this takes the form of saying the phrase "'aoudibilah" which means "I seek refuge with God" and oftentimes doing it in a tone that indicates emotional disgust. Usually this practice has been modeled by adults in the lives of Muslim children, and there is plenty of precedent for using it in the Qur'an and Sunnah. Qur'an 113:1 https://quran.com/113/1, Saḥīḥ al-Bukhārī Book 80 Hadith 68 https://sunnah.com/bukhari/80/68

[159] Ancient Egyptian civilization has frequently been a part of elementary school curriculums ever since the publishing of the Core Knowledge curriculum of E.D. Hirsch in the 1980s. It is extremely common that Egyptian American kids growing up in the American public school system are confronted with stereotypes being assigned to them by other kids based on conceptualizations of ancient Egypt as it exists in the school curriculum as well as American pop culture. For example, kids being asked if they "walk like an Egyptian" or if they will be mummified after they die or if they worship the Sphinx. The beliefs and practices of ancient Egypt are entirely antithetical to the teachings of Islam, the overwhelmingly predominant religion of Egypt today, and these stereotypes are extremely offensive to Egyptian people when made upon them. Instruction about Ancient Egypt must be balanced with instruction about the religious makeup of what Egypt is today.

So curriculum is connected to this matter as well. The benefits for teachers in having this religious knowledge is that the potential for these phenomena to occur with students can now be anticipated, which enables proactive as opposed to reactive measures. Before studying materials that might trigger sensitivities, preemptive talks at an age-appropriate level that frame the study's approach as one of a clinical examination of history should be had. Distinction needs to be made very clear to students between where the learning is of something that actually occurred in history vs. when it is of mythological stories that ancient civilizations had. It should be acknowledged beforehand that the mythological and religious beliefs and practices of some cultures might be something in opposition to the religious beliefs that some people have today, and for some people it is important for them to express those beliefs, and the opportunity to do that ought to be provided for in the classroom. Also, students should be talked to explicitly from young ages about the fact that part of education in America is that you study things with which you disagree. This is what teachers usually end up saying anyway after a sensitive reaction has already been incurred. It is much more preferable to anticipate when these sensitivities will arrive in the curriculum and have the discussion *beforehand*. This makes the whole experience less emotional for the student whose beliefs conflict with the topic of study.

It is also paramount for many Muslim students that considerations are made and provided for to help set the student up for success in articulating their own differences of belief in a mature way. If the student is a struggling learner or has emerging skills in English they might experience anxiety about talking to classmates in general. These anxieties are likely to be compounded if they are a minority student in the classroom in a heterogeneous environment. It might be the case that the best scenario is for the teacher to articulate to the class some of the ways in which the beliefs and practices of the historical area of study differ from worldwide religious beliefs and traditions of today. In an environment that is more homogeneously Muslim a comprehensive comparison between the beliefs and Islam can be drawn out if the teacher has the appropriate background knowledge. Leaving these issues unaddressed and unconfronted has a suffocating effect on students and misses an opportunity for them to be trained in articulate and professional manners of expressing differences. Muslim students can often be put in a bind where they inherently know they are learning something that is offensive to their religious beliefs, but they are lacking for the confidence, opportunity, set up, and perhaps language skills with which to articulate their grievances. Sometimes a lack of skill and understanding on the part of the student, and also a lack of effective teaching on the part of the teacher, can leave Muslim students in a situation where they are learning about the pantheon of ancient Greek gods (as an example) and the creation stories thereof and the students think it is being taught to them as something that *actually occurred* in ancient history, as opposed to being an ancient civilization's story of mythology. Distinctions such as these need to be crystal clear. When they are not, students undergo learning experiences that can be confusing due to the stark clash they experience with the historical and human origins stories that they are taught are the truth in the religious context of their home culture.[160]

Imitation of Other Religions

Something else that is prohibited in Islamic practice is the imitation of the religious practices and beliefs of others that are foreign to Islam.[161] This principle and rule effects practices in school in a few different areas. As it relates to this first pillar it is important to understand that while there is no issue with students learning about religious and mythological beliefs, practices, and stories in a clinical fashion, a larger issue arises when students are compelled to partake in activities that involve imitation or direct participation of these practices. This can show up in a variety of school settings in ways both large and small. Some examples of such situations that I have known to occur include having students act in plays where they have roles as different Greek Gods, creating a mock Shinto shrine as a craft project, reading and presenting horoscopes as bona fide and encouraging students to take heed of them, and participating in the singing and dancing of a native American pow wow. There are numerous other things that can be listed here. Students partaking in class celebrations around the common holidays in the West are a whole other matter that has its own discussion under the upcoming section on the fifth pillar.

It is important to consider with these issues that there are precautions to be taken beyond simply asking the student if they are "ok" with participating in such activities, especially for younger students. By reading this book it has now been made aware to you that this is a potential area of concern for Muslim students and families. Only asking if the student is "ok" with participating in the activity fails to take many factors into consideration. Firstly, the student might not understand the full nature of the activity they are participating in (this is likely). Secondly, the student might not have a full understanding of the extent to which these activities

---

[160] Islam teaches the Adamic origins of man. The story of Adam and Eve (*Hawā*) is told in the second chapter of the Qur'an (Quran 2:30-39 https://quran.com/2/30-39). There are differences in the story from what is generally understood about it in Christianity. Perhaps most importantly is that Islam rejects any concept of original sin (Quran 30:30 https://quran.com/30/30, Sahīh Muslim Book 46 Hadith 36 http://sunnah.com/muslim/46/36, Jami' at-Tirmidhī Book 32 Hadith 2287 https://sunnah.com/urn/674410). Islam also does not have a concept of earth being a "fallen world" or the "fall of man". Muslims could certainly be categorized as creationists, in believing that Allah created everything, and therefore are likely to be skeptical of some of the attribution of cause that takes place in Darwinian epistemology. But Young Earth Creationism that has long had a degree of viability amongst Christian literalists based on interpretations of the book of Genesis are rare to non-existent amongst Muslims because Islam gives no hard dictates to understanding the precise age of the earth (Chang, 2009).

[161] Bulūgh al-Marām Book 16 Hadith 1471 https://sunnah.com/urn/2054330

violate Islamic teachings (this is also likely, especially if they are young). Thirdly, the student is likely to err on the side of taking the action that will not stigmatize them socially, which means capitulation. Fourthly, even in a class that is majority Muslim students, they will be hesitant to push back on teacher directives or make the teacher feel uncomfortable. Clearly, the next level of engagement to consider is having a discussion with the parents. Even with this many factors need to be considered. All of the same issues concerned with broaching the student could also be present with the parent as well, especially if it is a parent of a lower education level.[162] If families struggle to communicate in English this obviously indicates that extra efforts need to be made in order to communicate about a complex matter.

It is a general recommendation of this book that families should be asked about whether or not religious accommodations and considerations are something they would like the school to have for their students at the beginning of the year. Schools ought to be proactive in making sure that families are aware and educated upon what their and their children's religious rights are in school. This is true for all families, but it is very likely a more urgent matter with Muslim families who come from backgrounds with less experience and integration in the United States. Hosting an educational seminar open to all student families that informs about their religious rights in the public school system can open the door for more detailed conversations. *The Guidance on Constitutionally Protected Prayer and Religious Expression in Public Elementary and Secondary Schools* issued by the federal Department of Education can be used to anchor the educational content of these seminars.

The Islamic term used to describe violations of Islam's first pillar is *shirk*. Every thing I have described here that Muslim children are not suppose to do are acts that are categorized in Islam and in a Muslim's life understanding as *shirk*. For some families the most direct conversation to have may be to ask if they are okay with their child participating in activities that the vast majority of Muslim authorities and people would consider *shirk*. If this could be communicated effectively, you would be very unlikely to have a Muslim parent say they are okay with it. Having a cultural liaison, either hired at the school or contracted with, or perhaps a community volunteer or mentor family, could help dearly with facilitating these conversations. The idea here is not for public school educators to be in the role of telling families what is and is not religiously impermissible in Islam. But the benefit of knowing this word *shirk* is that there may be situations when having a family genuinely understand the nature of some school activities

---

[162] Knowing the education level of parents is something that educators need to strive to have some awareness about. The second chapter of this book gives something of a general outlay as to where many Muslim families might fall in this regard as relates to their process of immigration here in America, but still it must be investigated upon the level of individual families. Cultural liaisons and family engagement specialists should be employed to help teachers and administrators understand.

(like the examples given above) relative to Islam may be difficult for families to understand the full context of, especially if their own understanding of the nature of the activity is in question. However, virtually all Muslim parents and families will know what the word *shirk* is because it is so commonly known and used in religious teachings and is the word that embodies the meaning of violation of this first pillar. *Shirk* holds the place in Islamic teaching of being the *gravest* sin a person can commit.[163]

The First Pillar - Prophets and Messengers

Below the completion of the first pillar in the hadith has been added and is discussed thereafter:

> **Islam has been built on five pillars...**
> - **To bear witness that there is none worthy of worship except Allāh and Muahammad is Allah's Messenger.**

Amongst all the central figures of the world's major religions, the most recent in history to have existed is The Prophet Muhammad ﷺ. The same can be said for the Qur'an amongst the holy books of the world's major religions. An exhaustive discourse on the Prophet Muhammad ﷺ and his life is well beyond the scope of this book, but some central points will be made and illustrated that are usually relevant to the wonderings of non-Muslim educators I meet, and that also connect to classrooms and a comprehensive understanding of students.

Historical vs. Mythological

Related to what has been mentioned before about the importance of distinguishing between the historical and mythological in some areas of study, it is important to understand that the Prophet Muhammad ﷺ is a historical figure and not a mythological one. His life is well-recorded in texts, his impact on the course of human history is a well-documented area of academic analysis, and his bones rest in the present day in a tomb in the city of Medina in Saudi Arabia. There is no academic dispute as to whether or not he existed, and likewise there is no dispute as to what the actual text of the Qur'an is; the book he brought to humanity.

The importance of understanding this for educators lies in navigating the nuance of using Muslim student's referential background knowledge about Islam as a basis of comparison to the beliefs and practices of other cultures. These comparisons would be both inaccurate and irreverent to sensitivities when it ventures on comparing that which is only known by ancient

---

[163] Qur'an 4:48 https://quran.com/4/48

myth to that which is known by historical documentation. So for example, saying to a Muslim student something like, "The Ancient Greeks believed in the story of Zeus just like Muslims believe in the story of Muhammad" might feel like a natural way of attempting to draw on student background knowledge, but it would do more harm than good. It could give the student the confused idea that Zeus was someone (or something) that actually existed in history; as opposed to being only a product of mythological tales.

Other Prophets and Religions

The Qur'an does not tell the complete story of the Prophet Muhammad ﷺ, in fact his name is only mentioned in it five times. Rather, a large portion of what the Qur'an contains is recounts of the stories of the same prophets who are mentioned in the Old Testament as well as Jesus عـليـه السـلام.[164] It is part of the intellectual foundations of belief in Islam that the story and life of the Prophet Muhammad ﷺ consisted of him being faced with a series of trials, wherein God would reveal to him knowledge and insight from the stories of the previous prophets, and that knowledge and insight would then be used as guidance for his affairs which ultimately gave him success in his proclaiming the message of monotheism. In this sense, Islam teaches that all of the Prophets were Muslims[165], and the Prophet Muhammad ﷺ is but the final, confirmatory, and superordinate link in the prophetic chain.[166] In addressing the Prophet Muhammad ﷺ the Qur'an says:

> **We[167] have revealed to you the same as We revealed to Noah and the Prophets after him, and that We revealed to Abraham, Ishmael, Isaac, Jacob and the offspring of Jacob, and Jesus and Job, and Jonah, and Aaron and Solomon, and We gave to David the Psalms. We revealed to those Messengers the same that We have revealed to you, and also to Messengers that We have not told you of; and to Moses Allah spoke directly. [33:21]**

---

[164] It is part of Islamic ettiequte to say "upon him be peace" when mentioning one of the Prophets that came before the Prophet Muhammad ﷺ and that is what is indicated here in Arabic.

[165] Qur'an 2:127-128 https://quran.com/2/127-128, Qur'an 42:13 https://quran.com/42/13

[166] Qur'an 33:40 https://quran.com/33/40, Sunan an-Nasā'i Book 4 Hadith 37 https://sunnah.com/nasai/4/37, Sahīh Muslim Book 5 Hadith 7 https://sunnah.com/muslim/5/7

167 There are parts of the Qur'an where God is self-referential by the plural first person pronoun. This is done only as a matter of linguistically illustrating strength, power, and authority, not dissimilar to what a royal proclamation might read like. It does not connote at all any idea of God encompassing plurality. Even when God is self-referential by the masculine pronoun, it does not connote that God has gender the same as biological entities have gender, since God is incomparable to all things in existence.

The underlined names are familiar to the English speaking world. Many non-Muslim teachers go unaware that their Muslim students frequently have these same names, only in their Arabic forms.

Christians and Jews are addressed directly in the Qur'an and referred to as "People of the Book", because they are a people who believe in revelation and have a book that they follow. In Islam's regulations Christians and Jews are not considered pure monotheists[168], yet a differentiated status is given to how Muslims relate to Christians and Jews vs. people of other religions and faith dispositions. For example, Muslims are allowed to eat meat[169] that is slaughtered and

Translations of Qur'anic Names		
English	Arabic [pronunciation]	Somali Variation
Adam	Adam	Aden/Adan
Idriss	Idrīs	
Heber	Hood/Hūd	
Noah	Nooh/Nūh	
Methusaleh	Salāh/Saleh	
Lot	Loot/Lūt	
Abraham	Ibrahīm	
Ishmael	Ismael/Ismail	
Isaac	Ishaq [ʔɪs.ha:q]	
Jacob	Yaqoob/Yaqūb	
Joseph	Yousuf/Yūsuf	
Jethro	Shuaib/Shuayb	
Job	Ayoob/Ayūb	
Moses	Mūsa	Mūse
Aaron	Haroon/Harūn	
David	Dawood/Daūd	
Solomon	Sulaiman/Suleiman/Sulayman	
Elias	Ilyas	
Elisha	Alyasa	
Jonah	Yunus/Younus	
Zacharias	Zakariya	Zakariye
John	Yahya	Yahye
Jesus	Issa	
Mary	Mariam/Maryam	Marian

---

[168] Qur'an 2:111 https://quran.com/2/111, Qur'an 3:67 https://quran.com/3/67
[169] Qur'an 5:5 https://quran.com/5/5

offered to them by Christians and Jews[170], but cannot do so for followers of overtly polytheistic religions, such as Hinduism, or someone who is an avowed atheist. Also, Muslim men are allowed to marry Christian and Jewish women[171], but likewise are not allowed to marry a woman who is a polytheist or an atheist.[172] Islam only allows for Muslim women to marry Muslim men.[173]

There are, of course, many points of similarity between the teachings of Islam and Christianity and Judaism. For Muslims, what is important for Christians and Jews to understand is that Islam essentially teaches kindness[174] and neighborliness[175] in treatment towards people from different religions, while maintaining key doctrinal differences. The Qur'an says:

> **Allah <u>does not forbid you</u> from kindness and respect to those**
> **who do not fight you for your faith or drive you out of your**
> **homes, so deal kindly and justly with them for Allah loves those**
> **who are just.**
> **[60:8]**

While the English translation of the underlined phrase in this verse gives off a sort of connotation of passivity, the Arabic phrasing carries the connotation of being earnest in doing so. This is reinforced within the verse where the kind and just treatment is identified as something Allah loves, and Islam dictates that kindness and leniency is maintained towards people of other faiths even when they are rude and unkind towards oneself.[176]

---

[170] There is an exception to this rule if the meat offered was slaughtered for the purpose of celebrating a non-Islamic holiday. There are also some stipulations as to how the animal is killed. Namely, that the name of God is supposed to be mentioned over the animal and that it has to have been slaughtered in a manner that allows for blood to have flown out of it; carrion, pork, domestic donkeys, and land animals with carnivorous teeth are also forbidden in Islamic dietary law. (Qur'an 2:173 https://quran.com/2/173, Sunan an-Nasā'i Book 42 Hadith 80 https://sunnah.com/nasai/42/80, Qur'an 5:96 https://quran.com/5/96). So a Muslim cannot eat meat that has been killed by strangulation, beating, drowning, electric shock etc. However, if a Muslim does not know how the meat they are offered was slaughtered it is permissible for them to eat it without investigation. Sahīh al-Bukhārī Book 72 Hadith 33 https://sunnah.com/bukhari/72/33

[171] Qur'an 5:5 https://quran.com/5/5

[172] Qur'an 24:3 https://quran.com/24/3

[173] Qur'an 2:221 https://quran.com/2/221, Qur'an 60:10 https://quran.com/60/10, Mūwatta Imam Malik Book 28 Hadith 1104 https://sunnah.com/urn/411360

[174] Sahīh al-Bukhārī Book 88 Hadith 9 https://sunnah.com/bukhari/88/9

[175] Jami' at-Tirmidhī Book 27 Hadith 49 https://sunnah.com/tirmidhi/27/49

[176] Sahīh al-Bukhārī Book 88 Hadith 9 https://sunnah.com/bukhari/88/9

Islam teaches that following it is a balanced path between extremes in all matters that it enjoins. The Qur'an tells Muslims:

Thus, We have made you a justly balanced community that you will be witnesses over the people and the Messenger will be a witness over you. [2:143]

Islam's approach and teachings towards interactions and relations with non-Muslims gives an example and illustration of Islamic balance. It would be extreme to cut off relations entirely with outsiders, yet it would also be an extreme to not have limitations with those who share values and beliefs that conflict with Islam in key areas; due to the potential of such relationships to allow the Muslim to absorb beliefs and habits that Islam forbids. Regarding relationships with non-Muslims, Islam enjoins Muslims to kindness[177] and neighborliness[178], but also makes clear where the boundaries of differences in doctrinal belief lie. The Qur'an addresses Christians saying:

O People of the Book, do not commit excess in your religion or say about Allah except the truth. The Messiah, Jesus, the son of Mary, was but a messenger of Allah and His word which He directed to Mary and a soul created on command by Him. So believe in Allah and His messengers. And do not say He is Three; desist from that and it is better for you. Indeed, Allah is but one God. Exalted is He above having a son. To Him belongs whatever is in the heavens and whatever is on the earth. And sufficient is Allah as Disposer of affairs.
[4:171]

The Qur'an makes clear distinctions here between theistic Christian and Islamic beliefs. Any belief that connotes multiplicity of Gods (the trinity) or anthropomorphism (divinity of Jesus, sonship) is a rejected doctrine that violates the beliefs of God's oneness and uniqueness in Islam. Nevertheless, Jesus عليه السلام is believed in as a Messenger of Allah[179] who called his people to worship one God alone. The virgin birth is also believed in, yet without any idea of

---

[177] Al-Ādab al-Mufrad Book 7 Hadith 2 https://sunnah.com/adab/7/2
[178] Jami' at-Tirmidhī Book 27 Hadith 50 https://sunnah.com/tirmidhi/27/50, Sahīh Muslim Book 45 Hadith 99 https://sunnah.com/muslim/45/99
[179] Qur'an 19:30 https://quran.com/19/30

Jesus السلام عليه being of God's corporal or carnal lineage[180]; Mary's conception in Islam is only a miracle willed by God.[181]

So it is not taken from an Islamic perspective that a whitewashing, avoidance of, or blotting out of religious differences needs to take place before kind treatment and neighborliness are enjoined. When articulating such differences the Qur'an instructs Muslims to do it with the best of manners:

> **Invite to the way of your Lord with wisdom and good**
> **instruction, and dispute with them in a way that is in the best**
> **manner.**
> **[16:125]**

Muadh ibn Jabal رضـــي الله عـنه, a companion of the Prophet ﷺ who was sent to live amongst Christians and Jews in Yemen, said the last advice the Prophet ﷺ gave to him before his passing was:

> *Make your character good for the people.[182]*

That Islam calls to a level of engagement with non-Muslims based on good manners and character, but also not without restrictions and limitations, can be a confusing area for Muslim children and parents to navigate. This can especially be the case when their own religious education is underdeveloped. Muslim families and communities in the West are trying to bring children up in a way that maintains a distinct identity as a Muslim, while the children are in a society that dictates they are constantly around people for whom a Muslim identity and Islam are something foreign, or for all intents and purposes unknown. This creates a degree of need within the Muslim community to sometimes emphasize key differences to children in private while also maintaining respect with people and learning from the matters of Western civilization that are beneficial and Islamically permissible. This is a lifelong course of navigation charted for the young Muslim in the West.

---

[180] Qur'an 19:35 https://quran.com/19/35

[181] Jesus عـليه السـلام is referred to in the Qur'an as "The son of Mary" and the 19th chapter of the Qur'an is titled "The Chapter of Mary". The name Mariam (or Maryam) is the Arabic name for Mary, a name many students have.

182 Muwāta' Imām Mālik Book 47 Hadith 1636 http://sunnah.com/urn/416970

So can a Muslim child be friends with a non-Muslim? I have been asked this by educators who have had students tell them they cannot be friends with non-Muslims, as well as from Muslim students themselves. I have also known some parents who taught their children not to be friends with non-Muslims, though on the whole this is rare. Some insight into Islamic sources can illuminate some of the issue's nuance. The Qur'an says:

> **Let not believers take disbelievers as <u>allies</u> rather than**
> **believers, and whoever does that will never be helped by Allah**
> **in any way, except if you indeed fear a danger from them.**
> **[3:28]**

The apparent meaning of this verse is that a Muslim cannot take a non-Muslim as a friend. The word that is translated as" allies" here is *auliyah* in Arabic and it can be translated as "friends" but a more correct translation is "allies" or "guardians".[183] A study of the background of verses like this show that they refer to specific instances relating to opposing parties in conflict.[184] For example, a companion of the Prophet ﷺ, his name was Hatib رضـي الله عنه, had a letter sent to their adversaries, the idolaters in the city Mecca, to inform them that the Muslims' return to the city was imminent. This was in the final years of the Prophet Muhammad's ﷺ life after the idolaters in Mecca had exiled him and his followers a decade earlier, after which they settled in the city of Medina. Since the idolaters had previously attacked the Muslims in Medina several times[185], and also prohibited their attempts to return to Mecca to perform religious rites[186], the Prophet's ﷺ companion worried a battle would break out[187] upon their return, Hatib wanted to forewarn the idolaters in order to secure protection for his family members who still lived in Mecca but were not a part of the ruling tribe there. It was in this type of context that verses like this were revealed.[188] Further study[189] of this verse and others that use this phrasing shows that contextually the verses refer to unbelievers (any non-Muslim) who are either a combatant or

---

[183] See ولى in the Arabic-English lexicon of Edward William Lane http://arabiclexicon.hawramani.com//ولـى #de2c27

[184] Many of the injunctions of the Qur'an generally were revealed to address specific situations but also have general applications. Sahīh Muslim Book 15 Hadith 93 https://sunnah.com/muslim/15/93, Sunan Abī Dawūd Book 25 Hadith 6 https://sunnah.com/abudawud/25/6

[185] Sahīh al-Bukhārī Book 9 Hadith 74 https://sunnah.com/bukhari/9/74

[186] Sahīh al-Bukhārī Book 26 Hadith 6 https://sunnah.com/bukhari/26/6

[187] This did not end up taking place, the Muslims returned to Mecca and the idolaters surrendered peacefully. This event is thus referred to as the Bloodless Conquest of Mecca.

[188] Qur'an 60:1 https://quran.com/60/1, Sahīh al-Bukhārī Book 65 Hadith 4890 https://sunnah.com/urn/45670

[189] The Qur'anic exegesis (*tafsīr*) of ibn Kathīr can be referred to in his explanations of verses 5:51 https://tinyurl.com/yarpoucx, 3:28 https://tinyurl.com/y9xlhev4, and 4:144 https://tinyurl.com/y9trb6nn.

oppressor to the Muslim that endangers them, or one that mocks Islam. Another verse from the Qur'an says:

> **O you who believe! Take not as protecting friends those who take your religion as a mockery and fun from among those who received the Scripture before you, nor from among the disbelievers; and fear Allah if you are indeed true believers.**
> **[5:57]**

So do these verses apply to a Muslim kid and a non-Muslim kid playing together on the playground at recess? In general, the argument to say it does not is solid. Yet, it is still important to understand that befriending non-Muslims creates pressures for the Muslim student and their family to navigate, and there will frequently be limitations as to what the family wishes for the child to absorb from their non-Muslim peers. This dynamic can create a constant source of anxiety for parents, and that anxiety is likely to be compounded the more foreign the parent is to Western culture.

To give a practical example, I once knew a student who was in an English as a Second Language (ESL) class in 5th grade where she befriended a classmate who was originally from Russia. One day while playing at recess, it began to rain and the Russian girl told her that when it rains it means that God is crying. The Muslim girl then went home, still while it was raining, and repeated what her Russian friend told her to her mother saying, "Mom the rain means that Allah is crying". This is a statement of *shirk*, ascribing the attributes of creation to Allah. Naturally, her mother became very upset and upset with the entire situation as a result. The mother admonished the girl for saying that statement with an emotional reaction and then asked her from whom she learned it. Upon finding out, the mother told her daughter not to be friends with the Russian girl anymore. This all resulted in an upset and shameful feeling on the part of the daughter, but without the benefit of further and clearer understanding as to the exact reasons why the situation was wrong from her mother's perspective as a Muslim.

This type of situation is not simple. The difficulty between the parent and child was compounded by linguistic barriers between each other; the mother's lack of skill in English, and the child's lack of skills in the home language. It was also an instance where the mother knew in essence that what her child had absorbed from the non-Muslim classmate was antithetical to Islamic teaching, but lacked the knowledge and competency herself to transmit a comprehensive religious understanding about their belief and the proper Islamic etiquette to her daughter; which would have enabled her to distinguish and communicate effectively with non-Muslim peers in the future.

Adding to the complexity of the situation is that the girl knew intuitively that what she was absorbing from her Russian classmate was something inconsistent with Islam, but she felt too timid to bring up that part of her identity to her peer in the public school context, even in the innocent and free setting of the playground. She had also mistakenly assumed that she was not even allowed to bring up religion as a topic of conversation in school, and feared she could get into trouble for doing so. This was an assumption that was conditioned into her by the overall lack of any talk in school settings that has anything to do with religion. While this lack of discussion about religion might be the default mode of social interaction in America, and exists as a means to avoid sensitive topics and the risks of offending people, it passively signals to young students that such talk and reference is wholly unwelcome. Thereby suffocating an integral part of their home culture experience from ever surfacing in the school setting to the point that they construct the idea that it is explicitly disallowed when this is not the case. Repeating the comment about God crying later to her mother was actually a way of probing for her mother's reaction so as to navigate for herself what she was supposed to think, feel, understand, and do about the situation.

So what could have been a valuable teaching opportunity for the parent was unable to be taken advantage of, and both the mother and child were left confused and anxious but in different ways. In middle and high school this family chose to send their daughter to homogenous charter schools where they felt assured that she would only be around Muslim peers.

Would it not have been better if this child could have had the opportunity at a younger age to learn and know the skills of kind and well-mannered communication about religious differences? Surely a reasonable argument can be made that there is a compelling secular purpose for children to undergo such learning, especially in cases where parents lack the skills and familiarity with Western culture. Also not to mention lacking in time with their child that would be needed to inculcate these skills on their own, as most parents have their own time monopolized by long work hours, while the children in turn have their time monopolized by school. Is there anyway this girl could have learned the skills and knowledge necessary beforehand in order to socially interact with her non-Muslim peer in a way that would have been respectful of not only her peer, but also the limitations of what her parents wished for her to absorb? How hard would it have been for her to have learned how to have an interaction (and that she had the right to have an interaction in a school setting) that looked more like this:

> **Russian girl:** When it rains it means that God is crying.
>
> **Muslim girl:** Well, in Islam, my religion, we do not believe that God cries, or that rain means God is crying.
>
> **Russian girl:** Oh, why?

> **Muslim girl**: Well, crying is something humans do, and we do not
> believe that God is like humans. So we don't say things like that.

I have consulted with educators who learn the Islamic teachings of good manners and wonder why it is then that they have Muslim students who can be rather misbehaved and uncouth in school. They wonder if this indicates a lack of regard or care for the religion on the part of those students. For myself, having taught in the inner-city to kids who come from economically deprived backgrounds and familial backgrounds with a high experience of trauma, I have had my share of students who were greatly challenged with behavior problems in school, as well as with their own personal and peer-related turmoil outside of school from falling prey to societal traps such as gangs and drug abuse. These are kids that many teachers often want to cast off. In the case of Muslim kids who fall into these ills, I do not find in my conversations with them that they have a rejection of Islam in their hearts at all. Family members of these youth reaffirm the same sentiment to me as well. It is grossly mistaken to see misbehaved kids as having a flippant inward attitude about Islam. On the contrary, Islam is often something they care deeply about, but they are struggling through a variety of developmental and psychological factors that result in destructive behavior patterns. Something that cannot be ignored is that an awakening of Islam in their hearts and minds and connecting it to healthy and productive societal and interpersonal behaviors is what likely holds the most immediate key to rectifying their personal conduct and paths in life. So how does it benefit anyone when explicit talk about it is suffocated in the public school that monopolizes their time and childhood?

There is a large extent to which a lack of both an understanding of Islam, and the feeling of Islam having an active presence as a live choice in life in Western society, are core identifiable factors in these young people's self-destructive behavior patterns. Many of them explicitly express to me that they wish they could learn more about Islam and have more time to know it, but they are hindered by other distractions, of which government mandates that they attend secular public schools are no small part. This is a matter to keep in mind as you read this book. It is clear from the Islamic sources that have been shown here that Islam is intended to act as a vehicle to inspire good conduct and manners. For many Muslim young people, growing up in a society and being constantly put into environments where Islam and religious identity is implicitly suppressed and unwelcome has the consequence of cutting them off from the primary source of inspiration for good conduct that their cultural background operates upon. When these misbehavior patterns do occur, there is no doubt that normal developmental factors are at play. Yet, with Muslim kids, the issue is deeper than something that can be simply passed off as "kids being kids".

How Islam relates to the Bible

Many Christian teachers I have trained who learn about Islam find it exciting to see that Islam is much more similar to Christianity than they had previously thought or assumed. This is a good realization and there is a secular purpose in schools to teach and recognize similarities across faiths and cultures. In the case of Islam and Muslim students, and in the interest of objective truth, there is also an importance to knowing and being ready to acknowledge key differences as well. If boundaries are crossed in emphasizing similarities, it can trigger sensitivities and also have the effect of relaying false information which is not in the interest of secular or liberal education.

The general rule in understanding how the Qur'an and Islam relate to understanding the Bible and how it is viewed is as follows: If there is something told in the Bible that is confirmed and correlates with what is taught in Islamic sources, then Muslims believe in it and believe it to be something authentically from God and His Prophets. If there is something in the Bible that is contradicted by what is taught in Islamic sources then Muslims believe that to be a fabrication[190], and not something that is authentically from the teaching of any prophet. If there is something in the Bible that is neither affirmed nor repudiated by Islamic sources then Muslims simply say "Allah knows best[191]" as to whether or not it was something true or divinely inspired.

This renders the Bible to be something for which a Muslim has no need in order to understand their own religion and God's truth. Study of the Bible or parts of it that might be done in World History classes is something that some Muslim students might express reticence about doing; and there is religious justification for this reticence.[192] The United States Supreme Court has recognized that objective study of the Bible and other religious texts is an essential part of a

---

[190] The Islamic teaching is that the scriptures of Christians and Jews were corrupted by insertions and alterations made by men in positions of religious authority in generations subsequent to the time of the Prophets from whom those scriptures are said to be. Qur'an 9:31 https://quran.com/9/31, Jami' at-Tirmidhī Book 47 Hadith 3378 https://sunnah.com/urn/641040.

[191] This is another phrase that is part of the lexicon of Islamic etiquette and that Muslims use commonly with one another. It is a way of saying "I don't know" that shows reverence and humility towards one's own station of limited knowledge. Use of this phrase is not limited to discussions on religion.
Sunan an-Nasā'i Book 21 Hadith 136 https://sunnah.com/nasai/21/136.

[192] Sahīh al-Bukhārī Book 96 Hadith 90 https://sunnah.com/bukhari/96/90

liberal education.[193] It is, of course, important to emphasize that it is being done for the sake of historical and primary source analysis, with a clinical tone of observation set. The injunctions in Islamic texts against reading the scriptures of the People of the Book refer to reading it for the sake of informing one's own religious practice.[194] Islamic scholars have and do read these texts in order to engage in polemics with them, especially when confronted with proselytization from Christians[195], which is a relatable context for students as Muslims living in the West are inevitably confronted with this at some point in their life. I have also co-taught in World History classes where Muslim students have actually found it quite interesting to analyze the Bible for the sake of seeing where divergences from Islam exist. I found this to be an interesting area of engagement for the students, but I had to set up the appropriate framework in order for them to buy into it. Some key divergences are as follows.

The Joseph of the New Testament is not a figure that is accepted by Islam. In the Qur'anic story of Mary عـليها السلام she is unmarried. The Muslim name Yūsuf, which means Jospeh, refers to the Jospeh عـليه السـلام of the Old Testament, who was one of the twelve sons of Jacob عـليه السلام and whose brothers trapped him down a well where he was picked up by caravaners and brought to Egypt where he helped avert an economic depression and famine. This prophet's story is told in the Qur'an, and the twelfth chapter of the Qur'an is entitled "The Chapter of Joseph". This is an exalted story in Islamic theology with lessons of patience, redemption, and reconciliation with former foes. Some of the curricular text sources referred to in chapter six draw on it to highlight these values and themes while addressing issues of bullying and forgiveness of others.

The Christian figure who is referred to as St. Paul and is the author of the better part of the New Testament and the person who originally brought Christianity to Europe is a figure that is rejected by Islam. This is why there it has no correlating Muslim name to Paul. Paul actually holds a place within Islamic polemics as a figure who corrupted the message of Jesus عـليه السـلام and the other Prophets and spread it to Europe. In the World History class I taught the

---

[193] *Abington School District v. Schempp*, 374 U.S. 203 (1963). In this case which ruled **compulsory** prayer reading of Biblical passages in public schools unconstitutional, Justice Tom C. Clark said in the majority opinion, *"it might well be said that one's education is not complete without a study of comparative religion or the history of religion and its relationship to the advancement of civilization. It certainly may be said that the Bible is worthy of study for its literary and historic qualities. Nothing we have said here indicates that such study of the Bible or of religion, when presented objectively as part of a secular program of education, may not be effected consistently with the First Amendment"*

[194] Sahīh al-Bukhārī Book 96 Hadith 90 https://sunnah.com/bukhari/96/9

[195] A relatively well-known historical example of this is the letter exchanges between the Islamic scholar Ibn Taymiyyah (d. 1328) of Syria and a Christian author from Cyprus who invited Muslims to Christianity during the Crusades (Ahmed & Rapoport, 2010).

Muslim students were vastly interested in studying Paul's epistle to the Romans as an exercise in studying primary sources. This is because the letter to the Romans gives an opportunity to see both where Christian doctrine diverges from Islamic teachings[196] as well as where it has strong correlations[197], and thereby helps to illuminate the specific sources and points in history where differences in these religions developed.[198]

The First Pillar - Conclusion

Islam's first pillar is its most important and is the very heart of the religion. Violations of it can happen in both major and minor ways.[199] While these violations do have differing degrees of severity in terms of the sin they incur in Islamic teaching, the avoidance of falling into any of them is taught to be utterly important, and it is commonly a goal of Muslim families to have children conditioned into personal habits that buffer against falling into these violations. The term used for the type of sin that constitutes a violation of the first pillar of Islam is *shirk*, this term is typically translated as "associating partners with Allah."[200] The Qur'an teaches that Allah is Merciful and ready to forgive sins to anyone who repents and that Allah will even forgive the sins of those who do not repent to whomsoever He chooses.[201] But the Qur'an also warns that *shirk* is the one sin that man can be guaranteed Allah will not forgive if one dies unrepentant and having committed it, so avoidance of it is of the most serious matters to a Muslim.[202]

What all constitutes *shirk* and major and minor violations of it is typically something very difficult for Muslims to communicate and explain to non-Muslims. The modern day ethos of polite society in the Western world relegates talk about religion as being abnormal, controversial, and awkward. Thus Muslims sense that considerations of these concerns about respecting Islam's first pillar are not prevalent or intuitive to the intellectual schema of most

---

[196] Particularly his formulation of understanding the gentiles as being exempt from the Law of Moses and his doctrine of expiation through belief in Christ's blood. Qur'an 5:110 https://quran.com/5/110, Qur'an 2:136 https://quran.com/2/136, Qur'an 2:48 https://quran.com/2/48.

[197] Such as teachings about hypocrisy of not practicing what one preaches, when Paul says "You who preach that one shall not steal, do you steal?" in Romans 2:21 it correlates nicely with Qur'an 61:2-3 https://quran.com/61/2-3.

[198] abrahameducation.com has some of the resources I used for this study.

[199] Islamic jurisprudence has a technical categorization of sins as being either major or minor depending on the sin's quality and degree of severity. Qur'an 53:32 https://quran.com/53/32, Jami' at-Tirmidhī Book 47 Hadith 3595 https://sunnah.com/urn/643210

[200] The root linguistic meaning of the word *shirk* is "sharing", because when one commits it they "share" the attributes of God with something other than Him. See شرك in the Arabic-English Lexicon of Edward William Lane. http://arabiclexicon.hawramani.com/شرك/#633995

[201] Qur'an 39:53 https://quran.com/39/53, Qur'an 48:14 https://quran.com/48/14

[202] Qur'an 4:116 https://quran.com/4/116

non-Muslims. Accordingly, they stay quiet about it as a matter of capitulation while it privately causes anxiety and concern. This is especially the case in overtly secularized contexts such as public schools where expression of religious beliefs are implicitly shunned if the right environment of respect and awareness has not been nurtured.

There is maybe nothing that illustrates the difference in consciousness between Muslims and non-Muslims more than the place that the Prophet Muhammad ﷺ holds. To most non-Muslims little is known about him and he likely holds no larger place in their mind than being some general figure of the past from a different culture who many people are named after. While to Muslims he is the central figure of all human history. He lived and died in the past but his life lives on in the habits and beliefs that Muslims carry with them, which form their daily and lifelong relationship with God and one another. The Prophet's ﷺ behavior forms the basis for a Muslim's inspiration and guidance to observe good manners and conduct. His manners are also recorded to a degree of minute detail, which form the basis for many habits that Muslims exhibit and aspire to practice. Knowing these is essential to understanding how Islam instructs and influences what a Muslim does, considers, and is pressured to do in even the most typical and seemingly mundane aspects of everyday life. While belief in One God is the central belief of Islam, the outward practice of that belief emanates from understanding the pillars that follow.

The Second Pillar - Salāh (obligatory prayer)

Below the second pillar has been added to the hadith of the five pillars and is discussed thereafter:

> **Islam has been built on five pillars...**
> - **To bear witness that there is none worthy of worship except Allāh and Muahammad is Allah's Messenger,**
> - **Establishing the Salāh (obligatory prayer)**

The word *salāh* refers to the five daily prayers that Muslims are obligated to do. That Muslims pray five times a day is a piece of general knowledge about Islam that is known well enough by people in the West. What is lesser known is what these prayers actually encompass, their prominence in the religion, and the psychological place their performance holds within the schema of a Muslim's understanding of their own life.

There are two words in Arabic that can refer to actions that would be commonly connoted in the Western world with actions that are called prayers. One is the word *duā'*, which literally means "calling out", and is the term used to define the type of praying that one does when they call out to God, either with their voice or perhaps just in their mind, and ask God for any type of blessings, forgiveness, and beneficence. *Duā'* in Islam can be done at anytime and in any place. While there is specific phrasing and times with which the Prophet Muhammad ﷺ was known to do his *duā'*, there are not prescribed obligations pertaining to it being done, it is generally a supererogatory act. *Salāh*, on the other hand, refers to the five daily prayers that are full of specific rules in order to meet its obligation.

The next chapter will discuss the importance and the practical steps of how to provide accommodations for students and families to perform *salāh* in school settings in a manner that is competent and provides for maximizing academic priorities. What I wish to discuss in this chapter is an understanding of the psychological place that performance of the prayer holds for Muslims, and the implications that are had by being unable to perform it. To do this we will look at some more *ahadith* and verses from the Qur'an.

The first chapter of the Qur'an is seven verses that form a prayer that encompasses in terse terms the Muslim's relation to Allah in contemplation and prayer. After that, the chapters of the Qur'an are roughly organized from its longest chapters to its shorter ones.[203] While the first chapter is often described as summarizing the essence of the Qur'an, the second chapter is often described as summarizing the entirety of Islam's teachings and practices. These two chapters are generally considered the most important ones for a Muslim to know. While the first chapter is recited in each *salāh* multiple times, the second chapter emphasizes the importance of performing the obligatory prayers right away in its opening verses when it says:

> **This is The Book about which there is no doubt, a guidance for those who are reverent to God, Who believe in the unseen, establish *salāh*, and spend out of what We have provided for them**
> **[2:2-3]**

Salāh is mentioned over 100 times in the Qur'an, always with a positive connotation and the majority of its mentioning being direct commandments to establish it. The Prophet Muhammad ﷺ said about the *salāh*:

---

[203] Not exactly but generally it goes from longer chapters to shorter ones.

> **Indeed the first deed by which a servant[204] will be called to account on the Day of Resurrection is his _salāh_. If it is complete, he is <u>successful and saved</u>, but if it is defective, he has <u>failed and lost.</u>[205]**

The Day of Resurrection here refers to a tenet of Islamic belief that there will come a day when all souls are raised from the graves and called to account before God for the deeds they did and the beliefs they had in their ephemeral life on earth.[206]

It is the ultimate goal of a Muslim to succeed on this Day and avoid failure. When the hadith mentions being successful, it means being granted into the place of bliss in the afterlife. In Christian theology this place is typically referred to as *heaven*. In Islam the term that is translated to mean heaven or heavens does not refer to this, it refers to the sky and the celestial skies and worlds that one sees in the nighttime, and whose grandeur the human being reflects upon.[207] The place of bliss that one strives to be admitted to in the Hereafter is more correctly called *paradise* in Islam. The place of punishment that one wishes to avert in the afterlife is properly termed *hell* or *hellfire*, as it is in Christianity.

Islam is like the other monotheistic religions in that it teaches that one cannot reject its belief and still be granted into paradise[208], and that sincerely having its belief will ultimately place one there.[209] However, Islam does not make hellfire exclusive to those without Islamic belief. It is part of Qur'anic teaching that Muslims can be granted into hell for a period of time sufficient as to expiate for whatever unrepentant sins the Muslim committed, and for which Allah did not choose to forgive them.[210] There are certain actions that are of course sins, but also the inaction of failing to adhere to the obligatory acts in Islam are also major sins; and no act is more severe to neglect than observance of these obligatory prayers.

This illustrates the psychological weight that performing these prayers has on a Muslim. It might be fair to say that most Muslims in America struggle to perform these prayers with their

204 Meaning a Muslim
205 Jami`at-Tirmidhī Book 2 Hadith 266 https://sunnah.com/tirmidhi/2/266
206 Qur'an 4:87 https://quran.com/4/87
207 Qur'an 45:13 https://quran.com/45/13, See سمو in Lane's Arabic-English Lexicon arabiclexicon.hawramani.com/سمو/#22b4ca
208 Qur'an 3:19 https://quran.com/3/19, and Qur'an 3:85 https://quran.com/3/85
209 Sahīh Muslim Book 1 Hadith 47 http://sunnah.com/muslim/1/47
210 Qur'an 6:128 https://quran.com/6/128, Qur'an 11:107 https://quran.com/11/107, Sahīh Muslim Book 1 Hadith 364 https://sunnah.com/muslim/1/364

prescribed consistency. The unawareness and lack of knowledge of non-Muslims who create and manage the environments that Muslims frequent is a key factor in this struggle. The other key factor is the Muslims' own hesitancy to communicate with the non-Muslims around them about their religious accommodation needs due to the silent capitulation that arises from anxieties over being stigmatized, lack of linguistic competency in some cases, and the codes of conduct in polite society that render religion an uncomfortable topic of conversation.

There are some key things to understand about the Islamic prayer:

- In the Muslim world everything is structured around performance of the prayer.
- Performance of the prayer is deemed to be the backbone of keeping a person upright and well-mannered in Islam.
- Failure to perform the prayer can result in psychological stress, guilt, and feelings of self-loathing, whether religiously justified or not.

The third of these points was discussed above, regarding the hadith that dictates the prayer is the most important outward deed for a Muslim to have performed when they are brought before God to be judged in the afterlife. So I will elaborate a little more on the first two points.

Lack of Structure is a Pitfall

Societies in the Muslim world structure themselves in such a way that enabling the people to perform the prayers with ease takes the first priority in how all interpersonal interactions and civil organization are arranged. When businesses open and close, when meetings are held, the scheduling of a school day, the design of buildings, neighborhoods, and even large cities are all done with accommodations of the prayers in mind.

So Muslim adolescents in the West, especially those who are the children of immigrants, find themselves in a position where they have great pressure from the religion, their families, the Muslim community, and within themselves to perform the prayers. Yet, in order to have accommodations for it when they are in school, they typically have to advocate for it all on their own. Meanwhile, they are likely being raised by people who grew up in the Muslim world themselves where all the structure of accommodation is already met by the society. So the parents usually have no experience doing the type of self-advocacy that their adolescent children would need to undertake in order to successfully and respectfully perform their religious duties in the public school environment. Nor have the parents gone through the emotional and psychological experience of having to undergo this self-advocacy, and therefore they may struggle to do the type of metacognitive coaching that a young person would need to meet these challenges.

The main point here for educators is to emphasize that without proper and well-structured accommodations within a school, Muslim students will find it difficult and burdensome to pray. The result will often be that they will neglect to do it entirely. Even if they do advocate their right to pray and are granted it, the flip side is that the school staff's lack of knowledge of the prayer's specifics leads to a lack of structure in the accommodations offered, which in turn gives the students too much freedom and their adolescent lack of impulse control sets them up to fail. Often students will end up misusing the time allotted to them as a way to avoid class, which leads to negative confrontations with teachers and administration over their irresponsibility. This inevitably results in consternation between the two parties, and likely families as well. Scenarios that result in Muslim students not performing their prayers have a good chance of putting their emotional states into a downward spiral, which can in turn develop into having a degraded self concept and possibly manifest in destructive behaviors and depression. Therefore putting in good accommodations, which involves consideration for the time, place, and duration of the prayer *and its preparation*, is paramount for educators of Muslim students to be ready to implement. This cannot happen without the educators having knowledge of the details of how the prayer works and is actually done. All this will be addressed in chapter four.

Maintenance of Discipline, Character, and Well Being

Central to an Islamic understanding of the prayer is that it keeps one away from bad deeds, poor character, and emotional distress. The Qur'an says:

> **Recite, what has been revealed to you of the Book and establish prayer. Indeed, <u>prayer prevents immorality and wrongdoing</u>, and the remembrance of Allah is greater. And Allah knows that which you do.**
> **[29:45]**

The first purpose of the prayer is that it is the most important external act of worship that a Muslim does in order to be rewarded in the Hereafter. But its most immediate ancillary effect is that it inhibits the one who performs it from doing bad deeds. The prayer is understood to be the quintessential act of worshipping God where one stands, bows, and prostrates before Him. The position of standing is called *qiyam* in Arabic, the aforementioned Day of Resurrection is also referred to in the Qur'an as the Day of *Qiyam*, or the Day of Standing, because it is a day where everyone will stand before God. The standing in the prayer is set to be a reminder to the Muslim of when they will stand before God and be judged. The prostration that is done is the worshipper's act of demonstration to God that they submit to Him. Submitting means following His commandments, staying away from His prohibitions, and following the example of the Prophet ﷺ. Partaking in these potent reminders in a tranquil state of reflection has the real world effect of inculcating a healthy confidence in the performance of virtue for the sake of virtue, as well as a healthy apprehensiveness of partaking in bad deeds.

Breaks in the school day that connect students to meditation[211] and spirituality are known to increase student calmness, resilience, and self regulation (Erricker et al, 2001; Fontana & Slack, 2007; Dobmeier, 2011). The chance to emotionally and psychologically reset during the day has measurable benefits for young people in school, and it is recognized that this need is heightened with students who have experienced trauma (Neiman, 2015; Brunzell et al, 2016). Given all this, it is more than reasonable for educators to ascertain that there are compelling secular purposes for effectively accommodating the prayers for students (and families). This being a reason why school staff should be motivated to accommodate prayers properly when it is desired by students and families, in addition to the constitutional obligations that schools have to provide rights of voluntary religious practice, of which observance of prayers in school is well established as bona fide.[212]

The Second Pillar - Conclusion

What needs to be emphasized is that due to insecurities and the worry of feeling stigmatized Muslims often give in to passive capitulation when they are in environments that are controlled by non-Muslims. Thus, there ends up being a correlative relationship between the likelihood that a Muslim will voluntarily assert their right to pray in a given a context and the degree to which praying is accommodated and expected by others within that context. This is especially true for younger people with fragile egos and self concepts that make them insecure about

---

[211] One trend that has emerged in education from the recognition of the need for students to have relaxing breaks in the day to reset has been having kids do yoga in class (Neiman, 2015). Yoga is originally an orthodox Hindu tradition. Many Islamic scholars have ruled that Muslims are forbidden from partaking in it, even when doing so without any so-called "religious connection" because it still amounts to imitating the religious practices of others, which is also forbidden in Islam as previously discussed. There is no disagreement about the benefits of kids taking mental breaks to breathe, stretch, reset, and reflect. But we need to ask, if public school teachers are ready and willing *to lead* kids in doing Hindu practices for this, why should there be any inhibition about schools making proper preparations for Muslim kids to do their Islamic prayers in school on their own? Generally, if you do yoga with your students in your classroom and you have Muslim students, I believe it is best to at least be conscious of the terminology you use around those breaks and be sure it is something secular. Perhaps alter the poses and stretches to be something more religiously neutral, and certainly do not apply the Hindu religious terminology associated with them, nor have the kids say any Hindu religious phrases such as "namaste" or extended pulsations of "Om". Also, give those Muslim kids the chance to do their own prayers following the guidance offered in chapter four, which offer all the same benefits of these breaks in the school day.

[212] *Santa Fe Independent School District v. Doe, 530 U.S. 290, 302 (2000)*. Justice Paul Stevens in the majority opinion: *Indeed, the common purpose of the Religion Clauses "is to secure religious liberty.' Engel v. Vitale, 370 U.S. 421, 430 (1962). "Thus, nothing in the Constitution as interpreted by this Court prohibits any public school student from voluntarily praying at any time before, during, or after the schoolday."*

doing genuine self-advocacy. When the educators governing the school environment are uninformed and too uneasy within themselves to bring up the topic of religious accommodations directly with families, and to take proactive steps in providing accommodations, students and families default into sacrificing their religious rights and needs for the sake of maintaining the perceived expectations of politeness and normalcy in a secularized context. They are simply too timid about the idea of being perceived as a burden to others. These matters are frequently compounded when families have additional anxiety due to a lack of language skills or awareness of what their religious rights are in the public schools.

Similar to what was discussed regarding music class, asking parents directly if they would like religious accommodations for their students, specifically around accommodations for the prayer that are discussed in chapter four, is a very good starting point that signals respect and understanding to families. This could be done in the form of holding an informational seminar on religious rights of students and families in the public schools where the federal *Guidance on Constitutionally Protected Prayer and Religious Expression in Public Elementary and Secondary Schools* is reviewed for families. If the school has any reason to think that this may be a latent want within their school community there is nothing problematic at all with surveying for such information. Not doing so runs the risk of maintaining an always-present degree of dissonance between the school community's Muslim families and the teachers and administration, as well as passively contributing to suffocating the religious identity of young people and families at the cost of their partaking in a key practice that nurtures emotional well-being, calm temperament, and well-mannered conduct. All of which the school itself has a compelling secular interest in nurturing due to the association these attributes have with academic success.

The Third Pillar - Zakāt (obligatory charity)

Below the third pillar has been added and is discussed thereafter:

> ***Islam has been built on five pillars...***
> - ***To bear witness that there is none worthy of worship except Allāh and Muahammad is Allah's Messenger,***
> - ***Establishing the Salāh (obligatory prayer)***
> - ***Paying the Zakāt***

Zakāt is an obligatory charity with the technical definition of giving 2.5 % of one's excess wealth within a given year to the needy.[213] Excess wealth is generally defined as the amount of wealth

---

[213] Sahīh al-Bukhārī Book 24 Hadith 58 http://sunnah.com/bukhari/24/58, Sunan Abi Dawūd Book 9 Hadith 17 https://sunnah.com/abudawud/9/17

and property that one owns after fulfilling the needs of themselves and their family. Therefore *zakāt* is not obliged upon one who does not have excess personal wealth. So it will not apply to most students and is not something schools need to worry about accommodating for, but the opportunity will be used here to explain further the concept of charity in Islam and point to potential areas of utilization for engagement that builds upon students' prior understandings.

The word *zakāt* means purification and Islam holds strongly the concept that giving charity is a means to purify oneself from sins and have them forgiven.[214] Consider the following verse from the Qur'an:

> ### Certainly, successful are the believers who are humbly submissive in their prayers, and who turn away from <u>ill speech</u>, and who establish charity (zakāt)
> ### [23:1-4]

Purification from Ill Speech

Firstly, I share this verse pertaining to *zakāt* to also illustrate the value Islam places on humility and staying away from using bad language. The Prophet 鑪 said:

> ### *...whoever believes in Allah and the Last Day, should speak what is good or keep silent.*[215]

It is the case that some Muslim students come from cultures that are oral, highly social, and frequently from familial backgrounds where verbal banter between one another is not taken as something harsh, unsettling, or uncouth when they socialize. However, there is no social or cultural acceptance in these contexts of accepting outright rudeness[216], use of curse words or foul language[217], nor of challenging elder people[218] or people in authority.[219] I mention this because I have consulted with teachers and schools who had undergone training from various platforms in culturally relevant pedagogy, and sometimes these teachers had been instructed to dismiss and accept student abrasiveness, rudeness, and use of foul language as something that

---

[214]Qur'an 2:271 https://quran.com/2/271, Jami` at-Tirmidhī   Book 6 Hadith 71 https://sunnah.com/tirmidhi/6/71

215 Sahīh al-Bukhārī Book 78 Hadith 163 https://sunnah.com/bukhari/78/163

[216] Jami' at-Tirmidhī Book 27 Hadith 115 https://sunnah.com/tirmidhi/27/115

[217] Al-Adab al-Mufrad Book 56 Hadith 10 https://sunnah.com/adab/56/10

[218] Jami' at-Tirmidhī Book 27 Hadith 27 https://sunnah.com/tirmidhi/27/27

[219] Qur'an 4:59 https://quran.com/4/59, Sahīh Muslim Book 33 Hadith 52   http://sunnah.com/muslim/33/52

the students were merely culturally inclined to do. Therefore the behavior was not deemed worthy of reprimand or correction. I share this verse from the Qur'an to emphasize that this is not the case with Muslim students, all parents I talk to consider it to be insulting that someone would assign such behavior to the students' home culture. This does not mean there are not effective vs. ineffective ways to deal with redirecting such behavior, but dismissal and excusal are not the proper routes of action. Worse yet, such attitudes and approaches towards student misbehavior are likely to only enable the student to adopt poor character as acceptable. A discussion on recommendations and considerations for managing confrontational and disrespectful students is addressed in chapter five.

Supererogatory Charity, Small Deeds, and Food Sharing

Another term worth knowing pertaining to charity is the word *sadaqa. Sadaqa* in its root meaning means "truthful."[220] While *zakāt* refers to the obligatory mathematized charity, *sadaqa* is the term used for supererogatory charity in Islam that one is not obliged to give but is highly encouraged to do so. Sometimes students are more familiar with the term *sadaqa* than they are *zakāt.* When a mosque has a box by the doorway that is soliciting for donations to help support it or some charitable cause, the word *sadaqa* is put on it. It is not uncommon for fundraisers to be held in mosques after sermons or prayers are performed where someone stands in front of the congregation to solicit for donations to aid the mosque or some charitable cause. When this is done typically the term *sadaqa* is used by the speaker for what is being requested. So especially with students who speak English as a second language, when the topic of charitable giving comes up, the word *sadaqa* might be useful for the teacher to know.

The concept of charity in Islam extends well beyond monetary giving to include simple endeavors of everyday life that can be undertaken by anyone regardless of whether they are rich or poor. This is shown in the following hadith of the Prophet ﷺ:

> **Your smiling in the face of your brother is charity, commanding good and forbidding evil is charity, your giving directions to a man lost in the land is charity for you. Your seeing for a man with bad sight is a charity for you, your removal of a rock, a thorn or a bone from the road is charity for you. Your pouring what remains from your bucket into the bucket of your brother is charity for you.**[221]

---

[220] See صدق in the Arabic-English Lexicon of Edward William Lane
http://arabiclexicon.hawramani.com/صدق/#ac8e27

221 Jami` at-Tirmidhī 1956 https://sunnah.com/tirmidhi/27/6

The Prophet also ﷺ extolled planting trees and plants, and sowing seeds in a field as a means of charity:

> *If a Muslim plants a tree, or sows a field and men and beasts and birds eat from it, all of it is charity from him.[222]*

Shared in the proper way this hadith has the potential to stimulate motivation in Muslim students for partaking in varying projects related to environmental science.

These *ahadith* also illustrate a certain preeminence that Islam puts on small deeds that are done regularly. The Prophet ﷺ told his companions:

> *Take on only as much as you can do of good deeds, for the best of deeds is that which is done consistently, even if it is little.[223]*

Within this hadith there is a consonance with advice that is commonly given in the secular world for attaining success in life and achieving long term goals. Namely that long-term goals and success are best achieved through a build up of smaller actions and goals that accumulate on a daily basis over the course of a long period. There are many students in school who are full of intelligence but lacking success due to a lack of productive day-to-day habits and doing them consistently. Instilling a message of the importance of day-to-day consistently is a positive message to give students and correlates to the religious teachings of Islam.

The sharing of food is a highly lauded act in Islam and Muslim cultures, and is also considered a form of charity. Consider the following hadith of the Prophet ﷺ:

> *The food of one person is enough for two, the food of two is enough for four, and the food of four is enough for eight.[224]*

This hadith is more or less taken to mean that it is a matter of fraternal right for Muslims to share food with others when one has it and the other is without it. Thus, in Muslim cultures the implicit expectation is that being selfish and overly possessive with one's food is greatly frowned upon, and that others have a right upon it if they do not have any. So it is unseemly, if not beyond thought, that the one with food would not offer to share with those around him or

---

[222] Riyāḍ us-Ṣāliḥīn Book 1 Hadith 135 http://sunnah.com/riyadussaliheen/1/135
[223] Sunan ibn Mājah Book 37 Hadith 4381 https://sunnah.com/urn/1293430
[224] Ṣaḥīḥ Muslim Book 35 Hadith 245 https://sunnah.com/muslim/36/245

her. This can have a way of showing up in school where some teachers have seen Muslim kids to be abundantly eager to share food with their peers, especially ones who are fellow Muslims that they may know personally. The implicit expectations with these kids in these situations that they have garnered from seeing family and community members share food in a variety of social settings in their lives needs to be understood here.

If Hassan walks into the room with a bag of Cheetos and Hamza sees him with it, the line of thinking in Hamza's mind is not exactly, "well those are Hassan's Cheetos, I sure hope he will choose to give some to me if I ask." The line of thinking is more, "Hassan brought Cheetos, sweet! I can't wait to get mine" and it is just implicitly expected that Hassan will give him some, as if Hamza's right to the Cheetos are equal to Hassan's. There is not a strong concept of Hassan having individualized ownership of it and playing the role of arbitrator over its distribution. When this sharing is disrupted by teacher insistence, or in some cases even school policy that prohibits food sharing, it feels very unnatural and disturbing to these students. When schools do have a policy that prohibits food sharing, or mandate the use of sharing tables in the cafeteria while direct interpersonal sharing is prohibited, an important step in getting students to code switch into accepting these norms is explaining in a developmentally appropriate way the culture of liability concern that dictates so much about behavioral norms in the United States these days. This is further discussed in chapter five.

Prohibition of Ribā (Interest)

Another note on financial matters and Muslims, Islam explicitly forbids what is called *ribā*[225]; which means partaking in the use of interest as either a loaner or lender, or entering a contract that stipulates the use of interest.[226] The most apparent concern that this has is with taking out student loans. It is the case that many Muslims in America have capitulated on this concern for the sake of advancing professionally. There have been some Muslim organizations that have crafted limited justifications[227], under certain conditions, for taking out student loans under the guise that it is something Muslims are essentially compelled to do in the West.[228] However, these justifications are more commonly taken to be weak within Muslim polemic circles, and still there are many Muslims taking out student loans with the guilt of sinning riding underneath the surface.

---

[225] Qur'an 2:275 https://quran.com/2/275

[226] Jami' at-Tirmidhī Book 14 Hadith 3 https://sunnah.com/tirmidhi/14/3

[227] As an example see the Assembly of Muslim Jurists of America (AMJA) and a fatwa they issued in 2010. Refer to fatwa no, 81740 "Can We Take Student Loan for Study, If You Can't Afford It?" on their website. https://www.amjaonline.org/fatwa/en/81740/can-we-take-student-loan-for-study-if-you-cant-afford-it

[228] Islam does not place sin or fault on an individual for any action that they are compelled to do by force, which is generally meant to mean by physical threat.

I advise guidance counselors and AVID instructors and others involved with advising students through college admission decisions to simply pull back a little bit on the general push that takes place to get students to fill out the FAFSA. As with other matters, ask directly if they or their families have concerns over taking out interest-bearing loans. In my experience almost all Muslim students over the age of fifteen are well aware of the term *riba* and that taking out interest-bearing loans is forbidden in Islam. They have reservations about being pushed to do it, even if they end up doing so. High schools should be guiding all students these days towards real-world assessments over the true value of a college degree when measured against the modern day job market and standard amounts of debt that the average college student will incur; as well as the average amounts of debt that are taken on in specific fields of study and degrees. There are some schools and counselors who have been repeating the same mantra about the necessity to have a college degree in order to have a higher income in society for generations. While this still may be generally true there are several factors for students to consider with this, and it is not always ethical to simply run students through the college loan application conveyor belt.

One simple alternative to this is helping students map out what a savings plan would look like after high school in order to work and save to go to college either at a later time, or to attend college at a slower pace over the course of a longer period of time, as opposed to the standard four-year full-time continuum that students are typically told to follow. It is one of the benefits of the American post-secondary education system that one can enter it at any time. Real world matters pertaining to budgeting should be discussed. I have found that students, especially low-income students, love learning about the income tax brackets in the United States and figuring out what an hourly rate wage of a standard retail or fast food job actually earns per hour after taxes. Learning about federal and state income tax rates, FICA tax withholdings, and income brackets is illuminating and empowering knowledge because it is the beginning piece of actually being able to put together a personal budget. Once a personal budget can be put together a savings plan can be enacted.

One advantage in saving money that many Muslim students have is that culturally they are not stigmatized against living with their parents in early adulthood. This helps drastically with budgeting as a young adult, as rent or housing costs often do not need to be factored in (unless they contribute to paying their family's rent). Hence, opening up this discussion and type of planning can be a chance to honor the benefits of familial closeness into adulthood, upon which Muslim cultures place a high value.

Another piece to take away from Islam's prohibition on interest is that when students learn about how interest operates in math class teachers should avoid saying, "when you get a credit card when you're older you'll have to know about this…" It is in no way a given that a Muslim will get a credit card when they are older and most Muslims avoid using them. Credit card companies are often derided in Muslim circles as predatory and an evil to be avoided. Similar narratives exist about interest and lending in the current-day global financial system as well, but that is an extended topic I will not get into here. This is not to say that students should not learn about interest at all, they should, but attaching relevance to the learning ought to be done in a different way. Sometimes learning in school has to be about understanding how some societal practices and norms can be viewed as manipulative, and examining the ills of predatory lending is a way that can be done in math class. In upper grades, framing the learning about interest rates in this way can help protect students from becoming victimized by predatory lending in early adulthood when they are likely to be targeted for it (Todd, 2002; Norvilitis et al, 2003; Robb & Sharpe, 2009).

The Third Pillar - Conclusion

The obligatory charity in Islam has a precise financial definition. Executing this pillar is generally not of concern for school-aged children. However, understanding it and the broader concept of charity in Islam can illuminate areas where latent background knowledge can be drawn upon or cultural values reinforced. An interesting math activity might be to have students calculate what making an annual *zakāt* payment would look like for a hypothetical individual of a certain income level. Knowing that small non-monetary good deeds also carry the connotation of being charity in Islam, as well as being highly valued in general, creates the opportunity for educators to reinforce cultural values in a way that has mutual secular interest for school communities as well. Understanding the broader implications for financial regulation under Islam ought to prompt reconsideration for how students are advised and counseled to regarding post-secondary life options.

The Fourth Pillar - Fasting the Month of Ramadan

Below the fourth pillar has been added and is discussed thereafter:

> **Islam has been built on five pillars…**
> - **To bear witness that there is none worthy of worship except Allāh and Muhammad is Allah's Messenger,**
> - **Establishing the Salāh (obligatory prayer)**
> - **Paying the Zakāt**
> - **Fasting the month of Ramadan**

Similar to the five daily prayers, fasting during the month of Ramadan is a great act of worship in Islam that is obligatory, comes with specific rules attached to it, and carries heavy weight of religious significance. Thus, there are aspects to it that are both technical and spiritual, and implications for students and families that are both practical and psychological. Some of the technicalities of Ramadan are intertwined with those of the prayer, and they will be discussed in chapter four with correlating recommendations for schools. This section will focus on the religious significance of Ramadan, some of which cannot be separated from Ramadan's technicalities, and will be discussed here along with the implications for students and families in their relation to school.

Ramadan is the ninth month of what is often referred to as the Islamic calendar and is known to Muslims as the *hijiri* calendar, and can also be referred to as the lunar calendar. This is a twelve month calendar that differs from the standard calendar used in the West, known as the Gregorian calendar[229], in that it is calculated by the movement of the moon around the earth as opposed to the movement of the earth around the sun.

The practical result of this is that the *hijiri* calendar is ten days shorter in a given year than the Gregorian calendar, and eleven days in leap years. Therefore, when the months of the *hijiri* calendar occur in relation to the Gregorian calendar it is not the same from one year to the next. The Gregorian occurrence of the *hijiri* calendar months gradually recedes by ten or eleven days each year. As an example, this means that in 2018 Ramadan began on May 15th and in 2019 it began on May 5th. The beginning of a new lunar month is contingent on the sighting of the initial waxing crescent that is seen after a new moon.[230] If this is observed after 29 days of a month in the *hijiri* calendar the month ends and the new one begins. If the crescent moon is not observed after the 29th day then the 30th day is completed and the new month begins the following day.[231] Therefore Ramadan can be either 29 or 30 days in any given year, and projections of its starting date for the following year can be narrowed down to no better than one of two days. The start date of Ramadan can never be mathematically projected into the

---

[229] It is called this because it was introduced by Pope Gregory XIII in 1582.

[230] Saḥīḥ Muslim Book 13 Hadith 9 https://sunnah.com/muslim/13/9

[231] Sunan Abī Dawūd Book 14 Hadith 14 https://sunnah.com/abudawud/14/14

future within a 24-hour timespan; each year further out one tries to project it the more variability gets added to the timespan.[232]

Fasting in Islam means to abstain from food, drink, and sexual relations from the time of the first white light streak of the dawn in the eastern horizon until the time of the setting of the sun[233], which is defined as the disappearance of the top of the sun's sphere in the western horizon.[234] As with all matters that are obligatory in Islam, fasting is only obligatory upon those who have attained puberty.[235] Puberty is known by certain physical indicators as opposed to a specific age, however, if none of the physical indicators are present by age 15 the obligatory acts become obliged.[236]

More about Ramadan is explained by the following verse from the Qur'an in which the fasting is commanded:

> **The month of Ramadan [is that] in which <u>was revealed the Qur'an</u>,**
> **a guidance for the people and clear proofs of guidance and**
> **criterion. So whoever sights [the new moon of] the month, let**
> **him fast it; and <u>whoever is ill or on a journey - then an equal</u>**

---

[232] For specifics about why the crescent moon's appearance cannot be mathematically predicted with certainty within a narrower timeframe more can be read on the United States Naval Observatory's article entitled "Crescent Moon Visibility". As of the writing of this chapter their website - www.usno.navy.mil - was undergoing renovations due to be complete in April of 2020. But the article can be accessed at anytime at this web archive URL: https://web.archive.org/web/20190611151431/https://aa.usno.navy.mil/faq/docs/crescent.php. Factors they cite are the moon's elongation at the New Moon, the speed of the Moon in its orbit, the distance of the moon, and parallax relative to the observer's location. A mathematics or science teacher could dig into these matters more and use it in the classroom as a teaching tool for students about various astronomical phenomena. It would certainly be engaging to Muslim students as each year they witness their community anticipate the moon's sighting, while many people do not actually know the reasons why it cannot be mathematically projected. Robert Harry van Gent, A professor from Universiteit Utrecht in Germany runs a fascinating website that collects lunar crescent visibility maps in relation to the Islamic calendar that could be used as a classroom resource. URL: https://www.staff.science.uu.nl/~gent0113/islam/islam_lunvis_current_year.htm

[233] Qur'an 2:187 https://quran.com/2/187, Saḥīḥ Muslim Book 13 Hadith 40 https://sunnah.com/muslim/13/40

[234] Saḥīḥ Muslim Book 2 Hadith 27 https://sunnah.com/abudawud/2/27. Unlike the new lunar phases, the occurrences of these can be calculated and projected out with exactness. So while these are the rules of when fasting occurs and ends, Muslims do not need to look out into the sky for these things as they are already projected and the time frame is known. These times relate directly to the prayer times, so specifics about them are discussed in chapter four.

[235] Sunan Abī Dawūd Book 40 Hadith 48 & 53 https://sunnah.com/abudawud/40/48, http://sunnah.com/abudawud/40/53

[236] Sahih al-Bukhārī Book 52 Hadith 28 https://sunnah.com/bukhari/52/28

> ___number of other days___*. Allah intends for you ease and does not*
> *intend for you hardship and [wants] for you to complete the*
> *period and to glorify Allah for that [to] which He has guided you;*
> *and perhaps you will be grateful.*
> *{2:185}*

The second underlined part is an injunction that is another important ruling on fasting. Anyone who is sick, or has a medical condition as to why they should be, is exempt from fasting when they are under that condition. Also exempt from fasting are women when they are menstruating[237] or pregnant[238], as well as people who are traveling on a journey. So there are an array of legitimate reasons why a postpubescent Muslim may not be fasting on a given day during Ramadan. When the verse says, "an equal number of other days", it means that the days that are missed need to be made up by fasting on days outside of Ramadan. If one is not capable of fasting at all then they make the days up by feeding a meal to a poor person for each day that they missed.[239]

So while fasting is only obligatory during Ramadan, it is not restricted to this month. People may fast outside of Ramadan in order to make up the days that they missed. But in addition to that, fasting is a general act of worship in Islam and it was part of the Sunnah of the Prophet Muhammad ﷺ to do supererogatory fasts regularly throughout the year. In particular he would frequently fast on Mondays and Thursdays[240], as well as the middle days of the month[241] (the 13th, 14th, and 15th of the *hijiri* calendar months). This is why some may find that postpubescent Muslim students are fasting from time to time outside of Ramadan. Fridays[242] and Saturdays[243] are days where fasting is taken to be either prohibited or discouraged outside of Ramadan.

The first underlined part of the verse brings us to the month's religious significance and also an additional important practice that the Muslim community undertakes during the month. Islamic history teaches that it was in Ramadan that the angel Gabriel عليه السلام first visited the Prophet Muhammad ﷺ and revealed the first verses of the Qur'an to him in the year 610 AD.

---

[237] Sunan ibn Majah Book 7 Hadith 1739 https://sunnah.com/urn/1270730

[238] Sunan an-Nasā'i Book 22 Hadith 226 https://sunnah.com/nasai/22/226

[239] Qur'an 2:184 https://quran.com/2/184

[240] Jami`at-Tirmidhī Book 8 Hadith 64 https://sunnah.com/tirmidhi/8/64

[241] Bulūgh al-Marām Book 5 Hadith 684 https://sunnah.com/urn/2059330

[242] Jami`at-Tirmidhī Book 8 Hadith 62 https://sunnah.com/tirmidhi/8/62

[243] Sunan ibn Majah Book 7 Hadith 1797 https://sunnah.com/urn/1271290

The Qur'an was revealed cumulatively over time from that point up until the Prophet's ﷺ death in 633 AD. But Ramadan is also the month when he would be visited the most by Gabriel عـلـيـه السلام to learn the Qur'an.[244]

Therefore honoring the Qur'an is an integral part of Ramadan. A practice that was instituted by the Prophet ﷺ and his companions was for the Muslims to gather in the mosques late at night after the five daily prayers are done in order to perform extended supererogatory prayers where the recitation of the Qur'an in the prayer is vastly extended.[245]

This practice is called *tarawīh* and is continued by Muslims today, so every night in Ramadan there are large gatherings in the mosques that go until late. Typically, the gathering will begin at the time of the sunset prayer when the time of fasting is completed and a meal is eaten together by the congregants. People will socialize during the meal and up until the fifth and final obligatory prayer is performed in congregation. After this these longer congregational prayers will take place. This has the effect of keeping people up later at night. The particulars of when these times take place varies depending on which season it is, the given locale, and the amount of daylight that occurs; this is covered in more detail in chapter four.

This means that daily schedules for families can change drastically during Ramadan. It is not uncommon at all for whole families to go to the mosques, children included, and to socialize even after the extended prayers. Frequently community fundraisers, charity drives, and religious sermons are done in the time after the extended prayers as well. In general, whether from going to the mosques in the evening or not, many families find comfort and ease in having more of a "flipped" schedule during Ramadan where they are awake for more of the night hours and sleep more during the daylight hours. This can manifest in different ways and carry varying implications depending on the time of year in which Ramadan takes place. In the winter, it may not be so bad as the sun sets at an earlier hour. But the summer months or late spring can cause these events to extend past midnight. In the year 2020, as this is being written, Ramadan is projected to encompass the last week of April (beginning on the evening of either the 22nd or 23rd) and a little more than three weeks of May. It will be in the winter in its entirety, beginning in February but ending in March before the start of spring, in the year 2026.

At the time of my second editing of this chapter the precautions from the COVID-19 pandemic is due to cancel all congregations in the mosques during Ramadan in 2020, and most schools in

---

[244] Sahīh al-Bukhārī Book 66 Hadith 20 https://sunnah.com/bukhari/66/20, Sahīh al-Bukhārī Book 6 Hadith 63 https://sunnah.com/bukhari/61/63

[245] Riyād us-Sālihīn Book 9 Hadith 198 https://sunnah.com/riyadussaliheen/9/198

the country are closed and doing distance learning. One thing that I believe will come out of this is that even more families and people will want to attend the late night congregations during Ramadan in 2021, as a reaction to the emotional loss of having missed it the year before. Secondly, since the pandemic is causing schools to use distance learning like never before, we might consider giving students who will fast during Ramadan more distance learning options during that time. It could be a very effective and appreciated accommodation, as it might allow students the flexibility to do their school work during the night time when they are not fasting. Again, this is discussed more in chapter four.

Heightened Religious Awareness

There are no rule changes in the religion as far as what is permissible, impermissible, encouraged, and discouraged during Ramadan apart from the rules regarding fasting. However, at the core of religious reasons to perform the fasting is that one who completes it for all days of Ramadan is forgiven for all their sins in the previous year.[246] The Prophet Muhammad ﷺ said:

> **Whoever fasts in the month of Ramadan out of sincere faith and hoping for a reward from Allah, then _all his previous sins will be forgiven._[247]**

So Muslims enter Ramadan wanting to earn this immense reward of forgiveness by properly observing the fasting. While in its most technical sense regarding the human limbs, fasting means abstention from food, drink, and sexual relations; it also means to withhold from sin and to inculcate a disposition of humility. The Prophet ﷺ said:

> **There are people who fast and get nothing from their fast except hunger, and there are those who pray (at night) and get nothing from their prayer but a sleepless night.[248]**
> **Whoever does not give up evil and ignorant speech, and acting in accordance with that, Allah has no need of his giving up his food and drink.[249]**

This explains why many educators have found it to be the case that Muslim students who may not have been keen to perform the prayers during the school day outside of Ramadan, or

---

[246] Major sins excluded. Saḥīḥ Muslim Book 2 Hadith 19 https://sunnah.com/muslim/2/19,
[247] Saḥīḥ al-Bukhārī Book 30, Hadith 11 https://sunnah.com/bukhari/30/11
[248] Sunan ibn Mājah Book 7 Hadith 1760 https://sunnah.com/urn/1270930
[249] Sunan ibn Mājah Book 7 Hadith 1759 https://sunnah.com/urn/1270920

otherwise negligent of religious duties and habits, change during Ramadan and want to perform them. It is not because the rules of Islam are any different during Ramadan than outside of it, I found this to be a point of confusion for some people. These changes in habit occur because Ramadan prompts for a heightened religious awareness and sensitivity, and consideration should be given to students in this. Frequently with young Muslims it wears away at their their souls that they have so quickly in life acquired habits of neglect towards Islam's obligations and also find themselves partaking in matters that Islam forbids or highly discourages. Ramadan offers a chance for rectification from this. Every year there are Muslims in communities around the world who were steeped in habitual sin and negligence before Ramadan, yet they come out of Ramadan reformed, upright, and spiritually renewed. The desire of parents of Muslim students and many people with emotional investment in their lives is that being compelled into the environments of public school education on a daily basis would not have to deprive them of this opportunity. When it does, emotional and psychological instability can occur as a consequence, as well as the splintering of student homes and communities.

Therefore effective religious accommodations for the prayer, considerations towards scheduling school activities, providing alternative learning routes, and entering explicit conversations with students and families about matters that are of high value to them ought to take place around Ramadan. In addition to that, there are ways in which Ramadan could even be seen as an opportunity for positive school activities and community building to take place.

Prepubescent Youth During Ramadan

While Islam only obliges fasting once one arrives at puberty it does not mean younger Muslims are not effected by the season. Some educators have observed that there are younger Muslims who fast at times during the month. There is no basis for them doing this in the Islamic texts that I am aware of, yet there are families who have good reason for encouraging their child to do it.

Many Muslim families interpret the challenges they have in the West as a reason to place more emphasis on conditioning Islamic habits to be hardwired within children at a young age whenever possible. There are many casual and daily habits, such as using the previously discussed Islamic pleasantry phrases, for which they know children are paddling upstream to make habitual due to the secular and non-Muslim environments in which they have to spend so much time. So some larger matters that are isolated to the individual, such as fasting during Ramadan, are areas where a sense of control can be gained. Another example of this is seen in the practice many families adopt of having young girls wear the *hijab*[250] well before they have

---

[250] The *hijab* will be discussed in greater detail in Chapter four.

arrived at puberty. Like the other obligatory matters, wearing the *hijab* is not incumbent until puberty. Yet, some Muslims in the West prioritize girls wearing it at the youngest of ages possible in order to condition them to be so accustomed to wearing it that by the time they get older they will feel uncomfortable without it. It is not uncommon that families do this in the West whereas back in the home country they would maybe opt not to, though practices vary.

Concerning fasting during Ramadan and prepubescent youth, some different phenomena can take place. It is sometimes the case that families encourage the young ones to attempt a degree of partial fasting. According to what I have seen and discussed with families this typically means fasting half a day or some intentional portion of the day up until the child feels it becomes burdensome, and then breaking the fast at some point before sunset. Sometimes, perhaps at the older tween[251] ages, it may mean fasting some days in whole but not doing so every day of the month.

In pretty much any Muslim community there is going to be some families wherein prepubescent children partake in fasting to some degree or another. The impetus for this fasting can come from encouragement on the part of the parents and older family members, but it just as easily can come from the child's own volition. Especially as children enter ages 8-10 when they develop a desire to imitate adults and attempt to do so (Wood, 2007). The fasting can look honorable, mysterious, and desirably grown-up in the eyes of Muslims children at these ages, and they can thereby be self-motivated to try it. I myself experienced this with my nine-year-old daughter who, without any prompting whatsoever, asked her mother and I if she could try fasting for a day in Ramadan. To my amazement she completed a full day of fasting with little to no difficulty.

What I recommend to elementary schools where young students are found to be fasting is to bear with it and refrain from jumping to form any rash conclusions about it as an initial response. It is okay to call individual parents and let them know you want to support them and the child as they see fit. It is possible a conversation like this could bring to light that a student is fasting without permission from home (this has happened), in which case it is good for

---

[251] Islam does have a concept of what is called "the age of discernment" this is the age before puberty but when a child is developed enough mentally to be able to ascertain between right and wrong, generally beginning around age eight, up until the reach of puberty. This is usually regarded as an important teaching time in the child's life. The religion is explicit that parents are supposed to make sure they start praying at this age, usually deemed to begin at seven, and some families see it as the right time for them to start practicing some fasting. Sunan Abī Dawūd Book 2 Hadith 104 https://sunnah.com/abudawud/2/104

parents to know because a child should not be attempting it without their permission. But such conversations should not be approached in a manner where the educator will be interpreted by the parent as taken aback, confused, or worried. It is important to understand that while it might be culturally surprising as a non-Muslim, it is not a strange practice for children within the Muslim community. It can be beneficial for non-Muslim educators to acknowledge to parents that they have learned about these matters and want to be supportive.

Schools have to refrain from conducting any type of large scale communication home, such as sending a letter or email, that expresses concern about students fasting, and definitely not one that makes specific recommendations about how families should observe religious practice; even if the recommendations are couched in such language as "from our perspective as a school" etc.. Schools have done this and faced serious backlash from families who, due to the societal stigmas that are present, are highly sensitive to being misunderstood and even more so to being told how to practice Islam within their families (Morton, 2019). Again, it is recommended to use proactive communication that takes place before any specific incidents happen with families. Holding a community seminar that educates parents and families about their religious rights in public schools could be a chance to ask specific questions and survey families as to what specific practices they anticipate their children partaking in that could impact their child in school throughout the year. If school's learn from these seminars that they have many parents who expect their child to fast, it might be prudent to call another community meeting right before Ramadan to give parents a chance to discuss the support they need.

Secular Values of Ramadan

❖ *Self Discipline*
It should be clear at this point that the inculcation of self discipline is a recurring theme in Islam and fasting during Ramadan is no different. Self discipline is of course a skill that is generally commensurate with student success in school and life in general. Most teachers have learned about the famous marshmallow test done by Stanford University psychologist Walter Mischel in the 1970s that showed young children who could resist eating a single marshmallow for five minutes in exchange for receiving an extra one were more successful in life long-term when followed up with in adulthood (Mischel & Ebbesen, 1970).

Fasting during Ramadan, as well as just good deeds in general, are similarly taught in Islam as being an exchange of sacrificing in the near term for greater gain in the long term. Ultimately in the religious teachings the greater gain is earned in the life after this one on the Day of Judgement. However, it is still prominent in Islamic teaching that patience, self discipline, and a degree of self denial, are necessary for success in one's worldly life as well.[252] This teaching correlates very nicely with commonly taught and accepted ethos in Western traditions of delayed gratification and impulse control. Though the exact same terminology is not generally used in Muslim contexts, which would be more likely to talk about these values in terms of "patience". The word for patience in Arabic and in Islam is *sabr*, and that Arabic term is well-known to Muslims of all language backgrounds. Educators ought to reinforce the value of internal patience to students in a secular manner. Things can be said to students such as,

> *"The most successful people in life, and history, are people who can say 'no' to things that they might feel like they want. So you when you fast and say 'no' to food and drink you are teaching yourself to do that, and that will help you in the long run in life."*

Or...

> *"Fasting can be a very noble and beneficial practice, because if a person can teach themselves to say 'no' to food and drink, they will have an easier time in their life saying no to bad things and being patient through difficulty."*

What I have phrased as "bad things" here could be substituted for something more practical and nearer to whatever context one teaches in, such as drugs, getting into fights, lying etc.

When this type of teaching is valued in the school context and takes on a central focus during times like Ramadan it increases the likelihood that the home, cultural, and public school teachings are reinforcing one another for the betterment of young people's development.

❖ *Good Health*

Explicit within Islam is that fasting and moderation in eating and drinking is connected to good health. The Prophet ﷺ said:

> **A human being fills no worse vessel than his stomach. It is sufficient for a human being to eat a few mouthfuls to keep his**

---

[252] Jami' at-Tirmidhī Book 48 Hadith 119 https://sunnah.com/tirmidhi/48/119,Riyād us-Sālihīn Book 1 Hadith 428 https://sunnah.com/riyadussaliheen/1/428

spine straight. But if he must (fill it), then one third for food, one third for drink and one third for air.[253]

It has become commonly known in the Western world in recent times that there are many health benefits from fasting, and its connection to good health is something that can be shared and discussed with students during Ramadan. There may even be specific science lessons that can be drawn out from it.

Intermittent fasting[254], which mirrors almost exactly the practice of fasting in Islam, is widely recognized as a beneficial health practice, especially pertaining to weight and appetite control. Weight control is of course associated with numerous other health benefits and prevention of illness. The practice of fasting allows the body to have breaks from digestion. Since digestion necessitates greater blood absorption in the kidney and liver, fasting allows greater blood flow to the brain which encourages neurological health and can bolster resistance to stress and possibly injury and disease as well (Triplitt, 2012; Mattson et al, 2018).

Furthermore, the health benefits of appetite control are numerous. The most common cause of death in the United States is heart disease, which has been widely shown to be symptomatic of lifestyle choices that involve excessive caloric intake. Dieting and weight control are the most commonly assigned preventive measures of heart disease. Reduced caloric intake has also been found to reduce some of the negative effects of aging.[255]

While there are health benefits of fasting there can be negative consequences when it is done in certain ways. Having proper advice to avoid negative health effects of fasting might be the most important service that schools can provide for fasting students. In particular, extreme fasting that goes on too long can be associated with negative health effects. This is not of too much concern to Muslim students since they will normally be anxious to break the fast as soon as sundown arrives anyway, but not extending the fast too long is important for health reasons also (Zelman, n.d.). Fortunately, the religion also reinforces this, the Prophet ﷺ said:

---

[253] Sunan ibn Mājah Book 29, Hadith 3474 https://sunnah.com/urn/1274570

[254] Typically defined in medical research as the practice of restricting food intake into an 8-hour window within 24 hour time periods (Tello, 2018).

[255] While there are numerous articles and research reports to investigate into these matters one I like that shows the actual anatomical effects of over-eating can be found at mdanderson.org in an article entitled "What Happens When You Overeat" that has a visual graphic description as well. This could be shown to students. https://tinyurl.com/y7pqgbuo

***The people will continue to be well so long as they hasten to break the fast.*[256]**

So it is encouraged in Islam to break the fast as soon as sundown arrives and it is discouraged to delay it. The hadith about the stomach being the worst vessel to fill carries a warning against overeating in general. Avoiding overeating at the time of breaking a fast is more challenging, but also more important as it can result in the wreckage of the fast's potential health benefits. Since fasting puts the body's metabolism at rest it is best to be reactivated slowly at the time of breaking it. Consuming too many calories too quickly at this time can be shocking to the body's metabolic system, which can induce lethargy and cause stomach problems.[257]

Food choice that is made at the time of fasting and eating in the nighttime is another area where sound secular health advice can be given. Foods that are fried and high in processed sugars or sodium (i.e. junk food) generally will cause greater dehydration in the body during the day, and therefore make fasting more difficult the following day and increase the chances of experiencing headaches (Shaheen et al, 2018). It can be especially difficult to resist sugary foods when breaking the fast because the body's secretion of glucose decreases while fasting (Aronoff et al, 2004), and in many people this can cause a natural craving for sugar that occurs by the time of sundown. These cravings combined with tiredness can make a can of caffeinated soda seem quite appealing to adolescents, so they need to be armed with the knowledge that sugary soda actually dehydrates the body in spite of it being a liquid. The abundant sugar content in soda actually stops the body from absorbing water. The same is true for fruit juices that have a high sugar content, which many kids are duped into thinking is healthy. It should be reinforced to them that making the choice to consume these products when breaking the fast may be tempting in the short term, but will have longer-term negative effects by making their fasting more difficult the next day.

It is actually the practice of the Prophet 🕌 to break the fast by eating two dates and drinking water. Thus, in almost any context where a fast is being broken, either at home or in the mosque, the option of breaking the fast with dates will be present for Muslim adolescents because it is an ingrained part of the tradition. Many Muslim families stock up on dates from local ethnic markets at the beginning of Ramadan. Perhaps you have seen dates have more of a presence in your local corporate grocery chain in recent years, this is a direct result of corporate chains catering to an increase in the Muslim population. Dates satisfy the craving for sugars that

---

[256] Jami` at-Tirmidhi Book 29 Hadith 3474 https://sunnah.com/tirmidhi/8/18
[257] This has been studied by a hospital in the United Arab Emirates and a report on it can be found in the article "Break Fast Gradually to Avoid Stomach Problems" by *The National UAE.* https://tinyurl.com/y8jngjbx

is acquired while fasting with natural sugars as opposed to processed ones. They are also high in fiber content, making them more nutritious than processed sugary options, and therefore providing the glucose that the body craves while also allowing the sugars to be broken down slowly. This prevents the notorious sugar crash that people experience from consuming foods with high amounts of simple sugars and low nutritional value that the body metabolizes in a spike when consumed on an empty stomach (this is commonly experienced when eating donuts in the morning). Dates are called *timur* in Arabic and it is not uncommon at all for Muslim students of all language backgrounds to know them by that word. A discussion on the health benefits of consuming dates at the time of breaking the fast is something that achieves the secular purpose of promoting healthy habits in adolescents who are fasting. The option will be there for them wherever they are breaking the fast, they just need to choose it. Their parents might tell them to eat dates, but adolescents often like to not do what their parents tell them just for its own sake. If they are motivated to do it by information they got from a source that was not their parents, like a public school teacher, then they feel like the choice is their own.

There are other positive food choices that students can be encouraged to make for health reasons. Fruits and vegetables that contain high amounts of water are better for promoting hydration while fasting the following day. Foods such as tomatoes, cucumbers, grapes, and watermelon are all good choices, and eating them in the nighttime and for the pre-dawn meal (*suhoor*) can help greatly in reducing dehydration and headaches while fasting the following day (Shaheen et al, 2018).

Having dried lips is another common effect of fasting (Shaheen et al, 2018). It is a good idea to have several sticks of chap stick available for student use if they need it in the classroom. There is nothing wrong with using chapstick and lip balm while fasting since its use is only topical. This can avoid them having to make a trip out of class to the nurse's office if they need it badly. Having several new sticks, or just giving them away to students, can assure they do not have to share the same one, and having them available can endear the teacher to the students.

❖ *Charity, Giving, & Empathy*

It is also explicit within Islam that a benefit of fasting is that it allows the person to empathize with the poor, hungry, and needy. While charity is always encouraged to be given in Islam this encouragement is raised in earnesty during Ramadan. A companion[258] of the Prophet ﷺ said:

> *The Prophet (ﷺ) was the most generous amongst the people, and he*
> *used to be <u>more so in the month of Ramadan</u> when Gabriel visited him,*

---

[258] 'Abdallah ibn 'Abbas رضي الله عنه

> *and Gabriel used to meet him in every night of Ramadan till the end of the month. The Prophet (☀) used to recite the Holy Qur'an to Gabriel, and when Gabriel met him, he used to be more generous than a fast wind (which causes rain and welfare).*[259]

Charity drives and solicitations are common in mosques during Ramadan. Feeding a hungry person is an expiation of days where fasting was missed[260] for one who is unable to make it up by fasting outside of Ramadan. Towards the end of Ramadan there is an obligatory charity to be given by the head of household, called *zakāt al fitr*. This charity is given as food to a needy family or to an amount of needy people equal to the amount of people in one's own household. This charity is given to ensure that no one goes hungry on the day of the holiday celebration (*eid*) that follows Ramadan. While people nowadays commonly give this charity in the form of cash or other currency remittance, the Prophet ☀ and his companions gave the charity as a staple food item that is delivered by hand to the family in need.[261] This aspect of the charity giving is encouraged because Islam highly promotes visiting the poor and sick[262] for what it teaches of gratitude and perspective in the individual.

So it would be wonderful if schools or classrooms that have a high amount of Muslim students organized charity relief drives during this time. Service learning projects in general may be a good thing to do during Ramadan, such as visiting hospitals. Topics such as world hunger and famine also could be analyzed and studied during Ramadan.

The Fourth Pillar - Conclusion

Ramadan spent many years in the summer and school systems forgot about it. Even during that time the amount of Muslim students in many schools and districts increased, and these places are now finding themselves scrambling each year when Ramadan comes around in order to adjust to meet student and family needs. This adjustment will be ongoing as the arrival of Ramadan in the standard calendar is not the same from one year to the next, nor can its exact arrival in any given year be predicted with certainty.

This is a struggle for everyone involved and a key issue to success, avoiding pitfalls, and maximizing benefits for students is that school staff members have specific knowledge about

---

[259] Sahīh al-Bukhārī Book 30 Hadith 12 https://sunnah.com/bukhari/30/12

[260] Qur'an 2:184 https://quran.com/2/184

[261] Jami` at-Tirmidhī Book 7 Hadith 57 https://sunnah.com/tirmidhi/7/57, Sahīh Muslim Book 12 Hadith 24 https://sunnah.com/muslim/12/24

[262] Sahīh al-Bukhārī Book 56 Hadith 252 https://sunnah.com/bukhari/56/252

Ramadan and how it operates. When this knowledge is had, staff members can have the chance to function competently with student and family culture. Also, the potential will exist for Ramadan to be used as an area to increase student engagement and promote positive life skills and health.

Ramadan itself is not a holiday, even though it is commonly referred to as one, it is the ninth month of the lunar calendar. However, one of the two Islamic holidays follows Ramadan, *eid al fitr*. In leading up to a holiday and being a recognizable time of devotion, Ramadan can also be utilized as an area to discuss and learn about Muslim culture generally for all students. Some of the recommended resources in chapter six of this book can help facilitate that. More technical aspects of Ramadan pertaining to scheduling and their implications for school's academics is discussed in chapter four.

The Fifth Pillar - The Pilgrimage to Mecca (Hajj)

Below the fifth pillar has been added and is discussed thereafter:

> **Islam has been built on five pillars...**
> - **To bear witness that there is none worthy of worship except Allāh and Muahammad is Allah's Messenger,**
> - **Establishing the Salāh (obligatory prayer)**
> - **Paying the Zakāt**
> - **Fasting the month of Ramadan**
> - **Hajj**

The fifth pillar of Islam is what is called *Hajj*, it is known in English as "The Pilgrimage to Mecca" and it is commanded for Muslims to do in the following verse of the Qur'an:

> **And proclaim to the people the Hajj; they will come to you on foot and on every lean camel; they will come from every distant pass**
> **That they may witness benefits for themselves and mention the name of Allah on known days over what He has provided for them of [sacrificial] animals. So eat of them and feed the miserable and poor.**
> **[22:27-28]**

Making the pilgrimage to Mecca is something that Muslims are obliged to do once in their lifetime[263] if they are physically and financially capable to do so.[264] Successfully completing Islam in life in its most basic sense means to complete these five pillars.[265] Each obligation is unique in how it relates to time, duration, and means of performance, but when considered as a whole the five pillars are easily interpreted by Muslims to be comprehensive and holistic. The first pillar is something that resides in the heart, and the believer is challenged internally to hold onto at all times. The second pillar is performed externally with the body and done daily. The third pillar is performed with one's income and done annually. The fourth pillar is performed internally with the body and done for a month out of the year. The fifth pillar, Hajj, is performed externally with the body but also involves planning of time, travel, and income over the long term in order to complete. Hajj is the most practically difficult pillar to complete, especially for those who live in the Western hemisphere.

While Hajj and visiting the city of Mecca are not things the school system has to accommodate in and of themselves, awareness about them gives educators insight into something that has a prominent place in the lives of all their Muslim students and families, whether they are performing Hajj within a given year or not. Knowing about Hajj will also give insight into key cultural teachings that can be related to secular values of interest to school climates and academic topics.

Hajj is seasonal and takes place during a certain part of the Islamic calendar which, like Ramadan, recedes in the Gregorian calendar by 10 or 11 days each year. Outside of the Hajj season it is still an honorable act of worship to visit the city of Mecca and perform a process that encompasses some, but not all, of the ritualistic rites that are done in Hajj. Visiting Mecca outside of the Hajj season and performing these rights is called *umrah*. So while the Hajj season is the busiest time of year in Mecca, pilgrims still travel there year round. While the rights of *umrah* are done within a single day, and are also done in Hajj, all within the sacred mosque in Mecca, the rites of Hajj take place over a week and involve a series of travels in areas outside of Mecca city proper.

During the Hajj season Muslims who are not performing the pilgrimage around the globe are still impacted in several ways. Almost everyone will know someone who is performing it in any given year. It is altogether very likely that students will have a family member, or know an acquaintance, or a whole group of people in their local Muslim community, who are making the

---

263 Sunan Abī Dawūd Book 11 Hadith 1 https://sunnah.com/abudawud/11/1
264 Qur'an 3:97 https://quran.com/3/97
265 Sunan Abī Dawūd Book 2 Hadith 1 https://sunnah.com/abudawud/2/1

pilgrimage. A way to show interest in student lives could be to ask, "do you know anyone who is going on Hajj this year?" in the weeks and days leading up to its season, as well as during it.

Even for those who are not performing Hajj it is often the case that families have long term plans as to when and how they, and possibly their children as adults, will perform Hajj. I have known families for whom a trip to Hajj or *umrah* was a planned graduation gift from high school or college. There are others who plan to one day work in the Arabian Peninsula or a nearer country in the Middle East or Africa for a period of their lives so as to make the performance of Hajj easier and less expensive. Hajj tourism is a large industry around the world. The cost of a travel package to go on Hajj that is guided by a tourism agency with all necessary arrangements set up can vary in price depending on where the pilgrims are traveling from and the quality of arrangements. I know in the Twin Cities, a Hajj package averages around $5k-$6k per person. Every major metropolitan area in the West has travel agencies whose exclusive business is offering travel packages for Hajj and *umrah*. Perhaps you have students whose parents or relatives operate such a business.

So to perform Hajj from the West takes some long term financial planning in the least. An interesting math project might be to have students determine how much money, and for how long, they would have to save up on a biweekly basis in order to save up to go on Hajj over a given course of time.

The Hajj Process and the Islamic Calendar

The performance of the main rites of Hajj takes place from the 8th day to either the 12th or 13th day of the 12 month of the Islamic calendar, which is called *dhūl-hijjah*. On the tenth of this month occurs the second Islamic holiday, *eid al-adha*. These first ten days of *dhūl-hijjah* are referred to as the Hajj season and are also a time of year, like Ramadan, where the reward for performance of good deeds, and likewise the punishment of sins, are magnified.[266] Thus leading to the heightened religious awareness effect.

There are also some specific themes relating to brotherhood of mankind that are brought up and reflected upon during the Hajj season. So there is benefit in educators understanding the Hajj calendar and the day by day rites for how they relate to the practices of Muslims who are not performing Hajj at the same time. There is much to be drawn upon with this for the school climate.

---

[266] Sunan ibn Mājah Book 7 Hadith 1799 https://sunnah.com/urn/1271300

The graphic to the right[267] is a birdseye view map of Mecca and its surrounding areas. It gives a general representation of the stations and rites that are performed on each day of the Hajj. Day 3 represents the 8th day of *dhūl-hijjah*.

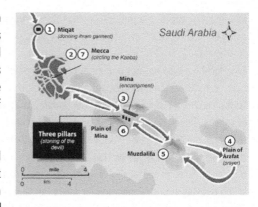

While the whole season is a special time for Muslims who are not performing Hajj the ninth and tenth day carry special significance. As stated before, the tenth day is the day of the second Islamic holiday that Muslims celebrate, *eid al adha*.[268] More on holidays is discussed further below. On the ninth day the pilgrims are all gathered in an open plain outside of Mecca which is called the Plain of Arafat. Thus this day is referred to in Islam as the Day of Arafat. While it is not an obligation, it is highly encouraged for Muslims who are not performing the Hajj to fast on this day.[269]

Also significant is that while the pilgrims are gathered on that plain, they will listen to a sermon[270] in which will be repeated a sermon given by the Prophet Muahammad ﷺ when he led his followers on Hajj towards the end of his life. This sermon is called the *khutbat ul wadā*, and is known in English as the Farewell Sermon. It is a very famous speech and well known to the Muslims for what it carries of summarizing Islam's teachings. During the Hajj season the *khutbat ul wadā* is frequently repeated and reflected upon in mosques around the globe as well. The sermon as it is delivered in Hajj[271] has been commonly listened to around the world on the radio, and nowadays streamed over the internet. Some of what is said in this sermon is monumental for educators to know about because of what it shows of the home-cultural and religious teachings in the lives of their Muslims students.

---

[267] Image attribution: Hajj *locations and rites*. By User:AsceticRose, CC BY-SA 3.0, https://commons.wikimedia.org/w/index.php?curid=39715975

[268] *Eid al-adha* translates into "feast of the sacrifice" the entirety of Hajj is essentially a reperforming of the rites and story of the Prophet Abraham عليه السلام in the Qur'an. In this story Abraham is commanded by Allah to sacrifice his son Ismael عليه السلام. When Abraham عليه السلام goes to sacrifice him Allah replaces him with a lamb (Qur'an 37:102-105). This is why the holiday is called "feast of the sacrifice" and also why it is part of the practice for both pilgrims and those who are not on Hajj to slaughter a goat or animal on this day, or to fund it.

[269] Jami` at-Tirmidhī Book 8, Hadith 68 https://sunnah.com/tirmidhi/8/68

[270] A sermon is called a *khutbah* in Arabic.

[271] Nowadays the sermon is given by the Grand Mufti or another eminent scholar from Saudi Arabia.

Islam and Race

In the *khutbat ul wadā* the Prophet Muhammad ﷺ said:

> *Oh mankind! Your Lord is One and your father is one[272], an Arab has no superiority over a non-Arab nor a non-Arab has any superiority over an Arab; also a white has no superiority over a black nor a black has any superiority over a white; except in piety and good action.[273]*

It ought to be apparent, the similarity between the words of the Prophet ﷺ here and those of Martin Luther King in his "I have a dream" speech, which are highly honored in the Western world. Yet the Prophet Muhammad's ﷺ statement came over 1300 years earlier. Islam is explicit in teaching what is essentially color blindness when judging the value of people. The Prophet ﷺ said:

> *Allah does not look at your outer forms or your wealth, rather He looks at your deeds and your hearts.[274]*

In Islam human beings are judged by their beliefs and their actions, which the individual can control and has choice over. They are not judged over their immutable characteristics such as skin color, gender, family lineage, or ethnic origins. He would admonish his followers when they were heard addressing one another in consternation by reference to tribal or familial lineage. The Prophet ﷺ would call such actions the "calls of ignorance[275]" and say that the one who used them was one who had not understood his message.

> *Whoever calls with the call of ignorance then he is from the coals of Hell...Even if he performs salāh and fasts. So call with the call*

---

272 This refers to Adam عليه السلام.

273 Al Musnad of Imam Ahmad 5/411, 'Abdallah ibn al Mubārak in al-Musnad (no. 239), and al-Bayhaqī in Shu'ab al Īmān 4/289. Refer to page 28 of the book *Prophetic Ahādith in Condemnation of Racism* by Dr. 'Abd al-Salām ibn Burjis ibn Nāsir Al-'Abd al-Karīm, 1st Edition published by Sunnah Publishing at www.sunnahpublishing.net.

274 Sunan Ibn Mājah Book 37, Hadith 4282 https://sunnah.com/urn/1292450

275 The call of "jahiliya" is translated as the call of ignorance, meaning the call used by someone who was ignorant of the Prophet's ﷺ message. This specifically means calling out to someone based on immutable attributes associated with lineage.

that Allah named you with: Muslims, believers, worshipers of Allah.[276]

This hadith shows that a Muslim is explicitly taught to identify themselves as a Muslim first and foremost before any other identity marker. So it can be dismaying to Muslim parents when children grow up in the West and are socialized by both the school system and pop culture into the idea that the preeminent signifiers they should identify with are skin color or gender. Schools will often adopt protocols of facilitating school conversations where they are explicitly told, even made, to identify themselves principally and exclusively by race. Meanwhile, nothing about the school environment makes it explicit that they can refer to themselves by religious faith, even though they 100% have the right to do so in the United States. In fact, if a conversation is explicitly set up with rules that limit the students to only identifying themselves by race it is very likely unconstitutional. According to the federal guidelines school authorities, "may not structure or administer such rules to discriminate against speech with a religious perspective".[277] This all has a psychological burden on the Muslim community as a whole. An authentic discussion on race in both America and public school settings cannot be had when parties are ignorant of these Prophetic teachings and their impact on the world.

Central to the Prophet Muhammad's ﷺ mission and success was that he unified the warring tribes of Arabia under the banner of Islam. He abolished all long-standing blood feuds amongst his followers, the type of which had previously been so common to Arab and many other cultures that perpetual war served as the basis of societal organization.[278] This unification spread as far east and west as terrestrial boundaries permitted at the time. So the Muslim world from its earliest of times has encompassed followers of a full-spectrum of diversity in colors, languages, social classes, and ethnic origins; and its message of non-favoritism to immutable human characteristics was central to this and continues to be an appeal of the religion today.

Race has always had a heavy focus in American society and in its education system. The development of critical race theory in the 1980s, the push for greater engagement in schools of African American students, and anxiety over the achievement gap[279], have put a focus on the implicitly racist dispositions of educators, whether actual or theorized, and fueled extensive examination of the school system through a lens of systemic racism. This along with the push

[276] Jami' at-Tirmidhī Book 44, Hadith 3102 https://sunnah.com/urn/630960

[277] See section C of "Overview of Governing Constitutional Principles" of the federal government's *Guidance on Constitutionally Protected Prayer and Religious Expression in Public Elementary and Secondary Schools.* https://www2.ed.gov/policy/gen/guid/religionandschools/prayer_guidance.html

[278] Sunan ibn Mājah Book 25 Hadith 3171 https://sunnah.com/urn/1280850

[279] Or "opportunity gap" if you prefer the demarcation of Gloria Ladson-Billings.

for nominal multiculturalism education has also brought a very explicit focus on race and anti-racist teacher practices into the learning curriculum as well.

Resulting from this, many urban school districts, as well as suburban ones that have experienced significant demographic changes in their student populations in the past two decades, have adopted racial equity training and protocols in their district's professional development. Principally among this is the Beyond Diversity training and the Courageous Conversations protocol and other resources from the work of Glenn Singleton and the consultancy agency Pacific Education Group (PEG) (Singleton & Linton, 2006). I believe this work has benefits to most people who undertake it, and can serve to honor the identity of students to a degree and encourage a disposition upon educators to challenge themselves and their attitudes towards students. Nevertheless, the reality remains that for Muslim students in these districts to be viewed *only* through a racial lens can serve the unintended consequence of suffocating an essential part of their identity, and clash with values taught at home. This is not to say at all that racial equity work is the principal agent of the suffocation of religious identity for Muslim students. But the point is that it is incorrect to limit considerations of Muslim students' identity to that of race or a "people of color" grouping, and it is in the vast majority of cases for Muslim students an incorrect point from which to initiate one's understanding and consideration of their identity.

I believe that the racial equity work in the school system has had the benefit of reshaping many minds and attitudes of educators. But a noticeable byproduct is that too often teachers are attempting to educate Muslim students solely as "black" or "brown" students or as "students of color". [280] Teachers today have more readily available resources to draw on for culturally relevant pedagogy of African American students that forms a basis of curricular engagement with students of color. The reality is that Muslim students have a mixed resonance at best with this type of teaching and the themes they elicit in the classroom, and to assume it ought resonate with their cultural backgrounds based on their skin color is a type of presumption that might accurately be called racism itself.

Singleton's Courageous Conversation framework, which has been adopted by schools and districts across the country, sets as a condition that teachers "isolate race" in their conversations with and about students. This is intended to serve a practical purpose under the theory that if participants in a conversation about race do not agree beforehand that they will stick to talking about race as the conversation's directive topic, it will inevitably veer off into other topics due to

---

[280] Students of Arab and Pakistani descent are often taught as "brown students", or perhaps Asian, or educators just remain confused in general about how to racially categorize them, mirroring the dilemma the wider society has always had with them that was discussed in chapter two.

the general discomfort and sensitivities that people, especially whites, have with talking about race that they might prefer to avoid. I believe Singleton is correct about this, however, the protocols of Courageous Conversations can be taken to explicitly dictate that other identity markers such as gender, religion, and ethnicity cannot be brought up in order to meet the stated condition of "isolating race" in the conversation. Thus, when a Muslim is either in such a conversation, or Muslim students are the subjects of them, a dilemma arises whereby the Muslim's religion is the explicit source of their understanding for how to view race in the world, yet they are effectively barred from bringing religion into the discussion because of prior set conditions in the conversation's protocols.[281] Sometimes teachers and equity coordinators use the same protocols when they structure conversations with and amongst students. Again, if students are explicitly told that they can only express themselves racially in a conversation, this sets up rules that explicitly discriminate against speech with a religious perspective and is unconstitutional.

How can Muslim students be expected to talk about solutions to racism if they cannot talk about Islam as being a solution to racism? As a matter of fact, how can Muslim students be expected to take a critical stance on anything when the whole basis of their own criteria between what is right and wrong is implicitly unwelcome in the school environment? I have been asked by teachers before if there is some reason that their Muslim students seem less capable of "critical thinking". While "critical thinking" can operate purely as buzzwords in education, there is research that suggests higher order thinking occurs when students are prompted to take a critical stance (Lan et al, 2014). For Muslim students, taking a critical stance would mean articulating arguments rooted in a religious way of looking at the world. Teachers need to be explicit that this is welcome, and also show that they have some background and competency themselves to understand and articulate religious perspectives, to thereby support students in their own development of doing it themselves. Certainly this affects students of other faiths to as well.

Personally, I am a religious person, but I understand atheistic and agnostic ways of looking at the world, and I have researched them and their historical development, explored and

---

[281] I will note here that I have attended many PEG trainings as well as their annual conference in 2015 and spoken to consultants from the organization about these issues at those events. Not one of them ever expressed that the training should be taken to mean that Muslim kids, or any kids, should leave their religious identity at the school door. Rather PEG consultants, as well as Singleton himself, will often acknowledge that the removal of God and religion from the culture of schooling has had a drastically negative impact on black communities over the course of generations. Gloria Ladson-Billings touches on this in her book *The Dreamkeepers* as well. The problem here is more about how participants can take the guidance of these conversations, and bring them back to students, when they do not have the appropriate background knowledge about Muslim students and their religion.

discussed them with individuals I know who hold them dear, and I do not shy away from articulating those views and their basis to students in my classes. I teach those perspectives and historical phenomena to my students out of the interest of being unbiased and serving the goals of a liberal education that takes into account consideration and understanding for all viewpoints. When doing so I do my best to keep a clinical disposition that shows neither favoritism nor flippancy towards the views I personally disagree with. Having a purely objective standpoint is of course not easy for anyone, but not impossible to strive for either. If teachers are unable to strive for the same type of disposition and knowledge towards teaching religious ways of looking at the world, they have to question their own competency towards serving the objectives of a truly liberal education (Nord, 2010).

There is no reason the exact words of the Prophet Muhammad 🕋 and Islamic teachings that have been shared above cannot be brought into classroom discussions about race. Same with facts about the racial make up the Muslim community in America, which is the most diverse in the country amongst major religious groupings (Bagby, 2011; Lipka, 2015). De facto racial segregation amongst church congregations is known to still be the norm in America, even in metropolitan areas where there are Christians of many different races and ethnicities (Lipka, 2014). But richly diverse heterogeneous mosques are the norm in places throughout Muslim communities in America where only 3% of mosque congregations are primarily of a singular ethnicity (Bagby, 2011). The heterogeneity of Muslim communities is a source of great pride for Muslims, and it is something that they are not given nearly enough credit for by mainstream society. This is of course not to say that racism does not exist within Muslim communities. Certainly it does, but the role religion plays is a mitigating one to racism that should rightly be examined for how it unites hearts of different backgrounds together.

I have had teachers who took my training and put the words of the Prophet Muhammad 🕋 that I underlined in the first hadith cited in this section, which are purely secular in their wording when they stand alone, on the wall or presented them next to the words of the Martin Luther King in their classroom. And of course the life of Malcolm X can be utilized as well, and the letter that he wrote back to his followers from the city of Mecca while he was on Hajj. Only a couple of weeks before going on Hajj Malcolm X had said that blacks should just start leaving religion at home. But while on Hajj he wrote back to his followers in the United Stats that *"if only America would look at Islam, it could fix its racial problem…"* while explaining the profound impact that the multi-racial unity and gathering of Muslims on Hajj had on his soul and worldview towards the possibilities of racial harmony. The transformation of Malcolm X brought his views away from the racist beliefs of the Nation of Islam which saw blacks as God's chosen people and whites as devils. In the sixth chapter of this book we have some sources that can be used across grade levels to touch upon the Islamic disposition towards race.

These are profound words, teachings, and historical occurrences that continue to directly impact the world today. There is nothing that prevents public schools from having discussions about how religious beliefs can influence people's attitudes towards race, especially in the upper grade levels. In actuality, excluding religious ways of looking at the world from discussion and instruction in public schools, whether that exclusion is explicit or implicit, in and of itself violates founding principles of liberal education and is possibly an advancement of a type of secular indoctrination that violates the establishment clause of the first amendment (Nord, 2010).

A part of Hajj itself is that the male pilgrims wear only two white towels when performing the rites. This is a removal of worldly demarcations of class, race, and ethnic affiliation and the gathering itself is a reminder of the Day of Judgement when all humans will be raised up naked[282] and gathered together before God to be judged individually for their beliefs and actions. The Qur'an says:

> *O mankind, indeed We have created you from male and female and made you into peoples and tribes so that you may know one another. Indeed, the most noble of you in the sight of Allah is the most righteous of you. Indeed, Allah is Knowing and Acquainted.*
>
> *[49:13]*

This verse makes clear that differences in demarcations and experience of race, ethnicity, and lineage can be acknowledged and learned about by a Muslim from other people. But none of it raises anyone above another person, and Judgement is reserved for what is based on beliefs and actions; that which falls within the realm of the human being's control and will, unlike the immutable characteristics. A Muslim is allowed to love the people they come from, but they are not allowed to let that love prompt them to pride and arrogance[283] or to assist their people in doing wrong.[284] In these teachings on race you see the balance of Islam, which gives clear guidance to human beings of the boundaries between right and wrong, while restraining them from extremes that people might think are common sense; yet that we see mankind fall into over and over again in history.

For a Muslim, any ideology or analytical framework that is not rooted in Islam is something that can only be accepted as valid to the degree by which it agrees with Islamic teaching. This

---

[282] Sunan an-Nasā'i Book 21 Hadith 267 https://sunnah.com/nasai/21/267
[283] Jami' at-Tirmidhī Book 27 Hadith 104 https://sunnah.com/tirmidhi/27/104
[284] Sunan ibn Mājah Book 36 Hadith 24 https://sunnah.com/ibnmajah/36/24

typically means that Muslims can agree on certain aspects of Western ideologies and analytical frameworks, but will be bound to disagree with other aspects of it. Critical race theory, which coats the current-day public school system's teachings about race, is an example of this.

Judiciously evaluating some past civilizations as oppressively hegemonic and chauvinistic can be easily done by the Muslim and is done in many Muslim circles. Same with recognizing that there are groups of people who are more subject to racism, mistreatment, and material disadvantaged in current-day society than others. At the same time, it is considered extreme for this evaluation to enter a realm of personal rancor towards the past.[285] This amounts to decrying what has been Allah's decree, and in Islam both good and evil are part of the predestination willed by Allah.[286] It is explained in the Qur'an that some will be granted more of the material world than others as part of the human condition, but a Muslim is not to be spiteful of this as wealth only gives man the illusion of strength and self-sufficiency.[287] The Prophet's ﷺ companions would admonish people who wished they had experienced something better in the past or could change past occurrences.[288] An increase in one's material wealth is only a test to see if one will have gratitude for it and use it righteously.[289] Islam allows the Muslim to pursue wealth by means that do not involve partaking in forbidden matters[290], and they should not seek to be impoverished.[291] However, if they find themselves in that state it is actually a blessing and preferable to one who is busied with riches.[292] Trial and tragedy are a test of the believer's reaction to it and their acceptance of Allah's decree. These challenges can even be blessings if they prompt one to remembrance of Allah when they had previously been negligent.

The Prophet ﷺ said:

> **Wondrous are the ways of a believer for there is good in every affair of his and this is not the case with anyone else except for the**

[285] Sahīh Muslim Book 40 Hadith 5 https://sunnah.com/muslim/40/5

[286] Qur'an 4:78 https://quran.com/4/78, While evil is part of Allah's creation it is against Islamic etiquette to verbally ascribe evil to Him. Rather, when evil befalls a Muslim they are to ascribe its fault to the evil within their own soul. Qur'an 4:79 https://quran.com/4/79, Sahīh al-Bukhārī Book 97 Hadith 17 https://sunnah.com/bukhari/97/17

[287] Qur'an 4:32 https://quran.com/4/32, Qur'an 104:1-4 https://quran.com/104

[288] Tafsīr ibn Kathīr 25:72-74 page 206 of the abridged English translation published by Darussalam. https://tinyurl.com/yc3lyeuf

[289] Qur'an 16:71 https://quran.com/16/71

[290] Qur'an 3:14 https://quran.com/3/14

[291] Jami' at-Tirmidhī Book 36 Hadith 47 https://sunnah.com/tirmidhi/36/47

[292] Sunan ibn Mājah Vol. 1 Book 1 Hadith 5 https://sunnah.com/urn/1250050, Sunan ibn Mājah Book 37 Hadith 4246 https://sunnah.com/urn/1292090

***believer, for if he has an occasion to feel delight, he thanks Allah,
thus there is good for him in it, and if difficulty befalls him then he
endures it patiently, so there is good for him in it.[293]***

These teachings coat a Muslim's understanding in discussions of historical injustices. It is a moderate path where racism can easily be identified for what it is, but both defeatism and rancor indicate an ill-measured and even pompous disposition[294] towards accepting that nothing occurs except by an underlying Wisdom. So some schools are very active in engaging students around social justice issues that are fundamentally about redistribution of wealth and rancor towards past injustices that caused social income disparities. Those injustices can be acknowledged by Muslims and an Islamic worldview, but Islam does not condone wealth redistribution that is not instigated by charitable giving and it protects private property.[295] To me, it is patently unfair for educators to enter Muslim kids into these discussion but to 1.) be wholly uneducated themselves about Islamic teachings towards race and social issues, 2.) not make any attempt to include or acknowledge those teachings and the fact that they might already or ought to have a place in the students' own attitudes towards social justice issues, not to mention their influence on history, 3.) not prompt them to also involve their parents in how they form their opinions on these issues, 4.) incline them towards practicing racism or reverse racism[296], and 5.) incline them towards joining the pursuits of activist groups without the explicit permission of their parents. I have known all of these things to happen regularly in public schools, all to the dismay of parents who experience these phenomena as a losing of proper influence over their child. In Islam, tending to the refinement of one's own soul and character takes precedent before laying concern over societal ills. In Islamic teaching the purification of one's own soul is the prescribed and perquisite first step for societal change to

---

[293] Sahīh Muslim Book 55 Hadith 82 https://sunnah.com/muslim/55/82

[294] Sunan ibn Mājah Book 33 Hadith 98 https://sunnah.com/ibnmajah/33/98

[295] Sahīh Muslim Book 53 Hadith 76 https://sunnah.com/muslim/53/76

[296] Critical Race Theory draws on Marxist lenses of critique by viewing everything that happens in terms of societal power struggles. As such, there is a line of thinking within it that dictates that only whites can be racist because they are the ones with power. Many educators know this line of thinking from it having been articulated in the popular book *Why Are All The Black Sitting Together in the Cafeteria* by Beverly Daniel Tatum (2003). I have known this idea to be taught directly to students as an absolute truth in some schools, classrooms, after school programs, and in-school mentoring programs. This idea is rejected in Islam, where it is explicitly defined that racism can and does occur at the smaller level of interpersonal interactions (Sunan an-Nasā'i Book 21 Hadith 47 https://sunnah.com/nasai/21/47), and there is no racial or hereditary attribute that voids a person from being susceptible to partake in it (Shamā'il Muhamadiyah Book 47 Hadith 336 https://sunnah.com/urn/1803180). When these types of ideas are introduced by instructors in a classroom, they should not be taught as absolute axioms. Rather their genealogical origins as an idea should be drawn out for students. There are many areas beyond just teaching about race where this applies.

occur.[297] When a Muslim does experience trial and poor fortune from outside forces Islam teaches to reflect on one's own self first.[298]

Indeed, Allah will not change the condition of a people until they change what is in their own souls.
[13:11]

Quite frankly, leaders[299] in American Muslim communities have spent a generation warding off the plots of social activist groups to recruit Muslim kids to be props in their causes by enticing them towards serving their own ambitions of creating the appearance of a diverse critical mass in protests and demonstrations that are antithetical to Islamic conduct[300], with this at times pushing kids into acts of civil disobedience that jeopardize their own safety. This is an especially patronizing phenomenon considering how many of these youth are being raised by people who escaped places of foreign-induced civil unrest and came to America in order to settle and raise children in a place of ostensible civic stability and security. Typically these groups give little to not attention towards engaging the parents of these youth, and sadly the public school system is often a conduit for this recruitment and enticement that is tearing communities apart no matter the ostensibly positive intentions of its provocateurs. The mistaken notions of these activists' plots only cause them to enact upon Muslim communities the same colonial machinations that they would profess to be against, but that have been devised to divide Muslim societies themselves for centuries.

Race and identity are of course deep issues. There is no doubt that many Muslim kids and their families have been victimized by racism and colonial oppression. Both current and historical. Without bringing Islam's views directly into these conversations, a more subtle persecution will occur to these children within the public schools that is brought on unwittingly by actors who think they are doing good. To immigrant kids especially conversations about race and oppression are often framed in schools as being conjoined with historical patterns of the West's colonization and manipulation of non-white countries and people, and rightly so. However,

---

[297] Qur'an 13:11 https://quran.com/13/11

[298] Qur'an 21:87 https://quran.com/21/87, Sahīh al-Bukhārī Book 97 Hadith 17 https://sunnah.com/bukhari/97/17, Sahīh Muslim Book 48 Hadith 99 https://sunnah.com/muslim/48/99

[299] Actual leaders, not people propped up by interests external to the Muslim community who are branded as Muslim leaders in order to serve others as mascots.

[300] Qur'an 13:11 https://quran.com/13/11, Sunan ibn Mājah Book 33 Hadith 98 https://sunnah.com/ibnmajah/33/98,Sunan Abī Dawūd Book 43 Hadith 28 https://sunnah.com/abudawud/43/28, Shamā'il Muhamadiyah Book 81 Hadith 351https://sunnah.com/urn/1903510, Sunan ibn Mājah Book 24 Hadith 2969 https://sunnah.com/urn/1277080, Sahīh al-Bukhārī Book 93 Hadith 8 https://sunnah.com/bukhari/93/8

consider that historically Western powers and colonialists would always make a point to demarcate Muslim lands and peoples by ethnic identity in a deliberate effort to suppress and downplay religious identity. This was done in both how they have managed their colonial subjects as well as how they appropriated them to the Western populace back home. So Muslim peoples would be referred to and known first as Turks, Arabs, Saracens, Berbers, Moors etc. In the 20th century colonial powers would push nationalist fervor in Muslim nation states that had been set up by Western powers in the first place.

This was a strategic way of fractionalizing Muslim peoples in order to employ a divide and conquer strategy that disempowered people, undermined their collective unity and strength, and allowed the Western world to exploit and monopolize virtually all natural resources in Muslim lands for their own gain. When Muslim kids are brought through the ringer of public schools and come out on the other end having been taught, whether implicitly or explicitly, to adopt the idea that their racial, ethnic, or national identity ought to take precedent over their religious identity, and that it must in order for them to effectively operate in Western societal discourse; then the educators who thought they were battling for equity and empowering the oppressed have actually carried out the colonial project themselves.

In Islam, it is taught unequivocally, that Allah did not give the human beings the will to decide their racial, familial, gender, or ethnic origins and identity. But He did give them the choice to choose their beliefs and actions[301]; so this is what the human being is judged by in Islam, and Allah's Prophet ﷺ told the Muslims explicitly to identify themselves by religious belief first.[302]

Holidays and Celebrations

As stated before, there are two Islamic holidays. One occurs immediately following Ramadan, on the first day of the 10th Islamic month, *Shawwal*, and the other is during the Hajj season. This makes for a distance between them of 65 days. The word for holiday in Islamic terminology is *eid*, the holiday following Ramadan is named *Eid al Fitr*, the holiday of breaking the fast, and the holiday following Hajj is called *Eid al Ādha*, meaning the holiday of the sacrifice. *Eid al Ādha* is named this because the practice and performance of the rites of Hajj are a re-enactment and commemoration of the Qur'anic story of Abraham عليه السلام.[303]

There is a major discussion to be had pertaining to holidays and school. School years in America are set up to accommodate Christian religious practices. Many schools have long held traditions

301 Qur'an 2:256 https://quran.com/2/256
302 Jami' at-Tirmidhī Book 44, Hadith 3102 https://sunnah.com/urn/630960
303 See note 268.

of incorporating celebration of both Christian and traditional American holidays in a secular manner within the schools. This usually involves things like class parties, specialized learning activities, and even varying modes of school-wide assemblies and events; not to mention staff-only celebrations as well.

These practices have been the bane of much private consternation for Muslim families in America. What educators need to know about Islam in this regard is that it forbids the celebration of any holiday other than the two Islamic holidays. When the Prophet 鑾 migrated to the city of Medina some Muslims there celebrated Persian holidays that they had also celebrated from the time before they became Muslim. The Prophet 鑾 said to them about those celebrations:

> **Verily, Allah <u>has replaced these two days</u> with two better days: Eid al-Adha and Eid al-Fitr.**[304]

Furthermore the Qur'an in many places describes the type of person that will be guarded from the punishment of hellfire and rewarded with paradise. In one such verse the description is:

> **Those who do not bear false witness, and if they pass by some <u>frivolity</u> they bypass it with dignity.**
> **[25:72]**

It is explained in the exegesis of the Qur'an, and in many statements from the early generations of Muslims, that the word that is translated as "frivolity" here (*zūr*) specifically is referring to the holiday practices of the non-Muslims. Thus this verse is an explicit command in the Qur'an to avoid celebrating the non-Islamic holidays.

But what is perhaps even more important to understand is that Islam also explicitly forbids *the imitation* of these holiday celebrations. These are based on the following hadith of the Prophet鑾:

> **Whoever imitates a people is from them.[305] "**

What is meant by this last hadith is an injunction against imitating disbelievers specifically in their practices that are particular to their religions as well as to practices that are sinful. What is entailed of "from them" is that one would be raised up with them on the Day of Judgement

---

[304] Sunan Abī Dawūd Book 2 Hadith 745 http://sunnah.com/abudawud/2/745

[305] Sunan Abī Dawūd Book 34 Hadith 12 http://sunnah.com/abudawud/34/12

when the unbelievers will be cast into Hell.[306] Specifically because of this the Prophet ﷺ would not allow any action that imitated celebrations of pre-Islamic festivals.[307]
It was further explained by one of the Prophet's ﷺ companions[308] that:

> "Whoever builds (a house, or takes residence) in the lands of the foreigners (non-Muslims), takes part in their holidays and celebrations, and imitates them, doing this until he dies (i.e. not repenting), he shall be raised among them on the Day of Judgment."[309]

It is because of this prohibition that it does not really work for Muslim families to change the name of the Christmas party in school to the "winter celebration" party, or to change Valentine's Day to "Friendship Day" and other such tactics that are employed in hopes of avoiding offending people's religious sensibilities.

Again, any school, and especially one that is experiencing recent demographic shifts in the religious makeup of its student population, will need to have a large discussion regarding what should be done around holiday traditions. Schools will vary on their practice based on their own history and the total make up of the community they serve. Some may have long held traditions that carry great weight with the majority of their stakeholders. Others may have already muted or altered celebratory practices for considerations of diversity long ago, but perhaps did so without the detailed knowledge of religious sensibilities that their Muslim families may have. In some schools practices may exist on a level determined more by individual teachers than any school-wide policies. My thoughts and recommendations on this are as follows:

Firstly, at least know that not every student and their family celebrates traditional American holidays nor goes through an exciting build up to them. So the pilgrim hat craft project and pine-tree coloring sheet that students are asked to do in November are not going to ring the same in the minds and hearts of Muslim students as Christian ones. If doing such projects and activities in school implants a seed of love and affection for these holidays within the child, then the school has nurtured something negative within the child according to the eyes of Muslim parents whose hearts are attached to Islamic teaching. Muslim parents in Western society have

---

[306] Yes, Islam teaches that anyone who disbelieves in Islam will perish in Hell (Qur'an 3:85 https://quran.com/3/85) and that one must have Islamic belief in God at a minimum to be granted into paradise (Saḥīḥ Muslim Book 1 Hadith 43 https://sunnah.com/muslim/1/43). But Muslims are still enjoined to kind and well-mannered conduct with people of other faiths as previously explained.

[307] Sunan Abī Dawūd Book 22 Hadith 72 https://sunnah.com/abudawud/22/72

[308] Abdullāh ibn 'Amr (d.684) رضي الله عنه

[309] As-Sunan al-Kubrā (v.9, p.234) of Imam al-Bayhaqī (Arabic) https://tinyurl.com/y7e7l3nl

to constantly strive against the desires that society at large implants within their children by making unIslamic things look alluring, fun, and to be pathways to social acceptance and status. It becomes a compound stressor when the school system, while nominally impartial to religion, does this implanting in its own right. I believe there is an argument to be made that having students do activities that are based on celebration and beautification of holidays infringes on first amendment rights of families and the dictates for non-favoritism in the public school system under the establishment clause, especially when those families are religiously opposed to that practice.

At the same time it seems to me there is an equally valid argument that a school could find a compelling secular purpose for having students do holiday-based activities around holidays that the school community knows the vast majority of its stakeholders celebrate. In schools where holiday and celebratory traditions are long-held parts of the school culture, I think an overhaul or canceling of these practices in response to a small, or even moderate, influx of Muslim families or other religious minorities might be too drastic an action step to take. It would likely run the risk of stigmatizing the Muslim families within the school community's majority population. At the same time, in these contexts it is also not correct or appropriate that Muslim children should just be swept along into these practices without any differentiating consideration.

It should be taken as a must that transparency and proactive communication take place with families. This means at the least that they need to be informed ahead of time about what activities regarding holidays will be taking place within the school; this ought to include school-wide activities as well as classroom-level activities that are perhaps only instigated by individual teachers. Precisely what the activities are should be communicated as well as the *foundational purposes* as to why the school does them. Will the students be studying historical facts about the history of these holiday's development for the purpose of learning factual history and practicing clinical examination of historical trends? Or are they doing a craft activity that involves making an ornament that can be hung on a tree, and the purpose is to learn artisan practices while drawing on the latent motivation stemming from the home cultural practices of students that celebrate holidays associated with hanging ornaments on trees? In the latter example the latent, or explicit, purpose is to do an activity that students will think is "fun" under the assumption that they also find the holiday it correlates with as fun. But a Muslim family that not only does not celebrate these holidays, but likely holds views that directly oppose even imitative participation in them, will have opposite associations and sentiments. So articulation of the underlying purposes that the school and educators have in choosing specific activities is necessary to communicate with parents in order for them to genuinely discern how their child could potentially be impacted by being involved in it. This gives them the opportunity to make an accurate and honest assessment as to whether or not they want their child withheld. An activity on holidays that is based on clinical observation and learning of factual history or cultural exposé does not need any prior warning or approval, as this is totally consistent with objectives of non-partial liberal education. However, one that is based on "fun" and drawing on the holiday's "spirit" does need it.

At the very least proactive and transparent communication needs to take place, and it needs to be done in a way that is *authentic* so that the parents can actually be reached and genuinely informed. This needs to be mentioned because different forms of communication to parents are more likely to be reached based on the parents' own background. It is the case that traditional modes of communication done by the public school system, i.e. letters sent home in backpacks or emails, do not reach all parents, especially ones who come from more oral cultures and *especially* ones who may be illiterate themselves, even in their native language. Even with parents who are well-educated and perfectly literate in English, the "letters sent home" mode of communication is really very passive aggressive, which does not always sit well with families from Muslim cultures. Especially when it comes to issues that are serious, particular, in-depth, and oftentimes emotional; direct interpersonal communication is much preferable. This means phone calls home, invitations to informatory sessions at school, or even home visits, and with competent translators present as need be.

Once sincere communication is delivered the question of accommodation arises. There can be different approaches but the first one I will discuss is separation and opting out. It is important for me to emphasize that Muslim families may very well not mind at all the idea of separating kids from these activities. Educators can often be very sensitive and hesitant about the idea of doing this under the guise of wanting to be "inclusive", but sometimes creating separate spaces for different students is exactly what needs to be done in order to *properly* be inclusive. In many cases this could serve the school community as a whole much better than modifying or canceling practice of the activities themselves. Simply separating the Muslim students will not create consternation towards them on the part of non-Muslim families who have long enjoyed having holiday practices in their child's public school.

If we take the example of having a school party the day before winter break. The most basic level of accommodating for separation would be for families to keep their children home and for the school to allow the absence to be excused. Here the school gives a concession but the burden of execution still rests with the family. The next level would involve the school employing its own resources in creating the separation. This could be done by planning to have students whose families indicated they want their child separated to be in a separate place during the time of the class party. If schools are incapable or unwilling to do the latter accommodations, the proactive communication home that informs about the event and solicits for parents' preferences as to whether or not they wish to keep their kids home should be done at least two weeks prior to the event. This is typically the minimum amount of time that people need to request time off of work, which they may need to do if they have to stay home with their children.

If the school does facilitate separation within its walls it is not a bad idea, and would likely be appreciated by parents, to reinforce and validate for Muslim students the importance of honoring what one's family and home-cultural traditions are, even if they are not part of the school's (and society's) cultural mainstream. Sometimes this separation causes a conflict within the child because celebration of the Western holidays are always made to look appealing, and in particular are centered upon appealing to the sentiments and wants of children for the sake of driving consumerism around them. So the Muslim parent is positioned in such a way that the society has implanted simplistic wants within their child associated with the holiday's celebration, but the parent has to restrict the child from their own wants due to the considerations of higher truths and ideals from the family's religious beliefs. This can lead to an element of consternation between child and parent, and it is powerful for the child to have adults at school who reinforce the value of their parents' decisions with them, especially when that adult at the school is not from the parents' culture. This lessens the feeling that the child may have that their parents and family (and by extension themselves) are something strange that they should feel insecure and stigmatized about. When children go through a struggle, having that struggle acknowledged to them by adults is powerful for coping. Extolling the virtue behind the action they are taking (or that their families are taking upon them) is likewise powerful and helps to inculcate a confident self-concept. The virtue of simply being obedient to one's parents even when it goes against one's own wants is another value that can be reinforced at this time.

There are schools and teachers who come to the logical conclusion that if they are to have celebration and educational focus around Christian holidays, it makes sense to also examine and acknowledge the holidays of other cultures. This has been around for a while in schools and a way that it manifests is often with some acknowledgement or reading that is done about Hanukkah and Kwanzaa around the same time as Christmas. I have been inquired with by schools who also wanted to do some education about *Eid* around this time and used some of the books that I recommend to do so.[310] This is all well and good but schools should understand that there is a fair degree of pretension to only talk about Islamic holidays and other culture's holidays in the week before Christmas. As previously explained, the occurrence of the two *Eids*

---

[310] See chapter 6.

changes from year to year in the Gregorian calendar. Teaching about it in the second week of December can give the non-Muslim students, especially younger ones, the impression that it is a holiday that takes place at that time also, like Hanukkah and Kwanzaa. It is better for *Eid* to be educated about near the times they actually occur.

As far as celebrations go, I think it is best to keep them either totally randomized or occurring in response to student and class accomplishment. There is nothing wrong in Islam with celebrating accomplishments. Birthday celebration and recognition generally are considered holiday celebrations in Islam and follow the same rulings in Islam as described above, i.e. prohibition. However, this is an area where Muslims have capitulated to on a wide degree in America society and elsewhere. This is directly the result of the emphasis that the public school system puts on celebrating student birthdays in elementary school. Increasing globalization has even brought the practice to the Muslim world in some areas. I have known some Muslims who held the view that birthday celebrations were okay so long as they were not done every year.

I am often asked if there is a difference in perception between celebration of holidays that are blatantly Christian-based and ones that are apparently more secular. In Islam a holiday is defined as a celebration that occurs at a regularly recurring interval, especially annual. So whether it is based from a foreign religion or a holiday that has formed for nationalistic, consumer, or other secular purposes, Islam's position on the prohibition of celebrating it or imitating its celebration remains the same. However, it is true that Western holidays can vary in the degree of severity with which Muslims view them, and to which they would be perceived as blasphemous through the lens of the Islamic texts. One's that are centered upon what Islam would categorize as a false idea about God would be worse than one's that are purely commercial or nationalistic. Still, Western holidays with religious origins go well beyond Christmas and Easter. Many people know this, yet I find it regularly proposed to me by non-Muslims that Thanksgiving, Halloween, St. Patrick's Day, and Valentine's Day are holidays that "have nothing to do with religion". These assertions are simply inaccurate historically. Besides, for Muslim families who view life through an Islamic lens, the act of celebrating itself is a religious act. So this type of casual mental separating that the Western mind often does between religious and so-called secular life is not really applicable to the Muslim mind because Islam considers all acts a human being does in life to be taken into account in their final record before Allah.

It is important for non-Muslim educators to understand the dialogues that actually go on in Muslim communities around Western holiday times. I have been confronted with many people who are curious to know more about Muslim attitudes towards these holidays. They make the mistake of Google searching questions such as "Do Muslims celebrate Christmas?" and basing their impression off of what they find and, even worse, considering it an informed impression.

Doing this will bring up no shortage of headlines from news outlets with titles such as "Why More American Muslims are Celebrating Christmas"[311] and "Muslims Can and Do Celebrate Christmas" [312] etc. Such stories draw upon cherry-picked anecdotes from the minority of secularized Muslims who, in an eagerness to gain acceptance from Western society where they fear stigmatization and likely fantasize about gaining status in establishment ranks, capitulate beyond the bounds of what is acceptable in Islam and to the vast majority of people in the Muslim community. Since these stories glamorize the modern-day conception of liberalized tolerance in the West, they find an audience amongst non-Muslim readers. This is exemplary of a larger trend that takes place in how the Muslim community is packaged in the media for non-Muslim consumers who do not know, nor wish to make the effort to know, the community from the inside.

The reality is that Western holiday times in the Muslim community produce a vast array of polemical discourse against these holidays and religious warnings against celebrating or partaking in them at all. What is interesting is that these polemics not only entail warnings from Islamic religious texts, but they often involve elaboration upon the historical roots of the Western holidays as a means to expose to the Muslim public their historical origins that are considered to be nefarious in various ways according to Islamic principals. Typically, through teaching this history, Western holidays in the polemical discourse of Muslims are characterized as being rooted in pre-Christian festivals related to idol-worship that predate Jesus عليه السلام, thereby having nothing factual to do with him historically, and then undergoing a Christianized repurposing in the Medieval[313] period long after his life. Through an Islamic worldview this history easily lends itself to seeing these holidays as gross corruptions of True religion, and thus something evil and to be avoided, even if its celebration is aesthetically beautified by pomp and glamour.

Something amazing about this is that educators could actually draw upon these polemics by doing more clinical examinations and learning about the actual historical roots and development of these holidays in the West. This is a type of learning that Muslim students can actually take great interest in for what it offers in the potential to confirm or disconfirm, or to lend more clarity to, the polemical stances that are taken within Muslim communities, of which they are likely to have an at least peripheral sense.

---

[311] Such as here https://tinyurl.com/ycqwuh56
[312] Such as here https://tinyurl.com/yaxco5ev
[313] The book *Christianity: The Origins of a Pagan Religion* by Phillipe Walter, professor of French Literature at Université Stendhal in Grenoble, can be referred to for more information on this. Published by Inner Traditions. Rochester, Vermont. 2003.

Students can be prompted to investigate questions such as "To what extent do the practices of Christmas relate to the historical Jesus?" or "What are the origins of putting a pine tree in one's house as part of a winter celebration?" or "Why is Christmas celebrated on December 25th? Is it actually Jesus's birthday?" I am actually amazed in my life how much more likely I find adults in the Muslim community to be informed about these types of questions than non-Muslims. This is directly related to the education that goes on within Muslim communities, and teachers would be smart to accept it as legitimate background knowledge and draw on it for the purposes of practicing historical investigation.

The Tenets of Belief

The five pillars of Islam encompass the religion's central belief in the first pillar, and the core of what is obligatory to observe in external practice in the other four. Encompassed within the first pillar are tenets of belief that Islam obligates the Muslim to believe in, and that are learned through knowing the Qur'an and the Sunnah. Similar to the five pillars, these tenets can be articulated and phrased concisely, even down to a single word in Arabic, yet they entail a much deeper understanding that, when known, is revealed to touch upon many different real-world aspects of the Muslim's life, worldview, and intellectual schema, in ways that are direct and concrete. This section will walk through the tenets of belief, explain what they are, and make real world connections as to how they impact Muslim students and families, as well as offer considerations for teachers and educators.

The World of the Unseen

Just as the Prophet Muhammad ﷺ articulated the five pillars concisely and within a single hadith, he also articulated the tenets of belief in the same way. As I did in the previous section I will show the hadith piece by piece and explain each relevant part. It is told in a hadith narration where the angel Gabriel عليه السلام appears to the Prophet ﷺ and his companions in the form of a man. Gabriel عليه السلام asked the Prophet ﷺ, "What is Islam?" and the Prophet ﷺ replied by listing the five pillars. Gabriel then asked the Prophet ﷺ, "**What is faith?**"[314], and he replied:

> **To believe in Allah (and)...**
> - **His Angels...**[315]

---

[314] The Arabic word for "faith" is *Imān*, a common Muslim female name.
[315] Sunan ibn Mājah Book 1 Hadith 66 https://sunnah.com/urn/1250630

Angels in Islam are a part of what is referred to as *al-ghayb*, which means *the unseen*[316], but in Islamic terminology can be accurately translated as *the world of the unseen*. It is part of Islamic belief that there is a world that exists alongside the one human beings live in currently, but that is imperceptible to human senses. This is a belief that Muslims take literally and seriously and awareness of it forms essential parts of a Muslim's paradigm for understanding life. The Qur'an establishes in its very beginning verses that it is a book only for those who believe in the unseen:

> **This is the book wherein there is no doubt, a guidance for the pious. Those who _believe in the unseen_, establish salāh, and spend out of what We have provided for them.**
> **[2:2-3]**

Important and emphasized enough is this belief in Islam that it is mentioned in the Qur'an before the mentioning of establishing prayer. But how does the Muslim know what is encompassed in this world of the unseen? The Qur'an instructs Muslims that knowledge of the unseen rests with Allah only:

> **Say: None in the heavens and the earth knows the unseen except Allah, nor can they perceive when they shall be resurrected.**
> **[27:65]**

This verse shows that knowledge of the future is also part of the unseen, and that in Islamic belief mankind can only know about the unseen to the extent that the Prophet Muhammad ﷺ informed his followers of what Allah had revealed to him about it. Central to these teachings is knowing about three types of creatures that exist in the world of the unseen that are called Angels, *Jinns*, and Devils. These unseen creatures play explicit roles in the Muslim's pattern of understanding life and consciousness. The angels are described by the Prophet ﷺ as being made from light[317], having existed before mankind[318], and that they submit to Allah's command perfectly without having the will or choice to be disobedient to Him.[319] The principal role of the angels is to keep a record of the deeds of every individual human. It is part of Islamic

---

[316] See غيب in the Arabic-English Lexicon of Edward William Lane
http://arabiclexicon.hawramani.com/غي/#c94423
[317] Riyād us-Sālihīn Book 19 Hadith 39 https://sunnah.com/riyadussaliheen/19/39
[318] Qur'an 2:30 https://quran.com/2/30
[319] Qur'an 66:6 https://quran.com/66/6

belief that every human being has two angels that follow them at all times[320], one on their left side and one on their right side.[321] The angel on the left side records all of the person's bad deeds and the angel on the right side records all of the person's good deeds. It is taught that on the Day of Judgement the human being will stand before Allah and the records of their deeds will be placed against one another on a double-pan balance scale. If the good deeds outweigh the bad deeds they will be granted into paradise, with the Islamic testification of faith (the 1st pillar) being the heaviest of all deeds.[322]

So the Day of Judgement is conceptualized in the mind of the Muslim in a literal and concrete sense, and Islamic knowledge of the angels serves as a constant reminder to the Muslim about their accountability to God on the Day of Judgement. More on how the Day of Judgement relates to a Muslim's psychological schema will be elaborated upon in its own section below.

While the angels are made of light the Qur'an states that the *jinn* are made of a smokeless fire.[323] The angels of the unseen world and the animals of the visible world are creatures who submit to Allah wholly[324] and are unendowed with the choice or will to be disobedient to Him. On the other hand, the *jinn* of the unseen world and mankind in the visible world are the only creatures who are given the choice and will to either obey or disobey Allah's order and command.[325] The *jinns* who disobey are called devils[326], in Arabic it is *shaytān* or the plural *shayatīn*, etymologically the same word as "satan" in English. The evil *jinn* are also referred to in the Qur'an by the name *Iblīs*. The Qur'an teaches that when Allah created Adam عليه السلام, the first human, He ordered the angels to prostrate to Adam and they did. However, *Iblīs*, who was a *jinn*[327], would not prostrate due to arrogance[328], believing he was better than Adam since he was made of fire and Adam was made of clay.[329] At this, *Iblīs* avowed to go about misleading mankind away from obedience to God's order and command.[330]

---

[320] Qur'an 50:18 https://quran.com/50/18
[321] See Qur'an 50:17 https://quran.com/50/17, and Qur'an 80:10-12 https://quran.com/82/10-12
[322] Jami` at-Tirmidhī Book 40 Hadith 34 https://sunnah.com/tirmidhi/40/34
[323] Qur'an 55:15 https://quran.com/55/15
[324] Qur'an 22:18 https://quran.com/22/18
[325] Qur'an 51:56-60 https://quran.com/51/56-60
[326] Qur'an 6:112 https://quran.com/6/112
[327] *Iblīs* is not considered a "fallen angel" in Islam like some Christian theologies considers the devil to be. He is a separate creature from the angels.
[328] Qur'an 2:34 https://quran.com/2/34
[329] Qur'an 7:12 https://quran.com/7/12
[330] Qur'an 14:22 https://quran.com/14/22

So the devil, or satan, in Islam is not conceptualized as being a demon with horns who rules over the hellfire carrying a pitchfork. Rather satan is conceptualized as having an ever-growing and ever-evolving progeny[331] who work to trick mankind into seeing sinful deeds as alluring.[332] Specifically, the primary way that the *shayatīn* do this is by whispering[333] into the hearts of mankind. Thus, it is extraordinarily common for Muslims to think of one's inner monologue, when it pushes an individual towards following impulsive temptation that goes against religious teachings, as coming from *shaytān*. This is certainly conceptualized as the want to give into temptations of major deviance, but more commonly is spoken of amongst people in terms of a prompting towards smaller initial steps to vice and disobedience. Just the day before I wrote these pages I was discussing with one of my students about her older brother, who was also in one of my classes, and the struggles he had with getting up in the morning to arrive at school on time and how this was affecting his attendance. I asked her if she ever tries to wake him up in order to help him and she casually replied, "I do mister but the *shaytān* gets him every time."

So with Muslim students I have that fall into common youthful vices, such as lying or petty theft, I talk to them in a secular fashion that aims to correlate with this religious schema of temptation and trickery on the part of *shaytan* through whispering. I will tell the student that the vice is a "wicked trap" that tries to trick people, and I will relate it back to self-discipline and delayed gratification. I will say something to the student along the lines of the following:

> *"Ya know _____, lying is a wicked trap in life that plays tricks on people. Do you know why?"*
>
> *"Why?"*
>
> *"Because it makes you think you are going to get something for it right away, like maybe it'll get you out of trouble, but in the long run it traps you because it ruins your trust with people. So when your mind starts telling you that lying is going to be a good idea you need to pause yourself and pause whatever you are thinking...You need to take control of your own*

---

331 Qur'an 2:30 https://quran.com/18/50
332 Qur'an 35:6 https://quran.com/35/6
333 Qur'an 20:120 https://quran.com/20/120, 41:36 https://quran.com/41/36, and 114:5 https://quran.com/114/5

mind and develop inside your mind the strength to trust in telling the truth."[334]

When I do this talk I consider it a small form of culturally-relevant cognitive behavioral therapy (CBT). Naming of the short-term reward being tempted into and the negative consequence here can vary depending on the circumstances. For students who have developed the habit of lying perpetually it might be better to say that lying causes one to have to create whole webs of lies and then spend their life stressing about maintaining their lies while in constant worry of being found out. Sometimes it is appropriate to the discussion to point out to the student that getting away with a lie is an even bigger trap because it can cause the one who gets away with it to take even bigger risks and fool themselves into thinking that they can get away with doing wrong things.

Lying is not abnormal behavior for children and pre-adolescents but is associated with behavior problems if it is not nurtured out of them by later ages in high school (Evans & Lee, 2011). Effectively prompting children out of the behavior from young ages is healthy for advanced maturation.

Specifically about lying, the Prophetﷺ said:

> **Lying is never good...lying leads to immorality and immorality leads to Hell.[335]**

So I will say to my students whenever I get the chance, *"Lying is never good, and it always leads to something worse,"* and I will say it like I know it for a fact.

The Day of Judgement - Life is a Test

The next two items listed in the hadith on the tenets of belief are belief in Allah's Books (revelations) and Prophets. This aspect of Islamic belief was gone over in the discussion on the first pillar with the relevant implications for teaching. So I will go ahead here to the fifth tenet, belief in the The Last Day:

---

[334] Sometimes before giving this talk, when I know a student is lying, I will start by asking the student, *"Are you a truthful person?"*, they will almost always say *"yes"* without thinking about it. Then I tell them that it is wonderful that they think of themselves that way and that they value truth. And I will tell them that the true test of honesty is whether or not you can tell the truth even when it might hurt yourself.

335 Sunan ibn Majah Book 1 Hadith 48 https://sunnah.com/urn/1250460

To believe in Allah (and)...
- ***His Angels...***
- ***His Books***
- ***His Prophets***
- ***<u>The Last Day</u>***

The Day of Judgement has been mentioned already, and is of course constantly reminded of in the Qur'an. Much of Islamic practice and the five pillars is meant to serve as literal reminders of the Day of Judgement and one's accountability to God on that Day. Educators should understand about the Day of Judgement and its place in the schema of a Muslim's mind is the potential to draw upon and reinforce the explicit teachings in the Qur'an that life is a test of conduct. The Qur'an says:

> **He it is who created Death and Life so that He may <u>test which of you is best in conduct</u>, and He is the Exalted in Might, Oft-Forgiving.**
> **[67:2]**

And...

> **And most certainly We will test all of you so that we can distinguish which of you strive hardest and are patient in adversity; for we shall put to a test all your affairs.**
> **[47:31]**

The well-known child psychology book *Yardsticks* by Chip Wood gives summarized developmental indicators of children ages 4-14. In it Wood cites as an indicator for 13-year-olds that they can "think globally but not act locally". This means young people at this age can have a sense of larger issues related to idealistic principles, but they struggle to translate them into their own daily interactions and habits (<u>Wood, 2007, p. 153</u>). Wood attributed this to thirteen-year olds-but as he and other developmental psychologists acknowledge, these developmental indicators exist on a continuum for young people and the reality is that building this connection between the personal ideals one holds and one's daily action is something all young people, and even young adults, are working on and benefit from when this connection is made explicit for them by older people in positions of authority and influence over them.

Educators have a key role in imparting cognitive strategies upon young people that will help nurture these habits at a quicker pace. Being told that "life is a test" is something that is likely to resonate with Muslim students. It is important that children have this reiterated to them over small matters pertaining to manners, kindness, and treatment of others, and not just when faced with challenges that are more daunting and seemingly fraught with bigger life implications. This is especially true for children who have frequent behavior problems in school due to a lack of impulse and emotional control. Students often need help with being given a framework in their minds for understanding their own emotional processes. They are frequently burdened with the habit of compulsively acting out on negative emotions in ways that are either vocal or physical. They operate from the brainstem as opposed to the prefrontal context whenever something upsetting or distressing takes place, impacting their ability to make productive and positive decisions. Understanding these floods of emotion as a test of one's conduct is a productive framework that can encourage growth and maturity, and for Muslim students it would resonate with and support teachings in their cultural background.

For very problematic students it may not be a framework that would be adopted and change their behavior in the immediate term, but it is frequently a problem in school settings that educators become overly concerned about changing behavior in the immediate term only. Thereby they implement strategies to coerce student behavior quickly, at the sacrifice of nurturing more beneficial long term life lessons. This can be understood as focusing on coercing students through short term external motivation as opposed to focusing on inculcating long term intrinsic motivation. An example would be putting a student on some sort of reward system where they receive a material prize in exchange for desired behavior as opposed to teaching for cognitive realignment in a matter that connects their thinking process to larger life lessons. Positive Behavior Intervention Supports (PBIS) can often encourage educators to only rely on external-motivation strategies. While these strategies might have some use as placeholders in the near term, teachers and educators need to see the larger picture with students and stop conditioning them only to be reflexive to external stimuli and reward. Humans might share some biological wiring similar to animals that caused Pavlov's dog to salivate at the sound of a bell (Pavlov & Anrep, 1927), but this does not mean it is respectful to our students for them to be conditioned as if they were dogs.

Furthermore, the entirety of American consumer culture inundates young people with subliminal Pavlovian conditioning in order to churn them out as habitual consumers by the time they reach adulthood. This has caused a physical and mental health crisis in American society. Pavlovian conditioning done by the food industry has caused an overeating epidemic (Bongers et al, 2015; Boswell & Kober, 2016). Its use by tech companies is undoubtedly causing addiction to smartphones and social media whose long-term effects are as of yet not fully known but highly anticipated to be negative with the current generation of young people who will without a doubt bear the brunt of its detriments. Instead of allowing itself to get caught up in these business trends and methods of influencing and controlling people's behaviors, public education should be a place where teachers and mentors carry a nobler purpose about themselves by pushing back on some of these destructive societal trends. To be clear, I am not advocating that schools should go out and blow up their PBIS programs, as I do not advocate drastic action and believe the best work is done in incremental steps. At the same time, we need to be balanced and recognize when some educational trends have perhaps gone too far. When schools threw out corporal discipline and increasingly-so, guilt, as a tool of reprimanding and coercing student behavior, operant conditioning provided tools to still manage behavior in a way that felt less abusive. Certainly there have been numerous positives in this trend. However, as responsible and reflective educators we need to ask ourselves whether or not we are experiencing the pendulum of some trends swinging too far and to an extreme end. I am concerned that an over-reliance on PBIS and operant conditioning in the schools has replaced and deafened educators to the importance of sound moral teaching that helps people mentally navigate basic trials of life. Focusing on building cognitive realignment in students that delivers a sound universal moral message and builds the mental skills of self-discipline instead of depending upon rewards, even if it is done at the sacrifice of near-term alteration in the student's behavior, is a small step that can be taken.

There is often a sad factor at play in some situations where "problem" students are only seen as problems, and their teachers' sole focus with them becomes coercing their behavior in the short term to facilitate the already implemented classroom structure; as opposed to having a plan and practicing strategies where proper life lessons are reinforced to encourage and inculcate long-term mental outlooks that nurture the intrinsic motivation and self discipline the child really needs. Unfortunately, this is more likely to happen when there is a cultural or racial gap between the student and teacher because the teacher has a lack of understanding of the student's cultural background and the latent mental habits for the student to acquire from those values and develop in their life. In the case of Muslim students, this is where learning about Islam itself has high value, because there is no reason those values cannot become known and apparent to anyone. I highly encourage teachers and educators to make the idea of nurturing long-term life lessons, especially ones related to self-discipline and intrinsic motivation for learning, central to your goals and purposes with students. Do these ideas come up frequently in your staff meetings? Reflect on that question. Especially in the "data-driven decision making" culture of education that we now live in and that has been forced on the entirety of America's education world from the top town; local considerations and the deeper needs of children's minds and souls are often the expense that is paid.

Before talking about the sixth and final tenet of belief in Islam, I wish to go through two more Islamic teachings that neither fall categorically under the five pillars or tenets of belief but that I have still found pressing for educators to know about related to the inquiries that are brought to me.

Motherhood and attitudes towards females

In a famous hadith the Prophet ﷺ said:

> **Your entrance to paradise lies beneath the feet of your mother.[336]**

I am frequently asked about male student attitudes towards female staff. Gender roles in Islam and attitudes towards females are one of the most asked-about topics from my trainings' intake forms. Some of the educational research case studies have found that female teachers can at times have the complaint and perception that Muslim boys do not respect female teachers as authority figures. The female teacher in turn can interpret male student misbehavior as being cultural or religious in origin.[337]

There is a large discussion that can be had about this, but the discussion must include consideration of what follows. Firstly, in all my discussions about this topic with adult Muslim males who have grown up in the West, dismay is always expressed that this viewpoint exists. They frequently point out the disposition that Islam takes towards motherhood especially, and how it is not uncommon at all in Muslim families that children grow up seeing the mother as the ultimate authority figure, and the one whose pleasure and approval must be sought above all else by the children. There is an explicit connection made in Islam towards pleasing the mother and parents as being akin to pleasing God because one's parents are chosen by God alone. The Prophet ﷺ said:

> **The Lord's pleasure is in the parent's pleasure, and the Lord's anger is in the parent's anger.[338]**

Secondly, teachers have to reflect upon themselves and consider the extent to which their interpretation of male misbehavior may be influenced by biases in their own disposition. This

---

[336] Sunan an-Nasā'i Book 25, Hadith 20 http://sunnah.com/nasai/25/20

[337] Bigelow (2008) notes that misbehavior in boys is a common stereotype amongst teachers of Somali male youth. A theme that correlates to Merry's (2005) findings of Moroccan boys in Flemish schools, Sarroub's (2005) findings of Yemeni boys in Michigan, and Iqbal's (2017) findings of Pakistani boys in the UK; in all of which the study subjects were Muslim. Farid & McMahan (2004) also found that behavior problems, particularly related to boys, were common complaints amongst teachers of Somali youth in Minnesota.

[338] Jami` at-Tirmidhī Book 27 Hadith 3 https://sunnah.com/tirmidhi/27/3

could be a latent bias that assumes Muslim, colored, or Eastern cultures are inherently disrespectful to women. This is a stereotype that the Western world has reinforced and propagated in its literary, academic, and media traditions for centuries[339], to such an extent that it can seep into people's subconscious without it being realized that it is indeed a personal bias.

Bias can take another form in that it is commonly an ethnocentric aspect of Western women (and people) that they are simply more likely to view the world and interactions through a *gendered* lens than are Muslims. I once shared my findings from my trainings' intake forms with Cawo Abdi, a Muslim female sociologist with the University of Minnesota, and showed her that questions about gender roles were one of the most enquired-about matters from my trainings' participants. She laughed and said, "that is so Western!" meaning that it is something typical of the West to view everything through a gendered lens. We have to understand that in the West a result of our own learning of different modes of critical theory in the education system is that we become prompted into taking on dualistic views of the world, where we are more likely to see varying identity markers, gender in this case, as in competition with one another, as opposed to being designed to work together in harmony; which is how the Eastenr world, and certainly the Muslim world to the extent it is informed by Islam, sees its own perspective on gender. Thus, in the West people go about interpreting their interactions with others through such lenses. So it is often the case that the role and dynamics of gender in these situations that are complained about are explicit within the female teacher's mind, but not the mind of the young Muslim male child. My investigations with both Muslim students and young adult Muslims who have grown up in the West confirms to me that gender bias against school staff is practically never an explicit consideration in the minds of these young people. It is extraordinarily unlikely to be the case that the student is thinking "I don't need to respect her because she is a woman[340]" but what is more likely is the teacher is thinking "he doesn't respect me because I'm a woman."

This is not to say that there are zero factors at play in situations where friction arises between female staff and Muslim male students. But these factors need to be considered in a proper and in-depth context. One thing that might be at play is that for some Muslim boys they are simply not used to being around white females, or perhaps just females at all who are not their family

---

[339] And I mean this to the extent that it is almost wired into Western society's collective consciousness about the Eastern World, whether or not individuals may realize it or not. Refer to the book *Orientalism* by Edward Said to understand this further, as well as the documentary *Reel Bad Arabs* based on the book of the same title by Jack Shaeen. These sources will also teach educators about critical lenses through which literature, media, and academic topics can be viewed that will have resonance with Muslim students.

[340] And nowadays if a student did think this it is altogether likely to be an attitude coming from the influence of misogynistic forces within the Western world itself; of which there is no sparsity on the internet and social media (Mantilla, 2015; Ging & Siapera, 2018; Thompson, 2018; Lee, 2019).

members. If they spend most of their time outside of school in home-cultural settings this is likely to be the case. In mosques the genders are separated and congregate and socialize in separate places (though prepubescent children can be conduits between the male and female sections in mosques). Likewise, at social gatherings in homes the males and females will socialize in separate rooms and spaces, and their socializing will be intra-gender and rarely inter-gender. What results from this is some Muslim boys come to school and they are simply not used to being around women, perhaps even more so non-Muslim white women. There is a phenomenon that takes place in the world where people are more dismissive of people from a cultural or racial outgroup to their own in social settings. Just ask black people about their experiences in frequenting white social spaces, and many women understand this themselves with their experiences navigating male dominated spaces. The elderly experience this in many spheres of Western society as well. I already discussed the complications of interpreting emotions from others of a racial outgroup in chapter two, this is another factor that plays into these situations.

When there is concern about the relationship dynamics within these types of situations there may be times when female teachers have to make extra effort to build relationships with some of their Muslim male students, and they must avoid common pitfalls in trying to manage these students in a tense environment. Muslim males are raised to have the highest regard and respect for their mothers, anyone who has seen a young Muslim male have his mother insulted to his face knows this. I have had many trainees who have observed their male Muslim students being responsive to strict reprimands from their mothers. Oftentimes this is misunderstood by the teacher to be taken as a cue that it would make sense for her to use strict admonishment with the same student in the classroom under the theory that they would be responsive to the same mode of communication that they receive at home. While such theorization has some *minimal* basis in educational psychology and research (see Howard, 2002, as an example[341]), it greatly misses the mark under these circumstances.

What is missed is that the responsiveness of those students to their mothers comes after having received a firmly established foundation of love, trust, and affection; something the student does not have with their public school teachers. Strictness in tone and mannerism is rarely advisable when the student teacher relationship is cross-cultural, and in my opinion even in most cases that are intracultural. The teacher's ability to maintain calmness with troubled students even when tested is one of the biggest keys to earning relationships with such students; this is something that has been explicitly identified to me by Muslim students who exhibited behavior problems in school.

Teachers who are concerned about these dynamics need to reflect on how they can build a connection and relationship with these students very early on in the school year. Too often teachers are nervous about building these relationships, especially when they have had previous bad experiences with similar students of the same background. If this nervousness causes teachers to shy away from proactive action steps in the beginning of the year, a looming problem is being inflated and kicked down the road instead of being prevented in the first place. If a teacher anticipates early on that they may have a student who they would typically struggle to build a relationship with, that needs to be *the first* student with which the teacher arranges to have some one-on-one time. This needs to be done in a proactive manner that is *not* done under the context of the student being in trouble or having done anything wrong. Too often these students do not have one-on-one time with their teachers until they have done

---

[341] Tyrone Howard, with UCLA, observed and conducted study groups with African American students, and his findings have been cited in educational research focused on cultural responsiveness to African American students. He found that students interpreted stern and strict modes of interaction from teachers as wanting them to put their best effort forth, with several of the students citing that the stern tone their teacher put out resembled family members. I have seen it where research and findings like Howard's, among others, are often referred to by teachers as justification for "mimicking" home modes of interaction, or more simply justifying stern and strict tones with students when it is speculated that their families use strict tones as well. The pitfall with this type of reasoning is that people usually do not know the wider context of the research they are referring to, and the theorized conclusions they are using to justify their practice is maybe not something they have not looked into in depth themselves, but is rather something they have only been told or picked up from colleagues or in some training along the line. While Howard did find that African American students said that strict and stern tones were reminiscent of their family members and they were "quite comfortable" with these interactions, this took place in a wider context of a teacher who built a community atmosphere in the classroom based on respect, which made the classroom "feel like home" in general, not exclusively by using strictness in reprimanding. Perhaps more importantly, this was all observed in a context where the students and teacher were *racially the same*. When a teacher is unfamiliar with the home lives and culture of the student and is an outgroup member from the student these dynamics change entirely.

something wrong, making it so a context gets set up early on for the student to associate their one-on-one relationship with the teacher alongside the consternation of being in trouble. This consternation can in turn manifest in outright anger or hostility in young children who are still developing impulse control and emotional regulation, and may have compounding factors working against this development as has been discussed.

Oftentimes it is found with boys who experience behavior problems year to year that even outside of the context where they have done nothing wrong they will come into any one-on-one conversation with a teacher having their defense mechanisms built up very high and being automatically under the assumption that they are in trouble. So mitigating these defense mechanisms needs to be the first consideration for building a connection in a conversation. Some students with consistent behavioral problems may have issues with want of power in the classroom, and the misbehavior becomes a way of asserting it. Another underlying factor at play is typically academic insecurity within the student about their own ability to perform in the class, and misbehavior becomes a way to cover up their own deficits.

Treating these underlying psychological factors is paramount for teachers to consider. As with most things, I advise you to start small. A common pitfall I see when teachers recognize that they have a student with a power complex, in order to treat it they go about asserting something too formal onto the student like giving them a class job. It has to be considered that while giving them more responsibility might also be giving them a sense of power and authority, if the class job involves too much responsibility and they lack the job's necessary soft skills, or the motivation within a classroom where they are struggling to do the job effectively and as directed, it could be that they are being set up for failure and the strategy is at risk of backfiring.

What I recommend frequently as an initial first step to empower the student is acknowledging explicitly with them the power and influence that their behavior has in the classroom. Especially with students whose misbehavior feeds into garnering social attraction from their peers. It can be said to the students that they are individuals with strong personalities, and that this is a good thing because people with strong personalities often have the ability to influence and attract the attention of others. So it can be said and acknowledged explicitly to the students that, "as the teacher I know I want you to be on my side with most things and I want you to be engaged in learning because I know that the way you are in the classroom has a powerful influence over the way other kids are in the classroom, do you know what I mean?" I have even told some students that I probably need them more than they need me. This can be especially appreciated when students have the "why does this matter?" complex towards the learning.

It can further be acknowledged that, "I know following along in class is not always easy because school can be very boring sometimes" because this acknowledges the typical difficulty that the student has with exhibiting on task behavior, as they see it. They think it is boring. It is also beneficial, I find, to set up the expectation with students from the beginning of the year that the learning in school *will be boring* more often than not, and this is a challenge that we all need to overcome. This brings the lessons that we are inculcating on students back to the "life is a test" theme, and this is better for the student in the long run as opposed to obsessing too much over whether or not the learning is actually fun. While there is no problem in wanting to do fun learning activities in the classroom to engage students, it can be mistaken to set up the expectation of students that the learning should always be fun, or that fun learning is something they have a right to. Plus, there is usually an incentive for the misbehaved kids who have high social influence to cast the teacher's attempt at fun learning as being uncool in order to leverage the situation to assert their power complex and increase their own social status among peers. When a teacher overemphasizes to themselves that the learning should be made fun, it can also rob students of the opportunity to learn important life lessons and advance their maturation. At the end of the day, school is never going to win against what kids consider fun. It is not a game we should try to play. We should want kids to enjoy school because they have developed an appreciation for the fruit of learning.

After acknowledging with the difficult student that the learning may be boring it can simply be said, "I hope we can work together on it." This sets up a framework of understanding between the teacher and student, and the reality is that they will have to work on it for the year, but when the proper framework of understanding is put in place on an individual level and the connection is made, it enables that work to be done without the tension of frustration towards one another. Maintenance of this always goes back to the teacher having a disposition of calmness. If a teacher cannot talk to a student in a calm voice that is released of tension in their face and body, then the words they say will have no use anyway because the student will simply read their own meanings into them.

Of course there is more that would need to be said than this in any given situation with a struggling student. The important thing is to treat the underlying psychological causes, which has everything to do with our interpersonal approach to students, the regularity with which we reflect on it, our willingness to try something different, and our willingness to learn about the latent values that students have in their background that can be drawn upon.

Islam exorbitantly honors the role of the mother in tending to the upbringing and education of the child. The Prophet Muhammad ﷺ said:

Each of you is a shepherd and is responsible for his flock. The ruler who is in charge of people is a shepherd and is responsible for them. The man is the shepherd of his household and is responsible for them. The woman is the shepherd of her husband's house and child and is responsible for them. Each of you is a shepherd and each is responsible for his flock.[342]

This teaching frequently manifests in Muslim cultures as women taking on a greater role in overseeing the education of the children, especially at younger ages. However, it does not mean that men check out of supervising a child's education altogether because education in general is highly valued in Islam.[343] But oftentimes women will be more likely to take on the lead role in managing the child's education because of the explicit honor that Islam gives her toward this, especially at younger ages. This can be somewhat of a reason why teachers might see that mothers are way more involved in communication with the school and attending parent-teacher conferences. I have been asked by teachers about this, but at the same time I am not so sure that non-Muslim fathers are any more or less likely to be involved in their kids education.

Kindness towards women is a foundational principle in Islam.[344] Mistreatment of women is pandemic to all societies and certainly Muslim societies and communities are not immune to this. However, if the West wants to analyze and make judgements about these issues it needs to consider whether or not the religion is actually a remedy to mistreatment of women where it occurs in the Muslim world, as opposed to a cause of it. Traditional analysis from the West has reflexively assumed that Islam itself is responsible for mistreatment of women. This is not the case, and abhorrent affairs such as honor killings[345], denying education[346], and domestic abuse[347] are all in direct contradiction to Islamic teachings. This is not to say that the treatment of women in the Muslim world is not a legitimate area for discussion and analysis in the classroom. But it should also be considered how the West's historical stereotyping of the Muslim world effects the lens through which American society sees Muslim men and women, as

---

[342]Al-'Ādab al-Mufrad Book 10 Hadith 1 https://sunnah.com/adab/10/1

[343] Qur'an 39:9 https://quran.com/39/9, Sunan ibn Mājah Book 34 Hadith 17 https://sunnah.com/ibnmajah/34/17, Sunan ibn Mājah Book 1 Hadith 229 https://sunnah.com/urn/1252230, Sunan ibn Mājah Book 1 Hadith 246 https://sunnah.com/urn/1252390 Jami` at-Tirmidhī Book 41 Hadith 3 htt ps://sunnah.com/tirmidhi/41/3

[344] Sahīh al-Bukhārī Book 60 Hadith 6 https://sunnah.com/bukhari/60/6, Sunan ibn Mājah Book 9 Hadith 1924 https://sunnah.com/urn/1261680

[345] Qur'an 17:31 https://quran.com/17/31, Qur'an 81:7-9 https://quran.com/81/7-9, Al-Ādab al-Mufrad Book 4 Hadith 8 http://sunnah.com/adab/4/8

[346] Sahīh Muslim Book 4 Hadith 150 https://sunnah.com/muslim/4/150

[347] Sunan ibn Mājah Book 9 Hadith 1924 https://sunnah.com/urn/1261680

well as how it biases the selection of news stories that show up in the media. There are resources in chapter six that can be used for such discussions. More issues pertaining to women and gender roles in Islam are discussed in chapter four as well.

Shyness

In another famous hadith the Prophet 🕌 said:

Shyness is a part of faith.[348]

While it is the case that virtually all teachers have some students who they wish were more shy, we can see by this hadith that with Muslim students there is nothing wrong if the teacher sees something good in reinforcing shyness as a value, this might be especially beneficial with middle schoolers. But some teachers frequently find that there are some Muslim students who seem to them as being extraordinarily shy, perhaps more frequently female students who are newer to the country.

A whole parlay of factors can contribute to a student being shy, but it is important to understand the place that shyness has as a positive value in Islam and Muslim cultures. This hadith applies to both males and females, and the Prophet's 🕌 companions described him as having been shy[349] in all circumstances except when it came to distinguishing the truth from falsehood.[350]

Many times Muslim students who are shy do well in school and are very responsible. It is common that what the parents of these students hear at conferences is that their child is very responsible, polite, and respectful, but the teacher just wished they would talk more, share more, or speak more in front of the class. In this situation the non-Muslim teacher often fails to understand that a strong cultural clash could very much be at play. The reality is that in most Muslim cultures shyness is a value that is positively reinforced. The student and family could very well have explicit religious reasons for wanting to be shy. Meanwhile, in contrast to these values, the education curriculum itself often gives an explicit impetus to discourage shyness under certain circumstances for students. Especially with requirements that students do public speaking, and thus the teacher is put in a conundrum with shy students.

Firstly, this is another situation where more explicit conversations need to happen with parents and families. Families will understand the intricacies of these situations and conflicting values,

---

[348] Sunan ibn Mājah Book 37 Hadith 4324 https://sunnah.com/urn/1292860
[349] Sahīh al-Bukhārī Book 78, Hadith 146 https://sunnah.com/bukhari/78/146
[350] Sunan Ibn Majah Book 9 Hadith 1999 https://sunnah.com/urn/1262430

and they will have differing viewpoints and goals for their children on it. Parents will certainly understand the importance of children learning presentation and public speaking skills in school and its necessity as a matter of college preparation. Yet, there will still be families who are explicit with their children in wanting them to be shy, or who consider an attitude and self-presentation of quietude to be appropriately respectful and dignifying. I have known of a situation where a student's mother was told in conferences by a teacher about how much the teacher enjoyed having her daughter in class because she was so smiley, outgoing, goofy, and made everyone in the class laugh. The teacher of course meant all of this in a positive way, but the student was later reprimanded by her mother for being so outgoing and being an impious "show off". I do not believe this story represents the majority of Muslim parents in the West insofar as reprimanding the child over this. However, it shows the importance of honestly knowing where parents stand in what they want for their children. Showing off is highly discouraged in Islam and associated with oppression. The Prophet ﷺ said:

Allah has revealed to me that you must be humble, so that no one oppresses another and boasts over another.[351]

So should shy Muslim students be exempted from presentational and public speaking assignments? No, I do not believe so. After all, it is part of the education curriculum. However, it does mean that extra considerations need to be made as far as building the motivation in students to take this specific type of risk, as well as to how the presentational assignments are expected to be done.

As far as motivation is concerned, I suggest drawing on the religious teachings in a secular fashion. So if the Prophet Muhammad ﷺ was shy except for when it came to distinguishing truth from falsehood, It can be discussed with the students that shyness is a valuable thing[352], but the student can also be told that most people come into situations in life where they are confronted with the need to stand up for the truth and when these confrontations happen even strong people can be overcome by internal nervousness. Set the understanding that the major purpose of doing presentational work in school is so the students can practice overcoming this internal nervousness within a smaller context to better prepare them for overcoming it in larger contexts that they well have to face in life and that will carry larger implications.

---

[351] Sunan Abī Dawūd Book 43 Hadith 123 https://sunnah.com/abudawud/43/123

[352] Western teachers may have to reflect to some degree on how to positively reinforce that as a value. Some secular benefits of shyness are that it maintains personal privacy, guards against vulnerability, prevents mishaps, and defends against the judgement of others.

As far as considerations for how the presentations are done, the number one principle to adhere to is that of incremental build up. It is a very bad idea to ask a shy student to go from rarely participating in class at all, to one day getting up in front of the entire class to give a presentation. Start by assigning the students to do the presentation in front of two or three classmates with whom they feel comfortable. The small group presenting can be done in such a way that perhaps all students in the classroom are participating in this type of presenting at the same time, and this draws even less attention to the shy student when they have to perform. Even within that small group structure there are different levels of incremental build up to be considered. For example, it may be best to have the student first present sitting down to two or three other students, and then to practice standing up. It can be very likely that students who come from the Muslim world have never had the experience of being in front of a mix-gendered crowd of sitting people while standing up, and thus having their body open to being looked at, even if they're wearing clothing that covers the body's shape. So just this act of standing can feel harrowing.

Of course, gender is another consideration here. Females especially may be more comfortable presenting only in front of females at first. The introduction to presenting in front of males is another thing that can be built up incrementally, but refusal to present in front of males as a religious matter is something that schools and teachers should be willing to accept as an accommodation of religious practice. Especially when families are on board with it. Teachers need to take all of these matters into consideration and work together and collaborate to provide appropriate settings. In my school a fellow Language Arts teacher was doing a poetry reading competition with his students that was focused on mannerisms and expressiveness. This is something that most Muslim cultures have in their oral and social traditions, but not as something that is done in front of the opposite gender, and the students expressed to him that they would feel more comfortable doing the poetry readings only in front of the same gender. The female students especially pressed on this. So he arranged with another teacher who had prep during that period to have the boys go to another room one day and work on an independent assignment while the girls did their presentations, and the next day the boys and girls switched spots. This accommodation was simple, effective, and responsive to genuine cultural concerns. Some of the expectations Islam sets up for inter-gender relations are discussed more in chapter four.

The Divine Decree and Critical Thinking

The sixth and final tenet of belief is in the Divine Decree or predestination:

> **To believe in Allah (and)...**
> - **His Angels...**

- ***His Books***
- ***His Prophets***
- ***The Last Day***
- <u>***The Divine Decree***</u>

The Arabic word for this is *qadar*. Predestination was also covered in our discussion on the first pillar, but since it is so central to everything that a Muslim's world outlook is based upon I will elaborate on it a little more here and use it to introduce a discussion on the participation of Muslim students in "critical thinking" in our schools, another topic I get asked about.

It is part of Islamic belief that everything comes from Allah's decree, both good and evil. Even the *shaytān* and his progeny are from Allah's creation. But as stated before, a disposition of fatalism and despair is not allowed in Islam. So belief in Islamic monotheism is to walk on a fine line of taking comfort in knowing that nothing happens that is not decreed by Allah, who is the Most Merciful, but also knowing that Allah has ordered man against complacency and has not absolved him from responsibility for the choices and actions that he makes within the limited sphere of choice and influence that Allah has granted him. That each human will face ultimate and absolute accountability for each of their choices is central to life's purpose. So it is out of God's Mercy that He sent Prophets and Messengers to mankind that they can be guided to upright conduct and know that their life is a test of their beliefs and actions.

For the Muslim, because they have been granted the insights and guidance of the Qur'an and the Sunnah, it is considered frivolous to partake in speculation regarding the how and why of what cannot be seen or known by the human being. Likewise it is pointless to conjecture over evaluations of right and wrong without being informed by the criteria of Allah's revelation; doing so is considered among the categories of ill-speech to be avoided.[353] So the Muslim is warned against dwelling on speculative questions such as "If God created man then who created God?" or "If God is so good why do bad things happen" etc.[354] To the Muslim such questions are pseudo-philosophical. The intellect already knows that the answer to speculation upon the unseen is either that what is knowable to humans about it is limited, or its answers are in the Qur'an and Sunnah. Therefore the speculation itself is a waste of the intellect which Allah has given to human beings as a tool to reflect upon His creation and revelation, and to then employ the intellect upon enacting good deeds once knowledge of the Wisdom revealed by God is ascertained.[355]

---

[353] Qur'an 23:3 https://quran.com/23/3
[354] Jami' at-Tirmidhī Book 7 Hadith 46 (Arabic) https://sunnah.com/tirmidhi/76
[355] Qur'an 3:190-198 https://quran.com/3/190-198, Qur'an 10:100-109 https://quran.com/10/100-109

So the underlying sense that a Muslim student can often have put into class conversations that might be considered philosophical, Socratic, or that "have no right or wrong answer" is that they are simply rubbish. If Plato pontificated over an alternate world of forms or René Descartes felt the only reliable knowledge was that he thinks, then all that is just conjectural speculation that is symptomatic of their own misguidance and lack of humility to follow divine revelation. To the Muslim, the musings of philosophical conversations or attempting to deduce right and wrong through probing dialectics without consideration for the criteria set out in the Qur'an and Sunnah are little more than conjecture that Allah has warned the Muslim against participating in; because all it will do is distract him or her from getting on in the test of life to worship God and perform good deeds. The Qur'an even directly instructs the Muslim to leave these types of conversations when others have them.[356]

So Islam conceptualizes learning for the Muslim as seeking knowledge[357] from those who have knowledge. Allah says in the Qur'an:

Say: Are those who know equal to those who do not know?
[39:9]

Islam conditions for an understanding where the teacher is to be the one with knowledge who bestows useful knowledge upon the pupil who seeks it. The teacher's direct transmission of knowledge to the student is the most efficient route of learning in Islam. When the student has put in the time to listen, study, and hardwire that knowledge they can then set about employing it for productive use. In Islam, truth is not arrived at through skepticism, it is arrived at by knowing evidences and reflecting upon them with an intellect that is sound and sober. This contrasts and conflicts with the methods of Socrates where truth is only arrived at through skeptical questioning, which much of what is considered "critical thinking" is ultimately based on in Western education (California, 1997).

So Muslim parents send their kids to school expecting that they will learn. That they will acquire knowledge that is proven to be productive and beneficial in science, mathematics, and history, which can then be employed for use to benefit themselves and humanity. The Prophet ﷺ told the Muslims:

---

356 Qur'an 6:70 https://quran.com/6/70
357 Sunan ibn Mājah Book 1 Hadith 229 https://sunnah.com/urn/1252230

Ask Allah for beneficial knowledge and seek <u>protection with Allah</u> from <u>knowledge that is of no benefit</u>.[358]

To me, this can play a role in what underlies the reasons why I have met many teachers who have interpreted Muslims kids as lacking the ability to think critically. It seems to them that when they prompt the class for a "critical thinking" discussion, some Muslim kids will just stay silent or only engage minimally in order to meet preset participation requirements. If they do participate it seems like they are just imitating what someone else said and are not really invested in the conversation.

This does not happen because they cannot think, it is because an Islamic world outlook produces the intuitive sense that a speculative conversation that systematically isolates itself from consideration of God's revelation and teachings is bound to misguide from the purpose and path that God has laid out for them. It will inevitably result in a waste of intellectual energy at best, or a blighted state of confusion at worst. For a Muslim to genuinely enter these conversations would mean for them to argue against the conversation's methods and foundations itself, for its lack of knowledge and reverence to God's revealed truths.[359] But for a student to assert in the public school setting that God has a revealed text whose teachings should be considered as truth would not harmonize with the environment's implicit expectations of politeness, nor the learner-readiness of other parties in the conversation.

Students are allowed to assert and advocate for the truthfulness of their religious world views in public schools.[360] But surely, it is instinctual for Muslims students in K-12 ages to know that to advocate in school that Islam holds keys to life's important truths would open up both themselves and Islam to critical examination in their own right. As young people who are still learning themselves, they are lacking in confidence and the necessary hardwired knowledge to be able to mount a full-scale defense of Islam in a Socratic discourse; and rightfully so, after all it is not like the teachers managing the environments who could help them form their arguments are aware of Islamic frames of thinking and its intellectual foundations. The preferable choice for them becomes to simply choose to just keep quiet in such discussions. After all, the Islamic worldview does not need them to advocate for it nor to defend it. If they

---

[358] Sunan ibn Mājah Book 34 Hadith 17 https://sunnah.com/ibnmajah/34/17
[359] Qur'an 31:20-21 https://quran.com/31/20-21
[360] See Section F on the Federal *Guidance on Constitutionally Protected Prayer and Religious Expression in Public Elementary and Secondary Schools*, "*Students may express their beliefs about religion in homework, artwork, and other written and oral assignments free from discrimination based on the religious perspective of their submissions. Such home and classroom work should be judged by ordinary academic standards of substance and relevance and against other legitimate pedagogical concerns identified by the school.*" https://www2.ed.gov/policy/gen/guid/religionandschools/prayer_guidance.html

were to try, it would be interpreted by others as religious proselytizing, and everyone knows that in the West people who do that are portrayed as lunatics or con artists. So advancing an Islamic worldview would be unwelcome, and besides, Islam does not give an overly strong impetus to convert others; at least, in my view, when compared to the associations that Westerners have with some factions of Evangelical Christianity (Stewart, 2012; Stetzer, 2017). Allah says in the Qur'an:

> **Say: The Truth is from your Lord, so whoever wills, let him believe; and whoever wills, let him disbelieve.**
> **[18:29]**

So teachers need to know that sometimes there is nothing wrong with just letting the Muslim kids stay quiet when the class is prompted into these "critical thinking" or speculative conversations. The reality is these conversations are not really meant for them and they often enough they feel that inside themselves, even if they cannot articulate it at their young ages. But please know that their quietude in those situations is not borne out of their own ignorance or stupidity. It is borne out of the parameters in which the conversation is taking place being unready to process the contributions that they would be most motivated to offer. Islam even teaches explicitly to just stay quiet when you feel you are incapable of defending the truth or advocating for what is right. The Prophet ﷺ said in a hadith that is well known to Muslims:

> **He amongst you who sees something evil should change it with his hand; and if he is not able to do that, then he should change it with his tongue, and if he is not able to do that, then he should detest it in his heart.**[361]

One of the most-learned companions of the Prophet ﷺ, Muadh ibn Jabal رضــي الله عـنه, said the Prophet ﷺ told him that controlling one's tongue was what held the foundation of all knowledge together.[362]

So I ask teachers who have this concern to please let these kids stay quiet and do not feel bad about it. There is clearly a deep conundrum at play for these students. If you belong to a school or district where you receive a lot of external pressure to engage your students in "critical thinking" conversations then there may be a conundrum for you as well. At the end of the day there is a high need in education for our conversations about our goals for students to enter a

---

[361] Sahih Muslim Book 1 Hadith 84 http://sunnah.com/muslim/1/84
[362] Riyad as-Salihīn Book 18 Hadith 12 https://sunnah.com/riyadussaliheen/18/12

more authentic level with a truly advanced understanding of who students and their families actually are; and for these goals to be cleared of the side agendas that are put upon school communities in the supposed name of best practice. The discussion on the learning habits of mind of our Muslim kids in the context of our modern-day education system is continued in chapter five.

Islam and Personal Subjectivity

While I find educators to almost always be energized and appreciative to learn about Islam and gain insights into their Muslims students, it is also the case that sometimes a feeling of confusion or frustration is sprouted as well. For many it is a concrete realization of just how actual the cultural clashes that take place in our schools are. Could there not be some way of making it simpler? This line of thinking can veer the Westerner toward wishing that Islam would be reinterpreted towards suiting their own comforts and preferences. If Islam seems austere to modern-day Western sensibilities and has all these restrictions and dictates that complicate what we do with Muslim students in schools, how about Muslims in the West simply reinterpret whatever it is that Islamic texts say in order to suit the relativistic ends that shape the norms of Western culture?

After all, the Western world had the Protestant Reformation, the Renaissance, the Enlightenment, and even the rigid and authoritarian Catholic Church buckled down and bent to the wants of the current-day by changing its rules with the second Vatican Council. Right? Should not Muslims just step up to the plate and reinterpret Islamic texts to fully assimilate into Western life like Jewish and Catholic immigrants have done before them?

There are two answers to this. The first and most obvious is that there is really nothing about being Muslim and living in the West that makes practicing Islam impossible. Muslims and non-Muslims just need to accept each other's differences, but they also need to *know* each other's differences. For the non-Muslims this means being informed while also simply accepting at times that boundaries exist that are better left un-prodded and pushed. For the Muslims this means being well-mannered and sophisticated[363] in how we inform others about ourselves while accepting that at times one might just have to risk and accept appearing strange.[364] For the most part there is nothing that stands in the way of this happening. You, the reader, are doing your part in this by simply reading a book like this, and Muslims ought to be grateful to people who make such efforts.

---

[363] Qur'an 16:125 https://quran.com/16/125
[364] Sahīh al-Bukhārī Book 81 Hadith 5 https://sunnah.com/bukhari/81/5

The second answer is that Islamic texts themselves have already tended to guarding against people changing them or reinterpreting their meanings to suit the subjective ends of catering to personal desires[365] at the cost of sacrificing what is clear and well known from the texts in the Islamic tradition that goes back to the earliest generations of Muslims. The Prophet ﷺ said:

> **Whoever innovates something in this matter of ours (i.e. Islam)**
> **that is not part of it, will have it rejected.[366]**

This means in the first instance that Allah will reject it on the Day of Judgement. But it is also a direction to the Muslims themselves to reject reinterpretations of Islam that clearly contradict its established teachings. The word that is translated as innovation here is *bidah* in Arabic. *Bidah*[367] means devising a new idea, meaning, or concept into Islam that contradicts its clearly established teachings. Doing this is especially severe when it comes to altering the Islamic understanding of God, bringing in new acts of worship that did not come from the teachings of the Prophet ﷺ, or altering the existing ones with no precedent in the early generations of Muslims. *Bidah* does not mean earthly innovations in technology or material human advancement, rather this type of innovation is welcome by Islam so long as it is intended to serve a noble purpose.[368]

The Prophet ﷺ warned sternly against *bidah*. He said:

> **The evilest of affairs are newly invented matters (in religion);**
> **every newly-invented matter is a bidah and every bidah is**
> **misguidance, and every misguidance is in the Hellfire.[369]**

When Muslims congregate on Fridays, which will be discussed more in chapter four, it is part of the requisite liturgy of that congregation for the leader to recite this hadith at the beginning of the gathering. So this warning is something that every Muslim is reminded about on every Friday, and has been since the time of the Prophet ﷺ.

---

[365] Qur'an 18:28 https://quran.com/18/28

[366] Sunan ibn Mājah Vol. 1 Book 1 Hadith 14 https://sunnah.com/urn/1250140

[367] See بدع in the Arabic-English Lexicon of Edward William Lane http://arabiclexicon.hawramani.com//بدع/#90f9bc

[368] Sahih Muslim Book 12 Hadith 88 http://sunnah.com/muslim/12/88

[369] Sunan an-Nasā'i Book 19 Hadith 23 https://sunnah.com/nasai/19/23

So Islam and its texts have their own internal self preservation mechanisms that fix themselves into the Muslim's psychology of faith. Learning and understating Islam is of course a lifelong journey for a Muslim. But reinterpreting it, or casting meanings into it that contradict what is apparent about it rarely gains a lasting foothold in this journey because doing so would amount to regarding the foundation of the religion's entire intellectual schema as meaningless.

Sure, there have been figures in history who have tried to innovate into Islam and to reform it to suit individual preferences and fancies. But advocates of such approaches are always met with round rejection by the Muslim masses. In the polemical circles of Muslim communities their reasonings fail to subdue the weight of evidence against them in Islamic texts that are well-known and easily made apparent to people. This is why traditional understandings always prevail over the arc of history in the Muslim world. To such an extent that nearly 1400 years after the death of the Prophet Muhammad ﷺ there is still high rates of religiosity and preference for literalist hermeneutics of Islamic texts in the Muslim world (Pew Research, 2012).

So public school educators of Muslim students find themselves at the forefront of a very real cultural clash. It is not a clash that should be made out to be a bigger problem than it really is, the clashes are mostly a collection of smaller problems and misunderstandings. But in many ways it is a challenge to the educators when lip-service is paid to the field's idealized conceptualizations of multiculturalism and respect for the values of home and family.
This will bring us to the technicalities of following Islam and what it means as far as action steps for educators to take in order to truly put their platitudes of respect for student home culture into practice. But first, after having shared many verses from the Qur'an and Hadith, I would like to share two hadith that any school or classrooms with Muslim students ought to use in them.

Two Hadith for the Classroom

Teachers and schools often use quotes from famous historical figures or celebrities and hang them on posters in their classroom to reinforce lessons that they want their students to imbibe.

While the Prophet Muhammad ﷺ is a religious figure he is also an undisputed historical figure. There are very few historians who argue that Moses, Jesus, or Abraham عــليهم الســلام never actually existed and are purely mythological figures; but there are some who take advantage of their chronological antiquity to put such speculations forth. With the Prophet Muhammad ﷺ such speculations are impossible. So there is no issue for a public school educator, or the institution itself, to put a quote from the Prophet ﷺ on the wall of a classroom or hallway that is secular in its wording. Work done by the initiative of students that includes religious wording can also be hung on the walls.[370] I have known teachers who do calligraphy art projects where the students paint a quote on a poster that then gets hung in the room, and have seen Muslim students use this as an opportunity to quote the Prophet ﷺ or the Quran or one of the Prophet's ﷺ companions.

The school and educators can put a quote up of a religious figure in the building so long as there is an objective secular purpose in doing so.[371] It can be a quote that does not mention God or religion, but rather reinforces a value that is of interest to the whole school community. This same thing is actually done in public schools across America all the time. Many schools have it encoded into their school rules or policy that students should *"treat others as you wish to be treated"* and this value is commonly taught to young elementary school students and students of all ages as a foundational rule by which students are to relate to one another in the school and classroom. *Scholastic*, one of the most influential companies upon the American education system, advocates that it be used as a general rule of conduct for all grades K-12.[372] In the West it is known as "The Golden Rule" and teachers will often refer to it as such and admonish students to follow "The Golden Rule" when they are in school. The state of Texas even has a consortium of public Charter Schools that are named after it.

So where does this "Golden Rule" come from? It is, of course, well-known that as an axiom that can be found throughout many world religions and cultures, but the common English phrasing of it used today is formulated from the book of Mathew in the New Testament in a recount of the words spoken by Jesus عـليه الســلام in the Sermon on the Mount, *"all things whatsoever ye would that men should do to you, do ye even so to them[373]"* (King James Bible Mathew 7:12). Added to that, in the book of Mathew is that Jesus عـليه الســلام said about it, *"for this is the law and the prophets."* So when we teach this to children in school we are teaching them the law of the New Testament and it would be dishonest to pretend otherwise. This is why I do not

---

[370] The federal *Guidance on Constitutionally Protected Prayer and Religious Expression in Public Elementary and Secondary Schools* says, "not all religious speech that takes place in the public schools or at school-sponsored events is governmental speech" and "Students may express their beliefs about religion in homework, artwork, and other written and oral assignments free from discrimination based on the religious perspective of their submissions" It cites *Santa Fe Independent School Dist. v. Doe, 530 U.S. 290*, which explains that "not every message" that is "authorized by a government policy and take[s] place on government property at government-sponsored school-related events" is "the government's own".

[371] *Abington School District v. Schempp*, 374 U.S. 203 (1963).

[372] See Scholastic's "General Rules of Conduct" at https://www.scholastic.com/teachers/articles/teaching-content/general-rules-conduct/

[373] The English Standard Version of the Bible has the wording as *"So whatever you wish that others would do to you, do also to them, for this is the Law and the Prophets."* The Revised Standard Edition says, *"So whatever you wish that men would do to you, do so to them; for this is the law and the prophets."*

entertain hesitancy about using the following two hadith of the Prophet 🖼 in the classroom that are secular in their wording, of universal appeal and truth, and need not even be used by citing the Prophet's 🖼 name if we do not want to (like the Golden rule is normally used, though personally I see no problem with telling students that that rule owes its origins to the Bible).

Kindness

Kindness is a value that all schools wish to inculcate upon their students and to see them practice in their social interactions in the school community. The injunctions to kindness are ever-numerous in the Islamic texts, and I recommend that teachers with Muslim students put the following quote up in their classrooms:

> **Verily kindness is not put into anything except that if beautifies it, and it is not removed from anything except that it disgraces it.**[374]

The beauty of this hadith and its teaching is that it can be used to prompt the student to be kind even when it is difficult or counterintuitive to do so. I keep a poster (see below) of this hadith on my wall that has the Arabic on it as well without the Prophet's 🖼 name on it. A colored jpeg of this poster is available on abrahameducation.com/twohadith.

إِنَّ الرِّفْقَ لاَ يَكُونُ فِي شَيْءٍ إِلَّا زَانَهُ وَلاَ يُنْزَعُ مِن شَيْءٍ إِلَّا شَانَهُ

"Verily, kindness is not found in anything except that it beautifies it, and it is not removed from anything except that it disgraces it."

The beauty of using a poster like this is that it gives students who can read the Arabic, even if just phonetically, the opportunity to demonstrate that skill. It also gives the students who know where the hadith comes from the chance to recognize that and explain it to others, fellow Muslim students or otherwise. Whenever I need to remind students about the importance of kindness I will

---

[374] Sahīh Muslim Book 45 Hadith 100 http://sunnah.com/muslim/45/100

simply direct my laser pointer up to the poster and tell them to remember what it says. It is responded to wonderfully.

Self-Control

The importance of self-discipline and self-control in both the development of youth and Islamic teaching has been much discussed in this book. The following hadith can help teach this:

> **The strongest person is not the one who is best at fighting. Rather, the strongest person is the one who controls himself when he is angry.**[375]

Having this posted in the school or classroom can be especially beneficial where there are students who struggle with aggression. There can be a conflict between the Islamic concept of strength articulated here and that of strength and masculinity in some cultures that Muslims come from, including Western conceptualizations of toughness. It is important to give young students with roots in these cultures the opportunity to know and reflect upon this Islamic perspective when learning in the real-world context of social interaction with their peers. Again a jpeg poster of this in color with Arabic text on it is available at abrahameducation.com/twohadith.

لَيْسَ الشَّدِيدُ بِالصُّرَعَةِ إِنَّمَا الشَّدِيدُ
الَّذِي يَمْلِكُ نَفْسَهُ عِنْدَ الْغَضَبِ

"The strongest person is not the one who is best at fighting. Rather, the strongest person is the one who controls himself when he is angry."

---

[375] Sahīh Muslim Book 45 Hadith 140 https://sunnah.com/muslim/45/140

Chapter 4: TECHNICALITIES OF FOLLOWING ISLAM - ACCOMMODATIONS AND COLLISION IN THE SCHOOLS

Islam is a very legalistic religion. The previous chapter explained the framework of its jurisprudence and how it assigns a ruling of obligatory, encouraged, neutral, discouraged, or forbidden to any act a human can undertake. These rulings are based on the life of the Prophet Muhammad ﷺ, which is recorded meticulously to such detail that many outsiders consider it banal, but to the Muslim its detail offers a way that one can be connected to the remembrance of God throughout all acts of life be they large or small.

Muslim students have the right to practice their religion in public schools and schools have the responsibility to accommodate them. When schools do not know what is necessary for these accommodations they fall short in their responsibilities and oftentimes consternation, either latent or explicit, exists between Muslim families and the schools. From this the Muslim children will absorb the implied message that their being Muslim is not welcome in school, and perhaps by extension Western society in general. This can cause an array of personal and psychological dilemmas to unwind in young people. Being able to properly accommodate Islam's religious practices and setting the expectation that there is no harm in Muslim students observing their religious practices has the potential to greatly simplify being a Muslim in public schools. This in turn can yield all kinds of benefits for these young people, the communities they belong to, and by extension the society at large. But it necessitates that educators be informed about the practical matters of what observing the religious practices entails. Otherwise they will not be able to properly make considerations for the specific context of their school in order to effectively accommodate them. This chapter sets out to bridge that gap.

The biggest religious accommodation needed for Muslim students and families is that of the *salāh*, the five daily prayers. As explained in the previous chapter, prayer is a precise process and cannot be properly accommodated without educators having knowledge of it. Proper accommodation necessitates consideration for time, place, duration, and the prayer's necessary requirements. While the prayer will be discussed in detail in this chapter, so will matters pertaining to bathroom habits, culinary habits, clothing, and gender roles. The discussion of some of these follow naturally from the beginning discussion of the prayer, as does some further detail pertaining to Ramadan beyond what was discussed in the previous chapter.

Salāh - Accommodations

Educators always want to know "how long" it takes to do the prayer. They want to be told that it takes something like 15 minutes to complete so they can then go and simply set aside 15 minutes in the daily schedule for students to do it and say to the students "okay if you wish to pray now is the time" and be done with it. Most pamphlet-type information that is available about accommodating religious practices for Muslim students also reduce the idea of accommodating the prayer to be a simple matter of setting aside a small amount of time. Unfortunately, this approach misses the mark, school contexts are all very different from one another, in terms of what is encompassed in their actual buildings as well as the size and nature of their Muslim student bodies. The prayer can not be effectively accommodated unless the school staff has a working knowledge of all that is necessary to be done for the prayer, this is what will enable adequate planning for accommodations within specific school contexts. Praying in school is a bona fide student right under the free expression clause of the first amendment, however, it can be taken away or barred as a right when it imposes an undue burden upon the academic environment.[376] School district attorneys or legal counsels for schools are often keen to advise administrators of this caveat, so when accommodating Muslim students religious practices becomes difficult it does get taken away or simply not considered for accommodation under this guise. This especially takes place when students are deemed to be "taking advantage" of asserting this right and being provided a time to pray in school. The caveat that students conducting the prayers not disrupt the academic environment is important, but this consideration also needs to be balanced against the dueling dictate of the courts that schools cannot unduly burden students from exercising their right to pray.[377] Again, school staff being informed, planned, and prepared to properly accommodate is the key to striking an effective balance that will serve the best interests of all parties.[378]

As was mentioned in the previous chapter, in the Muslim world everything revolves around the prayer. Muslim children in the West are uniquely situated in that they are under enormous psychological pressure to perform the prayers, yet have to advocate entirely by themselves for its accommodation. All the while they are likely being raised by people who did not have to do the same advocating growing up, and therefore are likely to lack the skill themselves to coach these students into how to effectively self advocate.

---

[376] See *Hazelwood School District, et al., Petitioners v. Cathy Kuhlmeier et al. 484 U.S. 260* (1988). Justice Byron White in the majority opinion, *"Educators do not offend the First Amendment by exercising editorial control over the style and content of student speech in school-sponsored expressive activities so long as their actions are reasonably related to legitimate pedagogical concerns."*

[377] See *Employment Division, Department of Human Resources Of Oregon, et al., Petitioners v. Alfred L. Smith et al. 494 U.S. 872* (1990). Justice Antonin Scalia in the majority opinion of the court, *"A regulation neutral on its face may, in its application, nonetheless offend the constitutional requirement for government neutrality if it unduly burdens the free exercise of religion."*

[378] The Texas Association of School Boards (TASB) has compiled a very good treatment on federal law related to student religious expression and rights in the public schools that I recommend educators read. https://tinyurl.com/yb9ou877

The biggest mistake schools make is that they allow students too much freedom when affording them the time to pray. They simply say "ok" when a student asks to pray and let them "go do it" and usually with zero or minimal supervision. This sets students up for failure, adolescents are simply too impulsive to be given the freedom to be let loose from their classes to perform a duty within a constrained amount of time, and to be expected to do it effectively without wasting that time, getting sidetracked, and giving in to the temptation to use the situation as an opportunity to avoid schoolwork. THE CHILDREN MUST BE SUPERVISED during the entirety of what it takes to execute the prayer. This supervision should be no less than what would be expected for supervising students in any given classroom. The adult to child ratio should be reasonable. Staff members at the school must not, and should not, feel shy or hesitant about supervising students while they go pray out of fear that it is something so private and personal that someone might feel "uncomfortable". There are some specific considerations to be had for doing the supervision in order to avoid doing something offensive, and knowledge of the prayer technicalities will illuminate those.

Time - When the prayer happens

First to clarify an important matter, the prayer times take place *within a time frame*, not at an *exact* time.[379] As alluded to, asserting religious rights in school is something that students can take advantage of for the wrong reasons, and this is set up to occur in the case of Muslim students when the process and rules of praying are unknown to their non-Muslim teachers. Some teachers have found that students seemingly tell them they have to pray only when a quiz is about to begin, and they insist that it cannot wait. One way I have known this to happen is students telling a teacher that they have to pray at a very specific moment, or minute, that cannot be compromised within a range. This is not the case, and for the teacher who does not know better they are set up to be duped.[380] That being said, there is religious evidence that dictates it is better to pray earlier within the timeframe[381], but what is obligatory and avoidant of sin is to pray *within* the time frame.[382]

There are five obligatory prayers in Islam and they are named as such:

Fejr (dawn)
Dhuhr (noon)
Asr (afternoon)
Maghrib (sunset)
Ishā' (evening)

---

[379] Sunan Abī Dawūd Book 2 Hadith 6 https://sunnah.com/abudawud/2/6
[380] Sometimes, the kids themselves do not fully understand it is a range.
[381] Sahīh al-Bukhārī Book 9 Hadith 6 http://sunnah.com/bukhari/9/6
[382] Jami` at-Tirmidhī Book 2 Hadith 24 https://sunnah.com/tirmidhi/2/24

These prayers also occur in the order listed here. *Dhuhr*, or the noon prayer, is primarily the prayer that students are dealing with performing during the school hours, although *asr* can come into play at times, especially during the winter. What makes the prayer times complicated in regards to consistency in school is that they are determined essentially by the positioning of the sun in the sky (or beyond the horizon) relative to one's position on earth, and the times do not remain static throughout the year. Just as the duration of the daylight has gradual change throughout the year and seasons, and two instances of drastic change in relation to the clock time when daylight savings occurs, so do the Islamic prayer times.

Listed below are the prayer times on September, 6th, 2019 for Hennepin County Minnesota, which I will use here as an initial example before showing examples from other locales. There is variation in the times based on where you are on the earth longitudinally, but a 150 mile span makes for differences of only a matter of minutes, and I will show you how to always look up the prayer times for your zip code further down.

Fejr (dawn)	5:18am
Dhuhr (noon)	1:10pm
Asr (afternoon)	4:51pm
Maghrib (sunset)	7:45pm
Ishā' (evening)	9:10pm

These are the minutes that the timeframes for these prayers begin. *Fejr* begins with the first light of the dawn in the horizon (or when it would appear if the sky is overcast, cloudiness and varying weather conditions *do not* have an effect on when the prayer times occur) and it's time frame ends when the tip of the sphere of the sun makes its first appearance in the sky assuming a clear cut view of the horizon. Things like buildings and trees blocking one's view of the horizon also have no bearing on when the prayer times occur. The precise minute of the prayers' arrival are all determined using calculation and their times are therefore easily predictable and mapped out. The timeframe for *dhuhr* (the prayer that students do at school) ends when the next prayer (*asr*) begins. Similarly the timeframe of *asr* ends a few minutes before *maghrib* begins (specifically when the sun is yellow and gotten close to its descent into the horizon), and the timeframe for *maghrib* ends when *ishā'* begins (when the sky has fully darkened from the glow of twilight), and the timeframe for *ishā'* ends halfway through the night.[383]

---

[383] Sahīh Muslim Book 5 Hadith 219 http://sunnah.com/muslim/5/219

So you might look at the time frame of *dhuhr* and think, "Hey! If it ends at 4:51 and the school day gets out at 3:30, then they don't even need to pray at school! They can just do it when they get home! Yes!" But just hold up for a moment. It is true that students might choose to pray at home in such situations, but it is not as simple as is wished by this line of thinking.

Firstly, as stated before, there is *plenty* of religious justification to the idea that praying closer to when the prayer's time frame begins is better than praying later.[384] As such, it is commonly the practice of families, and definitely the practice within mosques, that the prayers are done within 20-30 minutes after the beginning time comes in. Therefore, it is typically the case that students who pray are used to praying earlier in the time frame and wish to pray closer to the time when it comes in because the religious reward is greater when the prayer is done sooner. Students who want to pray *dhuhr* in school, even when the timeframe of *dhuhr* extends beyond the end of the school day, should still be allowed to do so and accommodated.

Secondly, even if the time frame of *dhuhr* extends past the hours of the school day there are many practical reasons to want to perform it earlier. It can be very hard for non-Muslims to appreciate just how hard it can be to find a private place and time to pray when you are generally out and about in the United States. All the more so if you are a young person who does not have total control over your own comings and goings. If a student leaves school at 3:30, even with an hour and 20 minutes remaining until the prayer timeframe ends, it is not likely to be a simple task for them to just find a time and space to pray before the timeframe ends. Their bus ride alone could be at least 30 minutes. They may have another activity scheduled for 4 o'clock or 4:30 that they have to get prepared for, or younger siblings to look after etc. For me, as a general rule, when I am in the United States if I am somewhere and need to pray and the timeframe is within an hour and a half of ending, I make my best effort to pray at the place I am at as opposed to going to somewhere else and expecting that I will be able to sufficiently get the prayer done. Between traffic, and the simple fact that there are not many places in public where one can expect the space and privacy needed to perform the prayer, it is just not realistic to expect that it is ever going to be convenient to get it done in whatever context.

Thirdly, the timeframes are going to change in such a way that there will be a sizable chunk of the year in which the timeframes dictate that the students *have to* pray the noon prayer (*dhuhr*) at school. Therefore, it is best to have the prayer accommodations at school be something structured, regular, consistent, and with clear and well-defined expectations and boundaries in

---

[384] Saḥīḥ al-Bukhārī Book 9 Hadith 6 http://sunnah.com/bukhari/9/6, Jami' at-Tirmidhī Book 2 Hadith 24 https://sunnah.com/tirmidhi/2/24

order to be the least disruptive and most respectful process possible for both the students and the overall school community. The prayer time frame between *dhuhr* and *asr* gets steadily smaller from the beginning of the school year until the solstice in late December. Consider how the timeframes for the prayers have changed by December 22nd, 2019 in Hennepin county:

	September 6th, 2019		December 22nd, 2019
Fejr (dawn)	5:18am	*Fejr* (dawn)	6:19am
Dhuhr (noon)	1:10pm	*Dhuhr* (noon)	12:10pm
Asr (afternoon)	4:51pm	*Asr* (afternoon)	2:16pm
Maghrib (sunset)	7:45pm	*Maghrib* (sunset)	4:33pm
Ishā' (evening)	9:10pm	*Ishā'* (evening)	6:03pm

The occurrence of daylight savings accounts in large part for *dhuhr* being an hour earlier than the September times. On November 2nd *dhuhr* came in at 12:56pm, the next day was daylight savings and the time for *dhuhr* became 11:56am. The time of *dhuhr* also advances by about a minute every five days until around the end of July when it starts to recede by the same rate up until around early November. The daylight length steadily becoming shorter causes the beginning of *asr* to creep up to 2:16! I do not believe there is a school in the state of Minnesota that will release early enough, even if the release time is 1:50, to where students can be expected to leave school and comfortably find a place and time to pray before the time of *dhuhr* expires in December. Definitely within the six months of daylight savings time during the school year, practically speaking, if the students do not take the time to pray at school, they will be unable to perform the *dhuhr* prayer within the appropriate time frame. I believe there is an entirely reasonable argument to be made that tangible practicalities like these render inaction to accommodate by schools unconstitutional because it would effectively prohibit the students from observing their religious practice.

Something important to identify here for the sake of accommodations is that 365 days a year from 1:30-2:00pm is a time period where, in Minnesota, the prayer time for *dhuhr* will be valid. It is beneficial to find a consistent time frame like this within the school's given locale and the school's schedule. Generally schools want scheduling matters to be consistent throughout the school year, so when it comes to scheduling a time for students to have a break to pray it should be a goal to identify a time that will not have to change and fluctuate throughout the year. Since the amount of sunlight in a day varies based on latitude each locale is a little different, but here are some timeframes where *dhuhr* is valid 365 days a year in different cities on varying lines of latitude.

City	Time Frame
Minneapolis, MN	1:30-2:00
Seattle, WA	1:00-1:30
Houston, TX	2:00-2:30
Knoxville, TE	2:00-2:30
Portland, ME	12:45-1:15

The good news also is that the prayer times are easily available to look up at anytime online, when they occur is entirely projectable mathematically so the schedules are laid out into the future. Anyone can look them up through a Google search of "Islamic Prayer times" or going to a website like islamicfinder.org where any zip code or city can be put into a search engine and the prayer times will be generated. There are also numerous phone apps, such as Muslim Pro, that will do the same.

Time - Wudū': Preparatory Ritual Washing (ablution)

The word *wudū'* (roughly pronounced like the word voodoo only with a 'w' in the beginning) is very useful for educators to know. Everyone is always very concerned to know how long the prayer takes for students to do, but the real issue with the prayer and time is not the duration of doing the actual prayer, it is the time it takes to conduct the ritual washing that has to take place *before* the prayer. This is called *wudū'*. In English, Muslims speak of "making" *wudū'*, in order to get into the proper state to pray, and "having" *wudū'* to indicate that one is in the proper state and ready to pray. After making *wudū'*, it can be "broken" by certain bodily functions; namely the production of urine, feces, flatulence, or sexual discharge.[385] Deep sleeping also breaks one's *wudū*[386], as does the touching of the opposite gender.[387] There is some difference of opinion in Islamic scholarship as to whether this connotes any touching at all or only touching that is purely of a sexual nature. There is sound evidence that non-sexual touching of an opposite gender family member does not break one's *wudū*[388], however, since cross-gender touching outside of family members is not at all an Islamic practice itself, most Muslim cultures

---

[385] Qur'an 4:43 https://quran.com/4/43
[386] Jami` at-Tirmidhī Book 1 Hadith 77 https://sunnah.com/tirmidhi/1/77
[387] Qur'an 4:43 https://quran.com/4/43
[388] Sahīh al-Bukhārī Book 8 Hadith 34 https://sunnah.com/bukhari/8/34

have taken to the approach that touching the opposite gender *does* break *wudū'*. I have been in a classroom where a female teacher put her hand on the back of a male student and he got mad at her and told her that she broke his *wudū'* (which she in turn felt very guilty about). What all this means is that it is possible to go from one prayer to another and hold one's *wudū'*, but overall it is rare, especially if one is accustomed to more American dietary habits. So it is unlikely to have a situation in the school setting where students are going to pray but do not have to make *wudū'* beforehand, so planning to accommodate for it is paramount for the school.

Simply stated, what is obligatory in the process of making *wudū'* is washing the face, mouth, nose (as in siphoning water into the nostrils and then blowing it out[389]), the arms to the elbow[390], wiping over the head, wet rubbing the neck[391] and ears[392], and washing the feet to the ankle[393], in that exact order[394] (see the pictures below[395]).

Those are the minimal requirements for making *wudū*. There is strong religious justification to practice washing each body part listed above three times[396], except for the head which is done

Ritual washing before Islamic Prayer - AKA *wudū'*

once.[397] This is what Muslim children are taught to do, and they may or may not distinguish between what is minimally required and what they have been taught to do by their parents or family members. There is also strong religious evidence that dictates for the appendages to be washed by being placed under a stream of water or immersed in a bucket as opposed to water

---

[389] Saḥīḥ al-Bukhārī Book 59 Hadith 104 https://sunnah.com/bukhari/59/104

[390] Saḥīḥ Abī Dawūd Book 1 Hadith 106 https://sunnah.com/abudawud/1/106

[391] Jami` at-Tirmidhī Book 1 Hadith 32 https://sunnah.com/tirmidhi/1/32

[392] Jami` at-Tirmidhī Book 1 Hadith 37 https://sunnah.com/tirmidhi/1/37

[393] Sunan ibn Majah Book 1 Hadith 492 https://sunnah.com/urn/1254550

[394] Qur'an 5:56 https://quran.com/5/6

[395] These are altered images from wikihow.com/perform-wudu, used under Creative Commons licensing. creativecommons.org/licenses/by-nc-sa/3.0/

[396] Sunan Abī Dawūd Book 1 Hadith 106 https://sunnah.com/abudawud/1/106

[397] Sunan an-Nasa'i Vol. 1 Book 1 Hadith 101 https://sunnah.com/urn/1001010

being wiped with a wet hand.[398] This is the same for wanting the foot to be placed under the stream of water and working the fingers in between the toes as they are being washed.[399]

Also, if someone makes *wudū'* and then puts on socks while they are in a state of having *wudū*[400], the next time they need to make *wudū'* within that day[401] it is not obligatory for them to remove the socks and wash the feet as described above. Instead it is permissible for them to get their hand wet and wipe over the top[402] of the sock on each foot.[403] The head, neck, and ear washing is also never meant to be total inundation, it is a wiping over of the head with wet hands, while washing the ears involves getting the fingers wet and sticking them in the ears.[404]

Firstly, just appreciate for the sake of the students that there are several rules to be followed just within this small process. So there is a real element of precision to be conscious of when one is doing it that necessitates some intentional focus. If one gets distracted or does it willy-nilly they could lose track of whether or not they got the process right and potentially have to start it all over.

Secondly, there are some things to consider about all of this time wise. First, when *wudū'* is performed the sink counter and the floor around the sink are going to be wet afterwards. When the hands are raised up to gently rub out the insides of the ears the elbows flare out. Considering the arms were just rinsed up to the elbows they are wet and are dripping all over the place. Of course washing the feet causes water to get out of the sink area. So, who cleans this up? If the students make *wudū'* quickly and it leaves the bathroom area wet, it must be clearly delineated whose responsibility it is to clean up afterwards. If it is the students' responsibility, that needs to be considered in *the amount of time* it will take for them to pray.

My suggestion is that the students are fully supervised when they have to do this and the expectation is set and practiced that they will dry up the bathroom when they are done. This would be a small step towards avoiding chaos in schools and creating peace on earth (Dupuy & Prather, 2015; Raghavendran, 2015). This is going to involve the use of paper towels. But the

---

[398] Saḥīḥ al-Bukhārī Book 4 Hadith 29 https://sunnah.com/bukhari/4/29, Saḥīḥ Muslim Book 2 Hadith 40 http://sunnah.com/muslim/2/40, Saḥīḥ Muslim Book 2 Hadith 40 http://sunnah.com/muslim/2/41

[399] Jami` at-Tirmidhī Book 1 Hadith 39 https://sunnah.com/tirmidhi/1/39

[400] Saḥīḥ Muslim Book 2 Hadith 99 https://sunnah.com/muslim/2/99

[401] Sunan an-Nasa'i Book https://sunnah.com/urn/1001290

[402] Jami` at-Tirmidhī Book 1 Hadith 98 http://sunnah.com/tirmidhi/1/98

[403] Jami` at-Tirmidhī Book 1 Hadith 95 http://sunnah.com/tirmidhi/1/95, Jami`at-Tirmidhī Book 1 Hadith 96 http://sunnah.com/tirmidhi/1/96,

[404] Sunan Abī Dawūd Book 1 Hadith 135 https://sunnah.com/abudawud/1/135

bathroom is not the only thing that will need to be dried. We do not want these kids dripping all over the building, creating who knows what kind of safety hazards, so they will also need to dry themselves. They are especially going to want to dry their feet, which, let me tell you, is much easier to do sitting down than standing up. Does the bathroom have a convenient place to sit near the sink? Have you ever put a sock on a wet foot? It is not a pleasant sensory experience. Water being absorbed into the socks from the feet could also be unsanitary because it could potentially cause bacterial growth if the wet socks are later put in shoes and unable to dry out. But with the arms, face, and head as well, it is ideal (not a religious obligation but we are talking comfort's sake here) to dry oneself off after making *wudū*.

In many of the arid and hot-weather countries in the Muslim world it may be common practice for people to leave the bathrooms wet and leave themselves wet as they would be in clothing that is made of light linen that dries easily. Bathrooms in the Muslim world typically have squeegees on the counters and drains on the floors to make for easy wiping away of any leftover wetness. In cold climate locales, people are making *wudū'* while wearing absorbent and heavy sweatshirts, you do not want to roll those over wet arms when you are all done. The point being, drying off is important and it has many considerations that necessitate proper set up.

Another thing about *wudū'* than can be sort of not fun: rinsing out your mouth and nose while standing next to a urinal that is full of…urine. It is gross and not fun to do. Generally, in the Muslim world there is a strong separation between the toilets and the sinks in bathrooms. The toilets there are contained in fully enclosed closets[405] and typically the sinks will be in a separate room entirely from those. Urinals practically do not exist in the Muslim world[406] because urinating while standing up is against Islamic practice.[407] So this is another aspect to consider, and if you are unable to accommodate students making *wudū'* in a place that is not next to a toilet, you can at least empathize with the unfriendliness of that a little. It would also take longer if students need to use the bathroom before they make *wudū'*. It is part of the directions of praying to relieve oneself beforehand if the urge to answer the call of nature is felt.[408]

Making *wudū* as described above, including a full washing of the feet, washing each body part three times, and a full drying off of the body and bathroom upon completion, takes me just under *three full minutes*. This means being timed from the point of standing in front of the sink,

---

[405] In America fire codes usually dictate that the walls around the toilet cannot touch the ground and ceiling for the sake of allowing escape in the case of an emergency. In the Muslim world such codes rarely exist.

[406] Outside of areas that are likely to be highly frequented by Western tourists or visitors.

[407] Jami' at-Tirmidhī Book 1 Hadith 12 https://sunnah.com/tirmidhi/1/12

[408] Sunan an-Nasā'i Book 10 Hadith 76 https://sunnah.com/nasai/10/76

it does not include time that it may take in the hallway to walk to the bathroom, and it entails only having to take off socks from slip-on shoes, meaning the time it might take to tie and untie shoes was not involved either. So while I can tell people that *wudū'* takes 3 minutes to perform, in reality it is only a frame of reference for how long you would use in planning the amount of time to set aside for each student to make *wudū'* given the relevant variables of your own school context. For example, if you give each kid 3 minutes and you have 10 students praying and a bathroom with two sinks, how long will that take? Does this affect the process by which they are dismissed from the classroom? Oftentimes it makes sense to have students dismissed in a staggered way. But this usually means that someone from outside the classroom has to be the supervisor. If students are going to pray during 5th period, it might make sense to have them do *wudū'* in a staggered fashion during 4th period so the interruption of one single class does not become too extended.

Of course the gender of whoever supervises students making *wudū'* is another consideration. Definitely, a male supervisor should supervise males, and a female supervisor should supervise females. Females also may take a little longer to make *wudū'* because they will usually have to disrobe to a greater degree in order to wash all the necessary body parts.

Time - The Process and Duration of Praying

Once one has *wudū'* and is ready to pray the prayer begins with the worshipper standing upright and facing Mecca[409] and then raising their hands to the side of the face and saying *"Allahu Akbar"*. This lets you know the prayer has begun, the saying of this phrase is called the *takbīr* and it is also used as an audible signal for the transfer from one position to another in the *salāh*. So if you are in a room with Muslims praying, you will likely hear it said several times. Once the initial *takbīr* is done the worshipper is in a state of prayer and has begun a precise liturgical process of conduct and speech that is meant to command full concentration and adherence. To interrupt them during this would not be taken well. So once this saying of *"Allahu Akbar"* has been done by the student who is praying or leading others in prayer, the staff member who is supervising should be careful to not say anything to those students or distract them until the prayer is complete in order to be respectful.

After saying the initial *takbīr* the worshipper then makes a specific invocation, which is five lines, and then recites the first chapter of the Qur'an, which is seven lines. Of the five prayers in the day there are two, *dhuhr* (noon) and *asr* (afternoon), where the Qur'an recitation is done quietly under the breath, and there are three, *fejr* (dawn), *maghrib* (sunset), and ishā' (evening) where

---

[409] The cardinal direction that this is on any place on the earth is determined by whichever direction is the most direct path to Mecca via aerial trajectory. This is Northeast throughout all of North America.

it is recited out loud. Your students will not be doing the prayers that necessitate the audible Qur'an recitation in school unless they are there after school, most likely in the winter, beyond the point of the setting of the sun, or are there early in the morning during the winter before the sun has risen. During the noon and afternoon prayer the only thing that is audible is the saying of the *takbīr* by the leader of the prayer. There is a benefit to this because it limits the likelihood that student prayer will distract others, even if it has to be done somewhere in close proximity to other non-praying students.

After reciting the first chapter of the Qur'an the worshipper must then recite at least one more verse of the Qur'an. This is a part where some variability in the prayer's duration can come into play. Reciting one verse of the Qur'an at this point is the bare minimum that needs to be done to meet the obligations of *salāh*. However, there is plenty of religious text dictating that it is better to recite the Qur'an longer[410], and just generally in Islam the more one recites the Qur'an the more reward there is for the worshipper. Furthermore, it is simply not the habit that is developed to only recite a single verse when doing this, and youth tend to go along with the habits that they have seen adults around them do when it comes to the religious acts. Nevertheless, I would say reciting the Qur'an for a duration longer than a minute here would not be common; reciting a short chapter that is only four lines is not uncommon. The important thing to understand is that in the initial standing position of the prayer there can be variability in the amount of time spent doing it.

Being informed with this knowledge ought to help educators appreciate why one person saying that it takes them three minutes to perform the prayer might not apply to another person. If they wish to recite the Qur'an longer or shorter within the prayer the duration of their prayer will expand or contract accordingly. If a supervising teacher notices that one student seems to pray or lead the prayer for a longer time than other students who they have seen, please do not accuse that student of intentionally trying to extend the prayer in order to avoid class. Please. At the same time, if the school has a regimented break time set aside that the students can use to pray and the students are taking so long in their prayers that they consume enough time to go beyond the break time's limits, some respectful discussion with the students about doing what is necessary in order to respect the time the school has allotted may be warranted. If discussions do have to go in this direction it is altogether reasonable to anticipate that students will be defensive. Therefore the teacher or staff member being calm in these discussions is of absolute importance. Calmness is discussed more in chapter five.

---

[410]Sahīh al-Bukhārī Book 10 Hadith 153 http://sunnah.com/bukhari/10/153, Sahīh al-Bukhārī Book 10 Hadith 152 http://sunnah.com/bukhari/10/152

After completing this second recitation of the Qur'an the worshipper raises his or her hands in the air again and says "*Allahu Akbar.*" They then bow and make another three-line invocation (there are supererogatory invocations that can be done here but the three-line one is the minimum, even doing a supererogatory invocation is not going to add significant time here). The worshipper then raises him or herself back up to the standing position and says "*sami allahu liman hamida*" and then says "*Allahu Akbar*" and then goes down into the position of prostration, preferably with the hands going to the ground before the knees.[411]

The position of prostration in the *salāh* is called **sujūd.**[412] It is the ultimate position of worship and submission to God in Islam, and the religious belief is that the supplication made in *sujūd* is more likely to be accepted by Allah, and that being in this position brings one "closer" to Allah.[413] Therefore, there can be variation on the amount of time spent in *sujūd* as some may prefer to make much extra supplication during it, perhaps more so in times of stress when they are feeling extra motivated to call on Allah's aid. Nevertheless, the time spent in *sujūd* is going to range from about 3 to 30 seconds. I would say, generally 30 seconds is a long *sujūd* and for a young person it is overall unlikely for it to last that long, but 15-20 seconds is still within reason and possibility. If they are praying in a group the leader of the prayer will in effect be determining the *sujūd* time since everyone else's actions will follow their lead. However, they will go to *sujūd* eight total times throughout the course of the *salāh*. Therefore time variation in *sujūd* does have the potential to add up to be a difference in minutes; and as we all know minutes in the school day (and life as well for that matter) are precious.

What is obligatory to do in *sujūd* is a three-line invocation. When *sujūd* is finished the worshipper says "*Allahu Akba*r" and raises to a sitting position (the knees do not move, they are sitting on their knees here), where they make a two line invocation, then say "*Allahu Akbar*" again, and make *sujūd* a second time, and then say "*Allahu Akbar*" again and sit up and rise to the standing position. At this point the worshipper has completed one unit of prayer, called a *rakah*, each of the five daily prayers has a certain amount of *rakahs* that are obligatory to make

---

[411] Sunan Abī Dawūd Book 2 Hadith 450 https://sunnah.com/abudawud/2/450, Sunan Abī Dawūd Book 2 Hadith 502 https://sunnah.com/abudawud/2/502 - yes there is direct guidance in the religion and its jurisprudence for matters as banal as to whether or not you ought to first touch the ground with your hands or knees, if one goes knees first however, it is not something that nullifies the prayer, that is to say: going hands first is not one of the prayer's obligations, but I want to give you an idea of just how meticulous some these matters can be for us.

[412] What is called a 'mosque' in English is not called a 'mosque' by Muslims. We call it by its Arabic name **masjid**, which means "place of **sujūd**". The root meaning of Arabic words is always found in the order and construction of its consonant sounds, with the vast majority of these roots having three consonants. You can see this in the relationship between the words *sujūd* and *masjid* where the order of *s-j-d* are consistent, but the vowel sounds have changed.

[413]Sunan Abī Dawūd Book 4 Hadith 245 https://sunnah.com/muslim/4/245

in it. At school it will be four *rakahs*, because the noon and afternoon prayers oblige four (the evening prayer is also four, but the sunset is three and the dawn prayer is two).

The *rakahs* happen fluidly, there is no break in between them and they are connected in a continual process with some slight variation in what is to be done to complete each one. At the end of the second *rakah* there is an extended sitting and invocation before rising for the third *rakah*. At the end of the fourth *rakah* there is a further extended invocation, and after that the worshipper may choose to make supererogatory supplications before finalizing the *salāh* with what is called the *taslīm*, which is turning the head to the right and saying "*asalāmu alaykum wa rahmatu Allah*" and then turning the head to the left and saying the same thing (in the sitting position). The *rakahs* that occur after the second one in all the prayers do not have a recitation of the Quran beyond the first chapter, like the first two do.

While it may not be what young students always choose to do, and it is not an obligatory part of the prayer, it is a supererogatory and common practice to sit quietly after the prayer is done and to recite additional invocations[414] quietly in the remembrance of God in a way to sort of let the prayer sink in. People will almost always do this after the prayers in the mosque so it is commonly what kids are used to seeing, and it can add to the time. It is also a supererogatory and common practice to perform two additional *rakahs* (individually, not in the group) of prayer after this sitting time is done. This is referred to as "praying Sunnah" and when done will definitely add at least a minute or two to the time. These additional *rakahs* are not obligatory, but it is common that people do them after they pray together and some students may consider doing them to be par for the course.

So how long does all of this take? When I timed myself praying *dhuhr* (the noon prayer) from the beginning of saying "*Allahu Akbar*" to the very end of saying "*asalāmu alaykum wa rahmatu Allah*" and doing only the minimum recitations and invocations as described here it took almost exactly **five minutes**, not including a quiet sitting period after the prayer.

To me the biggest variables for time in the prayer come in reciting the Qur'an after the first chapter in the first two *rakahs* and in making supplication while in *sujūd*. I would say usually Muslims make more supplications and recitation beyond the bare minimum requirements in all these situations, and generally you are talking about time variables between three and thirty seconds for these things, possibly longer for the Qur'an recitation. In total there are ten instances where time variability comes into play. Thus, we are talking about a **five to ten minute time frame** needed to perform the actual prayer. This of course does not take into

---

[414] Sahīh al-Bukhārī Book 80 Hadith 27 http://sunnah.com/bukhari/80/27

account making *wudū'*, nor the travel time from the classroom to wherever the prayer is taking place, this means five to ten minutes afforded for the actual performance of the prayer from beginning to end.

So if *wudū'* is a three minute process and the actual prayer we could consider to max out at ten minutes, it totals to an allotment of around **13 minutes,** which could reasonably be extended to **18 minutes** if we are to afford students time to do the supererogatory acts that follow the prayer. None of this includes considerations for traveling from the classroom to the bathroom to the place designated for students to pray, nor for cleanup time in the bathroom after making *wudū'*, or for using the bathroom to relieve oneself before making *wudū'*. All factors considered this could get close to at least **30 minutes**. In my experience in the Muslim world, when a break in a meeting happens or a business closes for the performance of prayers the standard amount of time taken for the break is **45 minutes.**

This illuminates a possible need to discuss with the students as to whether or not they wish to perform those supererogatory acts, or whether or not it is reasonable for them to do so within the time constraints that they are given, because if it is not reasonable then they will need some coaching that gears them towards not doing it or saving it for when they get home. Again, this can of course be a delicate matter because, due to a variety of stigmas, students will generally not like the feeling that the school staff is trying to tell them what to do in regards to the religious acts. I was once in a high school where I saw a student who was the known leader of the Muslim Student Association at the school get berated by the diversity coordinator because the students took too long to leave the auditorium, which had been given to them to perform the prayers, after the bell rang and this caused the theatre students to have to begin class late. This happened entirely because many of the students (they were a large group) had chosen to do these supererogatory acts that followed. If they had just done the obligatory acts and scrammed, the issue would not have taken place. It may be different from the prayer habits students absorb in mosques to just do the obligatory acts and then leave the place hurriedly; but in a public school setting it could very well be part of an appropriately negotiated agreement that students strongly consider only doing the obligatory acts in order to meet the time constraints afforded by the break time they are given. However, students need proper coaching and guidance around it, otherwise they will just do what they know and cannot be blamed for that. Staff in turn need to be aware that these issues actually exist and be diligent in setting up a proper school environment where these conversations can even have a chance to take place.

How do you have these discussions with students? Schools need to understand that there will be some trial and error for everybody. Set the purpose with students and families that the school wants them to be able to practice their religious rights if they so desire. Give them the choice at first as to how they go about some of these finer details, see how it goes, and always be calm with them. In setting the purpose of wanting to honor their religious rights it can be acknowledged that many schools do not do a good job properly affording Muslim students time and space to pray due to the society's general ignorance about Islamic religious practice, and that your school does not want to be like that, but you know it will be a learning process for everyone. This has the benefit of acknowledging that the school wants to take on responsibility in its own right, and it sets the expectation that all will have a growth mindset about the situation. Too often Muslim students are only given the "you need to be responsible about this" mantra in regards to observing their religious rights, and the whole thing becomes intimidating for them. They receive no coaching or authentic discussion about how to navigate these details of how to make the prayer actually happen in the school setting. Therefore they capitulate on the matter, do not end up observing their prayers, and thereby enter a downward spiral regarding their identity, religious self-concept, and quite potentially their emotional well-being as well.

Another important factor is the overall ethos that the school has towards the students' religious identity in general. Where is it addressed? Usually nowhere at all is the answer, and as shown in the previous chapter even schools that think they are making strong efforts to have conversations about diversity are making missteps that indirectly suffocate the religious identity of Muslim students. This is where integrating the books and suggestions in chapter 6 can be helpful. It is possible that some of these conversations can be planned around the integration of those books.

Space - Where the Prayer Happens

The space needs to be available during the prayer time. This may be self evident, but schools need to be sure that the room is not cross-scheduled with something else, and also that the prayer is not scheduled to be done in a space where an activity will be happening that might take too long, and overrun into the prayer time, or that will necessitate clean up that will run into the end of the time scheduled for the student break or before another activity is scheduled to begin in that room. So if the break time is scheduled to be done in the art room from 1:30-1:50, there should not be a clay moulding class going on in the art room up until 1:30 nor scheduled to start at 1:50. Such conflicts will leave the students who come to pray either bumbling around with their time unstructured and wasted and unproductive behaviors will be more likely to take place.

Enclosed and private is preferable. As far as the religious technicalities are concerned there are no dictates as to whether the prayer is done in an enclosed place or one that is more open, nor inside or outside for that matter.[415] Nevertheless, it is typical that people want privacy while they perform the prayers. Having other people around and in-sight or being in a place where there are other passersby, especially people who are noisy or socializing, is distracting and uncomfortable. Especially with our self-conscious adolescent students, it is likely to make them feel awkward and they may be uncomfortable about doing their prayers at all if their only option is to pray in a space that is a commons area or another space that is trafficked by other students. The number of students in the school who need to pray might be one factor in determining the spaciousness and privacy of the area where students will pray. A high number of students praying might dictate a bigger and more visible space has to be used.

Open and un-intruded floor space is crucial. If students are scheduled to pray during a certain time with a designated room and arrive there at the prayer time finding it full of desks, tables, chairs, or other materials that need to be moved around in order to create the proper space for praying, then the objective of having the prayer done in a concise and efficient time frame has been sabotaged. Students will need to take time to move desks around or stack chairs before praying. Afterwards they would have to choose between taking more time to put everything back as they found it, or to risk being accused of being disrespectful for having come into a room to pray, changing the arrangement of everything, and then leaving without putting everything back. It is often the case in middle and high schools that every classroom is full of desks and chairs. Elementary school classrooms might be more likely to have an open floor space, but less likely to have students who are praying (though not impossible, and family members of elementary school who need to pray when visiting need to be considered also). Schools have found that Special Ed rooms, dance rooms, wrestling rooms, stages or landings within the seating of auditoriums, or other areas used for physical education can be serviceable for this purpose; but of course it all depends on scheduling availability and other factors. In some settings a staff room might be the best place and could perhaps better accommodate supervision. Furthermore, if a physical education space is what is provided there will hopefully be a space where the surface in the area the students pray in is not entirely hard. There is nothing wrong with praying on a hard surface in Islam, but it is not exactly pleasant. Roll out rugs could be purchased and provided for the sake of setting up the prayer to accommodate this also.

It may be that there is not a perfect place to have set up for the students to pray and the students themselves will have to do some set up in order to make the room proper. There is nothing wrong with that, but if it is the case then it needs to be taken into consideration when

---

[415] Bulūgh al-Marām Book 2 Hadith 79 https://sunnah.com/bulugh/2/79, note that the bathroom is one place where the prayer cannot be done.

scheduling the amount of time the students will need, and expectations need to be made clear to the students as far as how the room is to be treated and rearranged upon leaving. And of course, all of this should be supervised, and like anything else the students would need practice, time, some explicit direction, and of course patience from the staff, in order to get it right.

The entry door would preferably be in the southwest corner of the room. This is not absolutely necessary but there are benefits to this if the room the students pray in is a smaller classroom where space will be tight. The direction in which students will face to [416] (towards Mecca) is northeast in North America. We want someone to be in the room supervising them, but it would be unbecoming and against Islamic etiquette if that person is standing in front of them facing the worshipper's face without any barrier in between them.[417] Any supervisor should also be sure to never walk directly in front of a person who is praying and over the area where they would prostrate.[418] It is part of the religious manners for the worshipper to put their arm up to block a person who attempts to walk in front of them while praying in order to prevent them from doing so.[419] If someone makes these mistakes around a Muslim who is praying the religion teaches that the Muslim is to consider their prayer "invalid", and they have to do the whole prayer over again in order to expiate for it.

Ideally, the person supervising the students who pray will be standing behind them as they perform the prayer. In many situations it will also be ideal that the person supervising the praying students will want to stand in the doorway, especially in middle and high school situations where there may be students coming to the prayer area from several different places, and therefore arriving in a staggered manner. The supervisor will want to have both the hallway and the room in their field of vision. The person supervising should know the process of praying, so they know when the students actually begin the prayer (because it would be rude to interrupt it) and will know when it has officially ended so that they can then give verbal reminders of the time remaining to get back to class if necessary.

An important note on supervision, there is no issue with a female staff member supervising male students or a mixed-gendered group of students praying, so long as they are behind them while praying. However, there are high sensitivities with a male supervising females who are praying. This is because the the bowing and prostrating that the prayer entails can be

---

[416] From anywhere on earth the direction facing Mecca is referred to as *the qiblah* by Muslims.
[417] Sahīh al-Bukhārī Book 8 Hadith 158 https://sunnah.com/bukhari/8/158
[418] Sahīh al-Bukhārī Book 8 Hadith 157 https://sunnah.com/bukhari/8/157
[419] Sahīh al-Bukhārī Book 59 Hadith 83 https://sunnah.com/bukhari/59/83

interpreted as quasi-sexual positions, and for a male to view a female doing it is considered inappropriate and Muslim cultures are highly sensitive and affronted by this. If a male has to supervise females it is best that they are basically not in the room when they are praying or at least turned in such a way that he will not be viewing them during the prayer. This might mean being in front of them and standing parallel to where the males are praying if it is a mixed group, and facing to the side or forward. Some schools find it most useful to simply have the males and females pray in separate groups and spaces with separate supervisors.

If students are praying in a mixed gendered group, it is done with the male rows in the front and the female rows behind them.[420] In such situations it will typically work best to have a male supervisor standing at the back or to the side of the male rows and a female supervisor standing at the back of the female rows. If students pray in a single gender group it is best that the supervisor matches the gender of the students biologically. If that is not possible a female supervisor of male students should stand behind them while they pray and a male supervisor of female students should not be in the room while they pray, but this situation is best to be avoided.

Some schools find it works best to have all the students who want to pray to do it as a group. Others find it best to have them do it individually perhaps in separate places within the building or in a staggered fashion. It is fine either way but do know that Islam definitely considers it better to do the obligatory prayers in a group[421], and it is basically considered to be part of the prayer's obligations to pray in a group if that is possible.[422] While this is an area that Muslim students capitulate on all the time, understand that some students may have a strong preference to pray as a group and the religious rules provide a strong impetus for that preference. When prayer is done in a group there is one individual who leads it, this person is called the *Imām* of the prayer, and the others stand behind him in rows as described here. For groups of males and mix-gendered groupings the *Imām* is always male. For female-only groups the *Imām* is a female. A female cannot lead males in prayer even in a grouping where the females outnumber the males.[423]

It is best that the person supervising is not someone who will feel indignant about witnessing the prayer's rules and structure pertaining to gender, and who would be tempted to press their

[420] Sunan ibn Mājah Book 5 Hadith 1054 https://sunnah.com/urn/1283490
[421] Sahīh al-Bukhārī Book 10 Hadith 42 https://sunnah.com/bukhari/10/42
[422] Qur'an 4:102 https://quran.com/4/102, Qur'an 2:43 https://quran.com/2/43, Sahīh al-Bukhārī Book 10 Hadith 41 http://sunnah.com/bukhari/10/41, Sahīh al-Bukhārī Book 10 Hadith 42 http://sunnah.com/bukhari/10/42
[423] Sunan an-Nasa'i Book 49 Hadith 10 https://sunnah.com/nasai/49/10

personal politics onto the students by prodding them with questions about why they do not choose a female to lead males in the prayer or why the genders are separated spatially as they are etc. The Islamic prayer is an institute that has been replicated generationally and served as a bonding glue and uniter of human hearts for civilizations and communities going back nearly a millennia and a half. Students themselves have experienced this firsthand in their own communities, so questions like these and carping criticisms are taken to be arrogant and ignorant by Muslims, and it would easily tick off students and families. When parents hear stories of students being antagonized with such questions it induces anxiety about sending their children to the school at all, and I have known concerns such as this to lead to parents moving their children to different schools altogether.

Ideally, there will be no pictures posted on the walls. Of all the issues I have heard and discussed with both educators and Muslim students alike I have never heard of the issue arising where a student complained that they could not pray in the room they were told to pray in because pictures of living things were posted. It is generally odd seeming to most non-Muslims, but there is religious justification to the understanding that prayers should not be done, and are indeed invalid, if they are done in a room where there is a picture[424] of a living thing that has a face.[425] If you ever visit a mosque you will never find one that has pictures posted in its prayer area, never. If the only room available is one where there are pictures this issue can be remedied by covering the pictures with a blank post-it note over the face. Furthermore, while this is an issue, I have never actually heard of students complaining about it, so it might be something a school administration is never prompted to worry about. But I mention it here so you can know that if it does come up, it is not something the students are making up out of nowhere.

Outside of the prayer, there are edicts in Islam against drawing and painting images[426], however, this specifically means images that are animate and have a face.[427] There is a rich tradition of art and design in Muslim cultures, but those traditions steer clear of creating facial

---

[424] Sunan an-Nasā'i Book 48 Hadith 308 https://sunnah.com/nasai/48/308
[425] Jami` at-Tirmidhī Book 43 Hadith 3036 https://sunnah.com/urn/630300
[426] Sahīh Muslim Book 37 Hadith 152 http://sunnah.com/muslim/37/152, Sahīh al-Bukhari Book 67 Hadith 116 https://sunnah.com/bukhari/67/116
[427] Jami` at-Tirmidhī Book 43 Hadith 3036 https://sunnah.com/urn/630300, Sahīh Muslim Book 37 Hadith 142 https://sunnah.com/muslim/37/141

images with only a few exceptions.[428] This is useful to know for art teachers and teachers in general who may incorporate art projects into their curriculum. I generally do not recommend that you should prohibit yourself from doing any project that is already part of your teaching repertoire. But be aware of this as some teachers have experienced having a Muslim student who was reticent to do drawings of living things. Always keep an option where not including a facial image is available, for portrait projects finding an artistic way to obscure the eyes can be a desirable idea.[429]

Another side note about pictures. Due to this dictate about praying, it is not part of Islamic etiquette nor Muslim culture for families to decorate the walls of their homes with pictures of families members and friends. Many schools and classrooms have adopted the practice of hanging up pictures in the classroom of students, and sometimes their family members as well, on the walls. There is no problem with this and I am not saying to not do it, but I like to point out to teachers that the underlying theory of this practice is that putting up student and family pictures in the classroom makes the room feel "more like home" to the student, based on the presumption that all students' families hang up family pictures in their home (Moos, 1979). This is not the case at all for Muslim students. For Muslim students in these classrooms it may be the first time they have been in a room where a photo of themselves or their family was hung up. Again, there is nothing wrong with this in and of itself in a school classroom, but it is important to understand that this practice may not have the same resonance with Muslim students as those from an Anglo-American background. Being in a classroom full of pictures might even feel over stimulating to some students who are used to being in homes and mosques where the walls are kept more plain. Whether or not the general busyness of the walls in many school classrooms is having an effect of overstimulating students is something

---

[428] Most notably the traditions of miniature paintings in Persian culture, which influenced similar traditions in Turkey and the Mughal empire of South Asia. Even in these traditions facial images were kept small, the paintings were kept in manuscripts and not hung on the wall, and images of religious figures excluded the face entirely. Western researchers of "Islamic Art" have a tendency to overemphasize these art forms in their characterizations of art in the Islamic world. This may be in part because Western academics of the Muslim world have been historically more likely to choose heterodox exceptions as their own areas of fascination and pedestalization while appropriating orthodoxy as small-minded (Said, 1978, see the subsection "Crisis" in Chapter one). This type of selectivity on the part of Western academics can be problematic for teachers at times when they go and research something like "Islamic Art" and find books or articles authored by Western academics. It often gives an impression of traditions in the Muslim world that is biased against the orthodox traditions that the majority of Muslims that people interact with in their daily lives actually adhere to. The term "Islamic Art" is a Western academic term that is itself nebulous and whose pertinence is disputed (Blair & Bloom, 2003). The vast majority of art in the history of the Muslim world is centered upon calligraphy or geometric and floral patterning precisely because those art forms exclude animate beings.

[429] Sunan Ibn Mājah Book 6 Hadith 1521 https://sunnah.com/urn/1288040

teachers may want to consider in the case of Muslim students whose homes and cultural spaces are much more likely to have plain walls.

Praying in congregation and consequences for students. As stated before, Islamic jurisprudence dictates that it is highly preferred to perform the *salāh* in congregation[430], and only done individually when absolutely necessary. One problem when schools take an approach that just leaves it to each individual Muslim student to figure out on their own about how, when, and where to go about doing their prayers during the school day is that it essentially denies them the chance to pray in congregation; which involves some level of coordination and cooperation with the school staff and administration to organize. Again, the viewpoint that praying in congregation is an obligatory component of the five daily prayers is a not uncommon position amongst Muslims, and there is plenty of religious justification behind it.

Furthermore, while each school has its own context and dynamics, where there are schools with a sizable population of Muslim students, having them pray in one big group at one designated time and in one designated space ought to lead to the most efficiency. Of course, if students do pray in congregation that is going to have all sorts of other implications because it will create a situation where students will be transitioning from one place to another en masse. This is another reason why supervision is crucial. Expectations for hallway behavior should be clear and explicit, and there are religious edicts that explicitly state that approaching the prayer should be done in a calm and solemn manner[431], consistent with the expectations schools typically want from the hallway behavior of students. This is not to say that it would be appropriate for schools to invoke these religious edicts in setting expectations for students in their hallway behavior when transporting to and from the prayer. But the point is that expectations should be set and it should not turn into a time for raucous socializing or galavanting for students. Families ought to support the school in this. It may be best to have a a pass issuance system for students to be executed during the prayer times; for younger and pre-adolescents it would be ideal that a staff member is assigned to go to rooms to excuse them from class with their pass, and then supervise those students in transport (perhaps in a line, which adolescents are typically reticent to). Otherwise hall monitors should be on guard and know and communicate clear expectations that students are to go nowhere but the bathroom for washing and the designated prayer area. I cannot stress enough that the more planned supervision the better. When I have had educators come to me who have had problems with students abusing their right to pray in school and I

---

[430] Qur'an 4:102 https://quran.com/4/102, Qur'an 2:43 https://quran.com/2/43, Sahīh al-Bukhārī Book 10 Hadith 41 http://sunnah.com/bukhari/10/41, Sahīh al-Bukhārī Book 10 Hadith 42 http://sunnah.com/bukhari/10/42
[431] Sahīh al-Bukhārī Book 11 Hadith 32 https://sunnah.com/bukhari/11/32, Sahīh al-Bukhārī Book 11 Hadith 33 http://sunnah.com/bukhari/11/33

probe them on their particular situation the most common pitfall that is unveiled is that there was not enough planned supervision of the students. This usually happens because the educators feel they want to respect student privacy and they are concerned about being invasive. These are legitimate concerns, but they are also rooted in a lack of understanding and knowledge about the prayer itself, which makes people afraid of making mistakes and insecure with how they might direct students while supervising them. It is rather strange in a way, when are there other instances in schooling when educators justify to themselves that students should not be monitored? It may not be intuitive for young people to like being supervised, but it is a basic need for them in order to be successful in almost anything they undertake.

It can be a good idea to have students sign off on a contractual commitment in order to pray where they agree to abide by behavior expectations. It can be acknowledged within the agreement that the right to pray could possibly be taken away if the student uses the time to cause disruptions. However, schools should not go into these types of contractual agreements with a "gotcha" mindset where they are overly-ready to cut off the students' rights. This creates animosity. It has to be approached with a growth mindset focused on mutual learning, cooperation, and the educators should model interpersonal patience for the students in how they conduct themselves with them; remembering that the students are up against many competing social-emotional factors in their quest to pray in school. There can be incremental systems of consequence in place. For example, if they misbehave once there could be a warning, if they do it twice they could be disallowed from joining the communal prayer the next day, if they do it a third time then maybe for two days, and so on. These types of things are reasonable, but their success is also contingent on the overall respect the students feel for themselves as Muslims. Including chapter six's recommendations with the curricula can help with this. School's should get the parents informed and on board with the details of any type of contract that is drawn up and need to make sure that only the specific offending students are reprimanded when misbehavior does occur and that not all of the Muslim students are punished and redirected collectively. Do not make the group suffer for the actions of a few. Also, females do not pray while [432] and will therefore go several days without doing so.

Having a specified quiet room in the school that students of any faith can use to pray or meditate in is another option. There are some public schools who have these and even label them "prayer rooms", though it seems to me that calling it a "quiet" room might be equally suitable and less controversial to some. This practice is extraordinarily common in hospitals, even ones that are the products of government funding. These rooms usually have barren walls and open floor spaces. Another option could be the room that is the office of the family or

---

[432] Sunan Abī Dawūd Book 1 Hadith 262

cultural liaison, so long as it works size-wise. This is discussed further in the section below on family involvement.

An important note on supervision is to know that staff members at the school cannot lead or partake in the prayers with students. This is a violation of the First Amendment. I am often asked if it is better to have a Muslim staff member supervise the students, and I think there is likely to be reasons why this makes sense. At the same time having someone supervise who is a good supervisor and good at managing children in general should be the higher priority. This may or may not be a Muslim staff member, and if it is a non-Muslim staff member who knows the process and needs of the prayer that I have taught in this book then they might be equally well equipped to supervise. Personally, I think usually the principal is the best person to supervise. They are the symbol of ultimate authority in the building. Muslim cultures tend to like their leaders to be readily available to people on an inter-personal level. The principals that are taken to the best by Muslim students and families in a school community are not the ones who confine themselves in their office throughout the school day. They are ones who are out and about and make themselves present and available to the students on a causal level. Being present before, during, and after the prayers as a supervisor is a way a principal could make that possible.

Jummah - The Friday Congregation

Friday is the day of congregation in Islam as Sunday is to Christians. Friday is called *jummah* in Islam and Arabic, as well as in most Muslim cultures regardless of whether or not Arabic is the native language. *Jummah* literally means "congregation" and the actual getting together on that day is also called *jummah*.

The rules and must-follows of *jummah* involve coming together in a setting where the call to prayer is made[433], then a religious sermon is heard and the *dhuhr* (noon) prayer is done in a large congregation.[434] The coming together can occur before the time of *dhuhr*, but in that case the sermon has to last past the time of *dhuhr* when the prayer is done, and just generally the jummah prayer is supposed to be done early in the time frame of *dhuhr*.[435] *Jummah* is typically done in a mosque and some jurists rule it must be done in one, but others rule it can be done anywhere that is a suitable place to pray, including the outdoors if the weather is nice. *Jummah*

---

[433] Sahīh al-Bukhārī Book 11 Hadith 39 https://sunnah.com/bukhari/11/39
[434] At jummah only 2 rakahs are prayed for *dhur* and the Qu'ran recitation is out loud.
[435] Sahīh al-Bukhārī Book 11 Hadith 64 http://sunnah.com/bukhari/11/64, Sahīh Muslim Book 7 Hadith 43 http://sunnah.com/muslim/7/43

is also an act that is obligatory for males to observe and supererogatory for females.[436] So there is a sin on post-pubescent males who do not observe *jummah*, but not on females.

Jummah is often referred to in English as "Friday prayers", which is fine, although there are no actual additional prayers that are done; what makes it different is the sermon that is listened to. There is nothing wrong with calling it Friday prayers, but I tell non-Muslims to just refer to it as *"jummah"*.

Jummah is not a sabbath. I have heard people refer to it as "their sabbath" in reference to the students. While Friday is a day off throughout the Muslim world,[437] unlike the sabbath of Judaism, there are no dictates in Islam that Friday has to be a day off or a day of rest or a day where work and fun cannot be partaken in.[438] Outside of having to observe the congregational sermon and prayer there are no additional obligations or restrictions on that day for Muslims, aside from it being a day where supererogatory fasting is highly discouraged.[439] An interesting side note, Saturday in Arabic and Muslim countries is called *yawm al-sabt*, which means "day of the Sabbath", in recognition of it being the day that is specially observed by Jews. It is very common in Muslim countries for families to observe the tradition of eating a meal together after the congregation on Friday.[440] Though they would like to, many Muslim families in the West are not able to do this due to work and school scheduling.

Accommodating Jummah

So how do the schools accommodate *jummah*? Generally, it will be the same as accommodating the prayers except the students will need at least an additional 15 to 20 minutes for the sermon that needs to take place, this could be as short as ten. At the same time, *jummah* often brings more participants than the daily prayers and that can make the initial process of the students gathering together last longer as well, including the time it takes for the students to all make *wudū'*. There are no time restrictions and mandates on the sermon that is given in the religion, however, there are obligations that the speaker giving the sermon has to observe as far as specific invocations that need to be said and other religious matters that need to be mentioned. Asking those delivering the sermon to be done in less than 10 minutes is stretching it. The

---

[436] Sunan Abī Dawūd Book 2 Hadith 678 https://sunnah.com/abudawud/2/678
[437] The typical weekend in the Muslim world is Friday and Saturday. In Saudi Arabia it was Thursday and Friday up until 2013.
[438] Sahīh al-Bukhārī Book 11 Hadith 27 https://sunnah.com/bukhari/11/27
[439] Jami` at-Tirmidhī Book 8 Hadith 62 https://sunnah.com/tirmidhi/8/62
[440] Jami` at-Tirmidhī Book 4 Hadith 38 https://sunnah.com/tirmidhi/4/38

sermon *cannot* be given by a Muslim staff member due to first amendment restrictions.[441] Therefore, the sermon has to be given either by a student or by a volunteer that has been invited by students or families to come into the school to give it.

The only actual religious dictates regarding who gives the sermon is that they be male and past puberty, they cannot be female.[442] Although, it should be someone who has religious knowledge and knows how to give the sermon, in the community this is done by someone who might be called an *Imām*. But there is no special ordination or formalized qualifications that have to have been bestowed upon someone in order for them to do the Friday sermon.

For a student to lead other students in a high school in the Friday sermon and prayer is a task with a lot of responsibility that will encompass a variety of pressures for that individual. In situations that I know of where Muslim students were able to effectively do the Friday congregation on their own in school, a solid leader of the process and deliverer of the sermon from the student body was a key factor. So the staff at the school could maybe coach the students a little bit around choosing the right person to lead the Friday prayer. It should be recommended to the students that they choose someone who others will be willing to follow and respect, and would also keep the students on track and responsible. No easy task for high schoolers, but it is a positive leadership opportunity for whoever takes the role on, and certainly a learning experience for them in its own right. Once the students choose a leader, that person should choose someone to serve as a backup in case they are absent for some reason on a Friday. Seniors usually work best for these leadership positions, and generally older people are given preference in leading the prayer[443], but they can also have the most reason to not be present in school sometimes. It might make sense for the students to choose as the backup an underclassman who would maybe be expected to take on the leadership role the following year.

---

[441] *Guidance on Constitutionally Protected Prayer and Religious Expression in Public Elementary and Secondary Schools* states, "*Teachers and other public school officials, acting in their official capacities, may not lead their classes in prayer, devotional readings from the Bible, or other religious activities.*" Citing *Engel v. Vitale, 370 U.S. 421* (1962). Note that staff leading their students in prayers or religious activities is not the same as staff supervising students while they conduct religious activities from their own initiative to ensure that the students abide by the school's expectations of conduct, for which there is a clear and compelling secular purpose.

[442] Sunan an-Nasā'i Book 49 Hadith 10 https://sunnah.com/nasai/49/10. Be aware that students cannot be compelled or pressured by the school to break these religious rules and told to have a female give the sermon based on the school's own perception and conceptualization of valuing "equity". The federal guidelines show that leadership choices are to be left with students of the religious group, "*...the Equal Access Act permits religious student groups to allow only members of their religion to serve in leadership positions if these leadership positions are positions that affect the religious content of the speech at the group's meetings. For example, a religious student group may require leaders such as the group's president, vice-president, and music coordinator to be a dedicated member of a particular religion if the leaders' duties consist of leading prayers, devotions, and safeguarding the spiritual content of the meetings.*"

[443] Sahīh al-Bukhārī Book 10 Hadith 27 https://sunnah.com/bukhari/10/27

If the prayers are conducted under the guise of a formalized student group, that group will have a staff member assigned as an advisor, which often enough is a non-Muslim staff member, and these are all pieces of advice than the advisor could give to the students.

When a student steps up to do the Friday sermon they open themselves up to a lot of critique and take on an intimidating job. They will have to be very self conscious of themselves and what they are saying. The Friday sermon is not something whimsical to be done. So preparation for it is a daunting task where the adolescent who is already overly-conscious of the judgement of their peers will have these stressors put on hyperdrive. There is a resource online called *Khutbah*[444] Bank from the United Kingdom; at https://khutbahbank.org.uk/. A contributor to this site has compiled about 80 sermons into a document that can be given in about 10 minutes. See the footnote for the exact link to the document.[445] The sermons are specifically designed to meet the needs of Muslim congregations who have to fulfill the rights of *jummah*, but are lacking in qualified people to do so and lead it. Muslim students in America are not always aware of this resource. So suggesting it to them or their families could be helpful because it would save the leader time and stress of having to prepare the actual sermon. There is nothing wrong with the person giving the sermon reading it from paper.

There are other options for accommodating *jummah* as well. If families wish to remove their students and children from school to observe religious rituals for a time, schools have the discretion to allow that according to the federal guidelines.[446] Families need to be made aware of this right because the most feasible choice for everyone may be for students to leave school in order to attend *jummah* in a mosque and then returning after. Loads of Muslims in American society do this with their workplaces. This may or may not be the best option depending on the specific community and the school's proximity to a mosque, as well as the trust and responsibility level on the part of the student that is perceived from the school and parents. The school can look up if there is a mosque nearby that can be reached in a few minutes time. Nowadays, there is a good chance the mosque will have a website and often enough they will post the time at which they have *jummah*. If they do it is probably a good idea to still give them a call or send an email to make sure the time posted on their website is actually correct and not outdated. Mosques usually operate via direct verbal communication with their congregants so they are not always keen to keep their digital presence up to date. Most mosques do have a set

---

[444] *Khutbah* is the Arabic word for "sermon".

[445] https://tinyurl.com/ybfdajry

[446] The *Guidance on Constitutionally Protected Prayer and Religious Expression in Public Elementary and Secondary Schools* says, "Schools have the discretion to dismiss students to off-premises religious instruction, provided that schools do not encourage or discourage participation in such instruction or penalize students for attending or not attending"

time at which *jummah* does start and the sermon and prayer together usually run from 30 to 45 minutes, probably closer to 45 in most cases. Because of daylight savings and the other changes in the prayer times that have been discussed, the exact start time of *jummah* will change in the year, becoming earlier after daylight savings in the fall. Also, while the mosque may have a stated start time they are not always exact in actually starting on that time. It could very well be normal at the mosque for them to say that *jummah* starts at 1:30 but on most Fridays the sermon does not actually start until around 1:45. Not being hyper concerned about to-the-minute punctuality plays a role in this, but sometimes there are simply very practical matters behind it. The *Imām* who is giving the sermon might very well work a normal job on Friday and simply get caught in traffic on the way. Due to this type of variability, while you will commonly find that mosques have a set time for the start of *jummah*, you will rarely find that they post a set end time for it.

If a school does reach out to the mosque to find out about their start time for *jummah* the consistency of the start time might be another thing to ask about. If students are going to leave school to attend *jummah* and are expected to come back it is important that the school has an awareness and sensitivity about these types of variables. If a student leaves at 1:20 to attend *jummah* at 1:30 at a local mosque and the school has it in their mind that *jummah* will take thirty minutes and end at 2:00, they might conclude that it is totally reasonable to expect the student back at 2:10. But if the student goes out to the mosque and it turns out that the sermon did not actually start until 1:45 and then it goes on for 45 minutes, the earliest the student is going to get back is 2:40. If they arrive back and are admonished for being late and accused of intentionally skipping class, those accusations are going to feel unjustified and insensitive to the student and then consternation is likely to ensue. So schools need to actually know about the cultural institutions that exist in the communities they serve. Reaching out to a mosque to find out about *jummah* or just to express a more general interest in what they do for the purpose of better knowing the places that the school's students are involved in is a very good idea. This can lead to discussions where the school might be able to position itself to offer the insight to the mosque about how consistency in punctuality would be helpful to the school as well and serve the mutual interest that they have in creating a productive environment to nurture young people. This could potentially act as some healthy pressure and advice that some mosques might need in order to become a little more punctual.

One advantage to know in this discussion is that mosques do not work like churches in some denominations where congregants are assigned or pledged to specific churches and then only attend Sunday services there. Generally, a Muslim can attend any mosque offering *jummah* to fulfill the religion's legalistic obligations. So it is totally reasonable to expect that a student could attend *jummah* at whatever mosque is in closest proximity to the school. It is not like they have to drive twenty minutes to go to the specific mosque that they study at on the weekends.

Another accommodation option is for the school to cut the student day short on Friday. This may sound far-reaching and for some school communities it definitely would not work. However, if the school community has a very large population of Muslim students, or if it serves primarily Muslim students, then this is something that should be considered and talked about with families of all backgrounds in the school community as a consideration. The mandates of given states as to how much students attend school is another matter that of course needs to be considered with this type of choice. In the state of Minnesota, for example, the mandates are done by hours, which opens up the opportunity for flexibility. So what some schools do is they add an extra 50 minutes to the school day on Monday through Thursday and then have a student half-day every Friday. The school I work at does this. This practice is highly appreciated by the families, and even we are finding that there is an appeal to it from non-Muslim families who feel that the weekend is often too short for their kids and do not mind them having the extra half-day time on Friday. Especially as new modes of distance learning become available, this could be an option for some school communities to investigate. Perhaps the schools even having Fridays off altogether is a good idea, in a fashion where the students do distance learning for half the day. This would save on transportation budgets as well. Another great benefit of it for staff is that consistent student half days or full days off can provide time for consistent staff collaboration or professional development. Not having enough time for these matters is a constant complaint amongst educators, and having a consistent half day or full day without students in the week I am sure most school staff would deem to be very helpful.

Ramadan Fasting Times

Since the prayer times have been explained I will now explain how the fasting during Ramadan correlates with them before going into some issues that may be auxiliary to these core practices but are nevertheless important technical issues in Islam for educators to know about.

Fasting in Islam begins at the minute when the *fejr* (dawn) prayer starts and ends at the minute when the sunset prayer starts. Taking our September 6th example in Hennepin County Minnesota, fasting would look like this:

Fejr (dawn)	**5:18am - Begin Fasting**
Dhuhr (noon)	1:10pm
Asr (afternoon)	4:51pm
Maghrib (sunset)	**7:45pm - End Fasting**
Ishā' (evening)	9:10pm

The meal that is eaten before the dawn prayer is called *sahūr* and the meal that is eaten to break the fast at *maghrib* (sunset) is called *iftār*. If one sleeps past the time that the dawn prayer comes in, they are still not allowed to eat until sunset and have to fast the day without having had breakfast. Adolescents struggle with this frequently. If you hear a Muslim student say to another Muslim student during Ramadan, "I didn't have *sahūr* today" it means they missed the pre-dawn meal and the day of fasting is more difficult for them. When the time to break the fast gets earlier in spring and winter in later years, it might be a cool community building idea for some schools to host a dinner (*iftār*) at sundown for families to attend. I am sure that would be greatly appreciated by families, well-attended, and a splendid way for families to teach about foods from their culture.

As of the year 2019, Ramadan has moved into the spring side of the summer solstice[447], which means that the amount of daytime for the fasting is still long but getting shorter each year. It also means that within Ramadan the first day is the shortest day of fasting and each day gets progressively longer by increments of a few minutes each day, the exact amount of which varies depending on a location's latitude. This will remain the case until the entirety of the month reaches the other side of the winter solstice, which will likely be in 2033.

Ramadan Beginning		Ramadan End	
April 12th, 2021	Prayer times (MN)	May 10th, 2021	Prayer times (MN)
Fejr (dawn)	**5:06am - Begin**	**Fejr (dawn)**	**4:10am - Begin**
Dhuhr (noon)	1:15pm	Dhuhr (noon)	1:10pm
Asr (afternoon)	4:59pm	Asr (afternoon)	5:11pm
Maghrib (sunset)	**7:56pm - End**	**Maghrib (sunset)**	**8:31pm - End**
Ishā' (evening)	9:23pm	Ishā' (evening)	10:11pm
Total fasting time:	**14 hours 50 minutes**	**Total fasting time:**	**16 hours 21 minutes**

---

[447] How Ramadan works in the calendar was explained previously in chapter three.

Let's look at some specific days to understand how fasting can vary in specific locales. In 2021 Ramadan will begin around April 12th[448] and May 10th will be towards the end of Ramadan. Let's look at the prayer times for these two dates in Minneapolis:

So over the course of four weeks during the spring time the fasting time in the Twin Cities increases by about ninety minutes total, and it does so incrementally by about three to four minutes a day with the fasting both beginning a little earlier and ending a little later each day. The more north one goes latitudinally the more this trend expands, and the more south one goes the more the trend contracts. So in Houston in the same time frame the same trend is observed, but there is only about 50 minutes of variation over the course of four weeks as opposed to the 90 in Minnesota because Houston is further south and closer to the equator.

Ramadan Weekday Schedule

Time	Activity
AM	
3:50-4:20	Wake up & eat *sahūr*
4:20-4:30	Pray *fejr*
4:30-5:30	**Sleep**
5:30-6:30	Get ready for work
6:30-7:00	Drive to work
7:00-3:15pm	Work
PM	
3:15-3:45	Pray dhuhr
3:45-4:30	Drive home
4:30-6:30	**Sleep**
6:30-6:45	Pray *asr*
6:45-7:45	Clean house
7:45-8:30	Read Qur'an
8:30-8:45	Break fast and pray *maghrib*
8:45-9:30	*Iftar*
9:30-9:50	Tea
9:50-10:10	Drive to masjid
10:10-10:30	Read Qur'an
10:30-10:45	Pray *ishā'*
10:45-11:45	Pray *tarawīh*
11:45-12:05	Drive home
12:05 - 12:20	Get ready for bed
12:20-3:50	**Sleep**
Total Sleep Time	**6 hours 30 minutes**

Scheduling Considerations for the School

Firstly, another life skill that can be emphasized to students during Ramadan is scheduling, daily organization, planning, and management of one's time. Life can get very tight during this month. The extra time devoted to spending in the mosque and reading the Qur'an are oftentimes tasks that people now want to perform daily while they might have been more likely to pass it up outside of Ramadan. For others who struggle to perform the five daily prayers outside of Ramadan, they will have a heightened desire to add that to their schedule as well. On top of that, daily sleep schedules are likely to go a shift one way or the other.

One thing I have done to try to directly help students is share with them my own personal daily schedule for Ramadan. My goal in doing this is to show them how I manage to fulfill all of my secular world obligations that I still have with work, while also making the time to read more Qur'an, attend the mosque at night, and still sleep at least six hours a day; though it may not be continuous. The most recent example of what I show them is to the left.

---

[448] The exact day cannot be known yet, how the days of the month are determined was explained in the previous chapter.

Students always ask me if I can print out copies of it and share it with them. I will make one of these out every year and post it on abrahameducation.com. If you like you can share it with students and tell them that this is how a Muslim teacher in Minnesota organizes his daily Ramadan schedule. Perhaps they can be prompted to make their own personal schedule before Ramadan that will help them accomplish their own personal goals and responsibilities with it in the time context of their given locale. The important thing with it is to plan in the schedule to get six hours of sleep, because this is the biggest struggle for most students. I will make a new one every year because what the schedule looks like can alter a little bit over the course of years as the daylight hours change.

While of course daily scheduling organization is a skill we want to teach students, and it would be nice if we can leverage Ramadan as a source of motivation for them to do it, the reality is schools are going to be dealing with the fact that most students will be staying up all night. For adolescents this is especially difficult as it is well known now in science that they are basically unable to go to bed and fall asleep at earlier hours due to the way melatonin regulates in their brains (Carskadon, 1993; Berger et al, 2018).

Let's consider first the different types of schedules that students will opt to operate on during Ramadan if they did not have to go to school. Let's think of these schedules as beginning when the sun goes down and the fast is broken, which is the actual beginning of the day on the Islamic calendar. The first schedule many students will run on is one where they wake up at this time having slept during the afternoon and stayed up all night. They begin the fast in the morning and continue to stay up until early afternoon. When they get to the early afternoon they go to sleep. They might wake up briefly to pray the afternoon prayer but go right back to sleep and wake up when it is time to break the fast. In the second schedule students would break their fast and stay up all night, and then when the morning prayer comes they will eat right before it and go to sleep after the morning prayer. Since the prayer takes place early in the morning this can entail a five to seven hour sleep session and still allow them to wake up before noon. When Ramadan was in the summer one of these two types of schedules is what they would normally run on. It is noticeable that both of them entail sleeping an extended period during the hours that would normally encompass the school day, if not all of it. During the summer, parents would mind this less because school was not in session. Now that Ramadan has fully come into the school year massive adjustments are needing to be made.

In my experience most students prefer the first schedule. I believe there is something natural about sleeping in the early afternoon. Neurologists have studied afternoon napping since at least the 1980s and determined it has numerous health benefits, especially with alertness and functionality, and is likely natural to the circadian rhythm of human beings (Broughton &

<u>Dinges, 1989</u>). Sleeping in the afternoon is a commonly known cultural practice throughout the world, it is referred to in the Spanish-speaking world as a *siesta*. There is precedent for doing it in Islam.[449] For me, even though I get to bed right after the prayers in the mosque and late in the evening and I am asleep around midnight, if I have the day off of work I greatly prefer to nap in the early afternoon during Ramadan. If I do have to work I will nap in the late afternoon as my schedule above indicates. When students do have to go to school during Ramadan they will inevitably be trying to steal sleep during part of the day, especially the afternoon.

So schools need to gauge their students and families and make a decision as to what time of day they choose to prioritize for academic work with students; the morning or the afternoon. I believe most schools will find that the morning is the time that works best to prioritize, because even if students stay up all night, the morning is still after they have recently eaten and drank. So the physiological aspects of fasting have not kicked in yet and the morning can feel like any other morning from the rest of the year. But by the afternoon the body is making its adjustments to not having eaten lunch and lethargy onsets.

As a general rule I advise schools to anticipate planning to prioritize academic work in the morning, and the afternoon for something else. But gauge the feedback of your students and families, and opening up the conversation proactively is the most important thing. In the afternoon, even though it is usually a time of tiredness, more physical type work might make the most sense. Moving around and getting blood circulated is one of the ways that a person can get more energy while fasting when they cannot nourish themselves. You might actually be surprised what people are capable of doing physically while fasting. It is common in the Muslim world for young people to play soccer all day while fasting. I know kids who love to play basketball in the afternoons during it. Husain Abdullah, a former player for the Minnesota Vikings fasted when Ramadan was in the long hot days of August in 2010 while participating in the entirety of NFL training camp (<u>Borzi, 2010</u>). Physical activity can help keep the mind occupied in a way that helps distract from the hunger and thirst. There are many Muslims who go running in the afternoons while fasting. Having students do rigorous sports in the afternoon is something that schools will probably have to consider carefully for liability reasons and make their own decisions about, as they do not want any student passing out from dehydration. But schools have implemented a variety of physical activity options in the afternoons with success.

If students are stuck in their regular classrooms during the afternoon, Ramadan is probably a good time to do more social learning activities that involve getting up and moving around. If they have to sit for too extended a period you are begging for them to go to sleep.

---

[449]Sunan Abī Dawūd Book 2 Hadith 697 <u>https://sunnah.com/abudawud/2/697</u>

While I think it is alright and logical that the afternoon classes during Ramadan loosen academic expectations to some degree, I advise to be cautious about being overly-ready to play movies for students just to pass the time. For one thing, they will still likely go to sleep during it. For another, while some people might resort to consuming entertainment as a way to distract themselves while fasting, there are still others who wish to avoid such activity for the reasons of heightened religious awareness that were discussed in chapter three.

If the school and staff do not mind if students nap during class for a portion of the day, then it might make sense to consider accommodating a nap time or having a nap room so students can take one during the school day that is structured and does not entail compromising expectations set by the school, nor dragging down a classroom atmosphere like students napping in class tends to do. If naps can be planned and relegated to a specific locale within the building, it helps to isolate the purpose of the nap for the student as something to help them recharge and focus on the rest of the day. When students steal naps during class their purpose for the nap can get meddled with the motivation to avoid learning. This makes the nap counter-productive and might even extend the time napping that they take. Sometimes a mere 15-20 minutes can be enough to recharge from a nap (Lovato & Lack, 2010). If a student sleeps for 20 minutes in an isolated room where nothing is going on, they may just get up and go back to class ready to focus. If they nap for 15-20 minutes in class and wake up to hear the teacher in the middle of a monologue that they have not been paying attention to, they will put that head right back on the desk and choose to nod off for longer.

The other options that need to be considered is giving students the choice of early release or late arrival to school. Now that almost every school in the country is versed with at least some type of distance learning platform after the closures from the COVID-19 pandemic, this should be something more reasonable. There are many students who would love to have a schedule where they are able to read and study overnight and do their homework, eat breakfast and pray, and then go to school to participate in live classes; but to then be able to leave at say 11:30 and go home to rest. Conversely there might be students who want to sleep in the early morning after the prayer but would be happier to arrive at school at 11:30 or noon and only participate live in the second half of the day and then do their schoolwork overnight.

If live testing has to be done, and Ramadan has snuck into April which is a heavy testing month, (of course all of the spring really is these days) then overall I would say definitely prioritize having options to do the testing as early as possible in the morning. The flexibility can be given to let students do testing in the afternoon for those who want to, but plan generally that the best option is going to be found to have testing in the morning.

Another consideration schools need to make is flipping their morning and afternoon schedule every other day. The major drawback that teachers always see in a school intentionally prioritizing the morning as the more rigorous academic time and the afternoon as more casual is that the academic rigor in classes scheduled in the afternoon will suffer. This is correct. So if the school could run on a schedule where instructional time in the morning is evened out amongst classes by flipping every other day this problem might be solved. During Ramadan, in a school with a very high percentage of Muslim students this definitely makes sense. But even outside of that consideration, most teachers will tell you that students have an easier time being academically engaged in the morning. The afternoon learning suffers from the after-lunch effect where students are digesting their food and have been buzzed up from socializing. They become distracted, tired, and their attention span bottoms out.

But in addition to that, we need to ask if there are not some general and natural physiological processes at play where people's circadian rhythm just makes them more lethargic in the afternoon, and then consider how this affects our students. If these effects do exist, it seems reasonable to think that when we have students who come from cultures closer to the equator where taking siesta is common they may be even more likely to experience these detriments. I am sure many of you have had the experience in your school of really analyzing a student and seeing that they are successful in their morning classes and failing in their afternoon ones. Could it not follow that flipping the students morning and afternoon schedule every day could at least better even out their success? Sometimes looking at the situations of specific cultural groups and their accommodation needs can help us consider changes in the school that could benefit everyone. It might help many students to run a schedule that flips every other day so each class can concentrate its instructional delivery into morning class periods, while making the afternoons more about student work, social learning activities, or rest and other accommodations that students might need. Aggregate reviews of different types of studies have shown that when schools intentionally accommodate student sleep schedules it has an association with better psychological health for them (Berger et al, 2018).

Family Involvement at School

Another one of the more frequent inquiries I get from my trainees is "how can we get more families involved?" There are many components that go into a question like this and there is an in-depth discussion to be had about it. Oftentimes parent involvement is measured by their attendance at scheduled school functions as well as reciprocation by parents from school communication to home.

I choose to talk about this issue in the section on technicalities of following Islam due to how intertwined it is with scheduling. As we can see from the discussion on the prayer times, practicing Islam gives ever-constant dictates over the schedule of one's life. When schools do not know how to consider things like the prayer times and having to perform the prayer, they will easily schedule school events along patterns that create dilemmas for Muslim families.

To illustrate this let's look back at the Minnesota prayer times for the first week of September:

Fejr (dawn)	5:18am
Dhuhr (noon)	1:10pm
Asr (afternoon)	**4:51pm**
Maghrib (sunset)	**7:45pm**
Ishā' (evening)	9:10pm

Now let's say that a school schedules a function from 5pm-7:30pm. The first thing you can notice is that it is going to be very unlikely that a Muslim family will want to show up precisely at 5pm. If it takes the family more than ten minutes to drive to school, not to mention getting everyone in the family ready to go out the door, there is no chance that they can both arrive on time as well as perform the afternoon prayer before arriving. If they do arrive at the school on time in lieu of performing the prayer early, and the function is something that will run close to the end of the prayer timeframe,[450] how confident can they be that they will be able to pray once they are at the school? Does the school set aside a regular place that families can go to pray when they visit? When they attended school functions before, was there a large clearly-labeled sign at the entry point or welcome table that pointed in the direction of the prayer room? Did the greeters themselves take the initiative to inform families that are clearly Muslim where they could go to pray once in the building? In the communication sent home from the school, was it noted that accommodations for the prayer would be provided? Will the event itself have a sufficient intermission or break that allows for families to do the prayer in a way that is not disruptive or that sets them up to appear to be rude or "ducking out" of the event? These are just some of the questions that come to mind. All in all, these situations often amount to it being an easier option for the families to just not show up at all.

If schools want to increase family involvement they have to consider the prayer times and accommodations for families, and this is true of all schools regardless of the age of the

---

[450] And this time frame between the afternoon and sunset prayer gets progressively smaller from the beginning of the school year until winter break, so for after-school functions that take place later in the year Muslim families are dealing with even smaller time frames.

students. If the families in the school's community are already in the habit of not regularly attending school functions, it may be that the school has to do some proactive communication with families about how they are trying to make the school more accommodating to the religious practices of the families they serve.

I will note here that punctuality itself is generally not stressed to the exact same degree in the Muslim world that it is in the West. In the West, punctuality is generally valued on a level that goes down to the minute. But in the Muslim world it is the schedule of the prayers that usually dictate when meetings, appointments, and social events occur. So in the Muslim world if there is an after-school family function, it will not be scheduled for 5 o'clock, it will be scheduled for "after maghrib" or after one of the other prayers. This means that families can show up after the city has done the maghrib prayer, the time of which will be known because all of the mosques in the city will make the call to prayer[451] through loudspeakers that ring through the neighborhoods. About 10 to 15 minutes after the call to prayer is done the actual prayer takes place in the mosques, which is signaled by another call.[452] So the expectation is that families will pray at the mosques near their homes and then after that they will start making their way to the school for the function. The reception and greeting at these events are long and extended because it is known families will be showing up in a very staggered fashion, and also properly conducted greetings are a highly valued matter in the Muslim world for which sufficient time and space are always afforded at social gatherings. There will be zero expectation that anyone shows up at any sort of precise minute. Even if the event involves the production of coordinated activities that necessitate scheduling themselves, they will be scheduled to begin at a time that occurs well after the prayer time and leaves plenty of space for people to arrive in a casual manner and greet and socialize at the event after their arrival before festivities take place.

Families not showing up to scheduled events is one concern that I have fielded from many educators. However, there is also an inverse concern of families who show up at the school unannounced, oftentimes seemingly with the expectation that they should be able to talk to their child's teacher, or whoever they came to see, just by virtue of having arrived. This causes a lot of anxiety for school staff.

When this occurs there is usually a clash of values regarding scheduling and punctuality at play beneath the surface. However, within that, and something that I believe educators are often missing in these situations, is that they are underestimating the degree to which those families and parents who show up unannounced may be willing to wait and sit around for an extended

---

[451] The call to prayer is called the *ādhan*.

[452] This second, more quickly done call, which signals the prayer's imminent commence, is called the *iqāma*.

period of time once they are there in order to see whoever they came to see. Again, precise appointment scheduling is usually not done in the Muslim world, whether it is with schools, businesses, hospitals, or any other formal institution. What does exist is a culture of showing up when one needs to and when one has the time to wait for the services they need. Alongside this there is a culture on the part of the formal institutions of always being ready to accommodate the comfort of guests who will need to wait when they arrive. Full guest rooms near the entrances of buildings are very common in all institutions in the Muslim world, these will often involve comfortable couches and guests will be offered things like tea and water and perhaps some dried fruit.

A mind shift that many schools need to start making in regards to family involvement and attendance at the school is to stop thinking so much about how to get people to arrive at scheduled events, and instead to start thinking about how to start creating an environment, community, and atmosphere where the sentiment is that anyone is free to show up at anytime and when they do show up they are not only welcome, but rather encouraged to stay around for a while. A first step towards doing this can be creating a large family room in the school. Especially in schools that have a family or cultural liaison, that person should not be given some small office in a corner somewhere. Rather, if possible, they should be given a large room similar to the size of a classroom, and they should also be provided some funds in order to set that room up in a manner that they deem to be culturally appropriate and welcoming. This may involve buying some couches, a hot water dispenser with dixie styrofoam cups, tea packets, a sugar dispenser, and perhaps some dates that people can eat. They could buy large carpeting and have a large floor space for families to pray in if need be. They could buy books for children and child toys as families often need to bring younger children along with them. Their room could have a computer that families could use while they are waiting. Staff members who are available, even if they are not the person who the family has shown up to see, can stop by this room and say hello, exchange pleasantries, and maybe even use it as an opportunity to teach them things like how to access the school grading system digitally. Creating this type of cultural change is not something that would be done overnight. It may involve some initial investment and commitment on the part of the school to put the structure in place. The school may have to constantly communicate and re-iterate to the families about the resources that are newly available before they start really being utilized and taking hold. In the long run it can have many ancillary benefits of creating warmer relationships between staff and parents, garnering more feedback from parents about the school, giving parents an increased sense of safety regarding their child, and an increased sense of empowerment regarding their own influence on the school culture.

Bathroom Habits

Islam has some particular etiquettes pertaining to use of the bathroom that educators should know about as they come up frequently for students in the school day; for teachers and school staff in certain positions the possibility exists that they will have to deal with bathroom issues in a direct way depending on their particular responsibilities in the school and the age and functionality level of the students they serve.

Firstly, It is against Islamic etiquette for males to urinate standing up.[453] Some Muslim boys in the West adopt it as a habit out of seeing others do it, and sometimes as a practical matter because the bathrooms in school and other public places may be set up in a way that essentially only allows for using urinals, but it is not something that is consistent with Islamic manners. In Islam, urinating standing up is something that is only to be done if there are no other choices, which may include situations where the only sitting options are too unclean to do so.[454] Since bathrooms in the West are not set up to accommodate the particulars of Islamic bathroom habits, oftentimes Muslims end up needing more time in their use of the bathroom. For example, if a public school bathroom has four urinals and two stalls, it is set up with the assumption that six males who need to urinate could all use it at the same time. But for a group of six males who are Muslim this could very well not be the case, they may opt to wait for one another and only use the stalls. This could cause a group or class trip to the bathroom to take more time.

Secondly, it is part of Islamic etiquette to wash the private areas with water after every single use of the bathroom, whether the act is urinary or bowel.[455] In the West this typically makes it necessary for some type of vessel that holds water to be filled up and brought into the bathroom and toilet area, commonly this takes the form of a bottle.[456] Therefore, many students have a need to perhaps search around and get a hold of a bottle before going to the bathroom; which will perhaps involve inquiring with peers or visiting a locker before going directly to the bathroom itself. When a person is unable to clean

---

[453] Sunan an-Nasā'i Book 1 Hadith 29 https://sunnah.com/urn/1000290

[454] Sunan Ibn Majah Book 1, Hadith 324 https://sunnah.com/urn/1253040

[455] Saḥīḥ al-Bukhārī Book 4 Hadith 16 https://sunnah.com/bukhari/4/16

[456] In the Muslim world the toilets will all have hoses hooked up to them as is seen in the picture.

themselves from their bathroom use as they are used to it can lead to feelings of discomfort, anxiety, and inner-embarrassment. If students do have a bottle it is common nowadays for them to contrive it into a spraying mechanism by poking holes into the top of its cap, typically by using a pen.

Schools could attend to this need by providing what are called medical cleansing bottles, these can be easily purchased online. They are commonly used for feminine hygiene, but they function perfectly for any type of bathroom cleansing. There is some risk that goes along with providing such materials as students could misuse them, so there would need to be coaching and regulations around proper and improper use, but this is no different than any other material that is used by students in the school.

Thirdly, it is part of Islamic etiquette to use the right hand for clean and honorable things and the left hand for things that involve filth.[457] This means that when one cleans themselves in the bathroom they use the left hand.[458] For the most part this is a wholly individual and private matter that does not involve staff members in the school. However, in the case of pre-K students, and some students who have special needs that are low functioning, it is not uncommon at all that school staff members have to deal with and instruct about these matters in a direct way. In the case of pre-K students this involves conditioning them into habits that they will be using for the rest of their life. So it might be appropriate for direct conversations to occur with parents and families about how they want these manners taught to their children, because there could very well be specific preferences that the parents have but would be too shy to bring up themselves.

Fourthly, because answering the call of nature breaks *wudū'* it is the habit of many Muslims to make *wudū'* after any instance of it, whether the prayer is imminent or not. This can mean a certain degree of disrobing and re-robing is involved, especially for females. The process of *wudū'* is the same for both males and females. So females who wear head coverings need to take those off in order to do it. It may be the case for all students that they have to take off footwear. This can add to the amount of time that a student takes when taking a bathroom break and creates the same implications for how the bathroom's cleanliness is left after their use of it as was discussed in the section above on *wudū'*. It is also a common practice in Muslim cultures to wet the face in order to wake oneself up.

---

[457] Jami` at-Tirmidhī Book 25 Hadith 14 https://sunnah.com/tirmidhi/25/14
[458] Sunan ibn Majah Book 1 Hadith 333 https://sunnah.com/urn/1253110

Fifthly, it is counter to Islamic etiquette to greet or talk to someone while in use of the bathroom.[459] It is outside of Muslim cultural norms to knock on a locked door and ask "is anyone in there?" and expect a verbal response as people in the West commonly do. These differing expectations can make it uncomfortable for some kids when teachers or other students yell at them into the bathroom or through the stall doors to tell them to "hurry up" and get out. As another side matter, in many parts of the Muslim world, especially poorer ones, the most commonly used type of toilet is a squat latrine. This consists of what is essentially a dip in the flooring of the stall that is covered in porcelain with a hole in the middle. A squat latrine necessitates the user to squat down to the ground like a catcher does in a baseball game. Using it actually involves contracting different muscles when answering nature's call than one would use with a sitting toilet. So it is not impossible at all that some students who are newer to the country, especially if they came from poorer regions, may be getting used to different ways of using the bathroom entirely. An adjustment that can lead to all sorts of inner discomfort.

The most general takeaway with all this is that if you have students who seemingly spend too much time in the bathroom it is advised to be patient with them and think twice before you broach them about the subject. The intuition of many teachers is to suspect that students who take a long time to use the bathroom are intentionally trying to avoid class. While this certainly could still be the case, it is important to understand that there could very well be other real world matters at play that go beyond the student's control. So teachers should caution themselves before accusing students of wasting time and insisting that if they do not start arriving back to class sooner their privilege of using the bathroom might be taken away etc.

Culinary Habits

In Islam a supererogatory act, and part of the practice of the Prophet Muhammad ﷺ, is to eat with the hands, particularly using the first three digits[460] of the right hand[461], instead of using utensils. This does not mean a Muslim cannot use utensils, but many Muslim cultures and families do not use them regularly for the delivery of food to one's mouth. It is also a common practice amongst Muslims for food to be eaten from one large dish and to sit on the floor while eating with all of the food on top of a

---

[459] Sunan Ibn Majah Book 1, Hadith 381 http://sunnah.com/urn/1253520
[460] Sunan Abī Dawūd Book 28 Hadith 113 https://sunnah.com/abudawud/28/113
[461] Sunan Abī Dawūd Book 28 Hadith 41 https://sunnah.com/abudawud/28/41

sheet. In modern times it is common to use a plastic roll out sheet.[462]

These customs can cause different things to take place when eating in environments where expectations are adjusted to the Anglo culture of table manners that most Americans are accustomed to by default. When Muslims are gathered together in a mosque to eat they will usually sit on the floor and eat on a rolled-out plastic sheet to put everything on, and perhaps use disposable plating as well. This makes it so that when one is eating, most likely using the hands, it is not so big a deal if a little bit of food falls off and lands on the plastic sheet.[463] If the meal is being delivered in big dishes that are eaten communally, it may even be more desirable that the food falls off to the side of the communal dish. Afterwards when everyone is done eating, the sheet that everything is on can simply be wrapped up and tossed in a disposal. If it is a non-plastic sheet the dishes can be removed and the sheet can be wrapped up and aired out outdoors or into the garbage. This form of cleanup allows for a single individual to efficiently clean up after a group of many.

The extent to which families eat this way in their homes as opposed to the Western modes of culinary habits varies from family to family. But I have received inquiries about the habits of Muslim students in the cafeteria. This is not overly common but some teachers seem to have observed that the Muslim students at their school left bigger messes than other kids. I tell those teachers that there is no need to have different expectations for the Muslim kids, but just understand that some of them may have been nurtured upon different eating habits, and therefore the habits that are expected may need to be communicated to them proactively, with explicit detail and explanation of purpose, to a little more of an extent than one might expect. Of course, communication of this type can be delivered to all students and it would be ill-advised to single out kids of a particular culture for this type of direction.

Clothing & Hijab

There are rules in Islam for how one dresses. These are not rules that mandate any specific

---

[462] See photo on previous page. Attribution: Creative Commons. balavenise. https://commons.wikimedia.org/wiki/File:Iftar_in_Istanbul_Turkey.jpg#/media/File:Iftar_in_Istanbul_Turkey.jpg

[463] Although there are specific Islamic injunctions against wasting food. Sahīh Muslim Book 36 Hadith 177 https://sunnah.com/muslim/36/177

garments per se, but rather they are dictates over what is covered and exposed of the body. It is accurate to say that Islam mandates for its followers to observe conservative and modest dress. As with the other matters in the religion there are things that are obligatory and other things that are supererogatory to observe as part of the Sunnah.

For women, the obligations mean covering everything except for the hands and the face, including the shape of the body.[464] For males the obligations are covering everything from the navel to the knee. So the obligations are different, however, if a male observes the supererogatory customs of the Sunnah, they wear a style of dress that is essentially the same as the woman's obligations. Growing a beard is a part of Islam for Muslim men who are able to do so, and this takes the place of wrapping a garment underneath it as a women does.[465] There is also some religious evidence to determine that it is preferable for women to wear black or dark tone colors due to the fact that they are less likely to draw attention, and many of the women around the Prophet ﷺ and his companions would wear them.[466]

With Muslim youth, and Muslims in general, especially in the West, the edicts of religious clothing clearly interplay with differing social, societal, and psychological pressures. The Western mind upon observing Muslims can become almost compulsively concerned with whether or not Muslim females have the right to *not* observe Islamic dictates of modest dress if they so choose. It should be clear just from knowing the Islamic dictates of dress and then observing Muslims in America that this obviously is the case, or instances where it is not the case are extraordinarily rare. Surveying has found that

[464] The Islamic rulings on the women's coverings come from the Qu'ran verse 24:31 https://quran.com/24/31. There are some scholars who take the position that covering the face is obligatory, and it was certainly the practice of many amongst wives of the Prophet ﷺ and his companions that they would put their garments over their faces when in the presence of non-familial men, Saḥīḥ al-Bukhārī Book 65 Hadith 274 https://sunnah.com/urn/44290. But there is a clear and authentic statement from the Prophet ﷺ that he told his sister in law that what is restricted once a female reaches the age of menstruation is covering everything *except* the hands and the face. See Sunan Abī Dawūd Book 34 Hadith 85 http://sunnah.com/abudawud/34/85.

[465] Jami' at-Tirmidhī Book 43 Hadith 2990 https://sunnah.com/urn/629840

[466] Sunan Abī Dawūd Book 34 Hadith 82 http://sunnah.com/abudawud/34/82

as high as 40% of Muslim women in America do not wear hijab at all outside of the mosque, while a near-equal 36% say they wear it at all times while out in public (Pew Research Center, 2011). Many others wear some type of head covering to signify that they are Muslim, but will still wear heavily stylized clothes that display the shape of the body or front of the hair.

What is clearly visible from this is that there is a range of choice and freedom for Muslim women generally. At the same time, Muslim women are disproportionately burdened with the pressure of having to be "visibly" Muslim in public, and worry about the stigma that comes along with that is only one concern with which they are faced.

What is not often considered by the Western mind is that there is a reverse phenomenon where many Muslim women dress less modestly in order to meet the societal pressures of adhering to fashion, beauty, and professional standards that the Western world puts on women in order to gain acceptance from society at large and to avoid being stigmatized by wearing traditional Islamic clothing. Educators simply ought to know that a variety of phenomena exist and it is not always, or even typically, along the pattern of yearning for more liberation in the sense that the ethnocentricity of the Western mind usually perceives it as.

In the Muslim world a variety of patterns exist. Certainly there are plenty of Muslims in more economically advanced societies that value popular culture of fashion, both for men and women. In Islam there is nothing wrong with a man or woman enjoying fashion. Only that such enjoyment is supposed to be done within the boundaries of what is permissible and impermissible in the religion. So if a man or woman wishes to adorn themselves with clothing that reveals more of the body than the Islamic guidelines described above, they can do this but only in front of the same gender or members of the opposite gender that are within their family circle. These rules make socializing in gender-separated contexts very important for Muslims to have.

It so happens that Saudi Arabia, the Muslim country where conservative dress is most highly valued, is also the Muslim country that loves fashion the most. The Western fashion industry makes a killing off of the Saudi market, and frequenting malls and shopping is perhaps the most commonly done leisure activity in Saudi's two biggest cities. Why is this? Certainly fashion is a status symbol in Saudi Arabia. But it is also the case that because Saudi society is structured around facilitating gender separation in nearly all its public and private edifices and institutions, there are more contexts there where women can display their fashion sense without violating Islamic dictates of exhibiting the body to the opposite gender. They can attend restaurants, malls, parties and social gatherings, beaches, gyms, and swimming pools assured that there will be a space where men are excluded. Muslim women in the West might have the right to dress however they see fit, but they rarely have the right and opportunity to do so in a public setting where they can be assured of being separated from men. So the Muslim woman in the West is faced with a constant paradox in her public life where she has to choose between either partaking in fashion or observing religious teachings on dress. She is unable to have it both ways. If she chooses to follow the religious rules to the letter, she risks being stigmatized and having to carry the fear of being judged by others along the West's common patterns of stereotyping Muslim women. If she chooses fashion she risks drawing unwanted attention from non-familial men and triggering sensitivities both within herself and likely her family that are fostered by Islamic teaching. There is basically no way for them to win and this greatly affects the ability for many Muslim women in the West to live a fulfilling life. They have to choose between pleasing pressures from their family, the Muslim community, and the religion itself, or to choose to not follow these rules and display themselves to a degree where they have less risk of being stigmatized or sticking out for appearing in a way that triggers stereotypes in the minds of Western observers. Which of these dueling pressures do you suppose most Muslim women fear would be harsher towards them? The answer is of course specific to the individual, but to assume it is always the case that the pressures coming from within the Muslim community are meaner would be pure ignorance.

The stereotype of the over-bearing, hostile, and close-minded Muslim father no doubt exists in some limited contexts in the real world, but overall it is very stupid, and so is its place in the Western consciousness. There very well could be many Muslim fathers who wish their daughters to wear more conservative clothing, and Islam does teach that there is a close connection between the father's dignity and his daughter.[467] But at the end of the day Islam teaches them to love their daughters and be merciful and kind towards them.[468] So for the Muslim man when his daughter makes the decision to capitulate to Western expectations and pressures by dressing more liberally in public, he might wish for her to make a different choice, but the daughter can still rest assured that he is going to be patient and kind with her and love her. That same assurance does not exist with the non-Muslim strangers that she has to be around.

Of course there are exceptions to the narrative that I am drawing out here. But I draw it out in order to illustrate what I know to be more common in the Muslim community from the inside in contradiction to the typical stereotypes. I also draw it out so we can have a feeling for the depth of the constant tension that is at play for Muslim females in the West. Obviously this conundrum has huge effects on children and adolescents. Many of them will go through

---

[467] Sunan ibn Mājah Book 9 Hadith 2031 https://sunnah.com/urn/1262740
[468] Al-Ādab al-Mufrad Book 10 Hadith 3 https://sunnah.com/adab/4/3

periods of life of having very strong feelings about these issues one way or another. Some teachers ask me about handling situations where two Muslim students enter into an inter-religious dispute with one another in school. The most commons scenario that I am asked about with this is girls arguing over each other's chosen styles of dress with the most frequent manifestation being that a more conservatively dressed girl gets mad at or insults another Muslim girl who is dressed more liberally. At times, teachers have seen male students tell female students or their sisters to dress more conservatively. Teachers find these situations to be very harrowing for themselves, not just because the students are in a dispute, but also because they know that there is a deep level to the dispute and they themselves do not feel equipped with the appropriate knowledge to deal with it and foster a more positive interaction.

The common impetus that teachers feel in these situations, or any that involves inter-religious dispute between Muslim students, is to go to the instigating student and give them a "it's none of your business" talk. While minding one's own business is actually an Islamic manner[469], it is not an absolute principle and does not entirely connote the same understanding that this phrase does in the modern-day West. Especially, when it comes to fellow Muslims openly violating the religious rules[470], Islam encourages the Muslim to advise their brother or sister in faith against it.[471] If they are displaying this violation openly they have effectively made it the business of the community.[472] However, what is difficult for young people to grasp and practice is that this advice giving in the religion has a protocol to follow in doing it; of which being gentle[473], well-mannered[474], not hypocritical[475], careful to not further expose the other person publicly[476], and doing it privately[477] are all a part.

So when these inter-religious disputes take place I advise teachers against automatically going to the "it's none of your business" line of redirection with the instigating student. Doing this can have the negative unintended consequence of resonating in the student's mind as, "actually teacher, it's *you* who doesn't get it", because the teacher might fail to realize that for Muslims

---

[469] Sunan ibn Mājah Book 36 Hadith 89 https://sunnah.com/ibnmajah/36/89, Sunan ibn Mājah Book 36 Hadith 51 https://sunnah.com/ibnmajah/36/51

[470] Qur'an 24:19 https://quran.com/24/19

[471] Jami' at-Tirmidhī Book 27 Hadith 32 https://sunnah.com/tirmidhi/27/32

[472] Sahīh al-Bukhārī Book 78 Hadith 99 https://sunnah.com/bukhari/78/99

[473] Sunan ibn Mājah Book 33 Hadith 33 https://sunnah.com/ibnmajah/33/33

[474] Jami' at-Tirmidhī Book 41 Hadith 40 https://sunnah.com/tirmidhi/41/40

[475] Qur'an 2:44 https://quran.com/2/44, Sunan ibn Mājah Book 20 Hadith 2643 https://sunnah.com/urn/1268630

[476] Qur'an 24:19 https://quran.com/24/19

[477] Sahīh al-Bukhārī Book 59 Hadith 77 https://sunnah.com/bukhari/59/77

enjoining one another to adhere to Islamic rules is considered a virtuous and noble deed.[478] Rather, the line of redirection that the teacher should use is one that focuses on the efficacy of good manners. The line of talk that should be given to the student should be something more along the lines of:

> "If you think so and so is doing something wrong and you want them to change and to accept the idea you have of it, it is not going to work if you are mean and harsh with them, or if you embarrass them in front of other people. That will only make them want to argue back with you, or even fight you. What you need to do is to give them advice in a way that is warm, and does not embarrass them. In life, when you approach someone with kindness and respect they become open to what you have to say, but when you approach someone with harshness and anger they become defensive and turn away. It is not always easy to do that, especially if you feel strong emotions about the choices your friend is making. In that situation, controlling your own anger inside yourself is what actually takes a lot of strength to do and you might need to focus on first."

Culturally, there is certainly a difference with the outer styles of clothing in different parts of the Muslim world as well as to the extent of which they are conservative. There can also be differing expectations of conservatism between rural and urban settings, as well as class divisions, not unlike other societies. The clothing dictates in Islam are not obligatory until puberty, just like the praying.[479] Some cultures and families prefer to have their children observe these dictates before puberty in order to have them conditioned into observing them by the time they get there, while others wait.

Again, it is important to understand that concerns about social stigma play a large role in this. There are many families who would maybe like for their daughters to wear the Islamic dress from a young age, but do not want them to bear the burden of sticking out. These families might reach a sort of dilemma when the child reaches adolescence. In modern Western society adolescence and even young adulthood has almost become like an extended childhood, and families may find that it is not so easy for children to make a hard change in going from having not prayed and not observed Islamic dress when they were younger, to all of a sudden hitting puberty and doing it. Islam actually teaches to have a gradual induction[480] into observing these

[478] Qur'an 3:104 https://quran.com/3/104, Sunan ibn Mājah Book 36 Hadith 79 https://sunnah.com/ibnmajah/36/79
[479] Sunan Ibn Majah Book 10 Hadith 2119 https://sunnah.com/urn/1263600
[480] Sunan Abī Dawūd Book 2 Hadith 104 https://sunnah.com/abudawud/2/104

things for the children beginning around age seven. But families find that hard to do in the West, and the fact that children's time is monopolized by attending public schools plays no small part in this difficulty.

If a parent asks a school or teacher to report to them if their daughter does not wear the hijab in school should they do it? Personally, my instinctual reaction to this is to say "no", and I have a hard time imagining a scenario where I would do otherwise while in that role as a teacher. But the reality is this is a deep discussion with many factors to consider. I certainly err on the side of thinking that adolescents need room to develop and sometimes experiment with personal expression, and therefore are in need of having places with controlled freedom to make individual choices; and that families should appreciate that being overly restrictive upon them could bring on the negative compound effects of turning them off to the parents' wishes.

At the same time there are other factors to consider, especially related to the school or teacher's particular relationship with the student in question. If the teacher or school has a hard time with a student, and they are unable to motivate and control them and thus use calling the parents home as their go-to tool for motivating and managing them, then considerations change. This would be a situation where the school is relying on the parents to manage and motivate the child's behavior in school. If in the course of those conversations the parent happens to make a request about their child's conduct in school, including what they wear, it may be the case that the school community owes something to that parent because they are relying on them for management of the child.

This question also brings to light the fact that schools need to have a clear idea for themselves as to how they relate to parents and families when teaching their children. Do they consider themselves a place to reinforce and support the particulars of what the parents want inculcated upon their child? Or do they consider themselves a vehicle to push against and challenge parental indoctrination? Is the school willing to support parents' wishes for their children even when it clashes with the individual decision of the child? If not, why not? And based on what logic and science? If the school sees itself as being a place of balance between these points of tension, it is worthwhile to delineate some details about what that actually looks like and means. In what areas and matters does the school support the families' values and where do they not? If you have not gotten the sentiment already by reading this book, know that the extent to which your school honors parents' rights and authority is very congruent to the extent to which you will be respected by the Muslim families you serve.

If a school decides that they *do not* fully support reinforcing their families' values upon their students they need to 1.) examine the considerations they had in making that decision through the lens of potential biases that they may be asserting, 2.) also assess and examine what the effects of having this disposition would do in practical terms to their relationships with families, as well as the families' own sense of belonging, trust, and safety within the school community, and 3.) be ready to be honest about their stances, which may involve reevaluating the genuineness behind boilerplate statements made in the school vision or elsewhere about respecting families and diverse cultures.

Schools should have open discussions about these types of questions as a staff and be clear as to where they stand. When they are not, it creates a lot of confusion and frustration because the general approach to so many matters that come up is developed ad hoc. I have known of a situation where a mother went to her daughter's school in the middle of the day once without her daughter knowing it and came to find that her daughter was bringing an alternative outfit to school everyday and changing out of her home attire into something fashionable and revealing. Obviously it was very awkward and the mother was upset. She was even more upset to find out that the school knew the girl was doing this everyday. She asked the school to report it to her when the daughter did this and they said that they would and that they supported her wishes. The mother came to find later on that her daughter continued to do this but the school never informed her about it. When she confronted the school about it again they told her they decided they did not want to be intrusive into what they deemed to be a family-only matter. Yet they made no effort to apologize for effectively lying to the mother by deciding to change their approach. Needless to say, the mother felt unsupported, deceived, alienated, and lost her trust in the school.

Conversely, I have known a principal who would tell students that they need to wear the hijab in school after their parents had told him that they wanted him to tell them that, and the child knew that the parent asked him to do it. The rationale used by the principal is that the school is a place where the parents have entrusted the child to him, so he refuses to allow it to be a place where the child defies the parents right in front of adults to whom they were entrusted. This same principal was also not shy about disallowing students to listen to music at school under the same context, where the parents had specifically told them they did not want that to happen. This principle had the habit of asking parents, "what is something that is very important to you that you teach your child at home and that you would like me to reinforce to them while they are at school?" So he would not enforce these things to all of the Muslim students in the school, but he would for ones whose parents had specifically told him it was a concern, and he would also create the opportunities to elicit these concerns from parents. In any context, if a parent expresses a specific concern or a restriction on their child's behavior that they would like the school to support them with or report to them, and the school either refuses or fails to do so, educators need to ask, what type of message is sent to kids when we give them the idea that they can defy their parents right in front of professional adults to whom they have been entrusted?

Another thing school communities or classrooms can try to do is acknowledge that legitimate credence exists in the world to the idea that there is value and benefit to observing modest clothing. Education curricula are ever-ready to support and reinforce liberal ideas of not restricting individual choice. Stories of the Western world's women's movements and figures from the past like Amelia Bloomer[481] are highly lauded in schools, and their stories are told to children in the public school system from young ages. There is nothing wrong with this whatsoever, but if a liberal education is supposed to consider all points of view (Nord, 2010), balance can be brought to this teaching with some discussion at age appropriate levels that reinforce ideas and values that are part of a Muslim's home culture where conservative dress is valued. Some of the books recommended in the final chapter of this book can help with this.

The conservative clothing is seen as a means of protection, valuing, and self-respect. The fact that men sexualize women in their minds upon seeing their bodies is something that is explicitly acknowledged within Islamic teaching[482] and Muslim cultures. The existence of this impulse is something Muslims take to be matter-of-fact, and the conservative dress of both men and women are seen as a means by which to protect both individuals and society in general from its potential harms. So while it might be known as something "natural" per se it is not part of the schema of the Muslim mind to see it as something innocuous. Rather it is both something dangerous and exploitable by the *shaytān* in the unseen world, and in the seen world by nefarious profiteers of commercial industry. The fact that Western society exploits sexuality for profiteering is something that should be discussed in older ages in schools and the morality behind that should be assessed.

I believe public school educators need to consider the entertainment and advertising industries and their effects on youth very carefully. These entities' profits motives entice them towards

---

[481] Amelia Bloomer was an early 20th century feminist figure who chose to shun wearing the petticoats that were a staple of upper-class female fashion in the Victorian era. The book *You Forgot Your Skirt Amelia Bloomer* by Shana Corey (2000) is commonly used in elementary schools to give introductory lessons about the feminist movement. While the book and its title can give the impression that Amelia Bloomer was against skirts and dresses altogether, she actually advocated that instead of the petticoat, which was burdensome to wear because of the weight of the protruding frame underneath it, that women should wear a lighter type of baggy pants with a loose skirt over it that was modeled after the attire of Turkish women (Boissoneault, 2018). This came to be called the Bloomer suit. So Amelia actually used the dress of Muslim women as her model of what would liberate women in the late Victorian era. It is a side note but she was also a stern advocate against drinking alcohol, which she considered to be the great "foe" to women's peace and happiness because of how it would cause men to be abusive (*The Lily*, n.d.). These further details and historical facts escape the children's book that is used to teach about it, but if the book is taught in a class of Muslim children it would be culturally appropriate and affirming to point them out.

[482] In referencing the importance of lowering the gaze The Prophet ﷺ said, "**The eyes commit fornication**", from Musnad Imam Ahmad Hadith 3912 see page 419 of Volume 3 of the English translation published by Darusalaam. https://tinyurl.com/ybvabkhs

manipulating human psychology and impulse in order to entrap people into consumption of their products, regardless of whether that consumption is healthy or not. To do this, they employ all forms of media in order to bombard and entrap the populace with messages and imagery that preys on the iniquitous side of human impulse. These industries have an especial focus on children and adolescents because the neurochemistry of adolescents renders them more prone to addiction (Siegel, 2013). If they can become hooked to consumer culture at a young age these industries have customers for life. The era of social media is gradually making apparent that there are negative health and psychological effects of over consumption of media. Youth especially have been manipulated into being addicted to it at ages when their brains are still developing. It is altogether reasonable to believe that over-consumption of media will be seen in the future as something that was deteriorating people's health for generations while the public took no action against the industries that proliferated it on the masses with profiteering as their sole motive, similar to the course that played out with the tobacco industries and cigarette smoking in the 20th century.

Thankfully there can be reversals in these trends over the course of time. Youth smoking has gradually gone down in the past two decades after seeing significant rises in the 1980s and 1990s. But how did it go down? Oddly enough, while the 1980s and 1990s saw youth smoking increase it happened alongside increased efforts from the public to inform youth about the health risks of smoking. Yet, that information was not compelling to young people, because the makings of their neurochemistry causes them to downplay risk and danger when adjudicating life choices. In the early 2000s, the public campaigns against smoking switched their messaging to be one where youth were told that the executives within the tobacco industry were manipulating and lying to youth in order to profiteer. Once the message being given young people switched from "this is bad for your health" to "powerful adults are trying to manipulate you" the messaging started to work (Siegel, 2013).

Public school educators that are entrusted with so much of the nation's young people's time should take the same stance towards the entertainment, advertising, and social media industries today. Especially, they should talk about the use of sex appeal as a manipulative force upon youth, one that is trying to entrap them into addiction of constant consumption of media on their smartphones. Studies have found that the effects of sex appeal in advertising are especially averse for males (Wirtz et al, 2017). That online consumption of media is likely to lead to unwanted exposure to pornography in the majority of people ages 10-17 (Wolak et al, 2007). Consumption of pornography in turn is linked to higher rates of depression (Mattebo et al, 2018); and this is especially compounded in adolescents (Kohut & Štulhofer, 2018), and for people who hold a moral belief against it (Perry, 2018). Making this issue especially pressing for the case of Muslim students. This is only one of many lines of concern about health

226 • Engaging Muslim Students in Public Schools

detriments of addiction to media consumption that our youth are being manipulated into in the modern day by industry. Public school educators should take a stand against it and reinforce, or at least offer, a counter perspective to students. Given the constant struggle that teachers have nowadays with students constantly consuming social media on their phones in school, there is ample opportunity for every educator in the building to reinforce this message. It is not like offering this perspective will get young people to stop constantly using their smartphones, but it would offer them a needed alternative viewpoint that could moderate the negative effects of this consumption to some degree, and possibly resonate with them down the road in their lives.

It is not the case that Islam only puts the responsibility of observing modesty and protecting women upon women in how they dress. The man also has a responsibility to observe conservative dress himself and to be careful with his eyes as to what he gazes upon. The Qur'an explicitly instructs this when it says:

> **Tell the believing men <u>to lower their gaze</u> and guard their chastity. That is purer for them. Indeed, Allah is acquainted with all that they do.**
> **[24:30]**

A common feminist rebuke towards the arguments for conservative clothing is that it should not be a women's responsibility to regulate the sexual impulses of men. Islam has no problem with that because it also regulates the man to be modest, humble, respectful, kind[483], and careful with his eyes and imagination. But Islam also empowers the woman by giving her responsibility within these matters. The protective benefits of the conservative dress are actually confirmed by research of neural dynamics that show the male mind impulsively processes sexualized female bodies as objects in ways that preclude sexual assault (Awasthi, 2017). This is exhibited in a video on YouTube where two people did an experiment of having a young attractive woman walk through New York City, one time in clothes that revealed the shape of her body and the second time in conservative Islamic dress.[484] They counted the amount of cat calls and solicitations from men on the street that she received in each venture. The video illustrates clearly the lesser amounts of these types of advances that she received when wearing the conservative Islamic dress. This video could be played in perhaps a health class or another class

---

[483] Sahīh al-Bukhārī Book 60 Hadith 6 https://sunnah.com/bukhari/60/6
[484] Search for the video "10 Hours of Walking in NYC as a Woman in Hijab" on YouTube https://www.youtube.com/watch?v=mgw6y3cH7tA.

where feminism is discussed in schools.[485] If schools care at all about reinforcing or at least lending some credence to the values taught at home in Muslim cultures, discussions on feminism, health issues, and sexual responsibility will ask the question of what the responsibility is of both parties in inter-gender interactions where there are clearly sensitivities, and ask what are practical actions both males and females can take that are within their own power in interpersonal interaction to protect women from harassment and sexual assault.

A question in classes could even be asked explicitly as to whether or not the West has something to learn from Muslim cultures. Some companies in the West have considered instituting policies in the post MeToo era where men and women are no longer allowed to shake hands (Mills, 2019); those companies would be default observing an Islamic edict. Questions can be asked as to whether or not preventative measures are better in these concerns in society as opposed to only having remedial measures. It is generally a part of Islam to secure societal health, safety, and well-being in first principle through reasonable preventative measures[486], and the conservative clothing is a part of that, as is the general separation that is observed between the genders.

Any class involving physical activity is a place where clothing sensitivities potentially come into play for Muslim students. Part of the etiquette of modesty in Islam is to also avoid showing the nakedness of the body around the same gender as well, and it is likewise forbidden to look at the nakedness of someone of the same gender.[487] So some students can be reluctant about changing in locker rooms for gym class. When Muslim non-profits hold their own sporting events, such as basketball or soccer tournaments, they will do them in a gendered separated manner; separate times and places for males and females. It is taken as given that no one wants the opposite gender observing them partaking in sport, and the sensitivity is heightened with females. This can cause reluctance on the part of some students to want to partake in certain activities in a mixed-gendered gym class. In some settings observing gender separation in gym class may be ideal and most efficient while for other settings it would not be reasonable. Nowadays there is female athletic clothing available that keeps with standards of modesty for

---

[485] Some observers have expressed concern about the video because the majority of men soliciting the woman in the video are men of color; and they are concerned that it reinforces stereotypes about them. While I empathize with this concern it can be easily qualified in a classroom that white men, indeed men of all colors, do this as well, it can also be presented in the context of how historical injustices in housing have caused more men of color to live in places where the streets act as one of the lone places of social gathering and leisure. Therefore creating a situation where men of color are just the likely men to be passed by in this urban experiment.

[486] Jami' at-Tirmidhī Book 28 Hadith 2168 https://sunnah.com/urn/673390

[487] Jami` at-Tirmidhī Book 43, Hadith 3023 https://sunnah.com/urn/630170

almost any physical activity that can be done, including swimming. Helping students and families acquire these materials could be a helpful compromise.[488]

So the word *hijab* does not refer to just a single article of clothing that goes on a woman's head. Rather its meaning is "to protect" or "to preclude"[489], and refers to a broader concept of observing temperate but firm preventative boundaries of separation, physical contact, and eyesight that both men and women practice in their own right for the sake of maintaining personal and physical health and safety. Muslims see these measures as moderating, not shutting down completely, the individual's more animalistic impulses that can lead to a loss of one's reason, and as a consequence poor life decisions or violations of one person against another that will result in the most harrowing of emotional and physical consequences. So a Muslim perspective is that the experiences of human drama entailed in love and sex can bring people to the highest of highs and the lowest of the lows in their life, and practical rules that can be observed by the individual help bring the person to a balanced life experience with it and to avoid extremes.[490]

Another technical rule that Islam has in this vein and is important to know is that it is forbidden for a male and female who are not related to one another to be alone in a room together.[491] The Prophet 🕌 said about this:

A man is not alone with a (non-familial) woman but the third of them is Satan.[492]

Many schools and districts have adopted policies that disallow staff members to be alone with any student in an enclosed room together for liability reasons. So respecting this edict should not be difficult in our schools, but circumstances arrive where some find it to be. Schools should avoid situations where Muslim students are alone with a staff member or classmate who is the

---

[488] Some of these companies include Asiya Sport https://www.asiyasport.com/, Veil Garments https://www.veilgarments.com/, and Artizara https://www.artizara.com/collections/muslimah-sportswear-sport-hijabs none of these companies have paid or requested to be endorsed in this book, and the author and publisher of the book have no financial interest in them.

[489] See حـجـب in the Arabic-English Lexicon of Edward William Lane http://arabiclexicon.hawramani.com/حجب/?book=50#7b39f9

[490] Islam does not shun sex itself, only it regulates it to married couples who are committed to one another. The Prophet 🕌 said that having intercourse for pleasure with one's spouse is a good deed for which reward from Allah is earned. Sunan Abī Dawūd Book 43 Hadith 471 https://sunnah.com/abudawud/43/471

[491] Sahih Muslim Book 15 Hadith 476 http://sunnah.com/muslim/15/476

[492] Jami` at-Tirmidhī Book 33 Hadith 8 https://sunnah.com/tirmidhi/33/8 - This hadith is very well-known amongst Muslims, and its meaning is that Satan will tempt the man into illicit and improper thoughts in such situations. Non-Muslims need to understand for Muslims these types of teachings undergird interpersonal interactions that occur all the time.

opposite gender; if it has to take place *at least* the door should be opened. These situations trigger many sensitivities, especially for post-pubescent students, and certainly for students who had their cultural sensibilities nurtured in the Muslim world. Avoiding such situations is another way by which the entirety of Muslim societies and social interactions are organized, and a student who comes from the Muslim world likely would have never experienced being alone in a room with a non-familial member of the opposite gender.

Family Gender roles

Gender roles in Islam are another issue about which I am frequently inquired. In talking about this, I first want to remind that in understanding Islam one has to remember and consider their own ethnocentrism and understand that they have to know the matter within Islam and Muslim culture in detail, which this book is trying to help the reader take an initial steps towards. One cannot just assume words always carry the same connotation that they do in Western culture.

An Islamic lens sort of views gender roles in the West throughout history, especially history in the last two or three centuries, as one that swings between extremes. So there is a degree to which I can say to you that Islam dictates men and women to observe "traditional gender roles" and it would be true; but that tradition has to be understood within its own Islamic paradigm, and not one that carries along with it all the implicit assumptions that go with the same terminology in a Western paradigm. Let's consider some detail from history that informs the collective consciousness of the Western world's understanding of traditional gender roles.

Susan B. Anthony is a feminist figure who is often lauded in the West and in the education system. Her main bones of contention with society at her time were that women did not have the right to a divorce, to own property, and to vote. Her activism, as well as others, went against these aspects of traditional treatment of women in the West and set off a societal phenomenon that has spawned succeeding feminist movements and resulted in what some might interpret as an ever-increasing liberation of women in Western society.

From an Islamic lens, Susan B. Anthony's activism never should have been necessary because Islam has always given women the right to own property[493] and seek a divorce[494] since its inception.[495] Muslim woman also do not take their husband's name when they get married, a practice whose roots in the West were instituted to indicate the husband's ownership of his wife

---

493 Sunan Abī Dawūd Book 24 Hadith 142 http://sunnah.com/abudawud/24/142

494 Muwāta' Imām Mālik Book 29 Hadith 1204 https://sunnah.com/urn/412302

495 Republican style voting Anthony advocated for did not really exist in the Muslim world for either men or women until the post-colonial era in the 20th century. The most common form of rulership change in the history of Muslim societies has been dynastic succession.

(this is also why your Muslim students typically have a different last name than their mother). Within a Muslim family Islam gives both rights and responsibilities to the husband and the wife. The main responsibility given to men is that of provision for the entire family.[496] His main right is that of having the final say in most decision-making[497], so long as those decisions do not conflict with Islamic edicts, including his obligations towards his wife and family.[498] The main right of the woman is to be provided for[499] and to be consulted with.[500] Her main responsibility is to take care of the domicile and children[501], though the man is expected to assist with that.[502] These *are* traditional gender roles. However, there is nothing wrong or prohibiting in Islam with a woman working a job, owning and operating a business, or owning property to garner her own wealth. The Prophet Muhammad's ﷺ wife Khadijah رضـي الله عـنها herself was a businesswoman for whom the Prophet ﷺ actually worked.[503] Only, according to Islamic dictates, the husband has no right to own the wealth of his wife[504], whereas the wife does have rights over the wealth of her husband to the extent that he is mandated to provide for her and the family. This does not mean that a situation where a husband in a Muslim family does not work and instead fills the domestic role while the mother does work is not permissible, this is not the case at all. Only in Islam the woman in this situation is fulfilling responsibilities that she is not obliged to by God, therefore she receives the reward of charity[505] for the provisioning she provides for her husband. For the man's part, he is not allowed to compel his wife into this type of situation, it can only arise out of the wife's agreement.

When a Muslim man and woman get married they sign a contract together.[506] The man is obliged to pay a dowry[507] and the woman is appointed a guardian.[508] The guardian would be her father, and if her father is deceased or somehow unavailable the closest available male blood relative to him who would take his stead. If there are no male family members on her

---

[496] Jami' at-Tirmidhī Book 23 Hadith 36 https://sunnah.com/tirmidhi/23/36

[497] Sunan Ibn Majah Book 9 Hadith 1925 https://sunnah.com/urn/1261690

[498] Sunan an-Nasā'i Book 39 Hadith 57 https://sunnah.com/nasai/39/57

[499] Qur'an 33:28 https://quran.com/33/28, Sunan Abī Dawūd Book 12 Hadith 97 https://sunnah.com/abudawud/12/97

[500] Sahīh al-Bukhārī Book 65 Hadith 4785 https://sunnah.com/urn/44630

[501] Al-Adab Al-Mufrad Book 10 Hadith 1 https://sunnah.com/adab/10/1

[502] Sahīh al-Bukhārī Book 10 Hadith 70 https://sunnah.com/bukhari/10/70

[503] Sīrah of Ibn Hisham. See page 27 of English translation published by Al-Falah Foundation https://tinyurl.com/ycdlkmqe

[504] Qur'an 4:4 https://quran.com/4/4

[505] Sunan Ibn Mājah Book 8 Hadith 53 https://sunnah.com/ibnmajah/8/53

[506] Sunan an-Nasā'i Book 26 Hadith 158 https://sunnah.com/nasai/26/158

[507] Qur'an 2:236 https://quran.com/2/236

[508] Jami` at-Tirmidhī Book 11 Hadith 22 https://sunnah.com/tirmidhi/11/22

father side available then, in the Muslim world, a judge of the government is appointed to the position.[509] In the Western world this ends up being leaders, directors, and Imams of mosques. While in Islam it is technically only male members of the father's side who are supposed to fill the role of guardian, it is not uncommon for male members of the mother's side to take this role in situations where the father is absent in the West. Part of the reason that the woman has a guardian assigned to her is so he is able to act as an arbitrator on her behalf when the husband and wife have a dispute over the wife's rights not being met.

The woman giving her permission in the marriage is required for a marriage in Islam[510], as is the permission of the guardian.[511] Resulting from these stipulations is that high parental and family involvement in the process of meeting a partner and getting married has long been and remains to be a staple of marriage customs in Muslim cultures; though there is variation upon the exact way this looks amongst them, but Islam's framework forms the basis for all of them.

In the Islamic marriage process the contract is drawn up and signed by both parties and at least two additional witnesses and stipulates, at least, the specifics of the dowry, as well as any other special agreements that have been made and negotiated between the two parties. The signing of this contract amounts to what is essentially an engagement, and not a complete marriage. The marriage is complete when it is "consummated", which means the husband and wife have enjoined upon conjugal relations. By rule the dowry has to have been remitted to the bride prior to the marriage's consummation.[512]

In many cultures family involvement takes the form of "match-making" where two families arrange their children to meet, and then they gradually get to know each other in the presence and under the supervision of the families, particularly the female's family. This period is used for them to test out compatibility, and sometimes it is done in between the drawing of the contract and the consummation. This is a sort of "quasi-arranged" process where the families do the matching, but the children have the power of final veto and approval.

Many students' parents would have been married by a general process like this, especially if they are from the old country, but even in America I have known this general framework to be common amongst the range of different Muslim ethnic groups. Increasingly so, Muslim youths are identifying their own partners in this process as opposed to relying on families. Both the

---

[509] Jami' at-Tirmidhī Book Hadith https://sunnah.com/tirmidhi/11/23

[510] Jami' at-Tirmidhī Book 11 Hadith 28 https://sunnah.com/tirmidhi/11/28, Sunan an-Nasā'i Book 26 Hadith 65 https://sunnah.com/nasai/26/65, Sunan Ibn Mājah Book 9 Hadith 1947 https://sunnah.com/urn/1261920

[511] Jami` at-Tirmidhī Book 11 Hadith 23 https://sunnah.com/tirmidhi/11/23

[512] Qur'an 2:237 https://quran.com/2/237

advent of social media and, in the West[513], attending mixed-gendered schools have played into this. The idea of dating and concerns over children adopting wholesale the dating culture of the West is typically of high concern for Muslim parents. There are definitely generational dynamics at play here, and there are more and more second and third generation Muslim kids in our schools now whose parents would have experienced growing up with the pressures of American society themselves. Overall, for pretty much all Muslim families, the biggest concern is for kids to, at the end of the day, avoid committing premarital fornication. This is a major sin in Islam[514], and as such can bring a strong sense of shame and sorrow upon Muslim families who have children that fall into it.

Historically, the West is not unfamiliar with these types of shame. These sensibilities that Muslim families have can be accurately compared to sensibilities that the average American family had in the generations prior to the baby boomers and the sexual revolution of the 1960s (Allyn, 2000). However, what has to be understood is that the mechanism the West used for coping with a phenomenon of increased premarital sexual activity was *to have the sexual revolution*, which involved de-prioritizing and reinterpreting the West's own religious traditions in order to erode away the taboo of non-marital sexual relations from the societal consciousness. For Muslim families this same mechanism is not available, nor desirable, because of the relative immutability of Islamic texts. The intellectual schema necessitated for belief in Islam does not allow for the same type of de-prioritizing and reinterpreting that has taken place in the West. So even for Muslims whose families have been in America for several generations, they may have an increased confidence in helping their children navigate the West's social waters, but it is incorrect to just assume that they wish to abide by liberalized expectations regarding these religious rules.

How often do schools have open talks with their families about the families' values and attitudes towards dating? This is a conversation that affects all schools K-12, as it is not uncommon for children as young as second grade to start talking about it. Alongside the increased diversity in American society it has to be acknowledged that there is also an increased diversity in attitudes towards social matters such as this, and it is not appropriate for schools to just assume that families have the same values and expectations that their own parents did for themselves when they grew up in America; nor that families have the same expectations that are promoted by pop culture. Personally, I set an expectation with my elementary school-aged

---

[513] Even in the Muslim world social media is allowing more youths to meet their own potential partners since it offers an avenue of communication without the need of physical interaction; this is not to say there are not concerns in those society's about the propriety of non-familial members of the opposite gender communicating with one another electronically.

[514] Sahīh Muslim Book 1 Hadith 114 https://sunnah.com/muslim/1/114 - Sunan Abī Dawūd Book 40 Hadith 87 https://sunnah.com/abudawud/40/87

daughters that they are not allowed to partake in talking with peers about "crushes" or "who likes who" at all, and that such talk is a form of bullying. My personal sentiments as a Muslim father are that if they do partake in that in school I would like to know and for their teacher to report it to me. But admittedly, it is not an expectation I have talked about openly with their teachers. This is my own participation in capitulation to the comfort zone of the staff at the school and my own petty fears of being stigmatized as to how I will appear broaching a sensitive topic.

Studies on adolescent girls aged 12-14 have shown that the bullying that girls most commonly experience and exhibit are engendered by perceptions of how they relate to peer boys sexually. It shows that this bullying is typically executed through private communication between them, and that the common discourse on bullying that schools reiterate to students from educational psychology fail to adequately remediate these issues due to essentially ignoring them and simply passing off such behaviors as normal (Ringrose, 2008; Ringrose & Renold, 2013). It is warranted for schools to take a proactive approach to anti-bullying that sets expectations for these types of social interactions that are rooted in the values and desires of the families they serve. Connecting the importance of respect towards one another at school as a means of honoring students' home-cultural community is effective because it draws upon a sense of belonging that students most readily have available to them. Lacking a sense of belonging is the most common root cause as to why students commit bullying (Underwood & Ehrenreich, 2014). When schools permit social norms around inter-gender relationships that run counter to the home cultural values of Muslim students, the ability of them and their family to have a genuine sense of belonging in the school's social climate is greatly compromised.

At a more advanced level of honoring students' home culture, it can be taught to older students that there is sociological research that shows that having more partners prior to marriage increases the likelihood of divorce and is also a predictor of negative effects on marital satisfaction (Regnerus, 2017; Wolfinger, 2018). There is a fair argument to be made that a lesson learned from the experience of generations succeeding the sexual revolution is that chastity has real-world value for long-term relationship satisfaction in life. Children who come from a culture where they are the first generation growing up in a culture of premarital dating might benefit from this type of insight more than anyone, due to not only what it promotes of healthy lifestyle choices, but also how it validates home cultural teachings that pop culture pushes against. Marital ideas such as these naturally get caught up in people's minds within the context of the American culture war, and some educators might consider it their own priority to inculcate the opposite view upon their students. Those educators are free to make that choice, but they should be explicit with the families they serve about where they stand. It is not uncommon that teaching Muslim students positions educators and schools to choose between inculcating their own personal views and values upon children or supporting ones of their students' families. Educators need to become more explicit and transparent about where these divergences lie, be bold enough to open up the conversation with families, and practice introspection, self reflection and critique over their own dispositions, and err against being passive aggressive.

What rules does the school have about dating, peer pressure around sex and flirtation, and public displays of affection between students? These things take place constantly in public schools, and even they are seeded at the youngest of ages. The adults in positions of authority around these children can not merely hope to opt out of influencing the children's development and attitude towards these things. How teachers react when students talk about crushes and how they relate to the opposite gender sends a message to the children, even when the teacher's reaction is one of inaction or avoidance of the topic. So when do schools open up honest conversations about this with the parents of their students? It is easy to know that these are pressing and stressful issues for parents, so when do we ask them how they would like us as teachers and adults in authority around their child to react when they partake in these types of interactions?

Not dissimilar to informing families about religious rights, dealing with America's culture of sex and dating can be a topic that schools hold an informational session about for parents. This session can provide an opportunity to elicit feedback and responses from parents about their own desires for what they wish their children to adhere to while in school, and what they would like the staff members to reinforce to them. The informational session could inform parents about what is taught about and covered in sex ed and physical health classes. It can offer and brainstorm with parents on ways to talk to their children about sex and inter-gender relationships, many Muslim parents would love to have insight on that from people who have experienced growing up in American culture. The session could also talk about some of the themes that are brought up in books in the school's curricula; especially in literature and humanities classes. Frequently books that school's use deal with themes of love and sexual relationships in particular cultural contexts. Increasingly school's are moving towards introducing themes of sexual health to students of younger and younger ages. It is simply unscrupulous for school's to teach about these things without creating the space and opportunity to hear about the values and priorities of the students' parents. Especially when they know that there are heavy cultural factors at play for the families they serve who may already feel stigmatized, and therefore hesitant about advocating for themselves and likely to end up not doing so as a matter of capitulation.

Muslim families with conservative values regarding marital and sexual relationships can often feel like everything in the society is trying to pull and tempt their child away from their family's morals. These families would appreciate the chance to have a sense that their child's school, the real-world incubator of their child's social life, was on their side in this perceived battle to at least some degree. For the child's part, it is often stigmatizing to feel like these values their family's may hold are "strange" in a society that generally shuns them or sees them as antiquated, but without a global perspective on it. If the school can offer some objective perspective that runs counter to the modern-day pop culture norms, and allows them to appreciate their family's perspective in an objective and secular way, this can be reassuring and comforting to the child's self concept. Many Muslim students who are children of immigrants will belong to parents who may have been part of an arranged or "quasi-arranged" marriage. This can often be uncomfortable for Muslim youth to admit to non-Muslims, for whom such a concept is foreign. It can be helpful if in a school setting it is acknowledged that throughout the world family-arranged marriages are more common than autonomous marriages. Romantic spontaneity itself is very much a concept that is ethnocentric to Western culture. Ethnographic studies of South Asia have found that professional women find the arranged marriage process following Islamic guidelines to be empowering as a guarantor of rights (Khurshid, 2020), that marital satisfaction decreases over time in autonomous marriages but increases over time in arranged marriages (Gupta & Singh, 1982), and that satisfaction in South Asian arranged marriages have a higher marital satisfaction rate than autonomous marriages in America (Yelsma & Athappily, 1988). This research lends validity to the idea that heavy involvement of parents in partner choice produces healthy results. It lends credence to the idea that teachers should work with parents in monitoring their child's inter-gender social life if the parent expresses that they want help with that, and also giving credence to the idea that benefits can be had by involving one's parents in partner choice in health classes, or other classes where themes of love and romance are brought up.[515]

The Male as a Provider and Boy's Motivation

Islam and Muslim cultures being explicit about the male role providing for others has an effect on the way some Muslim boys show up in school. There are many concerns about the general disengagement of boys from school, and likewise many different aspects to it. For Muslim boys, despite whatever behaviors they might exhibit at school, whatever stage of development they are at, and no matter how far off on the "troubled" path they may seem, they all want to be successful in life. Pretty much all of them have an understanding and idea that it is the man's job to financially take care of others when they grow up. It is extraordinarily common that

---

[515] The reading of *Romeo and Juliet* especially has a way of castigating the idea of parental involvement in partner choice.

Muslim men living in diaspora in the West financially caretake for not only their own immediate family, but also other families who need help back home or in other places. Most Muslim boys will at least know men like this to one degree or another in their life, from within the community if not directly in their own family (and of course there are many women who fulfill these duties as well).

The West's colonial dominance over much of the Muslim world in the 19th and 20th century created what some intellectuals have theorized as an inferiority complex in Muslims as to how they relate to the West in material power and success. Especially in peoples who had direct contact and economic dependence on the West (Benlahcene, 2013). A way this manifests with our Muslim boys in school is that, to them, the secular school is where it is felt they are suppose to go and learn the West's secrets about having success in the material world so they can grow up and know how to earn money and provide for people. A major part of the disengagement of boys in school occurs when they do not see a purpose to the learning, and specifically when they do not see the connection to how the learning will help them earn money in the future. Making this connection is something that teachers need to think deeply about. They even might need to do their own research to figure out how to make concrete the connection between what they teach and earning money in the future, and not just rely on general platitudes of "you need to do good in school so you can get a good job". Pretty much all Muslim communities in America are supported financially by a strong base of small business owners. Many Muslims, both male and female but males especially, grow up not with the idea of wanting to "get a job" but rather with the idea of wanting to own a business.

One curriculum recommendation I will give. In 9th grade, in Language Arts class, classes should read the book *Think and Grow Rich* by Napoleon Hill (1937). Language Arts is often the class in which these boys are least interested. There is rarely an explicit and concrete connection made for how studying the field impacts their future earning potential. *Think and Grow Rich* is a historically influential piece of literature and merits analysis in Language Arts classes. After the industrial boom in America and the Great Depression Napoleon Hill studied all the major tycoons who made it big in that era, as well as several historical figures who had great success. His goal was to study the inner habits and attitudes of these people that correlated to financial success. So in this respect the book is a self-help book that teaches positive motivation and thinking to the reader. Self-help and how-to-be-successful books are now a major market of literature, but *Think and Grow Rich* is the original and foundational model of these books. So this book has the potential to offer young people the insight that success in life begins with one's inner attitude and outlook.

Hill organizes his chapters by personal traits that successful people carry and then goes over a figure of history who is emblematic in each one. Something that will be appreciated by Muslim students is that in his chapter on "persistency" the historical figure he chose to talk about was the Prophet Muhammad 🕌. In this sense the book offers students the chance to see a Western researcher characterize Islam's Prophet 🕌 in a way that is removed from all of the political implications that are seen in characterizations today. Making it a refreshing read. There are aspects of the book that can be critiqued as dated and engage students in general modes of literary analysis. But it can also offer students a break from reading fictional prose, which has traditionally not been a prominent or honored literary form in the Muslim world like it has in the West[516], and I believe this contributes to boys' general disinterest in Language Arts at school. Instead Hill's book can offer them true insight into the inner-habits that have led to material success by prominent figures in Western history, while perhaps easing the inferiority complex to some degree by demonstrating that those inner attitudes are not actually as distant from that which exists in their own cultural bank as it may seem to them. I recommend it be read in 9th grade because that way the book could potentially act as a vehicle to inspire positive attitudes and work habits for the rest of high school, but it could be read with higher grades as well.

---

[516] Poetry, parabolic vignettes, and polemical writing have been much more common and appreciated forms of literary expression in the Muslim world. The *1001 Nights* stories from the Arab world, which have been a subject of fancy and adulation in the West, were considered an inferior form of literature amongst the educated class of Arabs (Irwin, 2003).

Chapter 5: LEARNING IN MOSQUES & IMPLICATIONS IN MODERN EDUCATION

Many Muslim students spend a large portion of their time outside of public school learning in local religious institutions. Mosques are themselves learning environments where habits and perceptions about learning are framed for many of our young students. Yet there remains a long bridge to be crossed in understanding for public school teachers as to what type of learning goes on in mosques, how it is done, and how this can frame student perception of learning in public schools, as well as how the familiarity of Muslim students with learning habits that are nurtured in mosques can be utilized by teachers to draw on the students' background experience. This chapter will shed light on learning that takes place in mosques with a pedagogical lens that identifies common areas of incongruency that students may experience in public schools, while also illuminating factors that can be utilized to support student learning. In this chapter I will briefly review the literature that exists in educational research on learning in mosques, scant as it may be, and then go over how mosque learning can affect both student behavior and learning habits in the public schools; especially for EL students and struggling learners. Then I will demonstrate and discuss concrete strategies I take away from this, and some of the implications this has for us as public school educators of Muslim students in light of current trends in education. In this chapter I will use the word *masjid* and the plural *masājid* in lieu of the word *mosque* to give the reader the opportunity to be attuned to the use of the appropriate referents that Muslims actually use amongst themselves.

The masjid and attendance in Islamic weekend schools are a place where religious identity is fostered and encouraged within Muslim communities in the West. This is common knowledge to anyone involved in a Muslim community, and it has also been acknowledged in research on Muslim students and families across different ethnicities and continents (Berns-McGown, 1999; Farid & McMahan, 2004; Sarroub, 2005; Bigelow, 2010; Moore; 2011; Iqbal, 2017). In the Muslim world religious education is intertwined with the five-day a week[517] education where the secular subjects are learned as well. That education is typically funded, structured, and facilitated by the governments in those countries. When Muslims immigrate to the West and their children attend public schools, they find themselves having to work on their own as makeshift communities to try and bridge this educational gap for their children. This usually takes the form of creating weekend schools that take place inside the masjid, typically on both Saturday and Sunday, where the children will likely attend anywhere from four to six hours each day, and sometimes more. Night classes during the weekdays are not uncommon either. In the

---

[517] I say "five-day a week" here instead of "Monday thru Friday" because Friday is a day off in the Muslim world. The typical work week in the Muslin world is Sunday thru Thursday,.

Muslim world children are not shoved into the masjid for long hours on the weekends because their religious education is done concurrently with learning other subjects in the five-day a week schools.[518]

Learning in the masjid especially consists of memorization of the Qur'an and the decoding of Arabic phonetics, but also entails learning about Islamic belief and jurisprudence from other texts. This learning plays an important role in Muslim communities worldwide. However, despite being one of the most common learning environments in the world, very little is known about it or examined within educational research in the Western world. This is even more true when it comes to research on learning in masājid in the Western world itself (Moore, 2011).

One of the reasons for this is that access to masājid for Western researchers is difficult to attain (Wesselhoeft, 2010). Masjid learning is typically understood poorly by non-participants, and while it takes place in a variety of contexts, researchers have observed similar core practices within it in varying parts of the world (Moore, 2011). Leslie Moore (2012) of Ohio State strongly asserts that knowing about learning in the masjid will help public school teachers engage Muslim students more effectively. This dynamic makes the discussion and insights in the pages that follow to be of extraordinarily high value to the teacher of Muslim students in the West.

Since Qur'an memorization has an emphasis on learning that Western researchers typically characterized as "rote", it is often cast by outsiders as stultifying cognitive development of children who participate in it (Wagner, 1993). This is done by outside researchers, but also by educators in the students' non-religious schools (Moore, 2011). Negative characterization and assumption of masjid learning happens despite there being no empirical evidence in support of it, and when the reality is that little is known in educational research about Qur'anic schooling or the effects of this "double schooling" and how they impact Muslim children as learners (Moore, 2011).

Moore (2012) argues that the practice of Qur'an memorization is built upon guided practice and actually has many corollaries to public school teaching methods insofar as it is a process of modeling, imitation, rehearsal, and performance. Qur'an memorization also gives students a foundation in key reading concepts concerning phonemic awareness, decoding, language acquisition, and spelling (Bigelow, 2010; Mohamed, 2011; Moore, 2012). Sarroub (2005)

---

[518] Or they will go study the secular subjects in a different school for a shorter time period before going to a religious school on the same days (again typically Sunday-Thursday in most Muslim countries). In Somalia, for example, it is common that students spend the morning in a school studying the secular subjects and the afternoon in another school or masjid studying religion, or vice versa. In the Arab countries both religion and the secular subjects will typically be taught in the same school.

observed that students learn grammar principles and are then challenged to apply them in both discrete tasks and application in reading. Wesselhoeft (2010) found that question and answering was used as a technique to reinforce agreed upon ethical values.[519]

These conclusions from academic research are all fine in and of themselves. But the research still does little to answer the question as to what learning in the masjid actually looks like? And what are the academic and behavioral implications of pedagogy for public school teachers of double-schooled students? It is into these questions that I aim to give a deeper look and consideration.

There is also a commentary on the socialization aspects of masjid learning. Lewis (2007), who did not do observations within any masājid, argued that the amount of time British Muslim students spent in weekend Islamic schools hindered their development of English as well as their ability to socialize with non-Muslims. Niyozov (2010), again with no reported observations done in masājid, expressed concern that masjid schooling aligns the allegiance of Muslim students against neoliberal and pluralistic values that public schools ought to promote. Sarroub (2005) observed that Yemeni girls were taught some moral lessons and perspectives, such as the value of conservative dress, that ran counter to the liberal ethos of the public school they attended. Sarroub's observations of masjid learning takes on an ambivalent tone. On one hand she found Yemeni girls to be more social and lively within the masjid in comparison to their disposition at public schools, and on the other hand she expresses concerns over shaming methods of coercion she observed from some of the masjid teachers. Sarroub observed that teachers and students in the masjid came into conflict over the teachers' lack of creativity with the assigned learning tasks compared to the learning tasks the students were used to being given in their public school. Moore (2011) noted that a public school teacher who once attended a weekend school found it to be "chaotic" and disorganized. Negative perceptions of the social influence of masjid learning runs counter to what is generally found from the perception of parents and stakeholders within Muslim communities in educational research. Parents often express the conviction that attendance and positive participation in masjid learning will correlate with good conduct as well as better academic performance in school (Berns-McGown, 1999; Farid & McMahan, 2004; Sarroub, 2005; Bigelow, 2010; Moore, 2012; Iqbal, 2017).

I argue that much of the examination of Islamic modes of learning that does exist approaches it with a deficit mindset, preconceived skepticism, and sometimes even an insecurity on the part

---

[519] These being values that have been discussed in the previous chapters of this book, when the teacher can predict the students values and background knowledge, questioning and answering runs smooth and can go deeper.

of the researcher who is examining an environment of which they are lacking background knowledge of their own accord that would be necessary to give it a fair assessment. Thereby the research fails to garner lessons and draw on resources that could be used to further engage students and accommodate learning style.

My own research is based on experience managing a weekend school, advising masājid in management of children, observations, discussions and interviews with young adults and high school students and teachers in masājid, both those who have grown up in the United Sates and those who have not, and talking to them with the goal of reflecting on these dynamics; as well as my own study of Islamic learning both through books and partaking in classes and lessons in the Muslim world as well as in America. All of this examined through the lens of being a trained and experienced teacher in American pubic schools. Feel free to take from the pages that follow what you will. When I present on this material to public school educators of Muslim students the feedback I normally receive is that it provides highly valuable insight and is well-appreciated.

The discussion will talk about aspects influencing behavior, then areas of academic alignment and misalignment, with each part followed by lessons and strategies to be taken from this, including an extended explanation on a strategy for scaffolding reading comprehension. The final sections will discuss implications for pedagogical practice in public schools in light of current educational trends.

Behavioral Aspects

Consequences

The difference in consequences between weekend masjid schools and public schools is one of the most readily brought up topics by young Muslims I talk to who were double schooled growing up. Generally, they say that consequences in the masjid, as well as at home, feel stricter and come with a greater emotional attachment for the students than those that are received in public schools.

Why is this? There are two major factors. First, in the masjid they are with people from the same cultural group, oftentimes it may even be people who are close to their families either familially or socially, so there is simply by nature a greater emotional attachment to the people. The second is that in the masjid religion can be used as a tool of guilt, admonition, redirection, and reprimand; a tool not available in the public schools.

Is corporal punishment a factor in this? I am asked this question by teachers from time to time so I will take a couple pages here to discuss this issue and then return to talking about how the perception of having greater consequences with a stronger emotional impact in the weekend schools can affect the way students show up in the public schools Monday thru Friday.

Reality of Corporal Discipline

Some teachers have experienced Muslim students report to them, or overheard students talk amongst themselves, about experiencing corporal punishment in their weekend masjid schools.

There is nothing about Islamic education that makes corporal punishment a necessary part of its process. Reprimanding a child by hitting them is something that is allowed in Islam in circumstances of religious defiance after a child turns ten.[520] Baseline principals of Islam are that a Muslim cannot inflict harm onto his or herself or others[521], and that children are to be dealt with through mercy and tenderness.[522] So hitting is not a desirable course of action, and when it is done there are religious boundaries and guidelines to be followed that restrain it

from becoming abuse. Specifically, there can be no hitting of the head or face, which is forbidden altogether in Islam[523], and the allowable instances of hitting are numerically limited.[524] Hitting is also not supposed to be a first resort, it is explicit within Islam that giving sincere advice is an integral part of the religion[525], and it is stated explicitly by the well-known companion of the Prophet ﷺ Ibn Abbas رضـــي الله عـــنه, that hitting should not be done severely and that it should be done with a small bristle-ended stick called a

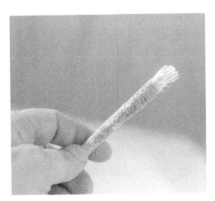

[520] Sunan Abī Dawūd Book 2 Hadith 105 https://sunnah.com/abudawud/2/105

[521] 40 Hadith Nawawi Hadith 32 https://sunnah.com/nawawi40/32, Sahīh Muslim Book 55 Hadith 82. https://sunnah.com/muslim/55/82

[522] Sunan Abī Dawūd Book 43 Hadith 446 https://sunnah.com/abudawud/43/44, Jami` at-Tirmidhī Book 27 Hadith 27 https://sunnah.com/tirmidhi/27/27

[523] Sunan Abī Dawūd Book 40 Hadith 143 https://sunnah.com/abudawud/40/143

[524] Sunan Abī Dawūd Book 40 Hadith 141 https://sunnah.com/abudawud/40/141

[525] 40 Hadith Nawawi Hadith 7 https://sunnah.com/nawawi40/7

siwak[526], that is used commonly in the eastern world as a toothbrush, it is pictured above. Based upon all these principals it is universally agreed in Islamic jurisprudence that when corporal punishment is used it is forbidden for it to incur any physical injury, disfigurement, scarring, or bruising. So Islam permits *regulated* hitting with strict guidelines.

These guidelines happen to correlate neatly with what is allowed under statutes of child abuse laws in many states. Many states have mandatory reporting laws for teachers that compels them to report a child to a protective services agency if they have reason to believe they are being physically abused. I have known it to be the case in some Muslim communities that there is a prevailing sentiment that this type of reporting is way over done and that the Muslim community is overly targeted for it. Teachers are obliged by their licensing agreements to fulfill certain obligations, and they cannot neglect those. At the same time they are also responsible for knowing *exactly* what child abuse laws say in their state, and considering a proper scope for choosing to report that includes cultural considerations.

For example, in Minnesota parents and guardians are allowed to spank or slap their children so long as it does not cause injury. The statute states explicitly, "*Abuse does not include reasonable and moderate physical discipline of a child administered by a parent or legal guardian which does not result in an injury*".[527] Minnesota also offers an example of a legislature that is sophisticated enough to recognize that mandatory reporters need to consider the child's culture in assessing the impact of physical discipline upon them. The same statute states in regards to mental or emotional injury that it means, "*observable or substantial impairment in the child's ability to function within a normal range of performance and behavior with due regard to the child's culture.*"[528] All of this correlates neatly to Islamic restrictions on the practice, which Muslims are more likely than not to observe. So educators need to have a holistic and well-informed perspective before they go about reporting abuse to government agencies and causing severe stress and possibly undue separation and government interference for families.

Furthermore, young adult Muslims have reported to me that at school as a child they would speak about being "whooped"[529] in the masjid, but that they did so in a way that was greatly

---

[526] Tafsir Tabari 4:34 (Arabic) https://tinyurl.com/y7439mg3

[527] Minnesota State Statute 626.556 https://www.revisor.mn.gov/statutes/cite/626.556. If one looks at the details of what the Minnesota statute considers to be "not reasonable and moderate" it would be found to actually be *less* restrictive than the Islamic guidelines. For example, the statute prohibits "striking a child **under age one** on the face or head" - Islam prohibits striking someone of **any age** in the face.

[528] Minnesota State Statute 626.556. See Subdivision 2 points F and G-9 for definitions of emotional harm and mental injury https://www.revisor.mn.gov/statutes/cite/626.556

[529] A term from American vernacular that they learn through consumption of American media, not a term taught to them by their parents.

exaggerated for the sake of attention. Rick Wormeli, a nationally recognized award-winning teacher[530], says in his book *Day One and Beyond* that a good axiom for teachers to establish with parents at the beginning of the year is that both parties "believe only half of what they hear [from the kids] about [teachers] and the class, and [the teachers] will believe only half of what [they] hear about [the parents]" (Wormeli, 2003, pg. 137). The separation of home and school itself is something that kids can and will manipulate for attention, and home-cultural spaces like the masjid are separated by a degree further than the home, making them even more pliable to this sort of manipulation.

So it is crucial for teachers to know what child abuse laws actually say in their state and the cultural context of their students. Mandatory reporting concerns should be based on whether or not the concern is over actual language of state statutes being violated as opposed to reactions to things kids say that could very well be overly conjectural or hyperbolic. A child talking about being hit in the masjid over the weekend might be one thing, actually seeing that they have bruising or emotional withdrawal as a possible effect is another. Social workers in schools and school psychologists are good resources for further understanding signs of genuine abuse and their expertise should be drawn upon. School or district's legal consultants should be sought to advise about the provisions and limitations of mandatory reporting laws in your given state.

In many Muslim cultures hitting is not an uncommon practice in raising children. Parents and adults will often describe it as a practice being done out of love and care for their children because, they will say, it is done in order to prevent their child from doing something harmful or immoral to themselves. This is where an emotional guilt is usually associated with it for the children. More often than not it is the emotion of reprimand that has the coercive effect on the child, as opposed to the actual physical reprimand. I have known some families where I felt the parents were overly reliant on hitting to reprimand their child as opposed to teaching them useful cognitive skills in an age appropriate way. These parents typically had numerous factors causing severe stress in their lives, which research has shown to have an autocatalytic relationship with both child misbehavior and physical punishment (Durrant & Ensom, 2012; Neece et al, 2012). I never found these parents to be lacking in love or hope for their child. The sad part is that a teacher aggressively acting on mandatory reporting laws towards these parents is predictably going to compound the stress in their lives, and thus compound the

---

[530] He was the winner of the Disney's American Teacher Awards Outstanding English Teacher of the Nation in 1999.

problem. Schools should ask what they are doing to offer formal educational opportunities for parents in soft parenting skills.[531]

This is also a matter where teachers may need to analyze their own ethnocentrism. Nowadays people in the West are very sensitive to the idea of any corporal discipline at all. I personally agree with this disposition and have found that most Muslims in the West do as well. I have spent countless hours in masjid weekend schools and youth programs and have only ever seen it done in a few instances and done so in a manner that was very light. I do believe there is a need within Muslim communities for more parents, caretakers, and masjid instructors[532] to learn about child development, and effective child-rearing practices that inculcate intrinsic motivation in children to choose compliance on their own.

But while educators try to help the families they serve adopt high-level parenting skills it should also be understood that there are alternative perspectives that exist. Muslims can view people in the West as being overly sensitive about physical discipline as a result of the West's own poor history of domestic and child abuse. It was not that long ago in American history when children were hit with sticks in school[533], and children and women were regularly beaten at home. Domestic abuse problems in America have always been exacerbated and intimately intertwined with abuse of alcohol (Gebara et al, 2015), which Islam forbids.[534] The perspective that a Muslim might have in analyzing Western society is that because Western society did not have something like Islam to regulate corporal discipline, it ended up occurring in a way that was inarguably abusive. Therefore, as a psychological *reaction to its own history* the modern-day West will connote any idea at all of a kid being hit in absolutist terms of abuse, and be unable to consider the idea of it taking place in a context of regulated discipline that prevents both abuse and misbehavior.

None of this discussion is to say that abuse does not happen at all within Muslim communities. Certainly it does as it does in all communities, this discussion is only a means to widen the

---

[531] A potential resource for this is the book *Positive Parenting in the Muslim Home* by Noha Alshugairi and Munira Lekovic Ezzeldine (2017). This book is a guide specifically for Muslim parents on implementing strategies that are based on Daniel Siegel's *The Whole Brain Child* (2011) in a culturally-competent way.

[532] A teacher in a mosque is usually called a *mualim*. In the West they are rarely people who are professionally trained in managing children; it is not unusual for them to be younger adults, or even teenagers, whose qualifications for being in that position are only that they know how to teach the recitation of the Qur'an.

[533] By the way, this practice, called caning, was exported by European colonial powers and inflicted upon Africa and Muslim majority countries, especially in countries where Britain overhauled the education system (Last, 2000; Ocobock, 2012).

[534] Qur'an 2:219 https://quran.com/2/219

scope of consideration and perspective for educators. For effective interventions to take place that will not run the risk of causing more harm when abuse happens in Muslim communities, the question needs to be asked as to what the proper role of Islam is to serve in these situations. Is it the source of abuse? Or is it a potential remedy? Ideally, the dictates from Islam that constrain physical discipline to a greater extent than the laws of the state of Minnesota would be used within Muslim communities as an admonition upon those who commit abuse of any kind. Without knowledge and consideration for the religious teachings, well-meaning interventionists can make major missteps and compound a community's anxieties and social isolation for no good reason.

It also needs to be noted that using organized positive incentives in the masjid is much more common for promoting student success and behavior. This often takes the form of masājid and organizations hosting Qur'an recitation competitions. These are fairly large tournaments where kids compete in their ability to have memorized and articulately recite the Qur'an. The students will win certificates and prizes for doing well, and be honored in festive ceremonies that Muslim organizations will often rent out banquet halls to host. The positive incentive provided by these competitions is something communities enjoy greatly. There are also large scale international Qur'an competitions held in the Muslim world, some of which have even been won by students from America (Dupuy, 2017). I have known masājid that do smaller competitions within the weekend schools and also ones that have systems where students can win material prizes such as toys for reaching certain stages of progression in their learning and memorization.

Considerations Regarding Problematic Behavior

Going back to our original point, whether reprimanding and consequences in the masjid involve corporal punishment or not, they are interpreted by kids as being harsher and carrying greater emotional weight than consequences in the public schools. Something that can result from this feeling of harsher punishments happening at the masjid is that some students come to school on Monday and feel, either consciously or subconsciously, that the public school is a place to "let loose" as it is the place of lesser consequence. Educators should appreciate that because of this many Muslim students with high behavioral issues who also experience double schooling commonly exhibit the worst behaviors that they do in life at the public school. Educators know and understand that at different developmental stages young people have a need to experiment with boundary-testing behaviors to some degree. In light of this we can appreciate the particular psychological phenomenon going on with some of these students that are perceived at school as "troubled."

It should not be taken from these insights that a route of solution with students like this is for the public school educators to be stricter and more harsh, even if this is advised by their parents.[535] Rather it should be understood that usually these students have had all kinds of consequences thrown at them before in their lives, and yet their behavior problems still persist. Therefore, the conclusion that should be drawn is that *nothing* is going to be "consequenced" out of them. This point should re-emphasize the importance of positive relationships being built with the students from as early on in the school year as possible, and the need to practice culturally-relevant cognitive behavioral therapy strategies (CBT) with them over the long haul. The strategies do not need to be overwhelming factors for the teachers, but they ought to inform how the students are spoken to, and such strategies have been provided in the previous chapters of this book and more resources are available on abrahameducation.com.

Another phenomenon that takes place from students feeling the need to "let loose" is that oftentimes there are students who exhibit very opposite behaviors between their weekend school and the public school Monday thru Friday. With these students their parents will often experience dissonance when the school calls them to report bad behavior. I have mentioned before that behavior problems with boys is one of the issues that I am asked about the most, as well as being asked how to better communicate with parents. I have noticed in my trainings that the inquiries about how to better communicate with parents often come from people from the same school where behavior problems are felt to be persistent. I tell these schools that it appears to me that these two questions are not divorced from one another, and it may be that the school staff is telling itself that somehow if the school could only communicate better with the parents that it would in turn resolve the behavior problems they are seeing. This very well could be the case, and I do not discourage communication with parents at all, however, I also believe that sometimes this view is mistaken, and certainly an approach that depends on this view is mistaken. It is often the case for the parents of children that exhibit behavior problems in school, and even more so with immigrant parents who grew up in a different culture, that their own frustration with the child's behavior problems have them at their wits end and they feel that they have tried everything and are at a loss for what to do themselves. Sometimes these parents suffer from feelings of deep embarrassment and simply stop answering the phone when they see the school's phone number calling them. This may be more likely to happen if they carry with them the weight of being a cultural outsider to the school community.

It is crucial with these students that they have a positive relationship with at least one person on an individual basis in the school building. Ideally, this will be with a *teacher* and not just support or behavioral staff. When the student's go-to relationship in the school building is a teacher their positive relationship is also associated with academics. A pitfall that many schools

---

[535] This is discussed in chapter three, I will add the point here that it is not uncommon for parents to see kids misbehavior at school as the fault of the school's own inability to be strict, because they know they have seen strictness discipline the child in other contexts, like the masjid.

fall into with students, especially ones who are cultural minorities within the building, is that the school depends on support staff or behavior deans to develop positive relationships and incubate motivation with those students. This is problematic because those staff do much of their work outside the classroom. When the student only has a positive relationship with them it creates a high incentive for that student to get themselves kicked out of the classroom. Thus the positive relationship actually contributes to their cycle of misbehavior. Sometimes the support staff needs to be used to monitor the class while the teacher steps out for a moment to talk to a specific student, as opposed to always having the student sent to the support staff's office.

In schools where a majority percentage of students are societal ethnic minorities, and perhaps even more so when they are Muslim students who are likely to have communal bonds with one another outside of the school; what sometimes takes place is a phenomenon where the students with high behavioral needs take on a place of high social status, influence, and instigation amongst their peers. This in turn results in more students partaking in the negative behavior in a sort of group-think fashion. This can happen to such an extent that the school's disciplinary system finds itself to be overwhelmed. Especially in contexts like these, it is of paramount importance that teachers develop relationships with students and use practices, both instructional[536] and behavioral, that are designed to keep kids in the classroom; some key ones of which will be discussed further down.

There are many different strategies out there for building relationships with students who exhibit problematic behaviors. For Muslim students, what I tell educators is that any consideration with relationship building has to begin from a place where *patience in temperament* is the number one consideration and priority. The students have to interpret the teacher as being a patient individual. Patience is a very lauded virtue in Islam. I mentioned briefly in chapter three that inculcating patience is an objective of fasting during Ramadan, and that the story of Joseph رضي الله عنه in the Qur'an is one that extolls it as a preeminent virtue. The teaching and importance of patience in Islam is extolled throughout Islamic texts, it is mentioned no less than ninety times in the Qur'an. This esteem given to patience is connected to Islam's belief in predestination. Since it is part of Islamic belief that every thing that happens is part of the decree of Allah, the way an individual reacts to adversity is understood to be a test for them, and Islam explicitly teaches to endure adversity with patience.[537] So the people in Muslim communities who are the most well respected leaders are very stoic individuals who

---

[536] And it is the instructional practices that are most important for mitigating troubled behavior. Usually students who instigate misbehavior are academically insecure, the strategies discussed later on are designed to treat exactly this dilemma.
[537] 40 Hadith Nawawi Hadith 19 https://sunnah.com/nawawi40/19, Sahīh Muslim Book 55 Hadith 82 https://sunnah.com/muslim/55/82

exhibit the virtue of patience with strong, near absolute, emotional control and calmness during stressful situations. Growing up in environs where individuals such as this garner community respect, and specifically respect as teachers, creates habits of mind in the conditioning of Muslim students that teachers need to draw upon with their own disposition that they exhibit in their classrooms.

It is also important for Western teachers to understand that there are large cultural differences regarding what is interpreted as worthy of getting stressed out about. For example, in many urban areas in America working as a taxi or bus driver is a common occupation for Muslim men of varying ethnicities. I have had many conversations in the masjid with drivers who express dismay about how exasperated non-Muslims can become over their ride arriving late by as little as two or three minutes. The internal clock that teachers run in their minds throughout the day in order to stay in step with the school day's tight schedule can sometimes work against them by sabotaging them into over stressing.

It is estimated that teachers make a decision every 15 seconds in the school day. Each one of these has the potential to trigger stress reactions (Starcke & Brand, 2012). These stress reactions in turn cause teachers to run all day on the release of adrenaline hormones. There are certain external behavioral responses associated with stress hormones that cue to observers (i.e. the students) that an individual is indeed under stress. Most common among these are strained facial expressions, a voice that is either shaky or suddenly raised in pitch, and tense posture. When stress hormones are secreted from adrenal and pituitary glands they provide feedback to the brain about the situation and put the brain in an initial "alarm" stage. While in this alarm stage the body's resistance to stress drops for about two to three minutes and the brain resorts to operating from its emotional center, the amygdala (Bernstein et al, 2003a). While making decisions during this stage people are more likely to rely on what psychologists call *mental sets*, which means a reliance on old patterns of problem solving even when they might not be the most efficient or effective for the given situation (Bernstein et al, 2003b). While some amount of stress hormones are necessary for basic human functioning, there are many negative health effects to excessive amounts of it, to which people in the profession of teaching are highly susceptible. Also, studies have shown that there is a correlative relationship between teacher stress and the secretion of stress hormones in students as well (Lever et al, 2017). So when teachers are stressed out it has cyclical and compound negative effects that directly impact the health of both the teacher and the students. The good news is that the secretion of these hormones can be aborted through breathing and taking control of one's own mental processing (Ma et al, 2017).

❖ *The Tongue Strategy*

For controlling the body's regulation of stress hormones psychologists recommend living a healthy lifestyle that includes a healthy diet, exercises, and meditation. But what can a teacher do in the moment of having a stress reaction provoked in the school day? What I have found to be most effective is what I call the tongue strategy. It is small to do but its benefits are numerous. The tongue strategy is to, when provoked, simply press one's tongue to the roof of the mouth. This prevents one's teeth from becoming clenched. There are two immediate benefits to this. The first is that having a facial expression with clenched teeth versus one where the teeth are not touching creates a subtle yet visible difference in the facial expression's external appearance that has been found to be the difference in having a facial expression that is interpreted by the onlooker as stressed as opposed to relaxed (Vlisides, 1994; Keady, 1999; Jones, 2000). This is because putting the tongue to the roof of the mouth actually prevents the face from becoming strained and switches the face's loci of stimulation from the jaw and teeth to the mucous membrane lining the inside of the mouth, which in turn keeps the face relaxed and prompts the brain to release oxytocin which induces relaxation and combats stress (Uvnäs-Moberg et al, 2015). You could even lightly massage the tongue back and forth on the roof of the mouth to increase the relaxing stimulation to the mucous membrane. This provides important input that the brain needs in a situation of provocation in order to abort the adrenaline process. To further give the brain feedback that signals relaxation after putting the tongue to the roof of the mouth, a relaxing breath can be taken through the nostrils. This breath should not be overly deep and preceded by a massive inhale, but still deep enough to release tension in the diaphragm; similar to how one might breathe when they casually relax from standing up to sitting down (Ma et al, 2017; Zaccaro et al, 2018). The other benefit of holding the tongue is that it prevents the teacher from saying the immediate thought that came to mind when they were provoked, and instead it allows them time to shift their own mental processing from the amygdala to the prefrontal cortex, and therefore put themselves in a situation where they are better able to think out the best words that need to be said to the students at that moment.

Practicing this strategy keeps the face calm and shows the students that the teacher is unaffected by the provocation that has occurred. For our Muslim students who exhibit problematic behavior patterns in school, as well as other students, this is a major key to casting upon them the idea that the teacher is a person of patience, which is the key to earning their respect and laying a foundation for a positive relationship.

Many students who I talk to who had behavior problems in school explicitly say that the negative behaviors are a test to see whether or not the teacher will "give up on them". Like other groups of students, the psychology of Muslim students are often influenced by societal stigmas with their personal and familial identity. This situates them to sometimes be necessarily suspicious as to whether or not they can trust their teachers. It is simply a part of the reality in which we work that problematic behaviors are often a child's way of testing where the boundaries of trust exist. The initial, most frequent, and most important way that teachers signal to these students that they can be trusted is by controlling their own emotions in stressful situations, and this is primarily signaled in direct yet subtle non-verbal ways.

❖ *Verbal Interruption*
I am frequently asked about student tendencies to interrupt during class. I have seen in masājid that when semi-formal discourse takes place between a teacher and students the conversational turn taking patterns can take on the same patterns that would take place in social discourse.

A semi-formal discourse in the masjid might include a teacher telling a small group of students directions about procedural matters, such as where to sit, or giving a short talk to a small group of students about some religious ethic or practical matter. But I have also seen that when small tutoring classes are done in masājid about secular subjects, there are many of them that offer tutoring programs for math, it is also more likely to take on semi-formal conversational patterns. This is different from how formal religious instructional classes or direct instruction in the recitation of the Qur'an are treated, which will be discussed later on.

Conversational turn taking is something that linguists have studied for a long time. Research has suggested that there are many common patterns and principles of conversational turn taking that are universal across languages and cultures (Stivers et al, 2009). However, there are definitely areas of variation that can have important implications for people's interpretations of others from cultural outgroups.

There is something done in conversation that linguists call back-channeling. It is essentially feedback that a listener gives to the speaker to let them know they are engaged in the conversation. English speakers tend to backchannel by saying things like "mm..hmm" or "yeah" and also by nodding. Cultures vary in the degree and extent to which back-channeling is verbal vs. nonverbal. In many Muslim cultures, I believe bachkchanneling is highly verbal and this can transfer to Muslim students' discourse in English. Observations of some researchers back up this notion (Tarone et al, 2009; Ward et al, 2007). But my specific takeaways about it are based on my own observation and experience, and are articulated here in a way to make it most helpful to the understanding of teachers who have issues with verbal interruption from students. I believe that interjectory comments and questions tend to operate as a form of back-channeling in many Muslim cultures.

So when a teacher in a masjid is interrupted in a semi-formal context the interjection is not treated as an interruption. Rather it is handled gracefully. They may simply signal to the student to be patient with a hand gesture and then go on with their own monologue, continuing the point they had to make and then bringing the monologue back to the question of the student and answering it; or they may choose to allow the interjection to redirect their monologue by answering it and then connecting the answer back to the original point they were making. They may also simply let the interjection pass without addressing it while continuing their monologue. One way or the other, a worthwhile general rule for public school educators to understand is that the orality of the home languages of many Muslim cultures handle interjections fluidly and in semi-formal contexts in the masjid a raise-your-hand system is rarely used. Due to the contrasting seriousness with which formal learning structures in the masjid are taken, I believe students often arrive at the public schools with a predisposition and sentiment where it is cued to them that the environment is meant to take on a more semi-formal structure, and therefore they treat it as such.

What does this mean? For some teachers who have students that are highly social, oral, and verbal the teacher might not mind simply going with the flow of these interjections and teaching in a similar manner where interjections are handled fluidly. Personally, I do not do this. I have observed classrooms where this is done and I often see very good learning being done for some students who are engaged in the learning and appreciate a highly oral format that is less regulatory of verbal input. But I also commonly see that the noise level of the classroom allows for a lot of side talking to be done by students who are disengaged, which goes unnoticed or unattended to because the noise level in the classroom is high. I run a classroom that generally *does* use a raise-your-hand system or at least an understanding that only one question is asked at a time.[538]

School always conditions students into understanding how a raise-your-hand system works, and that it only allows there to be one speaker at a time who is not to be interjected upon. But we have to understand that some students are more habituated to that type of format in their

---

[538] Whether or not it is specifically "raise your hand" varies with the age of students I teach as well as the class size. When I have taught older students, 11th graders, in class sizes less than twenty I have found allowing them to say "mister" in order to signal that they want to ask a question comes more naturally and can be done in a way that is non-disruptive. It is also common in Muslim cultures that teachers are addressed simply by the native language's equivalent to "Mister" or "Miss", and if a name is used following that it is the first name and not the surname. This is especially true in tribal societies where high numbers of individuals with the same last names exist. A side note, the Arabic word for "Mister" is "Ustadh" and it is from this word where the formal Spanish third person pronoun that is used to address a second person "Usted" comes.

home-cultural settings than others. So while caucasian students may be likely to experience a one person speaking at a time format at their dinner table, for many Muslim students this may not be the case. For my part, I do not believe this means we should abandon conditioning these students into a raise your hand system when they are at the public school, but we have to understand that for some it may take longer for them to take hold of it and show compliance. Therefore we must exhibit the utmost patience with them, and this understanding that they have an uphill battle in forming these habits relative to other students ought to promote within us enough empathy to be able to exhibit that necessary patience in our body language, tone of voice, and other non-verbal cues.

I will talk more specifically about learning in formal whole-class contexts in the masjid later on, but for the sake of this discussion, what is important to understand about those contexts is that they are so highly instructor-centered and focused that little to no student participation or questioning is expected during instructional time. American teachers today are taught to be sensitive about over monologuing and told they should prefer to have some ongoing student participation. So even during the lecturing or modeling time of a lesson where the students primary responsibility is to listen, most teachers will typically expect and do some prompting for verbal student participation and ask questions. This expectation can cue to the students that the class is really meant to operate in a more semi-formal fashion relative to what they have maybe been acculturated to in the masjid.

The majority of my teaching career has been in classrooms with students that were highly verbal and socially tight knit with one another, so quelling interjections and side-talking was always an important matter to be attended to. The number one principle I tell teachers in these types of contexts to abide by is that *you cannot talk over the students*, ever. This means that the teacher is going to have to allow themselves to be interrupted and then handle the interruption gracefully, with patience, and in a way that maintains respect in the teacher-student relationship; but also conditions the student into the appropriate expectations for the classroom.

Doing this comes down to very subtle matters. Firstly, teachers have to remember that whatever amount of side talking or interjections they allow with their actions is exactly how much of it will take place regularly over the long haul. When a teacher continues their teaching monologue while side talking occurs, their actions communicate to the students that the side talking is OK; it is the same with answering an interjection. Michael Grinder, the author of *EnVoy*, said that pausing is the greatest nonverbal cue that exists. I suggest teachers who are not familiar with Grinder's classroom management system, which is centered on body language and nonverbal cues, to specifically look up his strategies called ABOVE-Pause-(whisper) and Incomplete

Sentence (<u>Grinder, 2001</u>). What I will discuss here borrows from that framework, but I have added many additional considerations for the specific students we are talking about. I am going to talk through in narrative form a general scenario that commonly takes place in classes within the span of only a few seconds. The benefit of walking through it like this is for us to slow down the way we think about our interpersonal interactions with students for the sake of reflecting on the subtle matters at play. You are going to want to visualize in your mind the situation as it is strung out here.

When a teacher is giving their instructional monologue a common mistake that is made is that when they see a student turn their head to their neighbor to begin side talking, the teacher tells his or herself that it is just something small, that they should not make a big deal out of it, and then they continue on with their instruction. The problem with this is that the teacher's actions have communicated to the student that turning to their neighbor to talk during instruction is OK. It is small in the beginning, but this has now allowed a tiny spark to be lit that will quickly spread into a larger fire. Students are very aware of their peers in a classroom, when it is noticed that one student has turned to quietly say something to their neighbor, it cues to another student that they can do the same thing, and a downward spiral of the class's collective attention has begun. What has to take place in the moment that the first student's head turns is that *it needs to be stopped.* This is where the nonverbal cue of pausing becomes ever so important.

When a person is giving a monologue and they cut themselves off mid-sentence it does not sound natural at all and it immediately signals to the listeners that something is up, even if they are only listening passively and not paying close attention to what is actually being said. So when that student turns their head to talk to their neighbor and the teacher pauses their monologue, it immediately acts as a signal to that student and the rest of the classroom that the teacher is aware that someone is not listening. However, this signal has not been sent in any sort of way that calls the student out, and this is very important for maintaining respect in the teacher-student relationship. What the student will usually do is turn their head back to look at the teacher, often with their eyes a little wider than average, to assess the situation and see if the teacher is looking directly at him or her. When the student turns their head from their neighbor to see if the teacher is looking at them, it is okay for you to look at them but at this point it is best to avoid making it too obvious by turning your head, because that can non-verbally call the student out; so keep it to only a glance with the eyes. It should only take a second or two for the student to turn their own head away from their neighbor and back to facing the direction of the teacher. At this point the teacher has prevented the side-talk from taking place, and apparently gotten back the attention of the student whose mind was off task and not listening. But the student turning their head back towards the teacher is only a bluff at this point. That student still wants to side-talk and will be looking back at the teacher in wait of the opportunity to go back into it. Naturally, the student anticipates going back to the side-talk right as the teacher begins their monologue again. So how does the teacher prevent this?

The key is twofold, 1.) The teacher has to go back to the beginning of the sentence in which they paused, and 2.) The teacher must begin this sentence in a voice that is noticeably lower in volume than the one they were using when they were cut off, what Grinder calls a whisper voice. Starting the sentence again from the beginning allows any student who had lost their attention to regain it. If the teacher continues mid-sentence the monologue becomes choppy and disjointed and the attention of more students will be lost. When the student made a decision to side-talk, they had prepared themselves to do it at a volume level lower than whatever volume level the teacher was using in their monologue. So when the teacher lowers their own volume level after pausing the side-talking student is thrown off, because it has been cued to them that while the teacher has continued with their instruction they are also keeping an ear out for small distractions. The side-talking student is now effectively frozen, using nonverbal strategies that did not call them out, and they are left with only the choice to be listening. No, this does not mean that the teacher's voice will stay at a whisper, the volume will increase. It also does not mean that the student will not try to talk again, they will. But when they try it again the same process needs to play itself out again with diligence and consistency on the part of the teacher. When this happens the student eventually becomes conditioned to learn that in that classroom side-talking is not an option. The same is to be done for a student who interjects with questions or comments. The same strategy can be used when interrupted in a one on one conversation as well. Using this strategy is of course most effective when done intensely in the beginning of the year. If it is done as a change of habit mid-year, that is okay, but it will take longer to recondition the student(s).

For teachers who know this strategy and still struggle with making it effective, internal patience is usually the missing ingredient. It cannot be stressed enough that a disposition of patience and calmness is the foundation upon which forming a positive relationship, garnering respect, and making strategies effective with students is built upon. Many teachers will allow themselves to be cut off and use pausing as a cue maybe three or four times before slamming their foot down on the ground and berating the student telling them that they have "had it". There is a clear-cut cultural clash going on in these situations because usually the teacher's own acculturation from their upbringing has conditioned them to take the students actions as very disrespectful, and they feel like they cannot help but resort to admonition due to the tension and frustration that has built up inside themselves. This is an area where the tongue strategy comes back into play, because the student who is testing the teacher in this way is engaging them in a quiet power struggle and the teacher is provoked. Once the teacher gives the physical cues of being stressed out (a tense body, shaky voice, strained face) the student is getting feedback that they are in control. The tongue strategy allows the teacher to maintain a neutral facial expression that communicates to the student that the situation is nothing new to the teacher and they know how to handle it. Taking the relaxing breath through the nostrils allows the tension in the teachers body to relax, and allows their thinking to move from the amygdala to the prefrontal cortex where executive function takes place. This is key, because for students and classes that are very testy with these interruptions there does come a point within repeating the process and power struggle where the pesky student or the whole class will need to be addressed verbally. I have further broken down how to do this verbal addressing and its various caveats, please go to abrahameducation.com for detailed resources on that.[539]

There may also come select times in the year where a verbal address by the teacher might need to be stern with classes or specific students that struggle a little more with learning self control. However, sternly addressing a class is only effective when it runs counter to what the students have come to expect from that teacher. Therefore the teacher's sternness and apparent frustration comes as a surprise, and it affects the students because they have already developed respect for the teacher due to all the patience that the teacher has previously exhibited with them. This respect causes the students to feel appropriately ashamed at having disappointed them; not dissimilar to how one feels when having disappointed their beloved mother. With patient teachers, if students have gotten to the point where they are in need of a stern reminder, it is usually due to their youthful neglect and not due to an explicit desire to provoke the teacher. For the teacher who relies on stern intervention, the student's testiness becomes an explicit way to antagonize the teacher and bring on what they see as the inevitable meltdown. Usually one or two stern interventions a semester is what we should consider maximally appropriate for it to be effective as a tool.

Teachers need to understand that a part of exhibiting patience with this process is that it often needs to be worked beyond what feels natural, especially if they come from a cultural background of Anglo-American expectations. This is especially true at the beginning of the year when the relationship is being set with the students, a teacher may find themselves working this process to a point that feels ridiculous. But sticking to and being consistent with this process while maintaining a patient and calm disposition in regards to the subtle body language and nonverbal cues is exactly how respect is earned. When that respect begins to take hold, social pressure will begin to be pressed upon the very difficult students from their peers who want to pay attention. In the long run over the course of the year students' sensitivity and reactivity to these non-verbal cues increases and the process becomes simpler and easier.

---

[539] These may not be available until 2021.

Learning about the students home culture and learning about how it compounds the challenges they may face in being conditioned into the public school expectations, as this book aims to do, carries the benefit of providing the teacher with insight and a greater appreciation for where the student is coming from. This newfound insight and perspective in turn ought to provide the teacher with a prudently-measured[540] perspective of empathy that makes it easier for the teacher to be patient with those students.

❖ *Play Wrestling*

Teachers have often asked me if there is a cultural root to a sort of rough playing that they see students do in school where they engage one another physically in a fashion that sometimes appears to the teachers and staff in the building to be fighting. A staff member will usually interrupt this with loud vocal berating, if not physical intervention, and teachers find that the students will tell them "we were just playing". This type of playing is extremely common for low income children who live in close-quartered housing.[541] Since it is a type of play that involves exertion of muscle, it is an effective way for urban children to get their energy out. These children often do not have the means of partaking in cardiovascular play that a suburban child whose home has a yard and street with low traffic available to them can do. So this type of play is not only normal but very valuable for many kids.

For some Muslim kids there are compounding effects that add to the normalcy of this type of play. One is that Muslim families tend to live in homes with less valuable possessions around, and a higher value placed on open floor space compared to Anglo-American homes. There are specific religious edicts[542] that go against having too much vanity[543] in the home and that laud the value of having open space in it, especially in order to facilitate praying.[544]

---

[540] I say "prudently-measured" because we *do not* want to be empathetic to the point of being dismissive of student misbehavior and shunning accountability. This would be extreme, and is another pitfall that some fall into. We must hold students accountable, and Islam and Muslim culture values accountability very highly. But we have to employ the strategies that are most likely to be effective for the long haul.

[541] Muslim families are often large, increasing the likelihood they live in close-quartered housing. Especially if they are low income, and in some cases even if they aren not low income but prefer to live with the rest of their local community if it generally is.

[542] Qur'an 29:64 https://quran.com/29/64

[543] Sunan an-Nasā'i Book 48 Hadith 308 https://sunnah.com/nasai/48/308, Sahīh Muslim Book 37 Hadith 152 http://sunnah.com/muslim/37/152, Sahīh al-Bukhārī Book 67 Hadith 116 https://sunnah.com/bukhari/67/116, these ahadith also relate to the edicts on the prayers invalidation when there are images in the home.

[544] Musnad Imam Ahmad Hadith 3623. See page 296 of Volume 3 of the English translation published by Darusalaam. https://tinyurl.com/y8b6m5ln

Also, in Islam wrestling is normally *allowed* in the masjid and is commonly done during free-time breaks in weekend schools. It was actually a practice of the Prophet Muhammad ﷺ and his companions to wrestle for recreation.[545] A masjid, unlike a church, does not have pews and long rows of chairs set up, rather it consists of a wide open floor space. So when a break comes during the weekend schools, kids will often be allowed to let loose a little bit and play around. This often takes the form of this sort of play wrestling. Breaks frequently occur just before the prayer times, so the playing will be broken up by a natural audible signal in the call to prayer, and kids know from a young age that this signal means it is time to stop and line up for prayer. This creates a situation where the adults do not necessarily have to be active in getting the kids to stop playing, because a stoppage of all activity when the prayer occurs is built in naturally to the structure of how a masjid functions. So when kids do this type of play in the public school and it stresses out the staff members of the school and they get berated for doing it, what typically resonates with them is a feeling of "what's the big deal?", because they do the same thing in other situations around other adults and it does not incur that type of reaction.

So what needs to be told to these kids? It is pretty much outside the realm of consideration for schools to allow this type of play to take place, especially in a way where it occurs spontaneously throughout the building. When I ask teachers to ponder the underlying answer to the question *why aren't kids allowed to play fight in the school*? The answer I get is: because they could get hurt. So then I will probe further by asking, *what do you say when the kids tell you that they do not care if they get hurt*? And the teachers will say: someone else could get hurt. So I ask them to think further, and ask them to reflect upon why it *really* matters to us if someone else gets hurt? Sometimes I have teachers who get it, other times I have teachers who are at a loss with this line of questioning and never think about giving explanations for these types of school rules beyond these simple platitudes that their own home acculturation has trained them to give. The root answer as to why kids cannot play fight in school exists in one word: *liability*. Here is where the point of cultural clash meets in these situations.

While it is something that many Americans often fail to realize about themselves, and how it affects their own psychology, so much of the little rules and codes of conduct that we abide by in the West, especially the United States, is based on the culture of liability that has been developed in our society. Muslim societies and cultures do not have the same culture of liability

---

[545] Sunan Abī Dawūd Book 34 Hadith 59 https://sunnah.com/abudawud/34/59

at all.[546] When two parties enter into a dispute in these societies there is usually some sort of family arbitration that takes place. Even if a matter does get taken to the government there are very hard ceilings on the amount of money that someone can requite from another person for alleged wrongdoing; even in the case of causing the death of a member of their family. All of this being based on dictates in Islamic law.[547]

So what does this mean? For one thing, it means that the rules that exist in school often need to be contextualized for kids in a more in-depth way that goes beyond platitudes. So liability might have to be explained to the kids explicitly. This does not mean that a Muslim kid is less likely to know or understand the concept of liability than an Anglo-American caucasian kid; but the caucasian kid is more likely to have been habituated into behavioral practices that abide by the hidden codes of behavior that adhere to our norms of liability in the West.

Whenever a safety issue arises that students seem to not take seriously, they should be talked to about how liability laws put restrictions on all of us in the school setting that, as professionals licensed by the government, staff are avowed to enforce. That talk can be as simple as:

> *"Hamza, the school is a part of the government of the state of Minnesota. Myself and every teacher here is given a license by the state of Minnesota. When we accept that license we promise by law to make sure certain rules are followed. Not throwing pencils is one of those rules."*

The first benefit of talking to Hamza this way is that it de-personalizes the interaction. There is a fair chance that Hamza was only trying to loan a pencil to Yasir and sought an efficient route to transport it across the room. By making the issue about the system itself and not about Hamza specifically, it gives him the opportunity to see the teacher as just doing their job as opposed to

---

[546] Islamic law does have principals of fault and requisition that are not dissimilar to Western laws. But in Islamic law there is generally only two types of damages that can be claimed, property and personal injury. In the case of property the retribution is only equal to the amount damaged, in the case of injury there can be financial retribution but there are guidelines that limit it. There is generally no claim of damages such as mental anguish, cost of future earnings etc. that are allowed for in Western tort law. Although in the present day legal systems in Muslim countries are considering new approaches in tort law, but generally a climate of "liability anxiety" that pervades America is not the type of acculturation that people raised in the Muslim world will have. The juris doctorate dissertation *Compensatory Damages Granted in Personal Injuries: Supplementing Islamic Jurisprudence with Elements of Common Law* by Majed Alshaibani from the University of Indiana can be read for more insight and information on this. https://www.repository.law.indiana.edu/etd/35/

[547] Sunan ibn Mājah Book 21 Hadith 2731 https://sunnah.com/urn/1269460, Sunan Abī Dawūd Book 24 Hadith 1555 https://sunnah.com/abudawud/24/155, Muwāta' Imām Mālik Book 43 Hadith 1583 https://sunnah.com/urn/416422, Muwāta' Imām Mālik Book 36 Hadith 14 https://sunnah.com/urn/414640

being uptight. Even if he was engaged in tomfoolery, this talk gives him the chance to save face and say "oh, I didn't know that". There is a fair chance that Hamza will do it again, in which case the same talk can and should be had all over again. So long as the talk is done in a way that is relaxed, monotone, and boring, Hamza will be quicker and quicker each time to say "I'm sorry Miss I forget..." in anticipation of where the talk he has heard before is going, until the point is hardwired and has changed his impulse. If necessary, the talk that was gone over in chapter three about being tested against our impulses and immediate thoughts in life can be added to the liability talk. Remember that impulses take a while to change and we have to be patient with that.

Conclusion

Learning about some of these dynamics ought to help give educators insight into cultural causes at play that affect how students can show up at school behavior-wise. These newfound insights ought to form a foundation of empathy within the school staff that enables a disposition of patience to be externalized by them. This is key, the reality is that the solution to many of these behavioral and relationship issues begins inside the school staff themselves and their own ability to be relaxed, yet consistent with expectations. Once this disposition is practiced the execution of subtle yet clear-headed everyday practices concerning body language and how we talk to kids has a positive impact. When these practices are done on a consistent basis over time this positive impact compounds and becomes profound; and school and classroom culture alters for the better. It is not the case that the behavior management book needs to be rewritten, but we do need to be precise and accurate with our understanding, choice, and emphasis of tactics in order to avoid missteps and to, most importantly, exude a demeanor of patience to the students.

However, even effective practices that treat behavior are really only symptomatic treatments. The true anecdote to curing behavior problems is getting students engaged in academics. This will be the focus of the rest of the book and begin with a focus on clashes, or *incongruences* as I like to call them, that take place between the masjid as a learning environment and the Monday thru Friday public school.

Learning Incongruences & Areas of Utilization

Learning in masājid can look very different from place to place but there are two main modes in which learning is done. The first is Qur'an memorization learning, and this is what the majority of students do in their time in the weekend school. The second is lecture-based learning. I will discuss these two different modes and the implications and areas of utilization that can be taken out of them for children's learning in the public schools, before going over very concrete strategies I use and recommend based on this knowledge. But first I will go over some pedagogical principles that I see overriding incongruences between masjid learning and public schools.

First, generally, the learning style in the masjid is more relaxed, and with Qur'an memorization learning there is actually a high amount of autonomy given for students to self pace; how this exactly works I will explain further down. Second, lecture-style learning is in no uncertain terms *instructor-centered*. The field of education in America gives much discussion, and oftentimes adulation, towards "student-centered" learning. Classrooms that are highly committed to student-centered learning need to know and consider the implications this can have for dissonance with the learning style to take place between their practice and the cultural habits of learning that Muslims students have likely had inculcated upon them. It is also important to understand that modes of learning in the Muslim world that take place outside of the masjid, such as classroom learning of secular subjects and oral story telling in social settings, also have a basis in Islamic learning. So knowing how learning happens in the masjid can give the teacher insight into cultural background learning habits, even for students who may not spend a ton of time there.

Third, learning to memorize the Qur'an is done in an incremental, step-by-step, and very logical sequence. Learning the Qur'an involves first learning to read Arabic phonetically. Arabic, like English, is an alphabetic reading and phonetic system. It is not ideographic[548] or logographic[549] as are many languages in Asia Pacific. Unlike English, Arabic phonetics have very few irregularities, almost none. Also different from English is that Arabic reads from right to left, not left to right. This is the case for both how words and sentences are written on pages, the sequence of lettering to form words (however multi-digit numbers are sequenced left to right), as well as the organization of pages in a bound text. So the cover of an Arabic book appears with the binding on the right side.

Arabic has also been an intensely studied language ever since the advent of Islam. Therefore scholars of the language over time have developed a sequence for learning how to decode its phonetics that is incremental and logically sequenced to near perfection. They have also created instructional texts that lay this learning sequence out with exercises that allow the student to memorize these books lesson by lesson in such a way where each lesson builds upon the previous one in a manner that is, again, incremental and logical. By the end of going through

---

[548] A reading system where symbols represent ideas or concepts, such as Ancient Egyptian hieroglyphs.
[549] A reading system where individually written characters represent whole words or phrases. Chinese is logographic.

the book from cover to cover, if one has memorized each lesson and done its practice, they will be able to read Arabic phonetics perfectly. Some of these books have existed for hundreds of years and they are still used in masājid today. With this as a basis, the idea of orderly, incremental, logically sequenced learning pervades almost all instructional texts that are used for Islamic learning. So while the concreteness of learning the phonetic system of an alphabetic language lends itself to this type of sequencing, these principles are still held to in Islamic forms of instruction with concepts of higher-levels of abstraction as well. Thinking about how to transfer these principles to content-area instruction in secular schools has been a guiding principle of my work as a professional educator. These two principles of instruction are important for the public school teacher of Muslim (or any) students to always keep in mind: *incremental build up* and *logical sequencing*.

Also, while the masjid does not usually have well trained teachers in child management, what allows the student to be given autonomy to self-pace in the Qur'an memorization process is *the learning materials* themselves. This is because they are incremental and logically sequenced to such an extent that the actual instruction the student receives can be done in minimal spurts, after mastery of the previous lesson is completed and verified through a small one-to-one assessment. The learning is then hardwired through a much larger amount of independent repetitive practice of the instructed piece that is guided by the learning textbook.

In the next section I am going to attempt to explain what Qur'an memorization learning looks like in a masjid in such a way that I hope you will be able to ascertain some visual of it in your mind. Transferring this part of my training program to text is challenging but insha'Allah you will benefit, and to experience the learning of this chapter in a more visual form register at abrahameducation.com.

Qur'an Memorization learning

The basic structure of learning to memorize Arabic phonetics and then the Qur'an is that the students will be taught a lesson out of a book, usually individually, and will work on that lesson independently until it is memorized, and they will then tell their teacher that they are ready to be assessed on their mastery of the entire lesson. After passing the assessment, the teacher will then teach the next lesson to them immediately, which will be bite-sized enough to do in a small amount of time based on the level they have already attained, and the student will then work the process over and over again. This process works up gradually, going from learning single letter sounds in Arabic, to memorizing letter combinations, to words, to phrases, to sentences, to verses from the Qur'an, to small chapters, to pages, to larger chapters, and eventually to the entirety of the Qur'an itself.

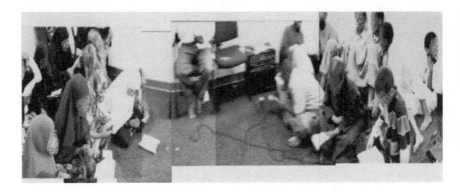

Let's use the image[550] above to walk through and discuss an example of what Qur'an memorization sessions in the mosque might look like. I know it is not the clearest of images, which is somewhat intentional, so take a moment to stop reading, observe it closely, and process for yourself what appears to be going on with each piece of it.

The first thing non-Muslims usually notice from this image is the gender separation. So first I will discuss that briefly. Gender separation is always observed in the mosque in one way or another. In America the particulars of what this looks like often has to do more with the practical aspects of available resources than anything else. In the Muslim world where masājid are in buildings that are purposefully built to be masājid, there is always strict separation in separate rooms, often in the form of the women having a balcony that is above the back end of the

Basic Qur'an Memorization Learning Process

Taught lesson

↓

Practice until memorized

↓

Tell teacher "ready" to "pass"

↓

Pass assessment

↓

Repeat.

men's section. But the vast majority of masājid in America are not in buildings that were built to be a masjid. They are in structures that are on their second or third repurposing. So the interior set up of many of them is makeshift to one degree or another.

---

[550] This image is single-frame shots from a video clip spliced together to create a panoramic-type view. Faces are blurred to keep with Islamic guidelines of picture-making and to respect the privacy of the individuals in it.

In the image above the class is actually using a room that is not the main room of the mosque (the prayer hall, which is called a *musallah*). This mosque is in a building that had previously been an old warehouse, and this room had been a side office. In the case of kids learning, sometimes the genders will have separate classes altogether and sometimes they are in the same room like you see here. The kids in this room are mostly of upper elementary or middle school age. Any kids older than this would not likely be in the same room. For ages younger than high school (i.e. prepubescent) communities and cultures will differ on their sensitivities as to whether or not boys and girls learn in the same class. But oftentimes the greater consideration is a matter of available resources and space in the facility. Even when they learn in the same class at young ages, they will still sit separately with some type of separation as you see here.

Another matter of resources for a masjid to consider is the teachers that they have available. In the image here the teacher is sitting in a chair in the center between the two groups. They have to instruct, give feedback, and evaluate each student. It can often be the case that the masjid does not have a female available to do this work in a girls-only class. There is an older woman who is also sitting on a chair in this room but she is only there to help supervise. Also interesting about this image is that the teacher is holding a microphone (off the frame of the picture) and has an amplifier next to him. This is not exactly regular, but what it illustrates to you is that the Qur'an memorization sessions in the weekend schools are typically very loud places. The Qur'an is recited out loud, younger students especially will often practice the repetition in a high-volume fashion to aid the memorization. There is an aspect of memorizing the Qur'an and Arabic phonetics, especially when Arabic is not one's native tongue, where muscle memory in the mouth and larynx play a key part. Making the recitation more audible aids this. So the weekend schools are not typically quiet places, on the contrary they are quite loud while students are practicing their learning.

There are some implications to this. If a Muslim student's primary cultural familiarity with literacy is reading and practicing the Qur'an, it provides a very different background experience than reading fairy tale picture books at bedtime or whatever other reading experiences Anglo-American culture tends to produce in early ages. Especially for students whose parents have low levels of formal education, reading the Qur'an out loud could very likely be the lone literacy experience that these students have seen modeled for them in their homes; and the silent reading model of Anglo-America culture that our education system frequently assumes children have seen is not present.

Students with this background may be less prepared to fall into the expectations of "silent reading time" or "read to self" periods that occur in the school day, often on a daily basis in elementary grades. These students may experience anxiety when they are first asked to sit in a room silently and read to themselves for 20 to 30 minutes. They will commonly look for a distraction as a coping mechanism. If those distractions cause them to be put in trouble and disciplined, their anxiety about the situation and perhaps reading itself will only be compounded. This insight should allow the teacher to exhibit increased patience with these students. I believe a helpful remedy for students in these situations can be to give them an assignment that is to be done concurrently with the independent reading, *not* done after it. While silent reading in English might be cognitively active, reading the Qur'an is more physically active than reading in English. Having an assignment that is straightforward, well scaffolded, and able to be done by the student while they read can help anchor their need for activity during these reading sessions. An example of a type of scaffolded reading assignment that follows this, and that I use all the time with my students, is discussed later on.

I will also warn teachers here against taking the lesson from this that you should always ask students to read out loud. Reading Arabic and the Qur'an is very different from reading English, as will be further discussed, and just because they do it out loud, reading of the Qur'an in the weekend schools does not mean that they are extra ready to read out loud in the public school. Especially considering that in public schools reading out loud usually means that you read to the rest of the class. In the masjid, they read out loud at the same time everyone else is, so one's own voice and articulation is indistinguishable from the din of the room. They only perform their reading for the teacher individually.[551]

The microphone and amplifier that the teacher has serves two main purposes. One is to redirect students who are off task into focusing back on their reading and memorizing. In the picture there are a couple of boys against the back wall on the right who may be distracted, although not looking at their book or paper in front of them does not necessarily mean this because at times it is necessary to look away from the paper in order to push oneself up to memorizing. But it can be plenty common that students will break from reading and memorizing to talk to one another and joke around. In this case they will be told to stop and get back to their work by the teacher. What you see in this case is that, because the room is so loud, the teacher is not going to bother moving from his seat or quieting everyone else in order to be able to redirect some students. The amplifier allows him to be heard even with all the noise in the room. Naturally, this can also have the effect of raising the volume level in general in the room. Again I am not saying that teachers should use this tactic with students to redirect them in their public school

---

[551] With students who are more advanced in reciting the Qur'an they will sometimes read out loud in a circle where others are listening, but this is more common with older adult or near-adult students of the Qur'an.

classroom. Only it is to drive home the point that this learning in the masjid is an academic setting centered on reading, but done in an environment that can be quite loud; paradoxical to how we think of reading practice in the West.

The second use this amplifier can have is that the students will actually do their recitation through it when they are being evaluated by the teacher so that he can hear them clearly. Again, I would not say using a microphone and amplifier is typical in these settings, but it is necessary during the student evaluations that the teacher can hear the student clearly. This needs to be accomplished in one way or another and is ideally done without the other students having to stop their own out loud practice. At the least it will almost always involve the teacher having some central position away from the students.

What the students are learning here is actually highly differentiated even though it may be hard to tell by just looking at the picture. Most of the students are not yet working on memorizing the Qur'an itself, they are working on lessons that are teaching them how to decode Arabic phonetics. Others who have moved beyond that are beginning to memorize short chapters and verses of the Qur'an.

The students who are working on learning Arabic phonetics will be looking at sheets, or a small book, with pages similar to the image above.

This is from a small book[552] that consists of 17 lessons over 27 pages. However, the actual lessons in the book are more numerous, as each one of the page's 9 rows is its own bite-size lesson that is built upon the one before it, and really even within one row there can be two or three lessons. The book operates in such a way that if a student goes through it and is taught each bite-sized lesson in the order the book lays out, and then practices it, and memorizes it, that learning will have the cumulative effect of enabling them to read Arabic phonetics perfectly by the time they are done with the book; and thus be ready to move on to reading the shorter chapters of the Qur'an.

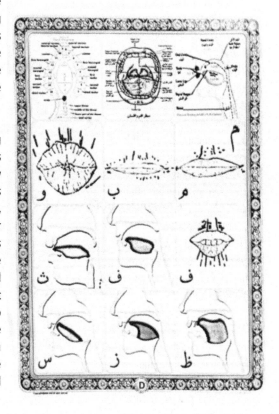

The book also uses color coding the whole way through. The rows are actually structured in a way where each time a new element is introduced it gets its own color, and then carries that color for several rows after it. These books make sure that elements are repeated in a spaced out and spiraled-type fashion throughout the book as well. Even if you do not know Arabic examining the color coding can sort of give you an idea of how the lessons are building up cumulatively, and repeating, throughout the pages.

The book also has an appendix in the back that shows diagrams of the human mouth and how to properly articulate the Arabic sounds. Learning to read the Qur'an comes with a high stress on correct pronunciation of classical Arabic. Oftentimes the feedback students receive from their teachers is about correct pronunciation and articulation found in very tiny bits. If you have Muslim students who struggle with pronouncing English, they should be totally resonant with

---

[552] *Noorani Qa'idah* by Shaykh Noor Muhammad ar-R'aee. NPP & MYA. 2nd edition 2010. See color images at abrahameducation.com/images

formal instruction on proper phonetic articulation. Proper articulation of language in general is something highly valued in the Muslim world. While it may not be just, it has been shown in research that having pronunciation errors in English relative to Anglo-American expectations can have detrimental effects on people's career prospects later in life (Celce-Murcia et al, 2010). The University of Iowa has put together wonderful modules for showing diagrams, very similar to what appears in this Arabic text, to teach the phonetics of both English and Spanish. They are available at https://soundsofspeech.uiowa.edu/home.

I should note here, that a negative consequence of the Muslim world's high priority on articulation is that being able to speak English well and without an accent is considered a status symbol in much of it. Unfortunately, a byproduct of this is that some of our Muslim immigrant students can be picked on by their Muslim American-born peers for having an accent. So be careful about correcting kids' pronunciation in front of their peers.

Within examination of this text lies the secret to how students in masjid learning can be independent and self-paced. The materials themselves are designed to anchor incremental progression and mitigate confusion. In Qur'an memorization the teacher might give whole group lessons only very rarely. Instead, in the format described above, each student will meet with the teacher individually when they feel they are ready to be assessed. After demonstrating mastery, the next lesson to learn is bite-sized enough that the necessary instruction can be done very quickly. The materials and this format also facilitate differentiation quite nicely as both feedback and instruction can be individualized. A more advanced student might be taught a group of the bite-sized lessons together at once, while another student goes piece by piece. The teacher can make these decisions at their discretion on an individual basis for each student. When students are being assessed they will generally be given corrective feedback on their mistakes with immediacy, nor are they allowed to progress with mistakes remaining in their prior learning. It is not set up for students to be allowed much time to flounder in error.

Western observers are ever-ready to characterize Qur'an learning as "rote" and demonize it as such (Moore, 2011). There is an extent to which the term "rote" might fit in describing this learning, but it also fails to do justice to the level of execution and integration that is necessary to learn and memorize the Qur'an. It would be wrong for an English speaker to imagine that learning to memorize the Qur'an is like looking at lines of poetry or sentences of a narrative book and simply repeating the lines over and over again. It is much different than this. The recitation of the Qur'an has a distinct science to it called *tajwīd* that involves learning precise phonetic articulation, as well as rules of annunciation of suprasegmental features such as prolongation, blending, and emission points. Even for native Arabic speakers, natively they will speak a colloquial dialect that does not share all of these same features as they exist in classical

Arabic. There is a level of complexity to this learning beyond monotonous mechanical repetition that is not done justice by applying the term "rote", and the connotations that term carries for a Western mind.

Also, the negative connotations of this term downplay the benefits of repetition in learning. Repetition has been called the first principle in all learning (Bruner, 2001). It is especially needed and beneficial for struggling learners (Levy et al, 1997; Denton & Otaiba, 2011). The National Institute of Child Health and Development (NICHD) showed the benefits of repetition in reading instruction unequivocally in the year 2000 with a large-scale review of scientific research literature on reading instruction. It determined that repetition is proven to help children know, memorize, and use independently, vocabulary, word and segment level phonics, and improve fluency and other critical reading skills; and that it helps students sustain higher-reading levels (Leung, 1992; Blum et al, 1995; Senechal, 1997; NICHD, 2000).

Controlled studies have also shown that giving students immediate and direct corrective feedback on science vocabulary and prompting the student to immediately repeat it increases student knowledge and performance with new science terms and concepts (Drevno et al, 1994), showing that repetition can form a foundation for higher-order academic tasks. It has been argued within the field of behavioral and brain science that a lack of spaced repetition that incorporates chunked tests within practice is at fault for the lagging skills in science and math of students in American classrooms relative to other countries (Kang, 2016). All of this lends credence to the idea that there is plenty of positives to draw on from the learning habits that Muslim students absorb in the masjid, and even that teachers may have something to garner from it.

As a youth, I took lessons on how to read music notation, play the guitar, and manipulate the vocal cords to sing. The supposed cognitive benefits of signing and playing music are highly touted by researchers (Miendlarzewska et al, 2014). Having practiced and undergone lessons on the recitation of the Qur'an in adulthood, I believe it is a more cognitively complex undertaking than learning musical notation. One aspect to this higher cognitive demand is the higher amount of integration involved in decoding the text, but also that learning the Qur'an comes with such a strong psychological pressure to get it right; after all, it is *the word of God*.[553]

It could be the case that this aspect of the learning reinforces the habits of mind that teach a child that in formal learning one must receive validation and approval from the instructor

---

[553] Please note that this discussion is in no way intended to compare the Qur'an itself to music. The Qur'an is patently not music, and suggesting the two are comparable is odious to Islamic sensibilities. It is a recitation and its recitation is a science and religious practice unto itself.

before continuing on in their learning progression. This could sometimes play out in a public school classroom as a student being constantly concerned as to whether or not something they have done is "right" or "good" before wanting to move on. It may also inculcate a hesitancy to take academic and scholarly risks in the classroom. This can rub up against what is known about the benefit of making mistakes in the course of learning and embracing them as learning opportunities.

But lessons that educators should take out of this learning are the principles of being incremental and logically sequenced. Again, it is my assessment that these principles override learning in the Muslim world in all subject areas and form the base of learning expectations and habits of mind as a learner for people from Muslim cultures. It is often very confusing for students and families who come with background learning experience in the Muslim world to be given textbooks in our public school classes, and to then find out that they will not be moving through the textbook from its first page to its last. Students and families experience confusion over finding that a subject's curriculum might not even be laid out in a textbook at all, but rather is delivered through an assortment of online articles and print-outs that are gathered and delivered by the teacher, and at times seemingly at random. Without a logically sequenced textbook that can be studied from front to cover, how can the students study ahead if they wish to? How can they anticipate what lessons will be forthcoming? Will it not be more difficult to find and look back at previous lessons in order to review and make the logical connections from one lesson to another? It is certainly the case in Qur'an learning that a student would not be faced with these questions, nor have to integrate resources given by the teacher from several different places in order to find their answers. If they wish to zoom ahead and have the volition and ability to do so, nothing will stop them and they will be handsomely praised for doing it. It is commonly the expectation that extra studying and review entails going back over what has already been studied in the book.

When there are textbooks used in America, which seems to be becoming more and more rare for better or worse, they are designed to be more of a resource index for the teachers as opposed to a well-sequenced learning continuum appropriate to the age and grade level for which they are meant (Klymkowksy, 2007). From what I have seen, textbooks in America are typically much thicker and less concise than textbooks that are used as curricula guides for subjects in the Muslim world, secular or otherwise.

Just taking as an example a standard geometry high school textbook used in ninth and tenth grade published by Holt Mcdougal and specifically designed for Common Core (Burger et al, 2012). There are 912 small print pages of instructional material in the book comprising no less than 84 different lessons. If a class were to study this book over the course of a 180 day school

272 ◆ Engaging Muslim Students in Public Schools

year with one 50 minute class per day, they would be allotted exactly 10 minutes in order to master each page and would have to master each lesson in only two days. That is incomprehensibly unrealistic, conundrums such as these likely contribute to the reasons why no one uses textbooks this way, and perhaps the diminishing value that teachers see in using textbooks at all. It would be much simpler, as well as correlate better to the cultural learning habits of students and families with roots in the Eastern world, if we had textbooks that were straightforward and designed to be gone through from the first page to the last.

Another issue worthy of addressing here is that learning in the masjid overwhelmingly conditions students to the idea that learning happens from printed texts as opposed to digital reading. There have been digital programs and eBooks made for all sorts of Islamic learning, but these are not used in the masājid. It is easily more cost effective and simple to stick with the printed texts that have been used for centuries, and besides, Islamic learning tends to prefer to stick to traditional modes anyway. So while tech companies bombard the education system with a massive push to turn everything digital, we have to keep in mind that some of our students come to school with the habit already inculcated that serious learning comes from text, and the electronic devices are used for entertainment and leisure.

Despite the push from the tech companies, research both over decades and more recently constantly shows that reading comprehension is better when done from printed texts vs. digital materials (Singer & Alexander, 2017a); even when students have the stated impression that the digital materials are better, objective assessment shows they actually garner better comprehension from the printed text (Singer & Alexander, 2017b). A major pitfall of the digital formats being that even something as simple as scrolling serves as a distraction to the reader and lengthens out the time it takes to process the text (Singer Trakhman et al, 2019). Educators also have to know that news reports that have come out informing the public that workers in the higher ranks of these tech companies send their kids to screen-less print-only private schools in Silicon Valley highly suggests that the tech industry is aware of print's superiority, but does not have the best interests of our students in public schools in mind when they push for each one of them to do all their work on a device (Weller, 2018).

Lecture based learning

Any form of learning in the masjid that is not Qur'an memorization is typically done in a lecture style. This can be a more informal lecture, typically called a *halaqa*, or a more formal lecture series that studies a book written for instruction of Islam, which is called a *dars* in Arabic but likely just referred to as an Islamic Studies class. The congregational sermons on Friday are lecture based as well. Lecture-based learning sessions are more likely to take place in the evenings compared to Qur'an memorization. It can often be the case for young students that they might spend the late morning to early afternoon hours in the masjid working on Qur'an memorization but then return in the evening with their parents to listen to lectures. Sometimes the masjid houses kids all day and they wait and hang out there during the time in between the end of their Qur'an memorization study and the evening lectures. However, having younger students undertake book study that is lecture based during the normal youth schooling time is commonly done also, and I would say it is becoming increasingly common in America. As the years go on and Muslim communities grow, the need for students to learn the faith and its tenets at a young age and not just learn to memorize the Qur'an is increasingly being recognized.[554]

A *halaqa* typically has a relaxed feel to it and focuses on some sort of moral lesson that relates directly to life and aims to inspire greater faith, whereas a book study session will likely be part of a more regimented course of learning instruction of hard facts, organization, insights about the faith, Islamic history, religious rules, and for advanced learners the methods of jurisprudence.

There are two main points to understand about lecture-based learning in the masjid: 1.) As stated before but worthy of repeating, they are instructor-centered, *not* student-centered, as far as the style of instructional delivery in the class, and 2.) typically, there is a distinctly unbalanced ratio between the teacher's verbal output and the reading of text in a book study class. First, I will discuss this second point, offer an illustration of how it can manifest, and discuss its implications.

Both *ahadith* and Islamic rulings are collected in large voluminous book collections better suited and organized as reference materials as opposed to instructional guides. So to compliment learning, Islamic scholars in history have written books intended for concise learning continuums and they still do today. It is these books that will typically be studied in a book study course. Just like the books that teach Arabic phonetics, they are designed to be gone through beginning at page one and going forward until the end of the book, and they will be taught this way in the classes. Also, like the Arabic phonetic books, it is not uncommon that still today books written hundreds of years ago are used for study. However, in the Western settings

---

[554] This is also, in actuality, the proper mode of Islamic learning, to learn the faith first before learning the Qur'an. See Sunan Ibn Mājah Book 1 Hadith 64 https://sunnah.com/urn/1250610. The Prophet's ﷺ companion, Jundub bin 'Abdullah رضي الله عنه, who was young during the Prophet's ﷺ lifetime, said, *"We were strong youths, so we learned faith before we learned Qur'an. Then we learned Qur'an and our faith increased thereby."* If you are a reading this as a Muslim in the West who is involved in your local community's Islamic education, please take heed of this statement as missing this point in our institutions has contributed heavily to the destruction of the character of so many Muslim youth in America.

an English translation would be used, and it is also not uncommon that an annotated version of the original book done by a scholar of contemporary times, whose annotated version is meant to give a more elaborate explanation, is what is studied. The principle of thorough explanation of each piece on a learning continuum is embedded throughout Islamic learning, as is the idea of not moving onto the next piece until the current piece has been thoroughly explained. Therefore, in a book study class, the book itself acts more as an anchor, guide, and prompt for the verbal output and explanation of the instructor, while the actual reading of the book is rather minimal. This means the book is gone through slowly over the course of time.

The book pictured above and to the left was written in the 18th century. The book in the middle[555] is an English translation of an explanation of the book on the left that was written by a contemporary scholar of the 20th century. The third image above and to the right is a flyer[556] produced by a masjid in America to advertise a book study lecture course that would occur regularly on Saturdays to study the explanation authored in the 20th century of the original book from the 18th century. I will use these as an example to illustrate some matters about Islamic learning and instruction.

---

[555] *Explanation of the Three Fundamentals of Tawheed of Islaam* by the Noble Shaykh Muhammad ibn Saalih al-'Uthaymeen. Translated by Aboo Talhah Daawood ibn Ronald Burbank. Al-Hidaayah Publishing and Distribution. 1997. Birmingham UK.

[556] The name of the specific institute and the instructor on the flyer have been deleted for privacy's sake. Notice that the flyer has spots to list digital mediums through which to access the lectures via tele link or live audio streaming (the specific domains have also been covered up). Live streaming and tele linking masjid lectures is very common in the Muslim community, and so is using those mediums for socializing, especially in diaspora communities. Schools might consider taking advantage of these mediums as a way to offer access to parenting classes or other educational seminars for parents and community stakeholders.

While the original 18th century book is 27 pages, the 20th century explanation of it is 150 pages[557]. The lecture series that studied the 20th century explanation[558] of the 18th century book was 46 different sessions, each of which was around 50 minutes in length, not including follow-up question and answer sessions. The first line of the original 18th century Arabic text is three words. In the 20th century explanatory text the explanation of those three words is roughly 16 sentences (none of which are simple sentences) and two full paragraphs. In the book study lecture series the explanation of those three words and of the contemporary explanation of them encompassed 25 minutes.

This illustrates the point of thorough explanation before moving on in Islamic learning. The priority given to thorough explanation is visualized literally in the image above where the explanation is under the line of the original Arabic text and the translation of it. The author of the explanation does not get through one sentence of the original text without stopping to provide an annotated explanation. Similarly, the teacher in the lecture course will rarely get

---

[557] And this is considered a very short and concise explanation of this book, there are other annotated explanations of the same book from the 18th century that run upwards of 900 pages.

[558] The lecture series was delivered in English but actually studied the Arabic version of the 20th century explanation.

through a single sentence in the explanation without stopping to provide additional verbal explanation.

Also, there is a layered explanation that goes on with this type of Islamic learning. In the lecture, the original text is translated from Arabic to English, as is the explanatory text. Just in this little sample the lecturer does this translating along with explanations of terminology, grammar and its effect on meaning, references to other sources that comment on the issue addressed in the text, explanation of context, and connection to everyday life, both past and modern. He will also emphasize and reiterate the main points the student is to take out of the learning to understand.

The ratio of verbal output to reading of the text is another lesson to take out of this. The lecturer reads the text but the vast majority of the teaching is the verbal explanation aside to that. Literally, neither a sentence in the original 18th century text nor the 20th century explanation is read without being followed up by some type of verbal explanation. So this type of study does not lend itself to the habit of extended silent reading, or the reading of extended pages or passages without breaking at all. It reinforces the idea that one does not move on without fully understanding what has been read and that each part of a text is important, purposeful, and well thought out.

There are numerous insights and lessons that a public school teacher can take from this if you consider that your students have maybe had a background of learning experiences of this type; or come from a culture that is rooted in this type of learning. I will point out a few key takeaways concerning application in public schools classrooms that I consider with my students in light of this, and that other teachers have told me they have benefited from considering.

First, it is typically better to focus on a shorter piece of a text and accomplish thorough comprehension of it in the students, even if this involves repeated reading, as opposed to reading a certain quantity or "finishing" reading material. This is doubly true in the case of students who are English Language Learners. Even those of us who speak English as a first language can recall experiences as young readers, or even as adults, where upon reading a book or text a momentary lapse in concentration caused us to go through the physical eye motions of reading some sentences but not actually internalizing or processing them. This results in a failure to comprehend what we were reading once we remind ourselves to put our attention back on the text. This happens as a result of a lapse in concentration while the eyes still carry through the reading process. For language learners, even when intentional concentration on the reading is present, the experience and risk of not comprehending phrases and sentences due to language barriers is ever-present. This occurs frequently for students in school, and when it does students tend to mentally check out of the reading altogether and a loss of comprehension is compounded.

This is likely to happen when students are asked to read an extended portion of a text without stopping to intentionally process or receive explanation, whether they are reading by themselves or being read to in class. So it is good to stop and explain in the course of reading. I do not recommend to any teacher that they move on in reading a text before all necessary terms have been explained and all necessary background knowledge to comprehend a text has been inserted. If you have a class with a large amount of Muslim students who have these types of learning needs, you can rest assured knowing that they will not be disturbed by frequent stopping in reading the text to provide verbal explanation, because the learning of their cultural background attunes for this type of expectation.

Second, this learning style habitualizes students to receive and expect direct instruction. It is a learning style where the teacher is known to be an expert, knows the material thoroughly, is confident in their demeanor, and is tasked with being a direct transmitter of knowledge upon the students. The students are vessels whose role is to receive this knowledge. Later on in the chapter I will have a discussion about instructor-centered direct instruction versus student-centered methods of learning.

Third, there is integration of language modalities[559] in both the lecture style and memorization modes of Islamic learning. In the book study format the students do not just read, but they read and listen, and go back-and-forth regularly between the two. It is also commonly expected that the students will have a notebook where they are writing down notes from the teacher's verbal explanation. There will rarely be guidance as to what these notes should look like, but note taking during these types of classes is considered part of the conduct of a student of Islamic knowledge. While the lecture format is heavier on listening and receptive modalities, the memorization learning consists of a constant back-and-forth by the students between receiving input, reading, and producing verbal output, reciting.

Questioning and Metaphors

Before moving on to demonstrating specific teaching strategies I use to engage students that draw on these learning aspects there are two more instructional strategies that are common to Islamic learning that are worthy of mention. One common form of questioning that is used is a type of rhetorical questioning where the question *does* have a straightforward answer, but the

---

[559] There are four types of language modalities under two categories. Under the productive category is speaking and writing. Under the receptive modality is reading and listening.

instructor is going to provide it after giving the students a moment to ponder the question. This means that it is often the case that the teacher in the masjid asks a question to students knowing the students will not answer, and the students know they will not answer, so the question is only being asked as a way to prompt the students to think about it before being provided the answer. There is a basis for this in the Islamic texts, some rhetorical questioning is used in the Qur'an.[560] Also in many ahadith[561] you read that the Prophet ﷺ asks his companions a question and they reply, "Allah and his messenger know best" as a way of showing that it would be irreverent for themselves and disrespectful to the one with greater knowledge to even try to answer. So in masjid learning this takes the form of the teacher asking questions, but with the students either staying silent or maybe saying "Allah knows best" in expectation that the teacher is going to provide the answer.

This device exists in the patterns of dialogue and prose of Arabs as well. When they are telling a narration, it is common that the speaker can be talking about something that happened to someone and before going to the next part of the story they will say to the listener, "So what did he do?" When obviously they are going to tell the listener what happened in continuation of the story while the listener has no ability to actually answer the question. So it might be that this aspect of Islamic teaching puts an expectation into Muslim students that if a teacher asks a question to the class, they are not necessarily expecting a response from the students, even it may be that they perceive the more respectful thing to do is to not answer the question and wait for the expert to provide the answer. In this sense, sometimes when teachers ask students a question and they get crickets from them, it may feel less awkward to the Muslim students than it does to the teacher because they are accustomed to this scenario playing out in a natural way in the masjid or other forms of prosaic discourse in their home cultural settings.

Another teaching method that is ubiquitous in the Qur'an and Islamic teaching is the use of real world objects or phenomena as metaphors to illustrate abstract concepts. In reference to this what English might call metaphors, similes, parables, proverbs, paragons, or examples can all essentially fall under the same word in Arabic, *mathalan*[562]; so whatever nuanced difference might lie between those terms is included in what is being discussed here.

---

[560] Qur'an 39:9 https://quran.com/39/9, Qur'an 75:3 https://quran.com/75/3, Qur'an 55:60 https://quran.com/55/60, Qur'an 29:2 https://quran.com/29/2

[561] Jami' at-Tirmidhī Book 40 Hadith 38 https://sunnah.com/tirmidhi/40/38, Al-Ādab al-Mufrad Book 24 Hadith 7 https://sunnah.com/adab/24/7

[562] See مثل in the Arabic-English Lexicon of Edward William Lane http://arabiclexicon.hawramani.com/مثل/?book=50#f12f28

The Qur'an actually states explicitly that it uses these as a teaching method.[563] It especially uses comparisons to the natural world. So in the Qur'an the resurrection on the Day of Judgement is compared to the earth's rebirth of spring[564], rejectors of faith to the deaf and blind[565], truth to the nourishment and purity of clean water[566], falsehood and vanity to the ephemerality of sea foam and dross[567], gossip to eating human flesh[568], polytheism to the flimsiness of a spider's web[569], disbelief to the deception of an oasis mirage in the desert[570], amongst many others of greater and shorter depth. This method of teaching of course transfers very strongly to any form of prosaic teaching in Muslim cultures. It is extraordinarily common for Muslim teachers to think of metaphors that take something from the concrete world to illustrate an abstract concept, and I have seen students be very responsive to this when teachers do it in public schools as well.

So I have long thought about these modes of learning undergone by Muslim students in the masjid, the habits and expectations they inculcate, and the students in public schools who have this type of learning in their background bank. As a result, I have developed my own way of doing reading, across subject areas, with students of varying age groups. It is not an exact mimicry of these masjid modes of learning, but it seeks to draw on the habits of mind they develop and build upon them as resources, as opposed to pushing against them. In the next section I will draw out a detailed example of how I do this in the creation of a reading assignment and the thought that goes behind it. It is a high school example, if you wish to see this drawn out in an elementary school example please register at abrahameducation.com.

Scaffolding Reading Comprehension

I will now go over in detail a strategy that incorporates the principles of learning that have been talked about, and that treats the underlying issues of academic insecurity that most students have who are disengaged at a base level. It can be used throughout grade levels and coursework of any subject in order to scaffold students to read and comprehend complex academic texts, even if they are above the students supposed reading leading level. It is

---

[563] Qur'an 2:26 https://quran.com/2/26
[564] Qur'an 30:19 https://quran.com/30/19
[565] Qur'an 2:17-19 https://quran.com/2/17-19
[566] Qur'an 13:17 https://quran.com/13/17
[567] Qur'an 13:17 https://quran.com/13/17
[568] Qur'an 49:12 https://quran.com/49/12
[569] Qur'an 29:41 https://quran.com/29/41
[570] Qur'an 24:39 https://quran.com/24/39

designed to build up incrementally to performance of higher-order academic skills that are dictated in benchmarks and standards. It could be applied, at least, to the grade-level textbooks or core texts that are used in the core subject areas of Language Arts, Science, Social Studies, and unit introduction of Math. It is designed to meet the needs of EL students and struggling learners, but is not necessarily only for them, I have found many advanced learners who found this mode of assignment to be engaging and rigorous.

Four Scaffolds

This scaffolding means having students read a text[571] with the aid of four scaffolds that are provided on a customized reading comprehension questionnaire. Customized here means it is generated by the teacher; it is *not* something pre-made by a curriculum developer or printed off of the internet. This questionnaire will be something the student does as a task, and it will feel like a task to the student. However, the questionnaire's true function is to be *an aid and guide to anchor analyzing the text and extracting information from it.* Extraction of information from a text is the base-level skill that is prerequisite to all other comprehension skills because it enables the student to acquire knowledge from the text. This scaffolding is designed to determine that students acquire this skill and are then incrementally prompted up to more complex ones.

The four scaffolds on the questionnaire are accompanied alongside or within each question. They are as follows:

1. Indicating the **paragraph number** where the answer to the question can be found.[572]
2. Indicating the **page number** where the answer to the question can be found.
3. **Matching** the **language** of the **question** to the **language** of the **text**.
4. Questions arising in the questionnaire **chronological** to the appearance of their answers in the text.

---

[571] Reading the text here can mean reading it independently, guided, or in small groups, etc. Determining the manner of reading to do in class with a given text and a given time in this regard is a separate discussion and would have a separate criteria. This reading scaffolding can be done in all of those forms. Ultimately the goal is of course building students to independence, which this scaffolding is designed to do.

[572] There is a system and method by which "numbering the paragraphs" is done that would need to be addressed separately on how to do it, and it would also need to be taught explicitly to students at the outset of using this scaffolding.

Scaffolds 1, 2, and 4 ought to be straightforward enough so I will start by elaborating upon and identifying the importance of the third scaffold, matching the language of the question to the language of the text.

Important points to understand about this third scaffold:

- The English language has an inverse relationship between interrogative statements (i.e. questions) and declarative statements. I will illustrate this in an example shortly, but the basis of this inverse relationship is the switching of <u>verbs</u> and **subject nouns** (or pronouns) between the declarative and interrogative forms. Here is a basic example that would be used in social language: *Where is **Steve**?* (interrogative) vs. ***Steve** is at home* (declarative). In academic language this basic inverse relationship is maintained, yet its appearance is made more complex through the use of expanded noun and verb groups, nominalization, and complex sentences. Understanding this inverse relationship between interrogative and declarative statements in English, and being able to process that relationship automatically, is at the core of all dialectic undertakings (<u>Barth & Krabbe, 1982</u>; <u>Smith, 1998</u>).

- Having an intuitive feel, developed through practice at a base-academic level, with this inverse relationship is essential for academic prowess across subject areas.

- Acquiring an intuitive understanding of this inverse relationship in academic language is a major hurdle for EL students that their native-speaking peers will struggle less to acquire, and have often mastered to a fair degree before their schooling even begins.

Let's look at an example of these scaffolds in action. Say I am reading the book *Guns, Germs, and Steel* by Jared Diamond (<u>1997</u>) with my students and I have some information I want them to extract from the text. We are reading Chapter 2 of the book, which is entitled "Farmer Power". On page 84 (paperback edition) in the third paragraph. It begins:

> In human societies possessing domestic animals, livestock fed more people in four distinct ways: by furnishing meat, milk, and fertilizer and by pulling plows. First and most directly, domestic animals became the socie-

Perhaps, as the instructor, the four ways that livestock fed people is some information that I want the students to extract and know from the text. So I am going to prompt the student to extract that information from the text in my customized scaffolded questionnaire that I create for them.

Let's look at two ways this question can be asked to the student on their assignment paper. First a non-scaffolded way, and secondly, the scaffolded way.

A non-scaffolded example:

> List the fours manners in which early agricultural humans were
> provisioned by farm animals.

What is the difficulty here? First of all, let's say the students were assigned only to read page 84, where there are five different paragraphs, 16 different sentences (most of which are compound or complex sentences, meaning the amount of clauses is probably over 40), and 433 different words. The page begins by talking about nutritional values of jellyfish, nuts, and larvae; and ends with a discussion of prehistoric European farmers that are known as (and called in the book) the Linearbandkeramik.

How does an EL student or a struggling reader wade through all that to find the precise spot on the page where it talks about the manners in which humans were provisioned by farm animals?

Furthermore, page 84 does not use the word "manner(s)" or "provision(ed)" which appear in the question. It does not use the word "farm" either. It does use the word "farmer" twice and the word "farming" once; but all of those appear in paragraphs different from the one where the answer to this question needs to be found.

This illustrates an extraordinarily common mistake that both teachers and curricula developers make when they create assignment materials that lack consideration for the needs of EL students especially. Oftentimes it is thought that a question like this is prompting for increased cognitive demand in finding details from the text, when what it is really prompting for is increased *mental language formulation*. The text does not use the word *manners*, it uses the word *ways*, which is a less complex word than the one used in the question. The text does not use the word *provision* it uses the word *fed*, which is also a less complex word than what is used in the question. The text does not use the words *farm animals* it uses the words *livestock*, which is a more academic and complex word than what is used in the question. The text does not use the words *early agricultural humans*, it uses the words human *societies possessing domesticated animals*, which is of roughly equal or greater complexity than what is used in the question.

In the study of academic content, what is the objective of the students reading this text and being prompted to extract this information? It is NOT for them to grapple with four different instances of second language formulation before even getting to selecting the appropriate detail from the text for recollection. Rather it is for them to intake content area facts, or gain knowledge, so that they can then use that knowledge for more demanding academic tasks that are built upon that knowledge as a foundation. The academic skill and mental habit we want them to exercise in reading this text is to find and recall the appropriate detail from the text. It is upon this skill that all other reading comprehension skills are built, and rigorous, consistent, practice with it yields a continuing sense of authentic success in the student is usually the foremost need for struggling readers and students who are academically insecure.

Now let's take a look at the scaffolded way of prompting the student to recall this detail from the text that takes into consideration the mitigating factors that EL students and struggling readers are often dealing with.

The scaffolded example:

Page 84 - Paragraph 3
1. What were the four distinct ways in which livestock fed more people in human societies possessing domestic animals?

Firstly, providing the page and paragraph number sufficiently narrows where the student needs to look in the text to avoid giving up on finding it at the outset. A questionnaire scaffolded like this will have questions running through the entire reading that is assigned and students will answer the questions *as they read*; not afterwards as the formatting of most textbooks tends to dictate.

Secondly, let's analyze how the third scaffold is utilized. Begin by observing how the inverse relationship between the interrogative statement (the question) and the declarative statement (in the text) is at play here. The subjective verb in the academic statement of the text is "fed" and we see in the question the same prepositional phrasing and noun group phrasing is used as in the text, but they are on the flip side of the verb, which is also the same as what is in the text. This is the same inverse relationship that is at play in common social language (i.e. *'where is*

Steve vs. *'Steve is at home'*) that EL students[573] will be familiar with at that level, but will need explicit practice and repetition with the more expanded and contextually abstract forms of academic language (Cummins, 1989).[574]

Language Formulation in Text vs. Question in Scaffolded Reading	
Prepositional Phrasing <u>in the text</u> (declarative statement)	Prepositional Phrasing <u>in the question</u> (interrogative statement)
"...**in four distinct ways**" "**In human societies possessing domestic animals**"	"...the **four distinct ways in** which" "...**in human societies possessing domestic animals**"
Noun Groups in the text (declarative statement)	Noun Groups in the question (interrogative statement)
livestock **human societies possessing domestic animals** **more people**	**livestock** **human societies possessing domestic animals** **more people**
Verbiage in the text (declarative statement)	Verbiage in the question (interrogative statement)
fed	**fed**

Phrasing the question with this inverse relationship explicitly where the language used in the question is *the same* as what is used in the text allows the student to experience a rhythm to finding answers and extracting detail from the text that forms the mental habit of processing this inverse relationship in a manner that is automatic. Just try reading the scaffolded questions

---

[573] So long as they are not beginners.

[574] If you are not familiar with the work of Jim Cummins in the 1980s, he found through longitudinal studies that students whose home language was not English were likely to catch up to their native speaking peers in *social* language fluency in English in 2-3 years, but it would take 5-7 years alongside quality instruction for them to catch up in *academic* language. Cummins research and this premise is foundational to the entirety of ESL as a field.

and then reading the beginning of the paragraph that the question directs you to read to get a feel for how this rhythm works.

If you are a native English speaker that rhythm and interchange comes so naturally that the question probably feels too easy to even ask. But for an EL student or struggling learner, experiencing that rhythm is at the base of forming the mental habit of connecting academic questions to a precise locale within an academic text. Providing these scaffolds for the student eases the cognitive load of the academic task and reaches the student at their zone of proximal development. Thereby answering the question correctly builds a mental association of confidence in performing the task. For many struggling readers the initial factor that needs to be addressed is their own propensity to give up and not put forth effort based on a lack of confidence. Providing these scaffolds remediates that. It makes the task doable for the student and forms the foundation from which greater complexity in academic performance will be built upon.

Removing the Scaffolds and Incremental Increase of Cognitive Demand

Finding the base level of achievement in academic reading comprehension skill is what has been identified and illustrated so far. Once that base level is found and reached with the student the goal is to build confidence and proficiency in performing the academic task at the base level through continual practice and repetition until the student(s) has attained what we would call mastery at the 80% level.[575]

Once that is attained the task for the instructor becomes to gradually remove the scaffolds in an explicit and incremental manner; gradually increasing academic and cognitive demand. Exactly how this is done will not look as uniform as finding the base level at which students are operating. It is a process that will always be subject to the idiosyncrasies of given learners and classes. What follows is an outline of incremental removal of the scaffolding and considerations to be made along the way.

Firstly, the order listed above of the scaffolds is the same order by which removal of them would be most incremental and accommodating to gradual increase of cognitive demand in future assignments. This begins with the paragraph marker, which greatly narrows the loci of attention for the student in finding the needed text to extract in order to answer a question. In the *Guns, Germs, and Steel* example above removing the paragraph marker from the scaffolding would increase the amount of text for the student to wade through in answering that one question

---

[575] This is based on a time management principle of economic productivity called the Pareto Principle.

from 127 words to 433; a 240% increase in text through which to grapple. It would be apt for the instructor to consider whether or not that is too big a leap to take in one step of removing the scaffold. An alternative that is more incremental might be to mark the paragraphs like this:

Page 84 - Paragraph 2-3
1. What were the four distinct ways in which livestock fed more people in human societies possessing domestic animals?

Now the possibility of where the answer will be found in the text expands from one paragraph to two. In the actual text this represents a change of narrowing the text from 127 words to wade through to 207; only a 62% increase in text to grapple through, a more gradual release. This is obviously something that a teacher can play with in how they do it.

The nice thing about having a uniform understanding in the class about how paragraphs[576] can be thought of in a numbered order of a text is that when the scaffold is removed and a student struggles with a question and asks for help, the previous scaffold that had been provided can now be delivered orally as a tool for the teacher to move the student along. When the student says, "teacher I need help with this one," the teacher can simply say "look at the third paragraph," and how paragraphs on a page correlate to numbers is a shared language between

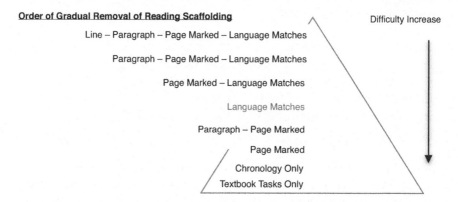

---

[576] The main rules that I use for understanding paragraph numbering are 1.) the paragraph numbering is done by page, when a new page comes the paragraph number goes back to one, so on the questionnaires I always indicate the page and paragraph number if there is more than one page in the assigned reading, 2.) If a page begins mid-paragraph that is still paragraph number one on that page, and 3.) Any indent marks the beginning of a new paragraph, even in narrative texts that include dialogue where as little as one word can be considered a paragraph. Indent might be replaced by line spacing, like I have done in this book, as it is common in science textbooks.

the teacher and student. This can act as another layer of the gradual release; perhaps the paragraphs will not be marked at all, but if a student struggles with that they can be prompted verbally to focus on a specific paragraph. The paragraph marking system sets up the verbal prompting to be concise and efficient, so the teacher does not fall into the trap of having to re-tutor instead of giving corrective feedback.

Certainly, as the paragraph and page marking is removed it will be an appropriate time to teach the skills of skimming and scanning the text; as well as repeated reading and rereading.

❖ *Removing the Language Matching*

So long as the language matches, the student will always be able to use the language that is given in the question as a cue for where they need to be looking in the text. Therefore removing scaffold number three is weightier than removing scaffolds one and two because making the removal gradual will involve further scaffolding around two core aspects:

1. Providing a ready resource for the student to reconcile the language difference.
2. Explicitly teaching of the cognitive process that one undertakes in discriminating the language difference and corresponding correlation between the questions and text.

So let's examine how this might look if we are using our non-scaffolded example from above.

List the fours manners in which early agricultural humans were provisioned by farm animals.

We have already analyzed that the following terms could trip up an EL student or struggling reader because their corollaries in the text are not exactly the same, they only correlate in meaning and not in form. These were the terms *manners, early agricultural humans, provisioned,* and *farm animals.* How can the student be set up to reconcile this successfully?

There are many ways this can be done, they may not be any different than several other strategies that are used to teach vocabulary. The most basic thing might be to front load the needed words by telling the students what those words mean before reading the text while verbally previewing the questions with them.

Another might be to set up a very explicit visual like this:

Vocabulary in Question	Vocabulary in Text
manners	ways
early agricultural humans	human societies possessing domestic animals
farm animals	livestock
provisioned	fed

A visual like this could be set up in the room as a poster, on the screen digitally, or could be included as a reference on the questionnaire itself. Maybe even a chalk or marker board could be used if those still function your classroom.

Another way this can be done is having the meanings of words explained in parenthetical statements after the questions. Like this:

> List the fours manners in which early agricultural humans were provisioned by farm animals. (remember *provision* means *fed*)

There are different ways in which students can be provided resources for reconciling the language difference by recognizing the similar meanings. The teacher of course can always provide the information orally when students get "stuck" which may be a scaffold provided further out. Another scaffold might be to always make sure the question words are less complex than their meaning corollaries in the text.

It is, however, quite important than when removing the language matching scaffold a resource *is provided* initially in order to make it a gradual step out. In all of the previous practice that will have been done up to this point before this scaffold is removed the students will grow to be heavily dependent upon using the matching language as a cue with which to locate themselves properly in the text. Therefore stepping out of reliance on that can not be done too drastically.

Providing a ready resource gets the student to first be ready to understand that an extra cognitive step is taking place. Having the ready resource at this point assures the cognitive process is not overwhelming, it involves recognizing the language mismatch, and applying the given information from the provided resource.

Order of Gradual Removal of Language Matching

Language Matches — Difficulty Increase

Page - Paragraph Marked - Ready Resource

Page - Paragraph Groups Marked - Ready Resource

Page Marked - Ready Resource

Ready Resource

Page - Paragraph Marked - Model Cognitive Language Process

Page - Paragraph Marked - Guided Cognitive Language Process

Page - Paragraph Marked - Independent Cognitive Language Process

Page Marked - Independent Cognitive Language Process

Independent Cognitive Language Process

Order of Gradual Removal of Reading Scaffolding

Difficulty Increase

Line – Paragraph – Page Marked – Language Matches

Paragraph – Page Marked – Language Matches

Page Marked – Language Matches

Language Matches

Paragraph – Page Marked

Page Marked

Chronology Only

Textbook Tasks Only

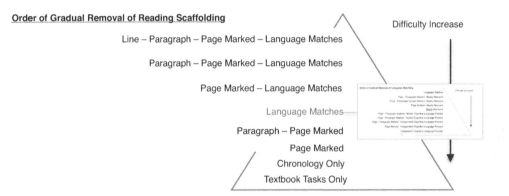

The next step out is much more cognitively demanding. The student has to be taught explicitly the cognitive language processing that should take place when they do not recognize any wording from the question with a match in the text. They have to be taught explicitly to stop and think and ask themselves, "so what does _____ mean?" or "What are some words that also mean _____?" or "What are some words that I do see in the text that might mean _____?" At this point a discussion about the use of technology as an outside resource might be prudent. If a student does not know a word, it might be the time that they exercise the use of their phone to search for a meaning or synonym.

Working at this cognitive level is one that is more demanding. It is a level and step where the instructor will want to back up and do increased explicit practice with the students, where going through this cognitive process is a central point and learning target. As we see from the last internal question prompt in the previous paragraph, part of the cognitive process that needs to go on here is scanning the academic text in exploration of words that might match in meaning to the words in the question; often this is what needs to be used when the student is not 100% sure of the meaning or synonyms of the words in the questions. Therefore bringing back the narrowness of the page and paragraph marking to the questions at this point is a good idea; and that sets off a whole new round and mode from which those scaffolds are removed again.

❖ *Removal of the Chronology*

Removal of the chronological arrival of questions in the questionnaire after the other scaffolds are removed just about equates to removal of the scaffolding altogether. This would mean transitioning from answering questions *while* reading to answering questions *after* reading. This may or may not be equivalent to doing the tasks assigned by a textbook itself.

Students will be at this point when confidence levels are very high and both comfort and stamina with reading academic texts in the subject area and successfully completing assignments like this has been thoroughly developed. Nevertheless transitioning to this phase will still need to be guided with explicit instruction and prompting into using the skills that have been developed through the scaffolding (i.e. skimming, examining the text closely, language processing) in a more independent manner.

The question that arises here also is what form of cognitive processing do we give the students that draws upon the learning and mental habits that the scaffolds inculcated unto them, but that they can take and use with any text at any time and without being given any assignment to aid them?

What I am in favor of is teaching a strategy that draws upon a skill that students learn in creating Cornell Notes in Advancement Via Individual Determination (AVID) programs. A part of Cornell Notes in AVID is creating questions on the margins that are answered by the notes taken within the margins. A cognitive processing strategy to teach the students could be to write questions in the margins next to each paragraph as they read that are answered in the paragraph. This makes it almost like teaching them to make a scaffolded questionnaire on their own, but acts as a form of independent note-taking and mental processing while reading. This induces them to reciprocate the learning form they have been habituated into.

❖ *Increase of Cognitive Demand **within** Scaffolding*

Even when the scaffolds are in place in a questionnaire it does *not* mean that recalling facts and details is the only skill that can be nurtured or prompted. The idea of the questionnaire is that it is a running guide to go along with the text and aids the student in processing the text's contents by prompting them to go over, look closer at, and extract certain details and knowledge from the text that are important for a variety of reasons.

Once a student has gone through a certain amount of text and some information has been extracted, the student can be prompted to stop and think deeper about the information and perform a more complex writing or reflection task in relation to it. These might be prompts that relate more closely to the type of prompts that are offered in textbooks or that more closely relate to the wording of academic standards. Only now the student will be doing them after the questionnaire has guaranteed that they have extracted the information from the text that they need in order to consider the more complex thinking prompt.

Let's look back at *Guns, Germs, and Steel* for an example. Further, let's consider the page and paragraphs we are working with along with the Minnesota Science standard 9.4.4.1.1. This standard is in the "Life Science" strand, the sub-strand is "Human Interactions with Living Systems" the standard itself is "Understand that...Human activity has consequences on living organisms and ecosystems" and the specific benchmark is, "Describe the social, economic, and ecological risks and benefits of biotechnology in agriculture and medicine. For example: Selective breeding, genetic engineering, and antibiotic development and use."

Wonderful. Let's use the *Guns, Germs, and Steel* text alongside a scaffolded questionnaire to guide our students to that benchmark. First we will have to look at the given paragraph in its entirety as well as the two that follow it:

In human societies possessing domestic animals, livestock fed more people in four distinct ways: by furnishing meat, milk, and fertilizer and by pulling plows. First and most directly, domestic animals became the societies' major source of animal protein, replacing wild game. Today, for instance, Americans tend to get most of their animal protein from cows, pigs, sheep, and chickens, with game such as venison just a rare delicacy. In addition, some big domestic mammals served as sources of milk and of milk products such as butter, cheese, and yogurt. Milked mammals include the cow, sheep, goat, horse, reindeer, water buffalo, yak, and Arabian and Bactrian camels. Those mammals thereby yield several times more calories over their lifetime than if they were just slaughtered and consumed as meat.

Big domestic mammals also interacted with domestic plants in two ways to increase crop production. First, as any modern gardener or farmer still knows by experience, crop yields can be greatly increased by manure applied as fertilizer. Even with the modern availability of synthetic fertilizers produced by chemical factories, the major source of crop fertilizer today in most societies is still animal manure—especially of cows, but also of yaks and sheep. Manure has been valuable, too, as a source of fuel for fires in traditional societies.

In addition, the largest domestic mammals interacted with domestic plants to increase food production by pulling plows and thereby making it possible for people to till land that had previously been uneconomical for

Now analyze below the accompanying scaffolded questionnaire that goes with these paragraphs. Notice how there are some questions labeled "Stop and Think", this indicates to the student, and it should be explained explicitly to the student, that questions with this label do not have answers that are found by pulling something exact from the text. Rather, the answers are explained by the student thinking about what they read. However, the student can look at previous answers they wrote to help them. On this particular questionnaire I have also indicated the answers that the student can look back to in emboldened parenthesis after the question prompt. Although more often than not if the student needs specific prompting to look back at certain ones I will prompt them orally. Most students do not need this help as answering the previous questions has ensured that they have extracted the needed information from the text and processed it.

Let's look through the questionnaire piece by piece, the answers the student would be expected to provide are in the italicized font.

Page 84 - Paragraph 3

1. What were the four distinct ways in which livestock fed more people in human societies possessing domestic animals?

Furnishing meat, milk, and fertilizer and by pulling plows

2. What did domestic animals become the societies' major source of?

Animal protein

3. What did some big domestic mammals serve as a source of in addition?

milk

4. What do some examples of "milked mammals" include?

The cow, sheep, goat, horse, reindeer, water buffalo, yak, and Arabian and Bactrian camels

5. What do these animals yield several times more of over their lifetime? (*yield = give off*)

Calories

These are all straightforward answers with wording extracted verbatim from the text. Now look at how questions 6 & 7 stops the student and prompts for more reflective thinking, yet integrates information the student has already extracted.

Stop and Think
6. Why does a cow produce more calories for humans than a chicken? **(look at #3 & #5 to help you)**

A cow gives milk and meat, and a chicken does not.

7. Why would it make sense for a farmer to breed more cows than chickens?

Because the farmer will get more calories and food from the cow.

Again the part in number 6 that says "look at #3 & #5 to help you" can either be on the paper or prompted by the teacher individually to students who need the prompting. Either way, because the teacher constructed the questionnaire, they will know exactly where to direct the student for help and can therefore do it in an efficient manner and not one that is time consuming, nor has the feel of "spoon-feeding".

This "stop and think" is also done here as a natural break at the end of the paragraph. The following paragraph has less questions accompanying it as it was deemed that there were less essentials to be extracted.[577]

The mention of breeding in question 7 prompts the student to integrate the information they are reading with a concept external to the text. The excerpt of the text we are reading here does not mention breeding. Therefore what breeding is and what the word breed means ought to be taught before the reading is done, or at least have been covered in a previous lesson. The reason that breeding is chosen as a concept to prompt the student to connect to the text here is because breeding is an example of a "biotechnology" that the standard dictates students describe the benefits and risks of, which we are moving towards as the assignment goes on.

---

[577] Though non-essential information can be asked for on the questionnaires also as an aid to anchor the student's attention on the reading. Typically this depends on the density of the text. Since *Guns Germs and Steel* is very dense and focuses on big concepts there is plenty to draw out that would be deemed essential

Page 84 - Paragraph 4
8. How can crop yields be greatly increased?

By manure applied as fertilizer.

Page 84 - Paragraph 4
9. How has manure also been valuable in traditional societies?

A source of fire

The following "Stop and Think" questions are much simpler to answer. Their purpose is to reiterate a point for the student that they can use when they answer the more extensive prompt at the end of the assignment.

Stop and Think
10. When farmers breed many big mammals and they want to increase crops and have fuel for fires, what do they use a lot of from the big mammals?

manure

11. **Complete this sentence**: *When farmers breed more big mammals they also use more __manure__.*

The "Stop and Think" questions here also reiterate a point that closely relates to what we want the student to take out of the text that relates to achieving the standard. The standard was "Understand that human activity has consequences on living organisms and ecosystems." The mass spreading of manure for crop production is such an activity. The excerpt of text that we are dealing with here *does not* connect that human activity to consequences of living organisms and ecosystems. But by reiterating this point seeds of background knowledge have been planted that can be drawn upon later.

In making the assignment it becomes apparent that teaching what the word "manure" means ought to go along with it. This can be done with an easy visual before the reading, another way to do this is to include a question that asks "what do you think manure is?" and encourage the student to use context clues skills to figure it out, or to simply give the answer if the assignment is being done as a class with explicit practice. In this case, if they are unsure they will likely ask. The following paragraph gets to a second factor in which large domestic animals affect crop production.

Page 84 - Paragraph 5

12. How else did large domestic animals interact with domestic plants to increase food production?

By pulling plows

13. What did pulling plows make possible?

For people to till land that had previously been uneconomical for farming

---

An important point to take out of these two questions is that the answer for both of them is from the same sentence. Sometimes it makes sense to ask separate questions for the student to extract separate pieces of information from the sentence. It is possible, depending on the student's own thoroughness, that they would write as an answer for number 12, "by pulling plows and thereby making it possible for people to till land that had previously been uneconomical for farming," exactly what the text says. In such a case their answer to number 13 will repeat part of their answer to number 12. Nothing wrong with that at all, again, processing and repetition.

The point of number 12 and 13 is to make sure that students are pulling out the information that connects to human impact on the ecosystem, because that is what will be used to execute the standard in the final prompt on the assignment, which you see here:

Stop and Think

Explain two reasons why farmers decided to breed more big mammals. Also, explain how this would change the land and environment. **(2 sentences) (look at number 12 and 13 to help you)**

Two reasons why farmers decided to breed more big mammals are to have more calories and to help grow more crops. This would change the land because they tilled land that had been previously uneconomical for farming.

The parenthetical part that says "2 sentences" is something I often put on prompts that are asking for more extensive writing, this is a way of making criteria clear and to make it clear that it is a full sentence writing part. Whereas previous questions could be answered with a short phrase or maybe even one word pulled from the text. The part that says "look at number 12 and 13 to help you, again, I do not normally put that on the questionnaire, but rather use it as a verbal scaffold given to students individually on a needs basis. It does have some importance here also for our targeting of the specific benchmark standard that speaks about "ecological risks and benefits of biotechnology" because the part about tilling in the text makes an explicit connection to environmental impact. This final prompt is also more akin to the type of prompts that are given in the textbooks at the end of sections, but that EL students and struggling learners are oftentimes hesitant to do all on their own. Especially when they have not had the appropriate build up.

This final prompt could also have variation in the students' answers, as some might write more about manure whereas the example here does not at all. Again, nothing wrong with that so long as they connect spreading manure to changing the environment.

So we see here how within one well-scaffolded assignment we set students up to be able to perform, and at least approach a manifestation of a standardized benchmark. The beautiful thing is that we now know something is in place to work upon. In the next class we can use the exact prompt we had at the end of this assignment as the warm up, providing some healthy repetition. From there we can look further into how tilling of the land impacts the environment in more specific ways, and thereby drawing out and extending the students' ability to perform the benchmark in a manner that is incremental and logically sequenced.

This type of scaffolded questionnaire is a piece of artwork for the teacher. Creating it can be the tool by which the teacher digests and dissects the texts that they are using with their students, and deepens their own knowledge of content. It can also be the roadmap by which they plan out the students' incremental learning to reach standards and benchmarks. Simply reading the texts that one is going to use with students and making questions to go along with it when your adult mind recognizes something important can kill the needs of both your lesson planning and familiarizing with content in one stone.

Review of Benefits of the Scaffolding

   1. *Anchors Student Attention on the Reading*
Since this scaffolding gives the student a narrow loci of attention in the text with each question, the student does not become overwhelmed with the idea of wading through the text and

getting lost. Because the questionnaire has questions continuously throughout the assigned reading it acts as a guiding hand to anchor attention and guide comprehension.

2. *Ensures Students Extract Needed Information*

Creating these questionnaires assures that both the teacher and the student dissect the text into pieces. The teacher's job in making the questions is planning out the specific and more important pieces and information from the text that they want the student to extract. By doing that and providing a correlating question or prompt with the scaffolds, they assure that the student is going to have an experience of mentally processing the information that will involve using it with both a receptive language modality (reading) and a productive language modality (writing). Since these will also be done frequently in an explicitly guided fashion the questioning creates natural breaks for verbal explanation from the teacher as well, which incorporates listening. The format also provides for frequent processing of information in the different grammatical forms (interrogative and declarative statements). This all amounts to reading being used to explicitly transfer knowledge to the learner, which is the necessary basis for any other academic task.

3. *Scaffolds for Increased and Incremental Build Up of Cognitive Complexity*

This has been demonstrated, both within a single scaffolded assignment as well as how it can be done overall through the gradual release of the scaffolds.

4. *Forms the Mental Habits of Grappling with a Text*

The scaffolds give the students a route by which to analyze specific pieces of complex text in a focused fashion, while also guiding them through its expanded density. Furthermore, that they will actually have to slow down and also process the text in writing encourages the mental habit of slowing down in reading a text and processing it in chunks. These are the mental habits that EL learners and struggling readers actually need to acquire in order to read complex academic texts. The scaffolding here sets up the acquisition of those habits through repetitive practice. This is how skills are hard-wired, more so than being told how to think about something. Going through the assignments will give the students the *feel* of reading, as well as the *feel* of processing the text and successfully connecting it to questions outside of it. This is the key to training students to read texts that are supposedly above their "reading levels".

5.   *Increases Teacher Knowledge of Content*

Teachers can often be reticent at the idea of having to create customized assignments for their students. But as professionals in the content areas and of academic learning, constructing these questionnaires alongside reading a text that will be used in class anyway can be done quite seamlessly. Furthermore, when the teacher has customized the questionnaire they are well-prepared to answer and verbally scaffold any question the student may come up with; because they will know the questionnaire and how it relates to the text thoroughly. Many teachers might be embarrassed to admit how often a student will ask a question about an assignment, and the teacher will have to go back into the reading on their own accord, on the spot in class, in order to find what is needed to help the student. This results from the teacher giving the student something that was pre-made by someone else, usually a curriculum developer. This does not happen when the questionnaire is fully composed by the teacher his or herself. Also, it works as an instrument by which the teacher can plan the learning of their students incrementally within one lesson or reading excerpt. Thus providing for further breakdown.

6.   Workable Uniform Academic Process
Teachers can not all do the same things within one building. But having some consistency in academic forms and routines creates predictability and comfort for students and sets them up for confidence and success. Creating these questionnaires is something all classrooms can do. Furthermore, all classrooms can anchor the questionnaires to their textbooks, providing a familiarity and predictability with academic texts. Even furthermore, it creates a very concrete, predictable, manageable, and productive way that the ESL departments can provide indirect support across many different classrooms; because if need be they or other auxiliary teachers can create these materials. Coordinating and co-planning time can be used to generate these out ahead of time, or they can be used as a proxy for co-planning when the time is not available.

7.   Correlation with AVID
Many students who will benefit from this strategy will also be AVID students. In AVID students are trained in the use of Cornell Notes wherein they are taught to design questions that would be answered by the learning that they took down in their notes. Here we have an inverse relationship with what this scaffolding does where it prompts students to find learning and information based on questions that are given. Once students get built up in their reading confidence, we begin taking the scaffolds away so we can teach the cognitive process of dissecting a text by thinking about questions that a text could answer as one reads it. Perhaps this takes the form of writing notes in the margins, while the student reads, in the form of questions that the paragraph answers; thereby combining a skill they learned in AVID with mental habits that were inculcated by our scaffolding process to create a cognitive framework for processing complex texts that can be done independently without any scaffolds or materials provided from anyone. From there, students can be taught to ask questions that probe for more detail or understanding. This is called self-questioning and meta-analytic research has found it to be the most effective metacognitive reading comprehension strategy to teach (Wong, 1985).

Metacognition Pitfalls

This reading scaffolding strategy is designed to build up the skills of understanding and recall through repetition, experiencing success, incremental increase of challenge, and by acquiring actual content knowledge by having repetitive practice with content information in both receptive and productive language modalities. Teachers need to value that building up understanding and recall and having success with it forms the basis for success in higher order thinking skills for all students. Educational trends that have placed high emphasis on higher order thinking skills and metacognition in reading comprehension has caused many teachers and programs to devalue this fact by employing teaching methods that overly focus on attempting to prompt and question students into "higher-order" thinking and metacognition.

Some research beginning in the late 1960s and up through the 1980s showed that good readers think about what they read and use metacognition (Smith, 1967; Haller, 1988).[578] This caused academics to ask the question as to whether or not comprehension can be taught; an appealing idea for its potential to act as a catchall approach that could in theory enable students to understand any reading passage, without necessarily having to teach them the requisite knowledge to understand given reading passages. This appeal only increased in the era of testing after No Child Left Behind, when testing became more closely linked to school accountability and funding. While at the same time creation of tests became more privatized and teachers became disallowed from seeing or knowing the reading passages that their students would actually read on the tests generated by private companies.

There is certainly research that shows that good readers use metacognition. There has been research that has shown in some context that training students in metacognition can be helpful. That is why today we have an endless amount of emphasis on it, and most reading programs center upon it. So reading in school has become about prompting and questioning students into "thinking" about what they read at the neglect of explicitly directing them to understanding and knowing what they read. Instead, the modern approaches hope that prompting the student to "think" about what they read will generate them to understand it essentially by osmosis. But this does not work, and there is a persistent problem in education today where teachers are constantly told and trained to teach reading this way because it has a trendy appeal, but it only leads to frustration for them and the students. The teachers end up

---

[578] There was much more research that examined a *correlation* of metacognitive skills and comprehension scores and theorization about metacognitive, or discussed theories of metacognition. Far less actually met a criteria of having examined whether or not interventions of metacognitive instruction actually improved reading comprehension against a control group. Haller (1988) gathered 150 scholarly references on metacognition in reading for possible inclusion in a meta-analyses, but only 20 studies met this criteria and they had mixed results as far as the efficacy of instructing for metacognition.

relying on explicit instruction, explanation, and transfer of knowledge anyway, only they do it in a way that was not planned for and thought out. Rather it is done in a way that is reactionary to the lack of engagement of the students that is caused by the metacognitive approaches. The strategies I propose above remedy this problem. In the case of Muslim students, the strategies build upon the cultural learning habits that are already inculcated in them upon their arrival at school, as opposed to rubbing against them.

This is not to say that metacognition cannot or should not be taught at all, but it must be built up to. After all, we have to consider that the original research that showed that good readers use metacognition was analyzing readers who were trained to read in an era prior to the metacognition movement (Smith, 1967). So just because they used metacognition does not mean that it came about by their being instructed in it. Metacognition and so-called higher-order thinking skills in reading is built upon a foundation of basic understanding and knowledge of content. It is only as competence in understanding excels that metacognition can be effectively approached (Haller, 1988). When this foundation is in place, students will often develop metacognitive strategies themselves. Indeed many of the best readers have developed metacognition this way, as metacognition is not a universal process, it is idiosyncratic to the individual.

When metacognition *is* taught it cannot be done so with an abundance mentality, i.e. thinking that the more that we prompt and question students for it the better the students will get at it. It has to be done with a principled focus on how it has been built up to logically upon a foundation of comprehension that has already been put in place. It should also be done with some detailed understanding of what the most empirical research on it actually says. What too often happens in education is there may be a single study or few, or a theoretician's paper, that say something general, like metacognition, works and then there is a rush to create programs and curriculum material that revolve entirely around the trendiness of the idea, and market them within the lucrative industry of the purchasing power for resources that public schools have.

Research on teaching metacognition says that it is better when done with higher grade levels, meaning there should be even more emphasis put on the basic comprehension of recall at lower grade levels. It is best done in small groups as opposed to the whole class level, and it is best to be done *less* intensely, with one or two days per week of metacognitive instruction being better than an everyday approach (Chiu, 1988). When prescribed questioning and prompting for metacognition is used it is best used for the purpose of revealing nuance in the text (Haller, 1988), but nuance cannot be approached without a solid foundation of basic understanding. Furthermore, when struggling learners or students with learning disabilities are examined it is clear that explicit direct instruction is paramount (Rupley, 2009), and it is essential to start simple in order to ensure initial success (Sencibaugh, 2005), because this sets students up to develop true confidence.

The best metacognitive strategy to focus on is self-questioning (Wong, 1985). Teaching this skill is a logical next step to introduce after the strategy that I described above, which ended with students creating their own questions about facts and details in the text.

The problem that is always made by curriculum developers is that not only do they over focus on metacognition out of a desire to appear fancy and advanced, but they will mix up and jumble the sequencing of the skills. This is why you will see reading textbooks that jump around from having the students practice comparing and contrasting, sequencing, describing, inferencing, etc. sometimes even within the same reading. The goal of the curricula developers is to make their materials appear complex, advanced, and feign that they are well thought out, all for marketing purposes. The reality is they are just confusing people, especially the students, while avoiding the detailed work of laying out a learning continuum that is incremental and logically sequenced.

If you would like to see an example of the same scaffolding strategy explained more visually or applied to an elementary school reader please register at abrahameducation.com.

Scaffolding Math

With math you want to stay with the same principles of being incremental and logically sequenced. Many aspects of math and science lend themselves to doing this in a more straightforward manner than perhaps social studies and language arts naturally facilitate. However, it is key to understand that concepts for EL students and struggling learners almost certainly need to be broken down to smaller increments well beyond what is offered by typical curricular resources. There are also at least two common mistakes in math instruction that I have seen made frequently and will address here.

The first is an overuse of what has been called summary graphics (Jones, 2000) as opposed to graphics that illustrate proper sequencing. The second is inconsistencies and mixing of what I call the "forms" of problems before one form is mastered, and I will demonstrate what this means.

What you see as the top image on the next page is what has been called a summary graphic of a math problem, it shows the completed product of a mathematical procedure but it does not show the steps that were taken in order to arrive at that final product. Oftentimes a teacher takes students through a mathematical procedure and teaches the steps along the way, but the visual that is left on the board is a summary graphic that shows the student the final product. The problem with this is the graphic does not make it clear how to retrace the steps that were made to get to the final product. So when the student is asked to do the task independently they can see a final product but have no clear roadmap as to how that product was arrived at. Summary graphics are also typically what are made into posters that are put up in classrooms and then called visual aids.

$$7\overline{)434} \quad \text{Long Division}$$

$$
\begin{array}{r}
62 \\
7\overline{)434} \\
-42\downarrow \\
\hline
14 \\
-14 \\
\hline
0
\end{array}
$$

Compare this to the type of graphic below where each step is clear and the change in the procedure from one step relative to the previous one is also clear.

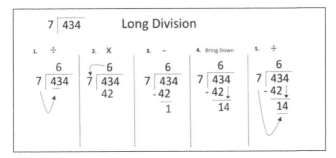

This type of graphic can be gone through step-by-step where each previous step is repeated, and a whole new illustration is generated with the students for each step. Usually these graphics are better generated on the chalk or whiteboard as opposed to the digital screen because that way they can actually be built in front of the students. These are what Fred Jones (2000) called Visual Instruction Plans (VIPs). Of all the instructional strategies I have researched there is maybe none better that I have found to engage EL students and struggling learners, whether of a Muslim background or not, though I see the strategy as being in harmony with the Muslim learning habits that have been discussed in this chapter already.

❖ *Considering Form*

The other issue with math is that students should be taught to master one "form" of a problem before moving on to others. So consider the long division problems below. While they both follow the same procedure to be solved, they are not what I would call the same form. The first problem is a three digit by one digit problem and produces a two digit answer. The second one is a three digit by one digit problem but produces a three digit answer with a remainder.

Long Division
inconsistent form
$\begin{array}{r} 62 \\ \hline 7 \, | \, 434 \end{array} \qquad \begin{array}{r} 247r3 \\ \hline 6 \, | \, 885 \end{array}$

So when students learn the long division process with three digit by one digit problems with a two digit answer, they should be given other problems that follow that same pattern until they have mastered doing long division in that form. See below.

Long Division
consistent form
$\begin{array}{r} 62 \\ \hline 7 \, | \, 434 \end{array} \qquad \begin{array}{r} 24 \\ \hline 6 \, | \, 264 \end{array}$

Once that form is mastered, then the form that produces a three digit answer with a remainder can be introduced, with explicit instruction about how the form has changed relative to the previous form that was studied. Once those two forms are mastered, *then* the students can be given assignments where the problems mix up those two forms. The problem with most assignments students are given, and certainly with the way that math textbooks are constructed, is that they mix up the forms of problems (and often the processes as well) and they introduce students to forms of doing certain mathematical operations and procedures without ever even providing explicit instruction about doing it in different forms. Again, this is something that the curricular developers think is a dynamic way to challenge students and they think they are enhancing the cognitive demand of students among other imagined benefits, when all they are really doing is creating confusion.

Phonics

Through teaching middle and high school in the second half of my teaching career it is both amazing to me and sad how many students are easily seen as arriving at these grade levels without a basic grasp of the phonetic system of English. The ability of these students to read and comprehend texts of anything close to grade level complexity is sapped by the anxiety that emanates from this.

This is especially sad in the case of Muslim students whose background learning in the masjid has given them a base for which to tap into a system of learning language phonetics. I have seen students in high school who could read Arabic phonetics fluently but failed to do the same in English despite having been brought up in the American public education system. Typically they have been through numerous expensive reading intervention programs throughout elementary school and even middle school and still do not have a solid grasp of the English phonetic system. Yet at the same time they can read Arabic very well, having only attended the masjid schools on the weekends in their life, and taught by untrained teachers from a book that might not have cost more than $10.

While I had thought to create a book that taught the phonetics of English in a style that mirrors the type of books I have shown in this chapter that teach Arabic phonetics in a linear, incremental, and systematic fashion; I discovered in my research that I did not need to because one already exists. I do not believe at all that Samuel Blumenthal considered that he was creating a teaching resource that correlated to the principles of Islamic learning when he created and published *Alpha Phonics* in the 1980s, but he may as well have.

Blumenthal was a critic of early sight word and whole language instruction. He argued that sight word instruction taught children at young ages to read English as an idiographic language as opposed to an alphabetic one. Inducing many of them to adopt the idea that any word that is going to be read in a text has to have been known beforehand for one to be able to read it, as opposed to being able to sound the word out; or at the least be confused about when to employ the proper strategy. This in turn caused children to guess-read and lack confidence in their own ability.

While phonics is not wholly neglected in schools today, it often lacks a fully systematic approach to hardwiring the English phonetic system in students at early ages. Blumenthal aimed to do exactly that by organizing his text in a lesson by lesson format with 126 lessons, one for each sound and phonetic construction in the English language and alphabet. By using repetition, direct instruction, reciprocation, feedback, and incremental progression, an instructor can take a student through the whole book cover to cover to commit the phonetic system to memory. Sight words are taught based off of phonetics as exceptions, as opposed to separate from them. Scrolling through its pages I see a book that mirrors the Arabic phonetic instruction books in its

```
4                        Lesson 2        Lesson 3                              5

                                         am    an    as    at    ax
                                         Sam   man   has   hat   tax
   S         am          Sam
                                              Sam sat.
   m         an          man                  Sam has an ax.

   h         as          has             Lesson 4
                                         a   d                        ad
   s         at          sat             d  ad                       dad
                                         w  ax                       wax
   t         ax          tax             D  an                       Dan

   S s                                       Dan sat.
                                             Dad has wax.

                                             Dd
```

accommodation of these teaching matters unlike any other English reading instructional text I have ever seen.

What I also like about Blumenthal's text is it's *lack* of visuals. He was critical of the visually-heavy "A is for Apple approach" to reading phonics. Reasoning that the visual the student should focus on when learning phonics is *the letter itself*; not pictures of apples, balls, or cats etc. He theorized that providing colorful graphics would only confuse the student and cause unnecessary stimulation and reinforce idiographic reading habits as opposed to alphabetic ones. Another benefit to the lack of visuals is the text becomes age neutral. Older learners who need to learn the phonetic skills can learn from Blumenthal's book and not feel like they are learning from a child's book.

Blumenthal thought his work was an anecdote to dyslexia, which he blamed on the progressive movement's influence on reading instruction. While that is almost undoubtedly a specious claim, I have been surprised in my life to have met high school students who thought that reading English was about guesswork and prior familiarization with words as opposed to phonetic decoding. Sometimes students who have studied in masājid have stated to me that they think English is hard because they think it "works differently" than Arabic. Saying that in Arabic you can sound it out letter by letter, but in English there are too many words to know and study. If a student thinks this is a fundamental difference between Arabic and English their English reading instruction was a miseducation.

One of the most influential reading programs of the last 25 years that students are likely to have experienced is the "Guided Reading" methods of Fountas and Pinnell (1996). This program is responsible for the "Daily Five" reading format and the proliferation of grouping, centers, and leveled reading in classrooms. Fountas and Pinnell's work spurred a whole industry of professional development, boxed leveled reader libraries, and coordinating digital testing systems. Even I have known of reading specialist licensure programs to be based almost entirely off of Fountas and Pinnell.

I would like for educators to critically examine and reflect upon the impact of this program and others like it on their students. Comprehensive reviews of reading interventions used in large urban districts have found it to be one of the most frequently used intervention programs yet wholly lacking in evidence of effectiveness (Klingbeil, 2013). This concern is compounded in the case of Muslim students in light of this program's incongruence with the formal learning background of Muslim culture. When we look at Fountas and Pinnell's foundational text *Guided Reading* (1996) we find that to them the "role of 'phonics'" is not touted as something that should be taught systematically through an intentional program that sets out to teach students to conquer the entire phonetic system in a logical order. Rather teachers are encouraged to think of it as only one component of "several layers of language". Therefore, Fountas and Pinnell encourage that phonics should be relegated to only being ad hoc mini-lessons delivered subordinately within comprehension teaching sessions whose primary focus is prompting for use of metacognitive strategies while reading silently. According to them, decontextualized phonics instruction that focuses on mastery of its alphabetic system is not a consideration. Rather students are to learn phonics during "interactive" writing when they "construct words in conjunction with other students and their teacher", or during a story introduction when teachers can "call children's attention to aspects of individual words", or "at the end of a lesson, teachers may spend a minute or two on word work" (Fountas & Pinnell, 1996, pp. 164-165). No argument is made as to why these ad hoc approaches are superior to a systematic approach of explicit instruction that ensures coverage and hard-wiring practice of every single phonetic piece of the English alphabetic system.

Furthermore, we need to understand that Fountas and Pinnell's guided reading is a program based only off of theory, as opposed to empirical research. They themselves state their work is based off of the work of New Zealand theorists Marie Clay and Donald Holdaway (Fountas & Pinnell, 1996), whose work in turn was based off of whole language theories that were ultimately rooted in the theories of the early 20th century psychologist Edmund Burke Huey[579] (Holdaway, 1979).

Despite its large influence on reading instruction and their annual seven figure sums garnered in grants, little empirical research has been done to assess the efficacy of Fountas and Pinnell's program. What research has been done has been disconfirmatory of its efficacy; especially when measured against direct instruction that includes decontextualized explicit instruction in phonics. A 2014 study that assessed Fountas and Pinnell's guided reading methods against a control group of students who received explicit instruction found that explicit instruction was "more likely to substantially accelerate student progress in phonemic decoding, text reading fluency, and reading comprehension" (Denton et al, 2014). A 2009 study compared the effects of Fountas and Pinnell's guided reading and a highly explicit program that provided direct instruction in phonics and comprehension strategies for first-grade students. It found explicit instruction was associated with better outcomes in oral reading fluency and that the results were consistent with several prior studies that demonstrated enhanced reading outcomes with explicit and systematic phonics approaches (Tobin & Calhoon, 2009). A 2007 study compared EL students and struggling readers in two groups, one that received a "balanced" literacy approach similar to Fountas and Pinnell's guided reading methods, and another that received "direct instruction" which "explicitly and systematically" taught phonological/phonemic awareness, letter-sound recognition, alphabetic decoding, fluency building, and comprehension skills. No surprise, it found gains that "significantly favored" students in the direct instruction group (Kamps et al, 2007). Leveled reading is another approach that has been thoroughly critiqued, and is not backed by empirical research. Refer to the review "Let's start Leveling About Leveling" by Australian academics Kathryn Glasswell and Michael Ford (2011).

I believe the over focus in education on getting students to "enjoy" reading, read silently, and "think" while they read has resulted in a bypassing and failure to teach phonics systematically. So students are being run through a reading instruction conveyor belt where a proper foundation for reading is never actually put in place for too many students. They are not set up

---

[579] Huey wrote a book that influenced later theorists called *The Psychology and Pedagogy of Reading*. In it he espoused that teaching phonics directly is a needless emphasis on the "geometry" of the letters. He thought that because experiments he ran showed people could read words when letters were taken out, phonics instruction did not really matter. Never mind that he was looking at people who already read well, and likely had undergone the traditional phonics instruction. He also thought academics should use their influence to create fundamental changes in the way people read English. He thought it should go from reading horizontal to vertical, and that some letters were useless altogether. He based these theories on what he saw as efficiency in Ancient Egyptian Hieroglyphs and Chinese; apparently missing the fact that the script of these languages function in a fundamentally different way than English, as they are ideographic and not alphabetic (Huey, 1908).

for success, and their initial reading experiences in school, rather than sparking interest and developing critical thinking as instructors intend, actually induces academic insecurity that only gets compounded throughout the years as they remain grouped into reading below "grade-level" texts all the time, and get told they are restricted to that. All the while constantly experiencing being "stuck" in group instruction where they are primarily prompted for metacognition for which the reading program has yet to build up the proper foundation. There is almost no doubt that this compounds inequities in education because the students who are successful in a system like this will only be the ones who come from a home environment that has the time and resources to fill these gaps for them.

Blumenthal's book can be purchased online for about $15. A pittance of an investment for the potential that it has to teach our students who are attuned to reading habits formed in settings of Islamic learning. I would love to see some schools or teachers try this book out, at least as a core part of their remedial program for struggling readers, but even as their base phonetic instructional program for early grade levels.

Direct Instruction vs. Student Centered Teaching

The knowledge of the learner is the absolute most important thing to consider when choosing instructional methods and approaches (Hollins, 2011). This remains an unaddressed, though not unacknowledged, issue in our public education institutes. There is no shortage of emphasis on the need to understand, or at least nominally respect, diversity, multiculturalism, and anti-racism. However, too often this respect and tacit acknowledgment of need does not translate into actual learning about students themselves and their backgrounds.

Because real efforts to actually know students are rare, teachers continue to fall into pitfalls and traps with their instructional methods. Oftentimes these traps are fallen into by assuming there is a best practice outside of consideration for who the learner is, or who the teacher is for that matter, that is "researched-based" by virtue of the fact that it was touted as such by some authority seemingly over the teacher's pay grade. The reality is that teaching methods that are often dubbed as best practices are fraught with conflicting interests; be they political, career, or private business. These interests frequently rub against authentically understanding and engaging the learner, and teachers need to have the appropriate background knowledge themselves to be able to recognize when that is the case.

This phenomenon is clearly at play with Muslim students. There is a popular saying in education, that has been around since at least the early 1990s, that a teacher should be "the guide on the side and not the sage on the stage" (King, 1993). Underpinning this mantra is the assertion that it is virtuous for learning to be "student-centered" and that learning is best when students "construct" their own learning. Thus teachers are pressured to run classrooms that feign the appearance of being student-centered by having the class do things such as sitting in groups, being prompted to talk to one another, and being asked questions that supposedly induce "higher-order thinking" apparently by some ill-defined apparition.

Maybe this is effective in some circumstances, but clearly from what I have demonstrated in this chapter, this philosophy clashes with the cultural learning background of Muslim students.

Unfortunately, many teachers are told in pre-service training, district initiatives, professional development, and other well-funded initiatives that are typically buttressed by handsome grants from the federal Department of Education and education foundations well-endowed by private enterprise, that student-centered and constructivist teaching methods are the route to equity, that they provide an opportunity to develop critical thinking, to creating problem-solving students, to close the achievement gap, or whatever other phrasing that gives off the sentiment of lofty ambition.

Maybe it is the answer in some cases, maybe, but it would be absurd to take this on as an assumption without consideration for the child's learning from their "immediate cultural and social context of family and community" (Hollins, 2011).

Just as an example, consider the Center for Culturally Relevant Teaching and Learning (CCRTL) at culturallyresponsive.org. It is just one of many consultancy agencies in the industry of culturally relevant pedagogy and equity. In Minnesota I have known of many schools and entire large districts that have taken on this organization's training as an initiative to better engage non-mainstream students, and sometimes with the explicit intent of reducing disciplinary referrals of students from particular races and ethnicities. Their own website boasts of having given professional development to over 200,000 educators in the country, if just three fourths of those were teachers that is a full five percent of the US teaching population.

All in all, it is a type of organization that I believe does quite a bit of good for both educators and students.[580] In fact one of their core texts, *Culturally and Linguistically Responsive Teaching and Learning* by Sharroky Hollie, is one of the better books teachers can get to learn about rule differences in the vernacular English of African American students relative to what Hollie calls "standard English", if one does not have the life experience to be familiar with that. But like

---

[580] And I do want to emphasize, I am not trying to "pick on" or overtly lambast or even make a critique of this organization. Only I am using them as an example to illustrate a conundrum, and I choose them because I have had many teachers attend my trainings who belonged to districts and schools that had also undergone CCRTL's professional development. So I have firsthand experience with this clash.

most agencies focused on equity and cultural-relevance, CCRTL also uses catch-all conceptualizations of understanding and approaching "students of color". For schools with high populations of Muslim students, it falls way short in teaching about actual specific cultural information and includes much that runs counter to it; even if those students could also be classed as "students of color". This results in some pitfalls and traps for educators who apply some of their methods with Muslim students.

CCRTL's vision says they achieve in making "teacher's skillsets develop so that learning is more **student-centered** and engaging". [581] According to their own texts, a cornerstone of this means having students do a lot of group work and conversation with one another. This is a problem when it is taken by the teacher to mean that they are absolved from having to do actual learning about culture.[582] Instead teachers are instructed to listen to the kids in order to learn about their culture. What this does is place the responsibility of teaching about the dynamics of cultural background on the kids, which in turn places kids and adolescents as the cultural representatives to educators of particular groups. There are many problems with this because young people are not equipped to do that adequately, and it also creates a conflict because it sets up a situation where parents are now sending their kids to school to be cultural educators to the teachers, as opposed to being there *to learn*. This clashes with the actual expectations of parents. Most parents, both Muslim and non-Muslim, are "learning centered" and not student centered (Steinberg, 1991; Ahmed, 2015). Muslim students are culturally-habituated to learning being a process of intake from experts, while conversation is a means of socializing and leisure. When classrooms are overly focused on student conversation it can cue to the student that school time is actually a social time to be used for fun, as opposed to a time of learning and study that is used for the increase of one's knowledge.

The reality is part of what allows for the success of organizations and programs like CCRTL is that they tell educators to use instructional methods that have long held favoritism with the progressive strand of education, which goes back to John Dewey and includes theorists such as Edmund Burke Huey. Proposals like those of CCRTL are doubly-attractive to academics who favor progressive instructional methods because it validates that their own methodological preferences must be right for what they deem to be oppressed minority classes. This type of fusion seems to have started in the 1970s with the book *Pedagogy of the Oppressed* by Pablo Freire and the esteem it garnered from academics for lamenting that traditional education treated children as "empty vessels" waiting to be filled with knowledge, and arguing that

---

[581] See https://www.culturallyresponsive.org/what-we-do

[582] And this is the message that I have found some teachers to have either taken out of this program, or concerned that their colleagues took out of this program. Weak motivation on the part of the teacher his or herself likely plays a role in this, as opposed to that being the actual message from CCRTL.

students instead should be "co-creators" in their own learning. Freire's arguments were simply a rehashing of Dewey's pedagogical theories, only with the added appeal of being branded as the route to lifting up oppressed classes of non-white students.

I lament the fact that seemingly nothing in American society can escape its own culture war. Unfortunately, the instructional methods we are told to apply in public schools are no different. The basis of this conflict in the field of pedagogy is the favoritism of minimally directed student-centered methods by progressives vs. direct instructional methods that the anti-traditional impulses of progressives would cast in a negative light.

This whole dynamic puts Muslim students, and Muslim communities, in a bind. It may be that they garner more favor and empathy from the progressives, who pride themselves on empathy for classes that are societal minorities. On the other hand, for the most part, both the cultural values and the instructional methods that Muslim children are nurtured to be more attuned to in their family and cultural spaces would have more harmony with the priorities and outlooks of traditionalists.

So a balance needs to be struck. If we truly want to be culturally responsive to Muslim students it has to be recognized that minimally directed teaching strategies clash with the learning of Muslim students' cultural backgrounds and are likely to **compound** academic insecurity and disengage struggling learners.

This **may** include strategies often given alluring titles such as…

- Inquiry-based learning
- Problem-based learning
- Discovery learning
- Critical Thinking
- Constructivism
- Student-centered learning

All of these labels are, in essence, either offshoots, reincarnations, or re-conceptualizations of the progressive pedagogical theories of John Dewey. At the core of their philosophies is that learning is only authentic when it is "constructed" from the learner's own mind and volition, and the traditional idea of bestowing a preordained curriculum of learning upon the student from an expert figure is admonished as oppressive.

It is not my aim to wholly lambast these instructional methods nor the progressives themselves. I have both used these methods as a teacher and experienced them as a learner, and there are aspects to both their pedagogical theories and societal critiques with which I agree. I believe they have benefits, especially in sparking interest and motivation in students, and I think they have a real role to play in our schools for that purpose.

But I also need to emphasize here, that when it comes to the actual learning of content, gaining of knowledge, and acquisition of skills, the minimally-directed student-centered approach not only clashes with the cultural learning habits of Muslim students, but they are also *not supported as practices that lead to success by empirical education research*. And these points are especially true when we are talking about struggling learners. Per my investigation it seems the foundational justification of the progressive methods is always limited to theory and not empirical investigation. I showed an example of this above with Fountas and Pinnell.

John Hattie, a statistician with the University of Melbourne in Australia[583], performed the largest synthesis of achievement research in education that has ever taken place. A synthesis of over 800 meta-analyses of studies relating to achievement. Hopefully you have heard of his work, but I am surprised at how rare it is for American educators to be familiar with it. His research confirmed what has been found in a large group of meta-analyses, that Direct Instruction is an instructional strategy that is consistently, and over a broad range of eras and contexts, above average in its effect size on achievement (White, 1988; Adams & Engelman, 1996; Schieffer et al, 2002; Borman et al, 2003; Przychodzin-Havis et al, 2004; Przychodzin-Havis et al, 2005; Hattie, 2009).

Hattie explains that the high effect sizes associated with direct instruction often come as a surprise to teachers who have typically been inundated with constructivist mantras. He shows

---

583 Previously he had been with the University of Auckland in New Zealand

that modes of instruction that are considered more traditional and less progressive are superior by the most objective measure of analysis that is attainable.[584]

Hattie found feedback[585], direct instruction, reciprocation, and mastery learning[586] to be four out of the top five[587] interventions for student achievement. When I look at Islamic learning in the masjid I see those methods as the foundation of learning, and that is a conclusion I drew before ever discovering Hattie's work. Too often, I have seen students who have undergone masjid learning in their life being put at unease in their public school classrooms due to the teacher's insistence of using student-centered methods out of a misguided notion that it is "best practice" or a route to equity and alleviation of oppression. The major benefits students get out of direct and incremental instruction is an increase in confidence and gradual build up of correct knowledge. The major pitfall of student-centered approaches is it causes cognitive overload.

Cognitive Overload

Even before Hattie's work was published debates had raged on in education over the student-centered vs. direct instruction approaches. I recommend teachers to read the article "Why Minimal Guidance During Instruction Does Not Work" by Kirschner et al from 2006. This article explains the pitfalls of student-centered strategies in light of the cognitive architecture of memory.

In short, it describes how items stored in long-term memory can be retrieved by a person with automaticity. The amount of items able to be stored in long term memory are ever-numerous,

---

[584] A meta-analysis looks at studies that quantify results measured against a control group. Social Science research, such as education, always has a degree of uncertainty to it because it seeks to measure that which can never be measured to exactness, unlike the mature sciences of physics and chemistry. Control-group studies are the closest that educational research can get to objective analysis that mimics the scientific process. Part of what contributes to the confusion around instructional methods and best practice is claims that are made based on research that is not done by control group experiment, or that research that shows "growth" but fails to discern between below and above average growth, or that is really just based on theory, such as Dewey's, but has not actually been proven by research. About growth, Hattie shows in his synthesis that almost any educational intervention can claim some sort of growth. It turns out that simply by attending school and getting older students will typically experience growth. So the approach Hattie took was to determine what was the median growth, or what statisticians call effect size, of all educational interventions overall, and then determine which interventions had below and above average effect sizes. It turned out the average effect size was 0.4 (effect sizes are articulated on a scale of 0.0-1.0).

[585] Specifically feedback that was explicit in distinguishing between what is right and wrong.

[586] Mastery learning means not moving on to one thing until the previous step is mastered.

[587] The fifth method was metacognition, though it has certain conditions to be successful as was previously discussed.

but it takes more time, practice, and repetition to store learning in long-term memory. The amount of items that can be stored in short-term memory, on the other hand, are severely limited. With any learning task a student undertakes they will have to mentally process at least the content information associated with it and the process of the task itself. If at least one of these is not stored into long-term memory for the student they will inevitably be set up to shut down and check out of the learning due to cognitive overload. For EL students, we can add language formulation as a third matter that needs to be processed. Cognitive overload in turn causes mental exhaustion and behavior problems in classrooms due to student frustration and disengagement.

The pitfall of student-centered approaches is that too often they assume that grappling through the learning tasks process will lead to long-term memory acquisition of the learning content. Again, knowing the learning content is not expected to be acquired through direct transmission of knowledge by an authoritative source, but rather the learning is meant to abstractly appear by osmosis that results from being prompted into a learning mode that sounds fancy but is not backed up by empirical research.

Foundations of School-based Learning

The arrival and increase of Muslim students in our classrooms over the past three decades might serve as a reminder for us to look back at some of the foundations that our school-based learning is built upon. If Western society is caught up in a constant tension between progressivism on one hand and traditionalism on the other, I believe it must be the case that there is good and bad to be taken from both standpoints. So we must practice well-informed analysis and critique of these points of view in order to develop a balanced approach that selects the best of both worlds. It may be the case that in many places of our educational world today it would be prudent to ask whether or not the pendulum has swung too far to the progressive end, and whether or not there are some benefits in balancing our approach by looking back at more traditional methods of learning and instruction.

Paradoxically, for engaging Muslim students there is an extended degree to which this would actually be a way of carrying out the progressive ideal of honoring the cultural background of minority students. The fact is, not only our traditional instructional methods, but also the structures of our schools and universities themselves in the Western world, were traditionally built upon learning formats that were taken from the Muslim world. Understanding this is a whole other large area to endeavor into, but if you wish to follow that venture I recommend reading the book *The Rise of Colleges* by George Makdisi (1981).

But to give a short, clear, and tangible example that illustrates how our learning traditions in the Western world are taken from the Muslim world, just consider the graduation ceremonies that students undergo when they graduate high school. The students are asked to wear a gown that covers the whole body, and they wear a square cap that is referred to as a mortar. Where does this tradition come from?

Centuries ago European explorers who traveled to the Muslim world observed practices at *Al Azhar* university in Cairo Egypt. They saw that when students of knowledge memorized a book they would receive a paper certificate verifying that they learned that book, and listing the the teacher who had taught it to them, and the chain of teachers who that book had been learned from in previous generations going all the way back to the original author; this chain is called an *isnād*. The Europeans, of course, observed that these Muslim students wore gowns because that was the traditional garb of the Muslim world at the time, and still is. It was also the practice at this University that when they would receive a certificate for memorizing a book they would tie the book to their head in the ceremony where they would receive the certificate, creating the mortar-like look. The students would use tassels as bookmarks that would hang down off the side of the book. Still today, the Qur'an is printed with tassels attached for bookmarking. So as Europeans developed their own universities they mimicked the university structure from the Muslim world, and along with that mimicked the Muslim's process of degree reception to form the graduation ceremony traditions that we still have today (Hussain, 2009). Now just think about how many of our Muslim students in the West graduate high school and go through the ceremony having never been taught about this connection of the ceremony to their Muslim heritage.

Conclusion

While an analysis of the learning backgrounds of Muslim students might nudge us towards considering more traditional instructional methods, it is still a true point to take from the progressives and the advocates of culturally relevant teaching that we need to include texts in the classroom that represent who the students are.

For Muslims, there are actually plenty of texts that can be acquired that feature Muslims. But for a teacher who does not have background knowledge about Islam and Muslim culture there are, again, many pitfalls that can be fallen into when selecting these texts. So the next chapter will not only recommend quality texts to use, but it will also survey the different types of texts that feature Muslims and are meant to be used for educational purposes. I will discuss the different implications and considerations for using these different types.

Chapter 6: TEXTS THAT FEATURE MUSLIMS

Texts that feature Muslims in them are not hard to come by in and of themselves. The challenge for educators is using them in a way that hits the mark to engage students. There are many dynamics to consider. I will begin this discussion on texts that feature Muslims with some illumination of certain types of pitfalls that can be fallen into when educators attempt to select texts without adequate background knowledge themselves. In this chapter I want teachers to think about ways in which culturally-relevant texts are commonly approached, and to have consideration for unintended consequences for Muslim students in what can result from those approaches.

The work of Toronto-based researcher Sarafoz Niyozov's, who we mentioned in chapter one, offers analysis for the intersection of teacher background knowledge and engagement with Muslim students. Niyozov received over $100,000 in grants from 2007-2011 to do case studies on teachers who work with Muslim students in public schools in Canada.[588] His reports reveal effort and good intention on the part of teachers, however, with complications still intertwined with a lack of background knowledge and perspectives still persisting. These complications are compounded by the fact that they go unacknowledged by Niyozov within his own analysis. All the teachers in Niyozov's study "acknowledged racism, and accepted that they may be contributing to it at the subconscious level" (Niyozov, 2010, pg. 26). A teacher is quoted as saying that she and her students discuss racism and anti-racism quite openly and the teacher said, "We have to acknowledge that we are all racists, and then cope with our racism" (Niyozov, 2010 pg. 27).

Most teachers quoted by Niyozov, including a "hijabi Muslim" teacher, referred to global geopolitical issues as a root source of difficulty between different ethnic Muslim students as well as between Muslim students and non-Muslim teachers. This includes a teacher citing it as being the root source of racist teacher attitudes towards students, as well as the root source of conflict between Afghani and Pakistani students, with the Muslim teacher stating that discussions over political conflicts taking place amongst parents are likely being absorbed at home by the students.

Niyozov says that while teacher voices acknowledge racism and bias in many areas it is important to understand that there is a need to further investigate and educate on different forms of personal and structural racism. In reference to this he emphasizes that according to

---

588 According to his staff page at the University of Toronto as of June 2020 https://www.oise.utoronto.ca/ctl/
Faculty_Profiles/404/Sarfaroz_Niyozov.html

teachers these exist on the part of not just teachers and Western society, but their students, and their students' communities as well. This is spoken of in reference to one teacher who said:

> Through my reading and meeting with Muslims, all state that Islam is about tolerance and not judging. But then we see and read about how Muslims have been using their sacred tradition against their Muslim and non-Muslim fellows in the predominantly Muslim countries, we wonder why there is this serious gap between the talk and walk. (Niyozov, 2010, pg. 27)

And another teacher who says:

> So you read all these things in the newspaper and it stirs people up but it's really people's daily experience of Muslims in the public schools and neighborhoods that normalizes their perceptions of Muslims as human beings similar to them. (Niyozov, 2010, pg. 27).

The questions implied here by Niyozov's study subjects are totally legitimate and ones that are not illegitimate to discuss in public school classrooms. Yet, while undertaking a polemic tone, Niyozov leaves these quotes unexamined for the particular conundrum that they lay on Muslim students. Namely, that Muslim students are disproportionately asked, expected, and told to be model representations for a wider community that holds a polemical standing in the Western world's geopolitical context. While the sentiments expressed by the teachers are most certainly genuine and not in ill nature, their words reinforce this conundrum and at the same time are direct products of it.

Is it possible for Muslim students to opt out of being burdened with representing Muslims in the world at large while in the public school classrooms without opting out of their Muslim identity altogether? What does facing such a conundrum do to the identity development of Muslim students? Especially ones who are bound to have their struggle with troublesome behavior patterns that are common to developing young people; but for the Muslim student normal developmental tendencies, such as arguing and having disputes, can get placed into a broader geopolitical context in the eyes of their teachers. What should schools do to validate the personal part of their identity in order to create a developmentally appropriate place to approach the discussions and questions that Niyozov and his study subjects are talking about? Virtually everything I have discussed in this book is attempting to offer answers to these questions.

Having culturally relevant texts that authentically honor the religious identity is something else that can help with this, but selection of these texts has to be on mark. It has to be done with appropriate background knowledge of Islam, Muslim cultures, and history; and it has to avoid the pitfalls of superficial selectivity.

Niyozov also touches on curricular concerns pertaining to representation of Muslims and teacher anxiety about not knowing where to find authentic sources, while also emphasizing the need for diverse perspectives to be represented and cautioning against the possible machinations of Islamist[589] agents and the effect this could have on public schools. Niyozov also feels that teachers are already making strong efforts to include Muslims in the curriculum, citing as evidence that one English teacher in a predominantly Muslim school that he talked to, "mentioned using texts, such as stories from Egyptian novelist Naguib Mahfouz, [and] the recent book *The Kite Runner* by Khalid Hosseini" (Niyozov, 2010, pg. 29) There is, again, a phenomenon at play here that warrants further critique than the treatment it is given by Niyozov in his reports.

Naguib Mahfouz is an Egyptian author, true, but he was also an existentialist author who was schooled and bought-into the ways of 20th century European philosophy, and this is what is represented in his books (Gordon, 1990). Khaled Hosseini is an ethnic Afghan raised primarily in the West. When *Kite Runner* was published in 2003 and sold over 4 million copies in the midst of the United States war in Afghanistan. It is a book that is part of a larger cottage industry of literature[590] that takes place in Afghanistan that spawned to popularity in the Western world in the context of the Western media's fascination with the take over of the Taliban there in the late 1990's and early 2000s. While this literature was popular in America, Hosseni's book drew protests and calls to be banned in Afghanistan for its portrayals of Afghan culture (particularly the book's portrayal of pederasty between Afghans). *Kite Runner* as well as Naguib Mahfouz's *Palace Walk* series are books that take place in the Muslim world, but they are ones wherein the themes that are drawn on are ones approved by Western philosophy and culture. Principal to that is the antagonistic portrayal of religious people and religiosity within the Muslim world. Thereby, central to these books' popularity in the West is their harmony to elements of the West's cultural appropriation and orientalist takes on the Muslim world (Said, 1979). Meanwhile Western teachers who use these books can tell themselves that they are practicing

---

[589] "Islamist" is a Western academic term. It is generally applied to militant or political activist groups in the Muslim world who advance a political ideology that purports to want to make a society more "Islamic". The term "Islamist" is used by academics to distinguish these groups from being characterized as "Islamic" because the machinations that they employ in order to gain power do not follow Islamic principles or methodologies at all.

[590] *The Breadwinner* by Deborah Ellis and *Three Cups of Tea* by Greg Mortensen are other examples.

culturally-relevant pedagogy with Muslim students on the superficial basis of the fact that the authors have Muslim names. This is not to say that there is anything wrong in principal in using these books in a public school, or to diminish their literary value, or to advocate their censorship in the context of teaching Muslim students. Not at all. But there are questions as to how to approach the use of such literature that needs to be asked. How does a Muslim student as a developing child deal with reading a text that positions the Muslim identity as a source of conflict? How is the child affected when their teacher mistakenly thinks that reading such literature is honorary to their Muslim identity? What are the most effective lenses of critical analysis for teachers to use when reading such texts to maximize academic engagement of Muslim students? This is a case where both a well-funded researcher and teachers think they are doing good work in engaging students in a culturally relevant way but are blinded to huge points of concern and consideration by either their own biases or lack of background knowledge.

The Muslim world has a fairly deep place in the history of Western literature. Most of this has followed patterns of stereotyping and demagogy, which has been notably catalogued by Edward Said in his book *Orientalism* (Said, 1979). On the other end of the spectrum there is a growing body of literature in the modern day produced by Muslims in diaspora in order to give proper portrayal to Islamic morals and values. Some of these were studied by Torsten Janson (2017) in the Sweden who found that Islamic literature produced in diaspora follows along cultural patterns of morality, and is a crossroads of local concerns and international tendencies that can provide unique depictions of the diasporic space that Muslim students exist in; providing the opportunity for much discussion that connects to student background knowledge (Janson, 2017). There is much to be drawn from such literature, while at the same time not all of it is appropriate for use in public school if they go beyond the realm of being cultural exposés and into the realm of direct teaching of religious indoctrination into young readers. Avoiding that is one of the criteria I used for selecting texts that I recommend forthcomingly.

Based on my own research, I propose to set up a framework of five categories in which books that feature Muslims can fall into and be categorized by in order to gain a broad understanding of how these books portray Muslims and religious identity. They are:

1. Books that are offensive to religious sensibilities
2. Books where Muslims are cast as victims
3. Books where Muslims are tokenized
4. Refugee and Immigrant narratives
5. Books that authentically honor and relate religious identity

The fifth category is the most rare to find, but is also the one with the most potential to draw upon latent background knowledge in students. These books are what I am focused on recommending. I will walk through the first four categories, explain some books in these categories that *are* commonly used in public schools, the pitfalls and considerations that go along with them, and offer alternatives that fit better into the fifth category but could accomplish the same goals these books set out to serve.[591]

Books that are offensive to religious sensibilities

Examples of books in the first category are *Persepolis* by MaryJane Satrapi (2003) and *The Kite Runner* by Khaled Hosseini (2004). In *Persepolis*, which takes place in post-revolutionary Iran in the 1980s, God is pictoralized and cursed at, something very offensive to Islamic sensibilities; and any character that is visually depicted as religious (the book is a graphic novel), by adorning a beard in men or conservative dress in women, is also portrayed as angry, arrogant, and hostile. There is a whole chapter of the book entitled "the veil" that is devoted to portraying wearing the hijab as being a tool of oppression (Elsherief, 2019). Women's rights in the Muslim world and geopolitical conflicts are certainly legitimate topics to address and discuss in public schools. However, approaching the topic through a book like this where they are characterized in an intertwined and extreme context can create emotional complications for Muslim students. There are more positive and effective alternatives for analyzing the same issues.

The Green Bicycle by Haifaa Al-Mansour (2015) is solid alternative to use for analysis of women's issues in the Muslim world in a non-politicized context. Haifaa Al-Mansour is a Saudi author. A movie was made for this book which was the first motion picture ever to be filmed in Saudi Arabia. The book is about a 13-year-old girl who wants to win her Qur'an recitation competition so that she can purchase a bicycle. Since she is coming of age in a very conservative culture she has to confront questions about whether or not her local society would consider it appropriate for a girl who has just arrived at puberty to be riding a bike in public. The book that addresses women's rights in the Muslim world in a context that is basic to real-life, not fraught with extremes, and authentic to the spectrum of debate that Muslims genuinely have.

In *The Kite Runner* there is similar casting of religious signifiers only being associated with people who are oppressive, simple-minded, and rigid; and also contextualized into an extreme

---

[591] Again, none of this is to say that the books I criticize here cannot, or should not, be used in classrooms. Indeed, I believe public schools can be a place for Muslim students to engage with texts that have malcharacterizations of Muslims. But the key questions pertaining to that are what critical lenses are best used? And how has their identity as a Muslim been previously honored in the classroom or school so that they will not feel put upon, and a safe relationships exists with the teacher?

geopolitical conflict. Such as when the book's protagonist returns to Kabul and witnesses the stoning of an adulteress by a member of the Taliban at a soccer stadium. The executioner pronounces before performing the stoning that, "We are here today because of the will of Allah and the word of the Prophet Muhammad, peace be upon him." Such jargon as referring to the will of Allah and wishing peace and blessings on the Prophet Muhammad ﷺ is something that belongs to the everyday lexicon of Muslims, as you have learned in this book. Yet, *The Kite Runner* only sees fit to utilize this lexicon in controversial situations with antagonistic characters.

Both *Persepolis* and *The Kite Runner* are compelling dramas and books that do contain value for literary analysis. I myself have co-taught in classrooms where these books were used as core texts with Muslim students. But it is difficult for Muslim students when these books are taught and the teacher is not able to have consideration for these types of malcharacterizations of religious people. So those characterizations themselves should be analyzed, and the agenda behind them on the part of the author should be questioned. What should also be questioned is the impact on Western society's perception of the Muslim world when books such as these are turned into bestsellers and made into major motion pictures.

Books where Muslims are cast as victims

A common example of a book where Muslims are portrayed as victims is *The Breadwinner* by Deborah Ellis (2000). Also part of the cottage industry of literature set in Taliban-ruled Afghanistan, this book is about a Muslim girl who has to dress up as a boy in order to go out and earn a living in the local market to support her family after their father is incarcerated by the Taliban. This book is common enough in school curriculums that reactions to it by Muslim students have been analyzed before by a researcher. This found that many students might find the book engaging, yet feel internally uncomfortable and confused about the negative portrayal in the book of Muslim females as belonging to an exotic culture that demonizes women who are in need of saving (Elsherief, 2019).

As mentioned before, *The Green Bicycle* can be used if the goal is to analyze women's rights issues in the class. If the goal is to analyze a situation centered on geopolitical conflict in the Muslim world, I recommend as an alternative *Where the Streets had a Name* by Randa Abdel-Fattah.[592] This book is set in the context of the Israeli-Palestinian conflict and it follows the plot structure of the quest narrative. It is about a Palestinian girl who lives in the occupied West Bank. The dying wish of her grandmother is to return to their home on the other side of the wall

---

[592] Randa Abdel-Fattah is a Muslim Australian author with several books that are worth checking out. In particular her first novel *Does My Head Look Big in This Thing?*, about the first person experience of a 16-year-old Muslim girl living in the West who decides to start wearing the hijab full-time might be especially interesting for some readers.

that encloses the Palestinian territories. So the girl sneaks to the other side to return to their home and gather soil from their old home to bring back to her grandmother. On the way she is aided by both Jews and Christians in her mission, setting up the context of cross-religious cooperation and empathy.

Unlike *The Breadwinner*, this book is written by a Muslim author, and it is apparent in the way the characters interact with one another and speak to one another that they come from a Muslim family. In *The Breadwinner*, which was written by a non-Muslim Canadian woman, there is nothing about the way the ladies in the protagonist's family interact with one another that would indicate that they are anything other than liberal white women from the West.

Another grossly tone deaf aspect of *The Breadwinner* is the fact that the main character chooses to dress up and disguise herself as a boy, and it brings up no moral conflict whatsoever within her family. This would almost certainly never happen in a Muslim family because Islam explicitly forbids and condemns for one to imitate the opposite gender.[593]

Books where Muslims are Tokenized

Examples of books that tokenize Muslims can be found in the "Salaam Reads" books published by Simon and Schuster. Simon and Schuster took on a project where they solicited aspiring authors to submit stories that featured Muslim characters, however, they provided a caveat that they did not want books that had anything to do with Islam actually (Alter, 2016); hence excluding as a prerequisite the most critical component of being Muslim. What results is books like *The Gauntlet* by Karuna Riazi. This book is essentially a take on *Jumanji* with Muslim child characters who partake in a "bewitched" board game and enter a parallel world (Riazi, 2017). There is a contradiction here that goes unattended to in the book in that Islam condemns witchcraft as forbidden in the strongest sense[594], yet the Muslim kids in the book partake in it ho-hum. There is much surface-level symbolism in the book's setting of the Eastern world, such as building types and food names, but its cultural depth stops there. This is the essence of tokenism, and the book's storyline also plays on old stereotypes of the Middle East as being a place of fantasy that Western literature has exhibited for centuries (Said, 1979).

Muslim students might enjoy such a book for the literary value it has as an adventure story and the quaintness exhibited by seeing cultural artifacts that they might relate to, especially if they are South Asian in this case. Yet, at the same time some of those artifacts might not be familiar

---

[593] Sunan Abī Dawūd Book 43 Hadith 158 https://sunnah.com/abudawud/43/158, Sunan Abī Dawūd Book 34 Hadith 78 https://sunnah.com/abudawud/34/78
[594] Saḥīḥ al-Bukhārī Book 76 Hadith 78 https://sunnah.com/bukhari/76/78

to a Muslim South-Asian child born in America who had not experienced the "old world" that their parents came from. In the cases of many such children it could well be that exposés of cultural practice directly related to religion are better suited for building upon already-existing background knowledge. It should be noted also that Simon and Schuster is the book publishing branch of the Central Broadcasting Station (CBS). CBS's television channels have been a main solicitor of television series that negatively portray Muslims, especially with portrayals of Muslims as being dangerous terrorists, that there has been in more recent times (Durkay, 2014; Teitelbaum, 2017). So there is more than a bit of smarminess to their claiming to produce a book project to honor Muslims.

Refugee and Immigrant narratives

There are many books that attempt to tell the stories of refugee narratives and several of these revolve around Muslim peoples. There are little to no drawbacks about these texts in and of themselves, however, the ones that feature Muslims are ones in which the religious identity is only something passive. Therefore the books lack the potential to draw on that aspect of background knowledge. Some of these may explicate a narrative that is overly pro-American and perceived as degrading by the home community that the author represents (Smith, 2018). There are a number of books that feature Somali refugee narratives. Among these are two that are geared towards young readers, yet, are not written by Somalis themselves. They are *Through My Eyes* by Tammy Wilson (2016) and *The Color of Home* by Mary Hoffman (2012).

Through My Eyes is written by a Principal from St. Cloud, MN and is a first person narrative about a Somali girl who migrates from Somalia to St. Cloud. Similar to the *The Breadwinner*, these books are written by non-Muslim authors who are attempting to write the story of people they know, but of whom they do not have the actual first-person experience themselves, in order to try to fill the market gap that exists in literature that tells these stories. There is nothing wrong with this in and of itself, but the degree to which these authors are removed from the communities whose stories they are trying to tell influences the degree to which the narratives can be taken to be authentic.

Another potential drawback about immigrant and refugee narratives is that they can be overdone in ESL classes or schools with high immigrant populations. This happens because, if the students are an ethnically heterogeneous group of immigrants, the fact that they are immigrants is seen by the school staff as a unifying identity marker amongst them. If the student group is ethnically homogenous, an immigrant identity is something that teachers have less nerves themselves about delving into, so these books might be read more for the comfort of the teacher than anything else. I have known it to be a problem for some students that they find every year in ESL classes or Language Arts that they are reading narratives and doing study units on immigration, and they come to find it to be patronizing. So I advise teachers to be wary about over-doing the immigration angle with students.

I have known some Somali students, particularly females, who were very interested in the book *Through My Eyes*, but only because it was so rare for them to see any book at all that featured a Somali protagonist. I use this book to prompt students into reflecting on the fact that there is a heavy interest that exists for their own story, and reading the book ought to reveal to them that they could do a better job telling their story than one that is already published. There is a career in writing waiting for whichever one of them wants to take it.

A nice alternative elementary school book for a refugee narrative is the book *Ayeeyo's Golden Rule* by Mariam Mohammed. It is written by a Somali fourth grade teacher from Minnesota. *Ayeeyo* is the Somali word for grandmother. The book is about a girl who immigrates from Somalia to America. She is nervous about it but the golden rule that her grandmother teaches her is that, "no matter where you go in life if you are humble people will respect you". So true. In this the book provides a wonderful opportunity to bring up the value of humbleness and humility in the classroom. The title of the book also brings up the opportunity to bring up the Christian golden rule and relate it in a context that provides for cross-cultural comparison of values.

Books that authentically honor and relate religious identity

Books that authentically honor the Muslim identity and connect to latent background knowledge on students have the potential to reach and engage a wide amount of students from a variety of Muslim backgrounds. Examples that could be used as central classroom texts will be summarized here.

Elementary School

- **It's Ramadan Curious George** by H. A. Rey and Hena Khan

This book is an excellent primer on Ramadan and some customs surrounding it that Muslims practice. It shows that even a lovable mischief-prone monkey can make friends with a Muslim kid named Kareem. I believe it is appropriate in the younger ages that inclusion of religion in curricula material is kept to the realm of examining celebrations and more cosmetic aspects of religious practice. This book can be nicely compared to *Curious George A Very Monkey Christmas*, a much older text. A notable difference between the two is that in the Christmas book George actually celebrates Christmas himself, implying that George is a Christian, whereas in the Ramadan one he only facilitates a friend's observance and celebration, implying that

George is not Muslim. And that is fine. We do not need Curious George to be a Muslim, he can just be our friend.

There are still several benefits and accurate portrayals in the book. We get to see the Man in the Yellow Hat wearing a yellow fez, as well as the comic relief of George mistakenly trying to put all the shoes of the local mosque's congregants into the charity baskets he is helping them put together. Don't worry, the Imam stops him before things get out of hand. Hena Khan, co-author of this book, has authored several other titles featuring Muslim characters that can be looked up and would be good to include in early elementary classroom libraries. The book *Happy Hanukkah Curious George* can be used to further the cross-cultural comparisons to include a Jewish holiday.

- **Night of the Moon** by Hena Khan

This is a great book to broach and educate about the traditions of Ramadan for a more sophisticated elementary audience. It follows the Ramadan journey of Yasmeen, an elementary school girl, through many of the traditions and technicalities of Islam during Ramadan. It shows how the moon sighting and phases work throughout the month, and how the Islamic calendar differs from the Gregorian calendar. It has a wonderful scene where Yasmeen is in her classroom and her teacher asks if anyone knows what fasting is and she gets to experience the excitement of being the one in class who knows and can share. When *eid al fitr* arrives at the end of the book Yasmeen's parents gift her a telescope. So she can now fulfill the interest in tracking the moon phases that Ramadan has stimulated in her, and have her interest in science nurtured as well.

- **Time to Pray** by Maha Addasi

Recommended by the *School Library Journal* and *American Library Association* for K-12 books on Islam[595] and books on Islam for Children and teens, *Time to Pray* tells the story of a young American girl visiting her grandmother in a far-off, but unnamed, Arab country.

The beautiful concepts illustrated in this work are numerous. The honor of cross-generational respect and tradition. A vivid portrayal and demystification of what the practice of praying in Islam actually looks like. The characterization of peace, community, and tranquility in the

---

[595] The *School Library Journal* has book recommendations for portrayal of the practices of Judaism as well. The American Library Association has books on the Hindu celebration of Diwali and there are many well known books that feature practices associated with Christmas and Easter. Teachers should select books that give students exposure to real world practices of a variety of global faith traditions.

developing world, as well as the longing hearts of family members separated by the distance of the world.

An interesting feature of this book is that it is written in both English and Arabic. Many of your Muslim students, even non-Arab ones, will know how to read the Arabic script from having memorized the Qu'ran in mosques or at home. You may have them read some lines from the book and give them the chance to display this unique skill to their classmates, if they are not too shy.

- ***Deep in the Sahara*** by Kelly Cunnane

The dress of Muslim women is long mischaracterized in the Western World; if not as a sign of oppression than at least a source of bewilderment and strangeness to the Western observer. This book portrays the very real ambition of young Muslim girls to one day be old enough to where the hijab (or *mulafa* as the full length garment is referred to in Mauritania where the book is set). The book portrays the many associations of beauty, maturity, and wisdom that Islamic dress represents to young Muslim girls, and would portray an alternative narrative to stereotypical impressions.

Interesting about this book is that it is illustrated by a Muslim lady, but the author is actually a non-Muslim who spent two years living in Mauritania. She arrived in the country carrying the impressions of Western stereotypes about Islamic dress, but came away from her time there with a fond respect for it that inspired her authorship of the book. Her story, told in the back, may spur as fruitful a discussion as the book itself in your classroom about cross-cultural experience.

- ***My Name is Bilal*** by Asma Mobin-Uddin

A book that can spur discussions about bullying, courage, race, accepting others, and the struggle of cross-cultural assimilation, all while respecting and showing an authentic portrayal of the heritage of Muslims. This book is highly recommended.

Bilal and his sister Ayesha move to a suburban town where being Muslim makes them stick out. Bilal is afraid to tell people his real name and says it is "Bill" and his middle name is "Al". Ayesha gets bullied for wearing her hijab. Thankfully, a teacher in the school is Muslim and mentors Bilal. He gives Bilal a book that is a biography of Bilal ibn Rabah رضــــي الله عــنـه, a famous companion of the Prophet Muhammad ﷺ who was and African slave that was freed by another of the Prophet's ﷺ companions after being tortured for accepting Islam. The Prophet ﷺ later appointed him to be the Muslims' treasurer, and he was the first Muslim ever to do the call to prayer. Through the biography Bilal learns courage and forgiveness. The next time his sister is bullied he stands up for her, but later on he makes amends with the bully. An absolutely beautiful story that gives a real life illustration of how the lives of religious figures in Islam inspire Muslims. A unique feature about this book that should not go unnoticed is that it is centered on *male* characters, which is harder to come across when it comes to children's books that feature Muslims.

- **Cinderella: An Islamic Tale** by Fawzia Gilani

Many teachers use the story of Cinderella to meet the #.9 reading standard strand[596] of the Common Core, which asks students to compare and contrast themes in similar stories from different cultures, as variants of the story of Cinderella exist in many different cultures. *Cinderella: An Islamic Tale* by Fawzia Gilani's is a *beautiful* illustration of Islamic values for children. This is a book that can bring cardinal features of the virtues and values that Muslim students are taught to honor and adhere to at home into the classroom. Many common Arabic phrases that are known as second nature to Muslims are used in the book.

There is a rich analysis to be done from this book in comparing and contrasting the virtues of Zahra (Cinderella) that are extolled, vs. the virtues of Cinderella in the traditional English tale, as well as others. Another example of a fine point to be made that richly illustrates cultural difference is that the story in this book is devoid of any "magic" or supernatural conjuring and figures, which would be deemed un-Islamic, in stark contrast to almost all other versions of the Cinderella story. This author has also written *Snow White: An Islamic Tale*, and an Islamic version of *Sleeping Beauty*. All of which are worth checking out.

This is one of the top books that I recommend. Despite being a picture book its lexile range is actually better suited for middle school. I think it can be used for any grade from fourth to eighth. I have taught it in 8th grade as part of a comparative study with a traditional English version and a Greek version. There are resources from that unit available on abrahameducation.com.

- **The Grand Mosque of Paris: A Story of How Muslims Rescued Jews During the Holocaust** by Karen Gray Ruelle

---

[596] The fourth grade version of this standard reads "Compare and contrast the treatment of similar themes and topics (e.g., opposition of good and evil) and patterns of events (e.g., the quest) in stories, myths, and traditional literature from different cultures". As grade levels increase the standard stays the same but the complexity of the standard's wording increases. http://www.corestandards.org/ELA-Literacy/RL/4/#CCSS.ELA-Literacy.RL.4.9

There is an endless array of topics we commonly examine in school to which this book can connect. But perhaps most importantly it is a vivid portrayal of one of the numerous historical instances of cooperation and mutual assistance taking place between Muslims and Jews. Instances that historically far outweigh those of confrontation that are often pointed at in the media. The advent of the Israeli-Palestinian conflict in the 20th century has unfortunately put us currently in a time where there is increased consternation between Jews and Muslims in the world. It is important that students learn that this consternation is a historical aberration and not a norm. This book, complete with vivid imagery, recounts how the central mosque in Paris, the oldest Islamic institution in Europe outside of Spain, was a central haven for Jews who were being hunted in Nazi occupied France during World War II. These Jews and Muslims both primarily came from Morocco where they had shared a millennia old history of living together in cooperation as neighbors. Teachers ought to read the book *Memories of Absence: How Muslims Remember Jews in Morocco* by Aomar Boum to know more about the historical background of the peoples featured in *The Grand Mosque of Paris*. Boum's book, as well as *Lives in Common: Arabs and Jews in Jerusalem* by Jaffa and Hebron Menachem Klein, and the article "How Islam Saved Jewry" by David Wasserstein, are all texts written by Jewish academics that inform about this important history of cooperation, mutual benefit, and neighborliness between Muslims and Jews that has characterized the vast majority of their history living side by side.

Informational Texts

- **1001 Inventions & Awesome Facts from Muslim Civilization** by National Geographic

This is the elementary book that was published essentially as a companion to a museum event done by National Geographic in London. This book is very appealing visually, it uses a variety of visuals and text boxes to categorically show the wide spectrum of contributions of Muslim civilizations to the world. A great text for research and teaching about text features in the middle elementary grades. There is also a teacher's guide developed by National Geographic available online for this.

- **1001 Inventions - The Enduring Legacy of Muslim Civilizations** by National Geographic

This is the more sophisticated text by National Geographic that can be used with high school readers. Organizing Muslim contributions to civilization into nine categorical chapters. This book is also very visually appealing and quite detailed in its history and drawing connections between the historical development of the Eastern and Western world. This book is also good for giving students the appropriate background information for understanding how certain historical narratives have played out in the Muslim world versus the Western world. In the Western world the Renaissance and the Enlightenment are periods that are highly lauded for their advancements in science and technology. In turn, they are also associated with sparking an initial unraveling of religiosity in the West, which would really start to gain steam in the 19th century after the French revolution, and then hit mainstream culture in America in the mid 20th century.

In the Muslim world the highly lauded era of scientific development and advancement preceded the time period of the Enlightenment. Unlike the Western world, advancement in science and technology in the collective consciousness of the Muslim world took route due to an increase and arrival of religiosity and not the opposite. A major part of this was rooted in the scholarship of Islamic sciences. So the Muslim world views the West's Renaissance and Enlightenment as something that resulted from their increased contact and borrowing with the Muslim world following the Crusades in the medieval period. This book can act as essentially a catalog of the details covering that confluence and borrowing that happened between the Muslim world and the West.

- ***The Genius of Islam: How Muslims Made the Modern World*** by Bryn Bernard

Written by Bryn Barnard, a western academic of the Muslim world, this book tells the history of Muslim's major contributions to the modern world in a more conscience narrative form. It also has beautiful visuals as well. Perhaps *you* did not even know that modern day hospitals, leather bound books, and optic surgery were all spawned from the inventions of Muslim scholars. Well, now you and your students can discover that and much more with this awesome book, which is well-suited for middle school.

- ***Lost History*** by Michael Hamilton Morgan

A trade paperback narrative telling of the history of Muslim civilizations contributions to the modern world. Published by National Geographic and written for a commercial audience, this book has an interesting and engaging style of mixing narratives into each given period that is discussed (with which the author takes some artistic liberty) while elucidating information and connections to our modern times. If not used with students, this book could be beneficial for teachers to read to advance their own knowledge about this topic to better prepare themselves for teaching the lower-level National Geographic books.

- ***Destiny Disrupted: A History of the World Through Islamic Eyes*** by Tamim Ansari

This is a decent book for world history teachers to have who want to get at least a window into how the Muslim world has experienced history differently than the West and I have found using select chapters from it to be useful in World History classes. If nothing else the introduction to the book is good for illustrating that this conundrum exists when the author recounts his experience of working on a counseling panel to advise a curricular developer on the creation of a world history textbook. He found that his own priorities as having been raised in the Muslim world for what should be emphasized in the book were vastly different than the other consultants who were from the West. The history recounted in the book can be a decent beginning place to learn about the historical developments that caused sectarian divisions in the Muslim world. Though the reader should be mindful when reading about these that the book is influenced by the author's own biases.

Secondary School

- **Sophia's Journal** by Najiyah Diana Maxfield

Perfect for middle school or early high school, this is a compelling novel that centers on a teenage Muslim girl with an interesting twist that makes *Sophia's Journal* an unmatchable book in connecting to Muslim students with an American identity. Sophia is a 16-year-old girl in 21st century Kansas who, upon falling into a river, finds herself back in time in the pioneer days of the 19th century during the historical era and locale that is known as "Bleeding Kansas". Still a Muslim, she must navigate explaining her identity to pioneer folk, with them being confused by her and mistaking her as Jewish. While also examining this historical period of America first hand through her own moral lens as a Muslim; weighing things such as treatment of Native-Americans and slavery in the light of the teachings of her religion. It is a book where her religious identity is prominent, but not the source of the book's conflict. The story's conflict is her attempt to free a slave from a neighboring family alongside the Christian daughter of the family that has taken her in. The slave they are trying to free it turns out is also a Muslim, and his story is loosely based on Abdurahman ibn Sori, who I taught you about in chapter two.

This book is an engaging narrative that easily intertwines to other academic topics and themes. Sophia's Muslim character comes out in her phrases and perspective that will be easily recognizable to Muslim students, but in need of explanation for non-Muslim students (just like it is unrecognizable to the people of the pioneer days that Sophia confronts). A creative way of approaching the issue of people in America being confused about one's Muslim identity, which of course still happens today.

Since this is one of the best books I can recommend, on abrahameducation.com I have a fully comprehensive teacher's guide to this book. It takes you through chapter by chapter and points out specific connections to be made with Muslim students, and gives the instructor background knowledge on them. I also have scaffolded reading assignments available there for each chapter following the format I laid out in chapter five.

- **The Autobiography of Malcolm X** as told to Alex Haley

Of all the books recommended here this is the one that schools are most likely to already have, especially urban ones. However, the use of this book in schools is almost entirely isolated to using it as a vehicle to focus on race. Nothing wrong with that use of it at all, in fact it is one of the best texts that can be found for that. It is a rather thick book, and nowadays teachers are generally afraid to have students read the entirety of any thick book. So it is used only by reading excerpts, and usually these are selectively chosen to focus on ones that are purely about race. Particularly common is excerpts from the second chapter, entitled "Mascot", where Malcolm describes the way he perceived white people looking at him as a youth.

With Muslim students the parts in the book about his various religious awakenings that went on in his life cannot be ignored, especially chapter 17 that recounts his visits to the Muslim world and the city of Mecca. The opportunity should not be missed to use this book to teach students about the whole history of Muslims in America, in which Malcolm X's life and the movements he was involved in hold a central place. Only very rarely do teachers have the appropriate background knowledge themselves in order to teach that. Thankfully, since you read chapter two of this book you now have it. There is a version of the history that I recounted in chapter two in article form available at abrahameducation.com that can be used with students to teach them that history as well.

- **The Road to Mecca** by Muhammad Asad

Novels from the first half of the twentieth century are often considered a high time in literature, and books from that era are often examined in AP or high school upper-grade literature courses. These books often play on themes of existentialism and other philosophical trends of the time in Europe and Russia that were heavily influential in the world of literature and elsewhere.

The Road to Mecca is a memoir of sorts written by Muhammad Asad, formerly known as Leopold Weiss, an Austrian journalist in the early twentieth century who converted to Islam during his ventures in the Arab World. In one part this book articulates the place and worldview of Islam within the philosophical discussions that took place in European academia during the early 20th century. But it is also a gripping tale of Asad's journey in serving the founding King of Saudi Arabia, assisting the native Libyan's in a resistance against colonizing Italy, and moving on to being Pakistan's ambassador to the United Nations; helping that country to write its founding constitution in the post-partition era.

Chapter 7: FINAL CONSIDERATIONS

Thank you for staying with me this long. I promise we are almost done but I do not want to let you go without talking about a few more things for us to consider. Every recommendation that has been made so far has been things that can be done at the school level or the level of teacher-student interaction within the classroom. It is not really my business to focus on institution-level reform, that is something that is much more political and frankly difficult for anyone to make changes in, while our smaller interpersonal interactions with students and families is where the heart and soul of education actually occur. Still, before departing I want to offer a few suggestions that maybe go a little beyond the school level of implementation.

The first is having a chaplaincy program. This can be done at the school level, but would almost certainly involve approval, planning and preparation at least at the district level in order to implement. To many, the idea of chaplains in K through 12 schools seems odd because, for the most part, schools have not wanted to touch it with a 10-foot pole. But we need to consider and understand that chaplaincy programs are approved by courts and funded by taxpayers for legislatures, the military, police forces, hospitals, medicare programs, and universities throughout the country.

I can find only a few cases where chaplains were invited to public school classes to give pep-talks, counsel, or in some cases lead prayers and invocations to football teams. It appears in these instances the schools had not set up the procedures to make the mentoring opt-in, so it raised alarms amongst some parents, or outside parties, and complaints ensued. Once the complaints came, schools did not want to deal with a court battle or even just bad press and they shut the programs down. So the legality of a chaplaincy program, opt-in or otherwise, in the public schools has never been ruled upon in the court system from what I can find. The status of chaplaincy programs in the legislature and military have been, and their legality has been overwhelmingly confirmed by courts. There really is no reason, from what I can tell, that a chaplaincy program in the public schools could not be ruled constitutional under the same grounds that it is ruled constitutional in these other governmental agencies. Nevertheless schools and districts who think this might be a good idea for their context ought not to take solely my word for it, they have to seek legal counsel that is available to them. Likely, a school district that did institute a chaplaincy program would want to prepare itself for a legal battle. At the same time I believe this likelihood would be greatly reduced if the program was only served to students whose families explicitly opted them into it.

The military especially has exhaustive protocols and criteria for its chaplaincy program that school districts can draw upon and perhaps alter the language of in order to apply to their own contexts. But among the duties of military chaplains is leading members in religious services and offering religious counsel. The Supreme Court has already ruled that when a governmental entity has an ostensible secular purpose to implement a policy or program there is nothing wrong if it correlates to the same desires of a sectarian interest within the body that the governmental entity.[597]

As I have recommended before, schools and districts should be proactive about seeking information and feedback from the families they serve about how they would like their children's religious rights to be asserted in the public schools. A good starting place for this would be to hold informational seminars that include community discussions to make families aware of what their religious rights are. The federal government's guidelines can be used for this. These seminars should be culturally competent and sensitive, use translators when necessary, and also give parents and families opportunities to offer inputs and make requests anonymously. It is my plan in the future to have translations of the federal guidance on religious rights in the public schools posted in Somali and Arabic on abrahameducation.com.

If the feedback districts take from the sessions informed them that they have an ostensible secular purpose to hire a chaplain due to the expressed desires of the families they serve, then they should consider doing it. It has the potential to greatly smooth out the issues associated with accommodating prayers in the school. The informational seminars give parents the chance to opt into the services explicitly, so the chaplain does not need to operate in any way where they service a student who is not explicitly opted in by either themselves or their parents.

A chaplain could also provide the service of counseling students in the school in a way that explicitly relates their conduct and choices to God and religion. That there are secular benefits to this is well-confirmed in scientific research. Brain scan studies that analyze the neurobiological components of religious belief have shown that being prompted to think about doctrinal concepts activates neural networks associated with intrinsic reward and motivation of positive behavior in religious individuals (Ferguson et al, 2018). Aggregate reviews of neuroscience studies on religion conclude that it acts as an effective remedy to anxiety induced by common life stressors, and does so better than scrutable systems of ascertaining meaning in life (Inzlicht et al, 2011). Holding religious moral attitudes shows consistent positive correlations with all executive functions measured, independent of demographic influences (Wain & Spinella,

---

[597] *Wallace v. Jaffree, 466 U.S. 924* [1984]. Justice Stevens in the majority opinion, "*...it is inevitable that the secular interests of government and the religious interests of various sects and their adherents will frequently intersect, conflict, and combine. A statute that ostensibly promotes a secular interest often has an incidental or even a primary effect of helping or hindering a sectarian belief. Chaos would ensue if every such statute were invalid under the Establishment Clause.*"

2007). Studies in the social sciences have shown that intrinsic religious motivation in students is correlated to higher GPA scores, academic success, and responsibility (Kahoe, 1974); that religion increases moral behavior when the religious see morality as a set of objective truths (Shariff, 2015); that individuals who have been prompted to openly profess themselves as religious are more likely to disapprove of lying in their own interests, and less likely to engage in fraudulent behavior (Stavrova & Siegers, 2014). That religious people are more likely to be honest in comparison to secular people has been shown in studies that analyzed females in particular (Arbel et al, 2014), as well as ones that compared people who believed in a God that dispensed punishment for sin to secularists and those who did not (Shariff & Norenzayan, 2011).

Brain scan studies also show that when individuals perceive threats to their religious identity it induces activity in neural networks associated with antagonism and consternation (Holbrook et al, 2016). It is more than reasonable to conclude that Muslim students are at greater risk for perceiving these threats on a day-to-day basis than other students. Whether from the society in general or from the school itself, where a lack of understanding of Islam on the part of the staff can cause well-intended people to fall into all sorts of missteps and be unequipped to provide appropriate accommodations, which in turn threaten student religious identity by implicitly telling them it is unwelcome.

Schools will of course always have the position of non-endorsement of any religious belief and can always make disclaimers to that effect. The goal of school is to educate and nurture young people to have a healthy and productive life that provides the opportunity to achieve success in the material world. But there is more than enough in empirical research to lend us to the conclusion that there are secular-world benefits for carefully considering how we approach students' religious identity and accommodate their religious rights in our schools. The reality is, at least one generation of Muslims in America has already been irreparably damaged by the school system's inability or unwillingness to engage in this discourse and make these considerations. I do not advise drastic measures. But I do believe that at least small incremental steps with due consideration for some of the propositions in this book, or to at least start thinking about them, is warranted.

Of course, a chaplain service is not something that would only benefit Muslim families, nor should it. The military surveys the religious identity of its members and uses the results to determine quotas for their hiring of chaplains of different denominations. The vast majority of course being Christian. The Medicare program, entirely funded by taxpayers like the military, requires that patients going into hospice care are given a spiritual evaluation and assigned denominational chaplains [598]

If the funding issue still scares schools and districts they could at least work with community organizations to see if they can find volunteer chaplain services. There are schools who have done this in coordination with police departments, and from what I can tell the state of Oklahoma has had chaplaincy programs in its schools for 18 years now. I recommend interested schools or districts look at the documents that are available publicly from the military concerning the regulations and implementation of their chaplaincy program as a basis from which to start exploring this. [599]

For the second and third recommendations I am going to make, I will take inspiration from the late Warren Nord who authored the book *Does God Make a Difference?*. Nord was a well respected academic of the humanities and professor at the University of North Carolina at Chapel Hill who published this book in 2010. He was stricken with leukemia as he authored it and passed away only 11 days after sending his final edits to Oxford University Press, and never lived to see it be put to print. From what I can tell this has affected the extent to which this book is known, as Nord was not around after its publishing to be able to promote it. To this day I have tried to bring the book up to many people who are in public education and academia and I have yet to meet another person who had heard of it before my mention of it to them. But I think what Charles C. Haynes, a well respected lawyer, director of the Religious Freedom Center, and leading scholar of first amendment issues in public schools, wrote in the book's introduction is probably correct. That the book is "the most important book ever written about the role of religion in American education" (Nord, 2010, pg. vii).

Nord argues for the inclusion of religious perspectives and ways of understanding the world as live options in life in the school curriculum, as well as the societal need for schools to set teaching basic religious literacy as a goal for students. Nord's argument is not made from a religious perspective, rather it is made as an educational, civic, and constitutional argument for giving students a truly liberal education, based on the ideals espoused by liberal education's advocates and founding principles.

---

[598] See the Centers for Medicare and Medicaid Services State Operations Manual
https://www.cms.gov/Regulations-and-Guidance/Guidance/Manuals/downloads/som107ap_m_hospice.pdf
[599] "Appointment of Chaplains for the Military Departments"
https://www.esd.whs.mil/Portals/54/Documents/DD/issuances/dodd/130419p.pdf
"Guidance for the Appointment of Chaplains for the Military Departments"
https://www.esd.whs.mil/Portals/54/Documents/DD/issuances/dodi/130428p.pdf?ver=2019-02-26-152326-953

Nord effectively argues that when students are provided in all disciplines of the academic curricula with only a set of secular conceptual nets that let all things religious slip through the mesh, then education indoctrinates them into a secular mentality that marginalizes and implicitly discredits contending religious interpretations of the world and various subjects in the curriculum. All of this done without due justification within the ideals of a liberal education.

Nord offers topical considerations for all academic disciplines. But an essential recommendation he makes is that high schools include a year-long required course in religious studies, and that districts have a religious studies department. Of course, these would be classes that observe the difference between religious education and indoctrination. Indoctrination, as Nord defines it, asserts concepts and ideas as absolute truths that are not to be contended with, and trains and socializes pupils into their adherence. Education on the other hand requires students to acquire critical distance from the subject matter that they study in order to practice the ability to articulate, compare, and analyze contending ways of understanding subjects. Nord argues that when only secular ways of looking at the world are offered and articulated in schools, without due consideration and examination given to religious ways of looking at the world and the conceptual resources that the world's religions have developed to sustain themselves in human history against potentially falsifying arguments; students are effectively inuring a secular indoctrination from the school system that is unconstitutional.

Currently, study of religions in schools, if treated at all, is usually relegated to the area of world history courses. The overall effect of the minimal treatments religious studies are given might do more harm than good, and no doubt contributes to the major problem of religious illiteracy in American society. A problem that produces violence, social discord, and all of the health issues associated with the atomization of our country's people. I suggest all educators read Nord's book, but even more so if they serve students and families for whom they know religion is important.

Religious Perspectives in Language Arts Curricula

Let's walk through a specific curricular idea to model thinking about diversifying content-area learning in language arts by including religious perspectives. Language Arts is probably the content area where learning philosophical worldviews has its most explicit place in the curriculum, and the prominence of secularist and anti-theist ways of looking at the world are ubiquitous within it. Just consider two of the most commonly read books in American high schools, the short novel *Night* by Eli Wiesel and the play *The Crucible* by Arthur Miller. I will add a third book to consider in this discussion, *The Plague* by Albert Camus, which is read in many high schools and colleges but does not appear as commonly as the other two in high school. However, since we are now teaching a generation of students who will have lived through the

COVID-19 pandemic, Camus's book is certainly going to be making its way into many curriculum plans. I myself read and studied these books in high school growing up, and have taught language arts classes as a teacher where these books were used as core class texts. When one studies what curriculum exponents urge to be taught with these books, and what students are supposed to be prompted to consider when reading them, inevitably with all three the teacher is supposed to ask questions that prompt the students to consider what the books tell us about the "nature of humanity". [600]

When I teach language arts to 11th graders at the beginning of the year and am setting up a framework for how we will study literature, I use a chapter from the 1917 textbook *A Brief History of English Literature* by Robert Huntington Fletcher called "How to Study and Judge Literature". The book is revealing because, 1.) it can inform us how educated people who wrote literature in the 20th century interpreted literature's purpose; and 2.) it still offers a good foundational framework for how to analyze and study literature, a framework that we should not deny students in the modern era.

Fletcher said the direct study of literature itself should "aim first to add an understanding of the literature as an expression of the author's views of life". So when we ask students what books say about the nature of humanity, what we should really be asking is "what is the nature of humanity according to the author's view of life?" But when we ask the question generally without relating it to the author's own subjectivity, which is generally what curriculum guides lead teachers to do with these books, we are implying that the author's view is an absolute truth. After all, the author is presented to the students as someone who is expert and skilled enough to have had their work canonized into the school curriculum and the bona fide institution of public schools. So instead of analyzing literature as a medium by which author's propagate their own subjective view of life by seeking to emotionally attach the reader to it, Language Arts study is often designed to induce students to imbibe the author's point of view as the nature of humanity. Indeed, classically the authors most honored in the tradition of English literature are ones who wished that their literature would be used to impart their own personal views of the world on the literate society, and in turn influence the direction of societal norms and ways of thinking. For a long time, centuries even, literature and the media has played this role in the Western world. In the Muslim world, this role has always been the domain of religion. In this sense, literature in the Western world and the inspiration it is intended to provide the populace is akin to being religious from a Muslim perspective.

---

[600] Just a few examples… https://tinyurl.com/ycaj4s5z, https://tinyurl.com/yymo5lks, https://tinyurl.com/25s9zcc

What is the common thread between these three books? The answer is the French philosopher Jean-Paul Sartre. Wiesel was a close friend of Sartre's during their time at Sorbonne University. Camus was a friend of Sartre's in the military and a political activist with him. Miller was from the other side of the ocean to Sartre in America, but Sartre was impressed enough with Miller's work that he chose to write the screenplay for the adaptation of *The Crucible* into a 1957 motion picture.

Why is it important to understand the link of Sartre between these three authors? Because the authors all share in the basic principles of Sartre's worldview and philosophy, and their books are mediums by which that worldview is propagated. This is why over a decade before *Night* or *The Crucible* were ever even written we find Sartre declaring "God is Dead" in an essay he wrote entitled "A New Mystic". Lo and behold, upon reading these books we find that the exact same phrase is declared and agreed to by the protagonists in both *The Crucible* and *Night*.[601] Where do you suppose Wiesel and Miller received the inspiration to include this as critical points in their books?

Sartre was a staunch anti-theist philosopher. This is why all three of these books emotionally connect the reader to a protagonist whose development in the novel causes them to consider and believe in the boilerplate atheist critiques of religion and belief in God; the monotony and uselessness of ritual, the paradox of a benevolent God allowing suffering and persecution, the sad burden of love desire being restrained by doctrine, the persecution and isolation of having heterodox thoughts in a religious society, and the superficiality and thoughtlessness of religious commoners fueled by the violent fanaticism of religious zealots in leadership. Meanwhile the protagonists who see these things clearly are themselves portrayed as innocent, scientifically objective, alone and persecuted in their sincerity, and noble fighters for the common man.

So as teachers and curricula developers we can pretend that these books are meant to prompt students to construct their own conclusions about the nature of humanity. But in reality, the conclusion the reader is meant to draw from the books has been predetermined and pre-ordained by the biases of the authors themselves: religion and religiosity is anti-intellectual and the root of all evil, and the noble and clear-headed ought to reasonably conclude its lack of purpose, hypocrisy, and destructive nature through the rigors of their own trials.

---

[601] In *The Crucible* see page 119 of the edition published by Penguin Books ISBN 978-0140481389, and in *Night* see page 34 of the edition published by Hill and Wang ISBN 978-978-0374500016

Of course the authors were very smart, sophisticated, and well-educated literaries when they wrote these books. So how is an adolescent who believes in God supposed to defend his or herself against them? Especially when no pro-theist way of thinking or rebuke of the linchpins of atheist reasoning is offered in curriculum. It is perfectly reasonable for someone to interpret this as biased anti-religious propagation in the schools that verges on indoctrination. It occurs in public schools all the time and has for decades, even if done so unwittingly by its purveyors, and I propose we stop pretending otherwise. We should instead be able to be professional enough to have honest discussions about the viewpoints that are put across in our curriculum and the implications of its impact upon all students, and perhaps Muslim students in particular; a class of students who come from families and a community that is wholly dependent on a religious way of looking at the world in order to sustain its health both as a community and as individuals, yet, is still a religious minority in the society that has to constantly drag through the detriments of being misunderstood, manipulated, and scapegoated.

No I do not advocate that these books in this discussion not be used, to the contrary, and as I said, I use these books in my own classes. In fact, they *should be* taught to students if for nothing else to know the influence that the philosophy they represent has had on Western society and its own ways of looking at the world, as well as their cultural impact. *The Crucible* has made the term witch-hunt, nomenclature that everyone uses. *Night* has contributed to nurturing society's deep empathy and sensitivity for Holocaust survivors. *The Plague* was a Nobel prize winning book, and after COVID-19 its full impact on Western societies collective consciousness and habits of reflecting on meaning in life and the nature of humanity have yet to even be fully played out.

But what I do when I study these books with my students is study them in light of the guidelines set up by Fletcher. So we do not ask what the books tell us about the nature of humanity, we ask what the author *is trying to get the reader to accept* about the nature of humanity. The difference here is crucial, and it is essential to observe in order to truly practice out the ideals of a liberal education. The goal is to undertake a type of clinical analysis where the student takes on critical distance from the subject to attempt to first fully understand it, and then analyze it as objectively as possible. It might be hard for anyone to be truly objective, of course, but no worldview can be looked at objectively without the inclusion and consideration of countering points of view. This is the real goal of a liberal education where all, or at least a spectrum, of viewpoints are authentically considered.

So I am not advocating that these books or the other books with similar themes like them be taken from the school shelves. Rather let's use them, but let's balance them with literature that can truly offer a wider spectrum of viewpoints, as well as give students the chance to look behind the curtain. So let's say we devote the entirety of 10th or 11th grade to reading these three books. For one year we can have students totally take in the canonical atheist literature. No problem with that as it has been influential on society and a truly liberal education is going to have them aware of it. But the following year I propose we have them do a study of autobiographies. Let's have them read four different autobiographies, written by people of the same tumultuous early-to-mid 20th century time period, but each of which articulates the author's own mental development of their view of theism in life. Each one arriving at a different conclusion, and each one coming from a slightly different place.

For the first biography I propose the students read *The Words* by Jean Paul Sartre. This is his own autobiography of his years aged 0 to 10 that talks explicitly about how his childhood experiences, especially under a doting grandfather who was a Catholic priest, led him to the anti-atheist dispositions that he held and propagated throughout his life; which would influence the authors of the books the students would have read the previous year.

For the second book, students can read the autobiography of CS Lewis, *Surprised by Joy*. Lewis was raised Christian, became atheist as an adult, and then went back to Christianity as a more mature adult with some different understanding of it from his childhood. He was a popular and influential novelist in his own right. Most famously having written *The Lion, the Witch, and Wardrobe*, which many students still read in elementary school. But when students studied that book in fifth grade they would not likely have been told that he was also one of the most influential writers and thinkers upon Christian theology and articulation of Christian thought in the 20th century. Having influenced Christian dialectics and discourse amongst Christians from a broad spectrum of denominations.

Third, I propose students read the autobiography of Ben Hecht, *A Child of the Century*. Hecht was born to Jewish immigrants in America in the early 20th century and was one of the most influential film directors in the history of Hollywood. His autobiography exhibits the struggle of religious identity in a diaspora immigrant community in America. One that experiences all sorts of societal pressure to suppress religious identity. Hecth finds the capitulation to these pressures of many members of the Jewish-American community to be a source of frustration and identity conflict for him. Hecht, for his part, chooses that his Jewish identity is very important to him, as well as his belief in God despite many around him choosing atheism. His articulation of his own belief in God comes from a place of being Jewish, but it is also one that incorporates personal subjectivity into what he interprets as right and wrong as opposed to a strict reliance on doctrine.

For the fourth autobiography students can read *The Road to Mecca* by Mohamed Asad, formally named Leopold Weiss. Weiss grew up as a Jew in Austria and became a journalist in Palestine and other Arab countries at a young age and eventually converted to Islam, and I discussed him and this book in the previous chapter. In it he reflects on the 20th-century cultural and philosophical climate of the West at the time. Doing so from having lived most of his adult life from afar in the East. He reflects upon the dueling history of the East and West and the continuing struggle to move forth and learn from one another in a tumultuous yet ever-globalizing world.

All four of these autobiographies are of men who came of age during a critical historical juncture. Just as the world was feeling the brunt of change from new technology of the industrial revolution, while in the midst of world wars, pandemics, and economic crises that rent the world asunder and caused people to deeply reflect upon the nature of their humanity and the future of the world. This time period and the philosophical ways of thinking that emanated from it have influenced who we are today. Yet, we are also far enough removed from it now that we can examine these ways of thinking with a critical lens during the present time when history is clearly repeating itself, and challenging us to both learn from and strengthen our intellectual battles of the past. We can and should ask students to consider the nature of their humanity. The critiques and dialectics of the anti-theist proponents can be brought to students in a liberal education, there is nothing wrong with that whatsoever. But if we pretend, or even are unaware ourselves, that the pro-theists have not considered and developed the conceptual and intellectual lines of thinking to address, rebuke, and cohabitate these critiques, we are being disingenuous to the goals and ideals of a liberal education; while also dis-servicing and patronizing the young but energetic minds of our students.

I offer the reading program outlined here in order to model a way of thinking about our curriculum that broadens our own horizons of consideration as public school educators. I recommend teachers to partake in this type of practice. It would give students the tools to see a spectrum of thinking about life's central questions, as it would also give them the tools to see that there is both commonality and rational thought in the way the world can be viewed and assessed by people of different dispositions towards proposed solutions to life's problems, as well as its ultimate meaning. When these tools and perspectives are offered to students is when we will begin to see them actually engage in the critical types of dialogue and inquiry that have energy behind them, that are built on a truly solid foundation of knowledge that makes use of the intellectual resources in their home-cultural bank, and that we all want to experience with students in our classrooms.

EPILOGUE

I would like to thank you, the reader, again for reading this book. The Prophet ﷺ said:

He who does not thank the people does not thank Allah.[602]

So accordingly, I thank you and I thank and praise Allah for giving me the ability to do this project. Any good that comes from this effort is due to Allah only and His Greatness. Any wrong that comes from it is due to the deficiencies in my own soul.

One after effect from this learning that my trainees experience is often the feeling that others need to know this information. If you feel that way please consider recommending the book to a colleague and leaving a positive review of it on Amazon, as this helps it spread.

Another after effect my trainees often felt was that there is quite a lot to digest. And that is okay. Sometimes being spurred with more questions is how one knows they are on a path to finding solutions. With any idea or strategy you chose to take from this book. I encourage you to start small, and focus on building up incrementally. This book may have taught you things that you realized you needed to learn. Just know that with each step you take in implementing something new, along with it will come the realization of even more things you need to learn. But trust that you can get to know the soul of your students, and you can come to know them and their families better than anyone else who is trying to influence your decision-making in your classroom. You can be empowered by that sentiment, and being empowered by that you can free yourself from the shackles of top down forces that are too commonly at play in our public schools, which are meant to serve local communities. As a colleague of mine once said, *sometimes it seems like everything in public education today is trying to prevent a natural conversation from taking place.*

I know from my great experiences with my trainees that the sentiment at this point is often that maybe the discussion has really only just begun, and it needs to continue. I share that sentiment as well. If you wish to be a part of this discussion as it goes on, you will not find me on social media, so please sign up at abrahameducation.com. May peace be with you.

---

[602] Sunan Abī Dawūd Book 43 Hadith 39 https://sunnah.com/abudawud/43/39

REFERENCES

Abdi, C. (2015). *Elusive Jannah : The Somali diaspora and a borderless Muslim identity / Cawo M. Abdi.* Minneapolis: University of Minnesota Press.

Abbas, T. (2003) The Impact of Religio-cultural Norms and Values on the Education of Young South Asian Women, *British Journal of Sociology of Education*, 24:4, 411-428, https://doi.org/10.1080/01425690301917

Abraham, S. Y., & Abraham, N. (1983). *Arabs in the New World: Studies on Arab-American communities.* Detroit, Mich: Wayne State University, Center for Urban Studies.

Abraham, M. (2019). "How Can The Cultural Funds Of Muslim Students Be Utilized By Public School Educators To Increase Academic Engagement?" *School of Education Student Capstone Projects.* Hamline University. 337. https://digitalcommons.hamline.edu/hse_cp/337

Abu El-Haj, Thea R. (2002). Contesting the Politics of Culture, Rewriting the Boundaries of Inclusion: Working for Social Justice with Muslim and Arab Communities. *Anthropology and Education Quarterly 33*(3), 308-316. https://eric.ed.gov/?id=EJ656738

Adams, G., & Engelmann, S. (1996). *Research on Direct Instruction: 25 years beyond DISTAR.* Seattle, WA: Educational Achievement Systems.

Ahlstrom, Sydney E. (2004) *A Religious History of the American People*, 2nd ed., Yale University Press, p.1067.

Ahmad, I. (2003). Muslim Children in Urban America: The New York City Schools Experience. *Journal of Muslim Minority Affairs.*

Ahmed, A. (2015). "Somali Parents' Involvement in the Education of their Children in American Middle Schools: a Case Study in Portland, Maine" *Electronic theses and Dissertations.* 2402. Retrievable from http://digitalcommons.library.umaine.edu/etd/2402

Ahmed, S., Rapoport, Y. (2010). *Ibn Taymiyya and his times.* Karachi: Oxford Univ. Press.Alegría, M., Canino, G., Shrout, P. E., Woo, M., Duan, N., Vila, D., Torres, M., Chen, C. N., & Meng, X. L. (2008). Prevalence of mental illness in immigrant and non-immigrant U.S. Latino groups. *The American journal of psychiatry, 165*(3), 359–369. https://doi.org/10.1176/appi.ajp.2007.07040704

Alitolppa–Niitamo, A. (2004). Somali youth in the context of schooling in metropolitan Helsinki: A framework for assessing variability in educational performance. *Journal of Ethnic and Migration Studies, 30*(1), 81-106.

Allen, M. L., Elliott, M. N., Fuligni, A. J., Morales, L. S., Hambarsoomian, K., & Schuster, M. A. (2008). The relationship between Spanish language use and substance use behaviors among Latino youth: a social network approach. *The Journal of adolescent health : official publication of the Society for Adolescent Medicine, 43*(4), 372–379. https://doi.org/10.1016/j.jadohealth.2008.02.016

Allyn, D. (2000). *Make love, not war: The sexual revolution, an unfettered history.* New York: Little, Brown & Company.

Alshaibani, M. (2017). *Compensatory Damages Granted in Personal Injuries: Supplementing Islamic Jurisprudence with Elements of Common Law.* Mauerer School of Law Theses and Dissertations. Indian University. 35. Retrievable from:

https://www.repository.law.indiana.edu/etd/35

Alter, A. (2016, February 24). Simon & Schuster Creates Imprint for Muslim-Themed Children's Books. *The New York Times*.

Anderson, C., Carnagey, N., & Eubanks, J. (2003). Exposure to Violent Media: The Effects of Songs With Violent Lyrics on Aggressive Thoughts and Feelings. *Journal of Personality and Social Psychology*, 84(5), 960-971. Retrievable from
https://www.apa.org/pubs/journals/releases/psp-845960.pdf

Ansari, G. (1960). *Muslim caste in Uttar Pradesh: A study of culture contact*. Lucknow: Ethnographic and Folk Culture Society.

Arab American Institute [AAI] (1997). Not Quite White: Race Classification and the Arab American Experience. Retrievable from:
http://www.aaiusa.org/not-quite-white-race-classification-and-the-arab-american-experience

Arab American Institute [AAI] (2019). Ensuring a Fair and Accurate Count in the 2020 Census: Promoting Representation of Our Communities. Retrievable from
https://www.aaiusa.org/2020census

Arbel, Y., Bar-El, R., Siniver, E., & Tobol, Y. (2014). Roll a die and tell a lie–What affects honesty?. *Journal of Economic Behavior & Organization*, 107, 153-172.
https://psycnet.apa.org/doi/10.1016/j.jebo.2014.08.009

Aronoff, S.L., Berkowitz, K., Shreiner, B., Want, L., (2004). Glucose Metabolism and Regulation: Beyond Insulin and Glucagon. *Diabetes Spectrum, July 17(3)*, 183-190.
https://doi.org/10.2337/diaspect.17.3.183

Awasthi, B. (2017). From Attire to Assault: Clothing, Objectification, and De-humanization - A Possible Prelude to Sexual Violence? *Frontiers in Psychology*, 8, 338.
https://doi.org/10.3389/fpsyg.2017.00338

Aziz, M. A. (2011). *The Kurds of Iraq: Ethnonationalism and national identity in Iraqi Kurdistan*. London: I.B. Tauris.

Bagby, I. (2011). The American Mosque 2011 Basic Characteristics of the American Mosque Attitudes of Mosque Leaders. *US Mosque Study 2011*, (1), 13–17. Retrieved from
https://www.cair.com/wp-content/uploads/2017/09/The-American-Mosque-2011-part-1.pdf

Benlahcene, B. (2013). *The Socio-Intellectual Foundations of Malek Bennabi's Approach to Civilization*. International Institute of Islamic Thought. London.

Barrett, P. (2007). *American Islam : The struggle for the soul of a religion* (1st ed.). New York: Farrar, Straus and Giroux.

Barth, E. M., Krabbe, E. C. (1982). *From Axiom to Dialogue: A Philosophical Study of Logics and Argumentation*. Germany: De Gruyter.

Basford, L. (2008) From Mainstream to East African Charter: Cultural and Religious Experiences of Somali Youth in U.S. Schools. *Journal of School Choice* 4:4, pages 485-509.
https://doi.org/10.1080/15582159.2010.526859

Beynon, Erdmann Doane (1938). The Voodoo Cult among Negro migrants in Detroit. *American Journal of Sociology*. 43 (6): 894–907.
https://www.journals.uchicago.edu/doi/abs/10.1086/217872?mobileUi=0

Berger, A. T., Widome, R., & Troxel, W. M. (2018). School Start Time and Psychological Health in Adolescents. *Current sleep medicine reports, 4*(2), 110-117. https://doi.org/10.1007/s40675-018-0115-6

Berns-McGown, R. (1999) *Muslims in the Diaspora : The Somali Communities of London and Toronto.* University of Toronto Press.

Bernstein, D. A., Clarke-Stewart A., Edward, J. R., Penner, L. A., (2003a). *Health, Stress, and Coping.* In *Psychology* (6th ed. pp. 494-495). Houghton Mifflin Company. Boston/New York.

Bernstein, D. A., Clarke-Stewart A., Edward, J. R., Penner, L. A., (2003b). *Cognition and Language.* In *Psychology* (6th ed. pp 283-284). Houghton Mifflin Company. Boston/New York.

Blair, S., & Bloom, J. (2012). The Mirage of Islamic Art: Reflections on the Study of an Unwieldy Field. *Journal of Art Historiography,* (6), 152-184. Retrievable from https://arthistoriography.files.wordpress.com/2012/05/blairbloomdoc.pdf

Blum, I., Koskinen, P., Tennant, N., Parker, E., Straub, M., & Curry, C. (1995). Using audiotaped books to extend classroom literacy instruction into the homes of second-language learners. *Journal of Reading Behavior, 27(4),* 535-563

Bigelow, M. (2008). Somali Adolescents' Negotiation of Religious and Racial Bias In and Out of School. *Theory Into Practice: Immigrant Families and US Schools, 47*(1), 27-34. https://doi.org/10.1080/00405840701764706

Bigelow, M. (2010). *Mogadishu on the Mississippi: language, racialized identity, and education in a new land.* Chichester, West Sussex, U.K.;: Wiley-Blackwell.

Boissoneault, L. (2018). Amelia Bloomer Didn't Mean to Start a Fashion Revolution, But Her Name Became Synonymous With Trousers. *Smithsonian Magazine.* May 24.

Bongers, P., van den Akker, K., Havermans, R., & Jansen, A. (2015). Emotional eating and Pavlovian learning: Does negative mood facilitate appetitive conditioning? *Appetite,89,*226-236. https://doi.org/10.1016/j.appet2015.02.018

Borman, G. D., Hewes, G. M., Overman, L. T., & Brown, S. (2003). Comprehensive School Reform and Achievement: A Meta-Analysis. *Review of Educational Research, 73*(2), 125-230. https://doi.org/10.3102/00346543073002125

Bornstein, M. H. (1995). Form and function: Implication for studies of culture and human development. *Culture and Psychology, 1*(1), 123-137. https://doi.org/10.1177%2F1354067X9511009

Borzi, P. (2010, September 05). In the Heat of Camp, the Hunger of Faith. *The New York Times.* Retrieved from https://www.nytimes.com/2010/09/06/sports/football/06fasting.html

Boswell, R. G., & Kober, H. (2016). Food cue reactivity and craving predict eating and weight gain: a meta-analytic review. *Obesity reviews : an official journal of the International Association for the Study of Obesity, 17*(2), 159-177. https://doi.org/10.1111/obr.12354

Brittingham, A., de la Cruz, P. (2005). We the People of Arab Ancestry in the United States. U.S: Census 2000 Special Reports. *U.S. Department of Commerce Economics and Statistics Administration U.S. Census Bureau.* March. Retrievable from https://www.census.gov/prod/2005pubs/censr-21.pdf

Broughton, R. J., & Dinges, D. F. (1989). *Sleep and alertness: chronobiological, behavioral, and medical aspects of napping.* New York: Raven Press.

Bruner, R. (2001). Repetition is the First Principle of All Learning. University of Virginia Darden School of Business. Retrieved from
https://papers.ssrn.com/sol3/papers.cfm?abstract_id=224340

Brunzell, T., Stokes, H., & Waters, L. (2016). Trauma-Informed Positive Education: Using Positive Psychology to Strengthen Vulnerable Students. *Contemporary School Psychology, 20*(1), 63-83.
https://psycnet.apa.org/doi/10.1007/s40688-015-0070-x

Burger, E. B., Chard, D. J., Kennedy, P.A., Leinwand, S. J., Renfro, F. L., Roby, T. W., Seymour, D. G., Waits, B. K., Holt McDougal., & Houghton Mifflin Harcourt Publishing Company. (2012). *Holt McDougal Geometry Common Core Edition.* Orlando, Fla: Holt McDougal.

California., & California. (1997). *California teacher preparation for instruction in critical thinking: research findings and policy recommendations.* Sacramento, Calif: Commission on Teacher Credentialing, State of California. Retrieved from
https://files.eric.ed.gov/fulltext/ED437379.pdf

Carskadon, M.A., Vieira, C., Acebo, C. (1993). Association between Puberty and Delayed Phase Preference, *Sleep.* Volume 16, Issue 3 May. Pages 258–262.
https://doi.org/10.1093/sleep/16.3.258

Celce-Murcia, M., Brinton, D., & Goodwin, J. (2010). *Teaching pronunciation : A course book and reference guide* (2nd ed.). New York: Cambridge University Press.

Central Intelligence Agency [CIA]. (2015). Iraq. *In The world factbook.* Retrieved from
https://www.cia.gov/library/publications/the-world-factbook/geos/iz.html

Chen, M., Miller, B., Grube, J., & Waiters, E. (2006). Music, Substance Use, and Aggression. *Journal of Studies on Alcohol, 67*(3), 373-381. https://doi.org/10.15288/jsa.2006.67.373

Chang, K. (2009). Creationism, Minus a Young Earth, Emerges in the Islamic World. *The New York Times.* November 02. Retrieved from
https://www.nytimes.com/2009/11/03/science/03islam.html

Chiu, C. W. T. (1998, April). *Synthesizing metacognitive interventions: What training characteristics can improve reading performance?* Paper presented at the Annual Meeting of the American Educational Research Association San Diego, CA. Retrieved from
https://files.eric.ed.gov/fulltext/ED420844.pdf

Clegg, C. (1997). *The Life and Times of Elijah Muhammad* (First ed.). New York: St. Martin's Press.

Cole, M. (1995). Culture and cognitive development: From cross- cultural research to creating systems of cultural mediation. *Culture and Psychology, 1*(1), 25-54.
https://doi.org/10.1177%2F1354067X9511003

Congressional Research Service (CRS), (2020). Global Refugee Resettlement: Selected Issues and Questions. *CRS Reports.*
Retrievable from https://crsreports.congress.gov/product/pdf/IF/IF10611

Corrie, B. P. (2015). *The Economic Potential of African Immigrants in Minnesota.* TheMcknight Foundation. Minneapolis: MN. Available at:
http://www.csp.edu/wp-content/uploads/2015/07/AFM-Report2015.pdf

Cottrell, A. (1980). *The Persian Gulf States: A General Survey*. John Hopkins University Press. Baltimore and London. pg. 309.

Cristillo, L. A. (2008). Religiosity, education and civic belonging: Muslim youth in New York City public schools. A research report. New York: Teachers College, Columbia University.

Cummins, J. (1989). *Empowering Minority Students*. California Association for Bilingual Education, Sacramento, CA.

Danielson, C. (2013) Rubrics from the Frameworks for Teaching Evaluation Instrument. *The Danielson Group*. Retrievable from: https://www.danielsongroup.org/framework/

Davison, R. H. (1960). Where Is the Middle East?. *Foreign Affairs*. July. Retrieved from https://www.foreignaffairs.com/articles/middle-east/1960-07-01/where-middle-east

De Voe, P. (2002). Symbolic Action: Religions Role in the Changing Environment of Young Somali Women. *Journal of Refugee Studies, 15*(2), 234-246.

Denton, C. A., & Al Otaiba, S. (2011). Teaching Word Identification to Students with Reading Difficulties and Disabilities. *Focus on exceptional children, 2011*, 254245149.
https://www.ncbi.nlm.nih.gov/pmc/articles/PMC4299759/

Denton, C. A., Fletcher, J. M., Taylor, W. P., Barth, A. E., & Vaughn, S. (2014). An Experimental Evaluation of Guided Reading and Explicit Interventions for Primary-Grade Students At-Risk for Reading Difficulties. *Journal of research on educational effectiveness, 7*(3), 268-293.
https://doi.org/10.1080/19345747.2014.906010

Diamond, J. (1997). *Guns, Germs, and Steel : The fates of human societies* (1st ed.). New York: W.W. Norton.

Dobmeier, R. (2011). School Counselors Support Student Spirituality through Developmental Assets, Character Education, and ASCA Competency Indicators. *Professional School Counseling, 14*(5), 317-327.https://doi.org/10.1177%2F2156759X1101400504

Douglass, T. (2005). Changing Religious Practices among Cambodian Immigrants in Long Beach and Seattle. In K. I. Leonard (Ed.), *Immigrant faiths : Transforming religious life in America* (pp. 123-144). Walnut Creek, CA: AltaMira Press.

Drevno, G., Kimball, J., Possi, M., Heward, W., Gardner, R., & Barbetta, P. (1994). Effects of active student response during error correction on the acquisition, maintenance, and generalization of science vocabulary by elementary students: A systematic replication. *Journal of Applied Behavior Analysis, 27*(1), 179-180. https://www.ncbi.nlm.nih.gov/pubmed/16795822

Dulong, J (2005). The Imam of Bedford-Stuyvesant, *Armco World: Arabic and Islamic Cultures and Connections*. May/June 2005, volume 56, number 3. Retrieved from:
http://archive.aramcoworld.com/issue/200503/the.imam.of.bedford-stuyvesant.htm

Dunst, C. J., Hamby, D. W., Howse, R. B., Wilkie, H., & Annas, K. (2019). Metasynthesis of Preservice Professional Preparation and Teacher Education Research Studies. *Education Sciences, 9*(1), 50.
https://doi.org/10.3390/educsci9010050

Dupuy, B., & Prather, S. (2015). Columbia Heights walkout protests anti-Muslim comment. *The Star Tribune*. September 17, 2015. Retrieved April 29, 2020, from https://tinyurl.com/y94genp5

Dupuy, B. (2017). Minnesota Somali students beat competition in Qur'an contest. The Star Tribune. April 3. Retrieved from https://tinyurl.com/yd7w3p5b

Durkay, L. (2014). 'Homeland' is the most bigoted show on television. The Washington Post. October 2nd.

Durrant, J., & Ensom, R. (2012). Physical punishment of children: lessons from 20 years of research. *CMAJ : Canadian Medical Association journal = journal de l'Association medicale canadienne, 184*(12), 1373–1377. https://doi.org/10.1503/cmaj.10131

El-Sayed, O. (2004). Engineering and Engineering Education in Egypt, Proceedings of the 2004 American Society for Engineering Education Annual Conference & Exposition. Kansas. 2004. https://peer.asee.org/engineering-and-engineering-education-in-egypt

Elsherief, H. (2019). Put Muslim characters who don't need to be 'saved' on school reading lists. *The Conversation*. April 30. Available at https://tinyurl.com/ycrccur8

Erricker, C., Levete, J., Erricker, Jane, & Levete, Gina. (2001). *Meditation in schools a practical guide to calmer classrooms* (Continuum studies in pastoral care and personal and social education). London; New York: Continuum.

Evans, A. D., & Lee, K. (2011). Verbal deception from late childhood to middle adolescence and its relation to executive functioning skills. *Developmental psychology, 47*(4), 1108–1116. https://doi.org/10.1037/a0023425

Fahlman, L. (1984) Toward understanding the lived-world of Lebanese Muslim students and their teachers. *University of Alberta PhD Thesis*. National Library of Canada.

Farid, M., & McMahan, D. (2004). *Accommodating and educating Somali students in Minnesota schools : A handbook for teachers and administrators.* Saint Paul, Minn.: Hamline University Press.

Felter, C., McBride, J. (2018). How Does the U.S. Refugee System Work?. *Council on Foreign Relations.* October 10. Retrievable from https://www.cfr.org/backgrounder/how-does-us-refugee-system-work

Ferguson, M. A., Nielsen, J. A., King, J. B., Dai, L., Giangrasso, D. M., Holman, R., Korenberg, J. R., & Anderson, J. S. (2018). Reward, salience, and attentional networks are activated by religious experience in devout Mormons. *Social neuroscience, 13*(1), 104–116. https://doi.org/10.1080/17470919.2016.1257437

Foley, G. N., & Gentile, J. P. (2010). Nonverbal communication in psychotherapy. *Psychiatry (Edgmont (Pa. : Township)), 7*(6), 38–44. https://www.ncbi.nlm.nih.gov/pubmed/20622944

Fontana, D., & Slack, I. (2007). *Teaching meditation to children : The practical guide to the use and benefits of meditation techniques.* London: Watkins.

Fountas, I. C., & Pinnell, G. S. (1996). *Guided reading: Good first teaching for all children.* Portsmouth, NH: Heinemann.

Frederking, L. (2007). *Economic and Political Integration in Immigrant Neighbourhoods:Trajectories of Virtuous and Vicious Cycles.* Susquehanna University Press.

García Coll, C., & Kerivan Marks, A. (2012). *The Immigrant Paradox in Children and Adolescents: Is Becoming American a Developmental Risk?* American Psychological Association. https://www.apa.org/pubs/books/4318097

Gebara, C. F., Ferri, C. P., Lourenço, L. M., Vieira, M., Bhona, F. M., & Noto, A. R. (2015). Patterns of domestic violence and alcohol consumption among women and the effectiveness of a brief intervention in a household setting: a protocol study. *BMC women's health, 15*, 78.

https://doi.org/10.1186/s12905-015-0236-8

Gilbert, D. (2004). Racial and religious discrimination: The inexorable relationship between schools and the individual. *Intercultural Education, 15*(3), 253-266.

Ging, D., & Siapera, E. (2018). Special issue on online misogyny. *Feminist Media Studies, 18*(4), 515-524. doi: 10.1080/14680777.2018.1447345

Glasswell, K., & Ford, M. (2011). Let's Start Leveling about Leveling. *Language Arts, 88*(3), 208-216. Retrievable https://core.ac.uk/download/pdf/143885072.pdf

Gordon, H. (1990). *Naguib Mahfouz's Egypt : Existential themes in his writings.* (Contributions to the study of world literature, no. 38). New York: Greenwood Press.

Grinder, M. (2001). *Envoy: Your Personal Guide to Classroom Management* (6th Ed.). Michael Grinder & Associates.

Guarini, T., Marks, A., Patton, F., & Coll, C. (2011). The immigrant paradox in sexual risk behavior among Latino adolescents: Impact of immigrant generation and gender. *Applied Developmental Science, 15*(4), 201-209. https://doi.org/10.1080/10888691.2011.618100

Guo, Yan. (2011). Perspectives of immigrant Muslim parents: Advocating for religious diversity in Canadian schools.(Researching Bias). *Multicultural Education, 18*(2), 55-60. Retrievable from https://files.eric.ed.gov/fulltext/EJ951848.pdf

Gupta, U., & Singh, P. (1982). An exploratory study of love and liking and type of marriages. *Indian Journal of Applied Psychology, 19*,92-97 https://psycnet.apa.org/record/1985-19991-001

Haller, E. (1988). Can Comprehension Be Taught? A Quantitative Synthesis of "Metacognitive" Studies. *Educational Researcher, 17*(9), 5-8. https://doi.org/10.3102%2F0013189X017009005

Hattie, J. (2009). *Visible learning : A synthesis of over 800 meta-analyses relating to achievement.* London ; New York: Routledge.

Hernandez, D. J., Denton, N. A., Macartney, S., & Blanchard, V. L. (2012). *Children in immigrant families: Demography, policy, and evidence for the immigrant paradox.* In C. G. Coll & A. K. Marks (Eds.), *The immigrant paradox in children and adolescents: Is becoming American a developmental risk?* (p. 17-36). American Psychological Association.https://psycnet.apa.org/record/2011-09286-001

Higgins, A. (2019). How an African Prince Who Was Kidnapped Into Slavery Outsmarted His Captors. *History.* February 08. Retrieved from https://www.history.com/news/african-prince-slavery-abdulrahman-ibrahim-ibn-sori

Hill, S., Lippy, C., & Wilson, C. (2005). *Encyclopedia of religion in the South / edited by Samuel S. Hill and Charles H. Lippy ; consulting editor, Charles Reagan Wilson.* (2nd ed. revised, updated, and expanded. ed.). Macon, Ga.: Mercer University Press.

Holdaway, D. 1979. *The Foundations of Literacy.* Toronto, Ashton Scholastic.

Hosseini, H. (2018). Dearborn-Detroit Michigan: Ethnography of Faith and the U.S. Domestic and Foreign Policy Axis. *World Sociopolitical Studies, 2*(1), 69-86. doi: 10.22059/wsps.2018.65219. https://wsps.ut.ac.ir/article_65219.html

Hosseini, K. (2004). *The Kite Runner.* (1st Riverhead trade pbk. ed.). New York: Riverhead Books.

Holbrook, C., Izuma, K., Deblieck, C., Fessler, D., Iacoboni, M. (2016).Neuromodulation of group prejudice and religious belief. *Social Cognitive and Affective Neuroscience,* Volume 11, Issue 3, March, Pages 387-394, https://doi.org/10.1093/scan/nsv107

Hollins, E. R. (2011). Teacher Preparation For Quality Teaching. *Journal of Teacher Education, 62*(4), 395–407. https://doi.org/10.1177/0022487111409415

Hoy, A. (2010). *Educational psychology / Anita Woolfolk*. (11th ed.). Upper Saddle River, N.J.: Merrill.

Howard, T. (2002). Hearing Footsteps in the Dark: African American Students' Descriptions of Effective Teachers. *Journal of Education for Students Placed at Risk (JESPAR), 7*(4), 425-444. https://doi.org/10.1207/S15327671ESPR0704_4

Hussein, F. (2012). Charter Schools: Choice of Somali-American Parents?. *Bildhaan: An International Journal of Somali Studies*: Vol. 11 , Article 16. Available at: https://digitalcommons.macalester.edu/bildhaan/vol11/iss1/16

Huey, E. B. (1908). *The psychology and pedagogy of reading: With a review of the history of reading and writing and of methods, texts, and hygiene in reading*. New York: Macmillan.

Human Rights Watch/Middle East. (1995). *Iraq's crime of genocide : The Anfal campaign against the Kurds* (Human Rights Watch books). New Haven: Yale University Press. https://www.hrw.org/report/1994/05/01/iraqs-crime-genocide-anfal-campaign-against-kurds

Hussain, A. (2009). Faith based Peacebuilding in Pakistan. In *Making Peace with Faith: The Challenges of Religion and Peacebuilding* (ed.) Garred, M., Abu-Nimer, M. Rowman and Littlefield. New York.

Inzlicht, M., Tullett, A.M., & Good, M. (2011). Existential neuroscience: a proximate explanation of religion as flexible meaning and palliative. *Religion, Brain & Behavior, 1*, 244 - 251. https://doi.org/10.1080/2153599X.2011.653537

Iqbal, K., (2017) *British Pakistani boys in Birmingham schools : education and the role of religion*. PhD thesis, University of Warwick. Retrievable from: http://webcat.warwick.ac.uk/record=b3064242~S15

Irving, D. (2014). *Waking up white: and finding myself in the story of race* (First edition.). Cambridge, MA: Elephant Room Press.

Irwin, R. (2003). *The Arabian Nights: A Companion*. Bloomsbury Publishing.

Janson, T. (2017). Islamic Children's Literature: Informal Religious Education in Diaspora. In (Vol. 7,p. *International Handbook of Religion and Education*)

Jay, G. (1994). Taking Multiculturalism Personally: Ethnos and Ethos in the Classroom. *American Literary History, 6*(4), 613-632. https://www.jstor.org/stable/489957

Jakubowski, K., Finkel, S., Stewart, L., & Müllensiefen, D. (2017). Dissecting an Earworm: Melodic Features and Song Popularity Predict Involuntary Musical Imagery. *Psychology of Aesthetics, Creativity, and the Arts, 11*(2), 122-135. Retrievable from https://www.apa.org/pubs/journals/releases/aca-aca0000090.pdf

Jamal, A. A., & Naber, N. C. (2008). *Race and Arab Americans before and after 9/11: From invisible citizens to visible subjects*. Syracuse, N.Y: Syracuse University Press. https://press.syr.edu/supressbooks/930/race-and-arab-americans-before-and-after-9-11/J

Jones, F. H., Jones, P., & Jones, J. L. T. (2000). *Tools for teaching: Discipline, instruction, motivation*. Santa Cruz, Calif: F.H. Jones & Associates.

Jordan, W. J. (2010). Defining equity: Multiple perspectives to analyzing the performance of diverse learners. *Review of Research in Education, 34*(1), 142-178. https://doi.org/10.3102%2F0091732X09352898

Kahoe, R. D. (1974). Personality and achievement correlates of intrinsic and extrinsic religious orientations. *Journal of Personality and Social Psychology, 29*(6), 812–818.
https://doi.org/10.1037/h0036222

Kamps D, Abbott M, Greenwood C, Arreaga-Mayer C, Wills H, Longstaff J, Walton C. (2007). Use of evidence-based small-group reading instruction for English language learners in elementary grades: Secondary-tier intervention. *Learning Disability Quarterly*. 2007;30:153-168.

Kang, S., Fiske, S., Levine, F., Mayer, R., Murphy, K., Newcombe, N., & Worrell, F. (2016). Spaced Repetition Promotes Efficient and Effective Learning: Policy Implications for Instruction. *Policy Insights from the Behavioral and Brain Sciences, 3*(1), 12-19. Retrieved from
https://www.dartmouth.edu/~cogedlab/pubs/Kang(2016,PIBBS).pdf

Keady, D. A. (1999). Student Stress: An Analysis of Stress Levels Associated with Higher Education in the Social Sciences. *All Graduate Theses and Dissertations*. 2598.
https://digitalcommons.usu.edu/etd/2598

Khurshid, A. (2020). Love marriage or arranged marriage? Choice, rights, and empowerment for educated Muslim women from rural and low-income Pakistani communities. *Compare: A Journal of Comparative and International Education, 50*(1), 90-106.
https://doi.org/10.1080/03057925.2018.1507726

King, A. (1993). From Sage on the Stage to Guide on the Side. *College Teaching, 41*(1), 30-35. Retrieved from www.jstor.org/stable/27558571

Kinsey, D. (1971). Efforts for Educational Synthesis under Colonial Rule: Egypt and Tunisia. *Comparative Education Review, 15*(2), 172-187. Retrieved from www.jstor.org/stable/1186728

Kirschner, P., Sweller, J., & Clark, R. (2006). Why Minimal Guidance During Instruction Does Not Work: An Analysis of the Failure of Constructivist, Discovery, Problem-Based, Experiential, and Inquiry-Based Teaching. *Educational Psychologist, 41*(2), 75-86.

Klingbeil, D. A. (2013). Examining the evidence-base for the interventions used in a large urban district. University of Minnesota. (Order No. 3599047). Available from ProQuest Dissertations & Theses Global. (1461395997)

Klymkowsky M. W. (2007). Teaching without a textbook: strategies to focus learning on fundamental concepts and scientific process. *CBE life sciences education, 6*(3), 190–19
https://www.lifescied.org/doi/10.1187/cbe.07-06-0038

Kohli, R., & Solórzano, D. (2012). Teachers, please learn our names!: Racial microaggressions and the K-12 classroom. *Race Ethnicity and Education*, 15(4), 441-462.
https://doi.org/10.1080/13613324.2012.674026

Kohut T, Štulhofer A (2018) Is pornography use a risk for adolescent well-being? An examination of temporal relationships in two independent panel samples. *PLoS ONE* 13(8): e0202048.
https://doi.org/10.1371/journal.pone.0202048

Kuran, T. (1997). *Private truths, public lies: the social consequences of preference falsification*. Harvard University Press. 1997.
https://www.hup.harvard.edu/catalog.php?isbn=9780674707580

Kurien, D. N. (2010). Body Language: Silent Communicator at the Workplace. The IUP Journal of Soft Skills, Vol. 4, Nos. 1 & 2, pp. 29-36, March & June 2010. Available at https://papers.ssrn.com/sol3/papers.cfm?abstract_id=1610020

Lan, Yi-Chin, Lo, Yu-Ling, & Hsu, Ying-Shao. (2014). The effects of meta-cognitive instruction on students' reading comprehension in computerized reading contexts: A quantitative meta-analysis. *Educational Technology & Society, 17*(4), 186-202. https://eric.ed.gov/?id=EJ1045530

Last, M. (2000). Children and the Experience of Violence: Contrasting Cultures of Punishment in Northern Nigeria. *Africa: Journal of the International African Institute, 70*(3), 359-393. Retrieved May 6, 2020, from https://www.jstor.org/stable/1161066

Lee, J. (2019). Mediated Superficiality and Misogyny Through Cool on Tinder. *Social Media + Society.* https://doi.org/10.1177/2056305119872949

Leung, C. (1992). Effects of word-related variables on vocabulary growth through repeated read-aloud events. In C. Kinzer & D. Leu (Eds.), *Literacy research, theory, and practice: Views from many perspectives: Forty-first yearbook of the National Reading Conference* (pp. 491-498). Chicago: National Reading Conference. https://eric.ed.gov/?id=ED351671

Lever, N., Mathis, E., & Mayworm, A. (2017). School Mental Health Is Not Just for Students: Why Teacher and School Staff Wellness Matters. *Report on emotional & behavioral disorders in youth, 17*(1), 6-12. https://www.ncbi.nlm.nih.gov/pmc/articles/PMC6350815/

Levy, B. A., Abello, B., & Lysynchuk, L. (1997). Transfer from Word Training to Reading in Context: Gains in Reading Fluency and Comprehension. *Learning Disability Quarterly, 20*(3), 173-188. https://doi.org/10.2307/1511307

Lewis, P. (2007). *Young, British and Muslim.* London: Continuum International Publishing Group.

Lipka, M. (2014). Many U.S. congregations are still racially segregated, but things are changing. *Pew Research Center.* Retrieved from https://tinyurl.com/y829zpld

Lipka, M. (2015). The most and least racially diverse U.S. religious groups. *Pew Research Center .* Retrieved from https://tinyurl.com/s65wbvd

Lovato, N., & Lack, L. (2010). The effects of napping on cognitive functioning. *Progress in brain research, 185,* 155-166. https://doi.org/10.1016/B978-0-444-53702-7.00009-9

Ma, X., Yue, Z. Q., Gong, Z. Q., Zhang, H., Duan, N. Y., Shi, Y. T., Wei, G. X., & Li, Y. F. (2017). The Effect of Diaphragmatic Breathing on Attention, Negative Affect and Stress in Healthy Adults. *Frontiers in psychology, 8,* 874. https://doi.org/10.3389/fpsyg.2017.00874

Makdisi, G. (1981). *The Rise of Colleges. Institutions of Learning in Islam and the West.* Columbia University Press.

Mantilla, K. (2015). *Gendertrolling : How misogyny went viral.* Santa Barbara, California: Praeger.

Mattebo, M., Tydén, T., Häggström-Nordin, E., Nilsson, K. W., & Larsson, M. (2018). Pornography consumption and psychosomatic and depressive symptoms among Swedish adolescents: a longitudinal study. *Upsala journal of medical sciences, 123*(4), 237-246. https://doi.org/10.1080/03009734.2018.1534907

Mattson, M. P., Moehl, K., Ghena, N., Schmaedick, M., & Cheng, A. (2018). Intermittent metabolic switching, neuroplasticity and brain health. *Nature Reviews Neuroscience, 19*(2), 63-80. https://doi.org/10.1038/nrn.2017.156

Matsakis, A. (1998). *Trust after trauma: A guide to relationships for survivors and those who love them.* New Harbinger Publications, Inc. https://psycnet.apa.org/record/1998-07279-000

Marzano, R. J. (2004). *Building Background Knowledge for Academic Achievement: Research on What Works in Schools*. Alexandria, VA: ASCD.

Mazawi, A. (2002). Educational Expansion and the Mediation of Discontent: The cultural politics of schooling in the Arab states. *Discourse: Studies in the Cultural Politics of Education, 23*(1), 59-74. https://doi.org/10.1080/01596300220123042

Merry, M. (2005). Social Exclusion of Muslim Youth in Flemish— and French—Speaking Belgian Schools. *Comparative Education Review, 49*(1), 1-23. https://dx.doi.org/10.3389%2Ffnins.2013.00279

Miendlarzewska, E.A., & Wiebke, J. T. (2014). How musical training affects cognitive development: Rhythm, reward and other modulating variables. *Frontiers in Neuroscience, 7*(8), 279. https://www.frontiersin.org/articles/10.3389/fnins.2013.00279/full

Michigan Department of Community of Community Health [MDCH], (2008). *Color Me Healthy: A Profile of Michigan's Racial/Ethnic Populations*. May. 2008. pg. 21. Retrievable from: https://tinyurl.com/ybcevv9k

Mills, J. (2019). Handshakes could be banned under new 'no physical contact' rules. *Metro*. April 24. Available at https://tinyurl.com/y3vwp27d

Mischel, W., & Ebbesen, E. (1970). Attention in Delay of Gratification. *Journal of Personality and Social Psychology, 16*(2), 329. https://psycnet.apa.org/doi/10.1037/h0029815

Moaddel, M. (2014). Is Iraq Actually Falling Apart? What Social Science Surveys Show. 2014, June 6) Retrieved from https://tinyurl.com/yb4nvpp9

Mohamed, W., Elbert, T., & Landerl, K. (2011). The development of reading and spelling abilities in the first 3 years of learning Arabic. *Reading and Writing, 24*(9), 1043-1060. https://doi.org/10.1007/s11145-010-9249-8

Moore, L. C. (2011). Moving across languages, literacies and schooling traditions.(Research Directions). *Language Arts, 88*(4), 288-297. Retrievable from https://tinyurl.com/ycudawal

Moore, L. (2012). Muslim Children's Other School. *Childhood Education, 88*(5), 298-303. https://doi.org/10.1080/00094056.2012.718243

Moos, R. H. (1979). *Evaluating educational environments*. San Francisco, Calif: Jossey-Bass Publishers. https://doi.org/10.1016/0191-491X(80)90027-9

Morton, N. (2019). Seattle school district apologizes for letter asking Muslim families to reconsider students fasting during testing season. *The Seattle Times*. March 14. Retrieved from https://tinyurl.com/ya5xc7l9

Naff, A. (1985). *Becoming American: The early Arab immigrant experience*. Carbondale: Southern Illinois University Press.

NAFSA: Association of International Educators, (n.d.). The Education System in Iraq: An Overview. Retrieved January 2, 2020, from https://tinyurl.com/y6u2bsxj

National Institute of Child Health and Human Development [NICHD]. (2000). Report of the National Reading (2005). *How students learn: History, mathematics, and science in the classroom (Committee on How People Learn, a targeted report for teachers*, M. S. Donovan and J. D. Bransford, Eds.). Washington, DC: National Academies Press. https://tinyurl.com/y9hfdskq

Neece, C. L., Green, S. A., & Baker, B. L. (2012). Parenting stress and child behavior problems: a transactional relationship across time. *American journal on intellectual and developmental disabilities, 117*(1), 48–66. https://doi.org/10.1352/1944-7558-117.1.48

Neiman, B. (2015). *Mindfulness & yoga skills for children and adolescents : 115 activities for trauma, self-regulation, special needs & anxiety.* Eau Claire, WI: PESI.

Nguyen, H. (2011). Asians and the immigrant paradox, in *Asian American and Pacific Islander Children and Mental Health,* edited by Frederick Leong and Linda Juang, volume 1, pp. 1 – 22, 2011. Santa Barbara, Calif: Praeger.

Niyozov, Sarfaroz. (2008). Understanding Teaching Beyond Content and Method: Insights from Central Asia. *European Education* 40(4): 46–69.

Niyozov, S., & Pluim, G. (2009). Teachers' Perspectives on the Education of Muslim Students: A Missing Voice in Muslim Education Research. *Curriculum Inquiry, 39*(5), 637-677.

Niyozov, S. (2010). Teachers and Teaching Islam and Muslims in Pluralistic Societies: Claims, Misunderstandings, and Responses. *Journal of International Migration and Integration / Revue de L'integration et de La Migration Internationale, 11*(1), 23–40. https://doi.org/10.1007/s12134-009-0123-y

Nord, W. (2010). *Does God make a difference?: taking religion seriously in our schools and universities.* New York: Oxford University Press.

Norvilitis, J. M., Szablicki, P. B., & Wilson, S. D. (2003). Factors influencing levels of credit-card debt in college students. *Journal of Applied Social Psychology, 33*(5), 935-947. https://doi.org/10.1111/j.1559-1816.2003.tb01932.x

Ocobock, P. (2012). Spare the Rod, Spoil the Colony: Corporal Punishment, Colonial Violence, and Generational Authority in Kenya, 1897–1952. *The International Journal of African Historical Studies, 45*(1), 29-56. Retrieved May 6, 2020, from https://www.jstor.org/stable/23267170

Parekh, B. (1995). Cultural Pluralism and the Limits of Diversity. *Alternatives: Global, Local, Political, 20*(4), 431-457. https://www.jstor.org/stable/40644843?seq=1

Pavlov, I., & Anrep, G. (1927). *Conditioned reflexes; an investigation of the physiological activity of the cerebral cortex.* London: Oxford University Press: Humphrey Milford. Retrievable from https://www.ncbi.nlm.nih.gov/pmc/articles/PMC4116985/pdf/ANS1017-0309-17-136.pdf

Peach, C. (2006). South Asian migration and settlement in Great Britain, 1951-2001. *Contemporary South Asia: The British South Asian Experience, 15*(2), 133-146.

Perry, S. L. (2018). Pornography Use and Depressive Symptoms: Examining the Role of Moral Incongruence. *Society and Mental Health, 8*(3), 195–213. https://doi.org/10.1177/2156869317728373

Pew Research Center, (2006). Lebanon's Muslims: Relatively Secular and Pro-Christian. (2006, July 26). Retrieved from https://tinyurl.com/ydcexwpx

Pew Research Center, (2009). Mapping the Global Muslim Population. (2009, April 7). Retrieved from https://tinyurl.com/y49kadm7

Pew Research Center. (2011). Pew Forum on Religion & Public Life Poll: July/August 2010 Religion & Public Life Survey.

Pew Research Center. (2012). The World's Muslims: Unity and Diversity. (2012, August 9). Retrieved from https://tinyurl.com/yage4pp2

Pew Research Center. (2013). A Portrait of Jewish Americans: Chapter 4: Religious Beliefs and Practices. (2013, October 1). Retrieved from https://tinyurl.com/yb9a8tzb

Pew Research Center. (2018). The share of Americans who leave Islam is offset by those who become Muslim. (2018, January 26). Retrieved from https://tinyurl.com/u28novw

Prado, G., Huang, S., Schwartz, S. J., Maldonado-Molina, M. M., Bandiera, F. C., de la Rosa, M., & Pantin, H. (2009). What accounts for differences in substance use among U.S.-born and immigrant Hispanic adolescents?: results from a longitudinal prospective cohort study. *The Journal of adolescent health : official publication of the Society for Adolescent Medicine, 45*(2), 118–125. https://doi.org/10.1016/j.jadohealth.2008.12.011

Przychodzin-Havis, A. M., Marchand-Martella, N. E., Martella, R. C., & Azim, D. (2004). Direct Instruction mathematics programs: An overview and research summary. Journal of Direct Instruction, 4(1), 53-84.

Przychodzin-Havis, A. M., Marchand-Martella, N. E., Martella, R. C., Miller, D. A., Warner, L., Leonard, B., & Chapman, S. (2005). An analysis of Corrective Reading research. *Journal of Direct Instruction*, 5(1), 37-65.

Public Affairs Alliance of Iranian Americans [PAAIA], (2013). Iranian Americans Are A Predominantly Secular Community. (2013, May, 1). Retrieved from https://tinyurl.com/ybjrw7xx

Pulcini, T. (1993). Trends in Research on Arab Americans. *Journal of American Ethnic History, 12*(4), 27-60.

Raffaelli, M., Kang, H., & Guarini, T. (2012). *Exploring the immigrant paradox in adolescent sexuality: An ecological perspective.* In C. G. Coll & A. K. Marks (Eds.), *The immigrant paradox in children and adolescents: Is becoming American a developmental risk?* (p. 109–134). American Psychological Association. https://doi.org/10.1037/13094-005

Raghavendran, B. (2015). Dayton praises the Columbia Heights walkout, calls on board member to resign. *The Star Tribune.* September 18, 2015. Retrieved April 29, 2020, from https://tinyurl.com/y92qtyq3

Ratcliffe, M., Ruddell, M., & Smith, B. (2014). What is a "sense of foreshortened future?" A phenomenological study of trauma, trust, and time. *Frontiers in psychology, 5,* 1026. Retrievable from https://www.frontiersin.org/articles/10.3389/fpsyg.2014.01026/full

Regnerus, M. (2017). *Cheap sex : The transformation of men, marriage, and monogamy / Mark Regnerus.* New York, NY, United States of America: Oxford University Press.

Riazi, K. (2017). *The Gauntlet*(Vol. 1). New York: Salaam Reads.

Ringrose, J. (2008). 'Just be friends': Exposing the limits of educational bully discourses for understanding teen girls' heterosexualized friendships and conflicts. *British Journal of Sociology of Education, 29*(5), 509-522. https://doi.org/10.1080/01425690802263668

Ringrose, J., & Renold, E. (2013). Normative Cruelties and Gender Deviants: The Performative Effects of Bully Discourses for Girls and Boys in School. *British Educational Research Journal, 36*(4), 573-596. https://doi.org/10.1080/01411920903018117

Robb, C. A., & Sharpe, D. L. (2009). Effect of personal financial knowledge on college students' credit card behavior. *Journal of Financial Counseling and Planning, 20*(1), 25-43. Retrievable from https://files.eric.ed.gov/fulltext/EJ859561.pdf

Roberts, S. (2004). *Who we are now : The changing face of America in the twenty-first century* (1st ed.). New York: Times Books.

Rupley, W., Blair, T., & Nichols, W. (2009). Effective Reading Instruction for Struggling Readers: The Role of Direct/Explicit Teaching. *Reading & Writing Quarterly: Direct/ Explicit Instruction in Reading for the Struggling Reader: Phonemic Awareness, Phonics, Fluency, Vocabulary, and Comprehension, 25*(2-3), 125-138. https://doi.org/10.1080/10573560802683523

Said, E. (1979). *Orientalism / Edward W. Said.* (1st Vintage books ed.). New York: Vintage Books.

Salih, M. (1989). The Europeanization of War in Africa: From Traditional to Modern Warfare. *Current Research on Peace and Violence, 12*(1), 27-37. Retrieved June 5, 2020, from www.jstor.org/stable/40725112

Sarroub, L. (2005). *All American Yemeni girls : Being Muslim in a public school / Loukia K. Sarroub.* Philadelphia: University of Pennsylvania Press.

Satrapi, M. (2003). *Persepolis.* New York: Pantheon Books.

Schieffer, C., Marchand-Martella, N. E., Martella, R. C., Simonsen, F. L., & Waldron-Soler, K. M. (2002). An analysis of the Reading Mastery program: Effective components and research review. *Journal of Direct Instruction, 2(2)*, 87-119.

Sencibaugh, J. (2007). Meta-Analysis of Reading Comprehension Interventions for Students with Learning Disabilities: Strategies and Implications. *Reading Improvement, 44*(1), 6-22. Retrievable from https://files.eric.ed.gov/fulltext/ED493483.pdf

Senechal, M. (1997) The differential effect of storybook reading on preschoolers' acquisition of expressive and receptive vocabulary. *Journal of Child Language*, 24(1), 123-138. https://eric.ed.gov/?id=EJ547516

Shaheen, N. A., Alqahtani, A. A., Assiri, H., Alkhodair, R., & Hussein, M. A. (2018). Public knowledge of dehydration and fluid intake practices: variation by participants' characteristics. *BMC public health, 18*(1), 1346. https://doi.org/10.1186/s12889-018-6252-5

Shariff, A. F., & Norenzayan, A. (2011). Mean gods make good people: Different views of God predict cheating behavior. *The International Journal for the Psychology of Religion, 21*(2), 85-96. https://doi.org/10.1080/10508619.2011.556990

Shariff, A. F. (2015). Does religion increase moral behavior?. *Current Opinion in Psychology, 6*, 108-113. https://doi.org/10.1016/j.copsyc.2015.07.009

Siegel, D. J. (2013). *Brainstorm: The power and purpose of the teenage brain.* Penguin.

Singer, L. M., & Alexander, P. A. (2017a). Reading on Paper and Digitally: What the Past Decades of Empirical Research Reveal. *Review of Educational Research, 87*(6), 1007–1041. https://doi/10.3102/0034654317722961

Singer, L., & Alexander, P. (2017b). Reading Across Mediums: Effects of Reading Digital and Print Texts on Comprehension and Calibration. *The Journal of Experimental Education, 85*(1), 155-172. https://doi.org/10.1080/00220973.2016.1143794

Singer Trakhman, L., Alexander, P., & Berkowitz, L. (2019). Effects of Processing Time on Comprehension and Calibration in Print and Digital Mediums. *The Journal of Experimental Education, 87*(1), 101-115. https://doi.org/10.1080/00220973.2017.1411877

Singleton, G., & Linton, C. (2006). *Courageous conversations about race : A field guide for achieving equity in schools / Glenn E. Singleton, Curtis Linton ; foreword by Gloria Ladson-Billings.* Thousand Oaks, Calif.: Corwin Press.

Spalding, P.S. (2010). GhaneaBassiri, Kambiz. A history of Islam in America: From the new world   to the new world order. *CHOICE: Current Reviews for Academic Libraries, 48*(4), 700. https://doi.org/10.1111/j.1468-5906.2011.01577_4.x

Smith, H. K. (1967). The responses of good and poor readers when asked to read for different purposes. *Reading Research Quarterly*, 3, 56-83. https://www.jstor.org/stable/747204

Smith, P. C. (1998). *The hermeneutics of original argument : demonstration, dialectic, rhetoric.* Evanston: Northwestern University Press.

Smith, R. (2018). Tensions in Seattle Somali Communities Lead to Author's Cancellation. *The Stranger.* September 13. Retrieved from https://tinyurl.com/y9fmxf4v

Starcke, K., & Brand, M. (2012). Decision making under stress: a selective review. *Neuroscience and biobehavioral reviews, 36*(4), 1228–1248. https://doi.org/10.1016/j.neubiorev.2012.02.003

Stewart, K. (2012). How evangelicals are making children their missionaries in public schools | Katherine Stewart. *The Guardian.* September 25. Retrievable, from https://tinyurl.com/ybcocsw9

Stavrova, O., & Siegers, P. (2014). Religious prosociality and morality across cultures: How social enforcement of religion shapes the effects of personal religiosity on prosocial and moral attitudes and behaviors. *Personality and Social Psychology Bulletin, 40*(3), 315- 333. https://doi.org/10.1177%2F0146167213510951

Stetzer, E. (2017). Why do Christians keep inviting you to church? April 14. *Cable News Network (CNN).* Retrieved April 28, 2020, from https://www.cnn.com/2017/04/14/living/christians-invite-easter/index.html

Steinberg, L. (1996). *Beyond the classroom: Why school reform has failed and what parents need to do.* New York: Simon & Schuster.

Stinson, D. W. (2006). African American male adolescents, schooling (and mathematics): Deficiency, rejection, and achievement. *Review of Educational Research, 76*(4), 477-506 . https://www.jstor.org/stable/4124412

Stivers,T., Enfield, N. J. Brown, P. Englert, C., Hayashi, M. Heinemann, T . . . Levinson, S., (2009). Universals and cultural variation in turn-taking in conversation. *Proceedings of the   National Academy of Sciences, 106*(26), 10587-10592. Retrieved from https://www.pnas.org/content/pnas/106/26/10587.full.pdf

Suárez, L. M., Polo, A. J., Chen, C. N., & Alegría, M. (2009). Prevalence and Correlates of Childhood-Onset Anxiety Disorders among Latinos and Non-Latino Whites in the United States. *Psicología conductual, 17*(1), 89–109.

Subedi, B. (2006). Preservice Teachers' Beliefs and Practices: Religion and Religious Diversity. *Equity & Excellence in Education, 39*(3), 227–238.

https://doi.org/10.1080/10665680600788495

Takeuchi, D. T., Alegría, M., Jackson, J. S., & Williams, D. R. (2007). Immigration and mental health: diverse findings in Asian, black, and Latino populations. *American journal of public health, 97*(1), 11-12. https://doi.org/10.2105/AJPH.2006.103911

Tarone, E., Bigelow, M., & Hansen, K. (2009). *Literacy and second language oracy.* (Oxford applied linguistics). Oxford ; New York: Oxford University Press.

Tatum, B. D. (2003). *Why are all the Black kids sitting together in the cafeteria? : and other conversations about race.* New York :Basic Books.

Teitelbaum, J.F. (2017). Combating Prejudice: Understanding Media Prejudice Toward Muslims and Advocacy Organizations' Efforts to Combat It. *Naval Postgraduate School (U.S.). Center for Homeland Defense and Security.* Retrieved from Naval Postgraduate School, Dudley Knox Library: https://calhoun.nps.edu/. https://www.hsdl.org/?view&did=808199

Tello, M. (2018). Intermittent Fasting: Surprise Update. *Harvard Health Publishing.* (2018, June, 29). Retrieved from https://tinyurl.com/yd39o2wx

The Lily. (n.d.). Retrieved from https://www.accessible-archives.com/collections/the-lily/

Thompson, L. (2018). I can be your Tinder nightmare: Harassment and misogyny in the online sexual marketplace. *Feminism & Psychology,* 28, 69–89. https://doi.org/10.1177%2F0959353517720226

Tobin K.G., & Calhoon M.B. (2009). A comparison of two reading programs on the reading outcomes of first-grade students. *Journal of Direct Instruction.* 2009;9:35–46.

Todd, R. M. (2002). Financial literacy education: a potential tool for reducing predatory lending? *The Region, Federal Reserve Bank of Minneapolis,* vol. 16(Dec.), pages 6-9,34-36. Retrievable from https://ideas.repec.org/a/fip/fedmrr/y2002idec.p6-934-36nv16,no.4.html

Todorov, A., Baron, S., & Oosterhof, N. (2008). Evaluating face trustworthiness: A model based approach. *Social Cognitive and Affective Neuroscience,* 3(2), 119-127. https://doi.org/10.1093/scan/nsn009

Triplitt, C. (2012). Examining the Mechanisms of Glucose Regulation. *American Journal of Managed Care,* (March 28). https://tinyurl.com/ycl2u32q

Underwood, M. K., & Ehrenreich, S. E. (2014). Bullying May Be Fueled by the Desperate Need to Belong. *Theory into practice,* 53(4), 265–270. https://doi.org/10.1080/00405841.2014.947217

Uvnäs-Moberg, K., Handlin, L., & Petersson, M. (2015). Self-soothing behaviors with particular reference to oxytocin release induced by non-noxious sensory stimulation. *Frontiers in psychology,* 5, 1529. https://doi.org/10.3389/fpsyg.2014.01529

Vega, W. A., Alderete, E., Kolody, B., & Aguilar-Gaxiola, S. (1998). Illicit drug use among Mexicans and Mexican Americans in California: the effects of gender and acculturation. *Addiction (Abingdon, England),* 93(12), 1839–1850. https://doi.org/10.1046/j.1360-0443.1998.931218399.x

Vlisides, C. E., Eddy, J. P., & Mozie, D. (1994). Stress and stressors: Definition, identification and strategy for higher education constituents. *College Student Journal,* 28(1), 122-124. https://psycnet.apa.org/record/1994-39275-001

Wain, O., & Spinella, M. (2007). Executive functions in morality, religion, and paranormal beliefs. *The International journal of neuroscience*, *117*(1), 135-146.
https://doi.org/10.1080/00207450500534068

Wagner, D. A. (1999). Indigenous education and literacy learning. In D. Wagner, R. Venezky, & B. V. Street (Eds.), *Literacy: An international handbook* (pp. 283-287). Boulder, CO: Westview Press.

Wang, Q., Chen, G., Wang, Z., Hu, C.S.,Hu, X. & Fu, G. (2014). Implicit racial attitudes influence perceived emotional intensity on other-race faces. *PLoS ONE, 9*(8), E105946.
https://doi.org/10.1371/journal.pone.0105946

Ward, N. & Al Bayyari, Y. (2007). A Prosodic Feature that Invites Back-Channels in Egyptian Arabic. In M.Mughazy (Ed.), *Perspectives on Arabic Linguistics*, Volume XX (pp. 187-208). Amsterdam: John Benjamins

Warikoo, N. (2013). 10 years later, Iraqi Americans feel gratitude, regret. *USA Today*. (2013, March 19). Retrieved from https://tinyurl.com/y9po4grn

Weller, C. (2018, February 18). Silicon Valley parents are raising their kids tech-free - and it should be a red flag. *Business Insider*. Retrieved from https://tinyurl.com/yculbey8

Wesselhoeft, K. (2010). Making Muslim Minds: Question and Answer as a Genre of Moral Reasoning in an Urban French Mosque. *Journal of the American Academy of Religion*, *78*(3), 790-823.

White, W. A. T. (1988). A meta-analysis of the effects of Direct Instruction in special education. *Education and Treatment of Children, 11(4)*, 364-374.

Willis, P., & Trondman, M. (2000). Manifesto for Ethnography. Ethnography, 1(1), 5-16.
https://doi.org/10.1177/14661380022230679

Winthrop, R., McGivney, E. (2015). Why Wait 100 Years? Bridging the gap in global education. *The Brookings Institute*. Retrievable from https://tinyurl.com/y7nk3x65

Wirtz, J. G., Sparks, J. V., Zimbres, T. M. (2018) The effect of exposure to sexual appeals in advertisements on memory, attitude, and purchase intention: a meta-analytic review, *International Journal of Advertising*, 37:2, 168-198, https://doi.org/10.1080/02650487.2017.1334996

Wolak J, Mitchell K, Finkelhor D. Unwanted and wanted exposure to online pornography in a national sample of youth Internet users. *Pediatrics*. 2007;119(2):247−257.
doi:10.1542/peds.2006-1891

Wolfinger, N. (2018). "Does Sexual History Affect Marital Happiness?" *Institute for Family Studies*, 22 Oct. 2018. Retrieved from https://ifstudies.org/blog/does-sexual-history-affect-marital-happiness.

Wong, B. Y. L. (1985). Self-questioning instructional research: A review. *Revjeiu of Educational Research, 55*, 227-268. Retrievable from http://www.psicothema.com/pdf/4204.pdf

Wood, C. (2007). *Yardsticks : Children in the classroom, ages 4-14* (3rd ed.). Turners Falls, MA: Northeast Foundation for Children. Pp. 153.

Wormeli, R. (2003). *Day one & beyond : Practical matters for new middle-level teachers / Rick Wormeli*. Portland, Me.: Stenhouse.

Yehuda, R., Daskalakis, N. P., Lehrner, A., Desarnaud, F., Bader, H. N., Makotkine, I., ... Meaney, M. J. (2014). Influences of Maternal and Paternal PTSD on Epigenetic Regulation of the Glucocorticoid Receptor Gene in Holocaust Survivor Offspring. *American Journal of Psychiatry*, *171*(8), 872-880. https://doi.org/10.1176/appi.ajp.2014.13121571

Yelsma, P., & Athappilly, K. (1988). Marital satisfaction and communication practices: comparisons among Indian and American couples. *Journal of Comparative Family Studies, 19*,37.
https://www.jstor.org/stable/41601406?seq=1

Yildiz, N. (2009). Skilled Immigrants and the Recognition of Foreign Credentials in the United States. *World Education News + Reviews*. December 1, 2009. Retrievable from
https://wenr.wes.org/2009/12/wenr-december-2009-feature

Yoder, B. (n.d.). Engineering by the Numbers. American Society for Engineering Education. Retrievable from https://tinyurl.com/lszn5e2

Yusuf, A. (2012). *Somalis in Minnesota / Ahmed Ismail Yusuf.* (People of Minnesota). St. Paul, MN: Minnesota Historical Society Press.

Zaccaro, A., Piarulli, A., Laurino, M., Garbella, E., Menicucci, D., Neri, B., & Gemignani, A. (2018). How Breath-Control Can Change Your Life: A Systematic Review on Psycho-Physiological Correlates of Slow Breathing. *Frontiers in human neuroscience, 12*, 353.
https://doi.org/10.3389/fnhum.2018.0035

Zelman, K. (n.d.). Diet Myth or Truth: Fasting Is Effective for Weight Loss. *Web MD*. Retrieved 2020, from https://tinyurl.com/y8wynbc9

Zine, J. (2000). Redefining Resistance: Towards an Islamic subculture in schools. *Race Ethnicity and Education, 3*(3), 293-316.

Zine, J. (2001). Muslim youth in Canadian schools: Education and the politics of religious identity. *Anthropology and Education Quarterly, 32*(4), 399-423.

Made in the USA
Monee, IL
09 September 2022

13680734R00215